THE DRUMS OF AFFLICTION

Completely adorned Novice in posture of modesty with her handmaid
before coming-out dance.

THE DRUMS OF AFFLICTION

A Study of Religious Processes
among the Ndembu of Zambia

BY

V. W. TURNER

CLARENDON PRESS · OXFORD
and
THE INTERNATIONAL AFRICAN INSTITUTE

Oxford University Press, Ely House, London W.1

GLASGOW NEW YORK TORONTO MELBOURNE WELLINGTON
CAPE TOWN IBADAN NAIROBI DAR ES SALAAM LUSAKA ADDIS ABABA
DELHI BOMBAY CALCUTTA MADRAS KARACHI LAHORE DACCA
KUALA LUMPUR SINGAPORE HONG KONG TOKYO

First published 1968
Reprinted 1972

Reproduced and printed by photolithography and bound in
Great Britain at The Pitman Press, Bath

TO EDIE

ACKNOWLEDGEMENTS

The material presented here was collected while I was a Research Officer in the employment of the former Rhodes-Livingstone Institute. First drafts of several chapters were written when I was a recipient of a Simon Research Fellowship at the University of Manchester. I am also grateful to the Center for Advanced Study in the Behavioral Sciences for affording me leisure to reflect on the field data and continue the writing. Thanks are due to the International African Institute for a grant towards the publication of this study. I am indebted to Professor Gluckman's seminar at Manchester and to the Intercollegiate Seminar at London University for many trenchant comments and criticisms. For skilled secretarial help at several stages on the way to the final draft I would like to express my warm thanks to Carmel Rosenthal, Jean Pearce, Lorene Yap, Susan Wilson, Julie Raventos, Linda Hickman, Carolyn Pfohl and Joan Oltz. My wife, Edie, from first to last, from fieldwork to index, has given me her careful and insightful help. To the many Ndembu who took us into their lives and explained with patience and good humour so many ritual minutiae go my deep thanks, especially to Musona, Muchona, Manyosa, Ihembi and Windson Kashinakaji.

I have disguised the names of certain Ndembu—villagers and chiefs—and Europeans who through no fault of their own have been discussed somewhat less than charitably by their opponents in factional or sectional struggles.

CONTENTS

CONTENTS

LIST OF PLATES

LIST OF FIGURES

I

INTRODUCTION

IN a paper on 'Ritualization of Behaviour in Animals and Man'[1] Dr. Edmund Leach first stressed that anthropologists are dominantly concerned with forms of behaviour which are not genetically determined. He then went on to classify such behaviour into three main types. These were:

'(1) Behaviour which is directed towards specific ends and which, *judged by our standards of verification*, produces observable results in a strictly mechanical way . . . we call this "rational-technical" behaviour.

'(2) Behaviour which forms part of a signalling system and which serves to "communicate information", not because of any mechanical link between means and ends, but because of the existence of a culturally defined communication code . . . we can call this "communicative" behaviour.

'(3) Behaviour which is potent in itself in terms of the cultural conventions of the actors but *not* potent in a rational-technical sense, as specified in (1), or alternatively behaviour which is directed towards evoking the potency of occult powers even though it is not presumed to be potent in itself . . . we can call this "magical" behaviour.'

Leach proposes to class (2) and (3) together as 'ritual', rather than to reserve the term, as most anthropologists do, for behaviours of the third type only. In this way he hopes to call attention to the highly important functions of ritual—including religious ritual—in pre-literate societies, of storing and transmitting information.

This is a fruitful way of approaching the data, and I have long considered that the symbols of ritual are, so to speak, 'storage units', into which are packed the maximum amount of information. They can also be regarded as multi-faceted mnemonics, each facet corresponding to a specific cluster of values, norms, beliefs, sentiments, social roles, and relationships

---

[1] 'Ritualization in Man in Relation to Conceptual and Social Development', *Philosophical Transactions of the Royal Society of London*, Series B, No. 772, Vol. 251, p. 403.

within the total cultural system of the community performing the ritual. In different situations, different facets or parts of facets tend to be prominent, though the others are always felt to be penumbrally present. The total 'significance' of a symbol may be obtained only from a consideration of how it is interpreted in every one of the ritual contexts in which it appears, i.e. with regard to its role in the total ritual system.

Each type of ritual, then, from the point of view of information theory, represents a storehouse of traditional knowledge. To obtain this knowledge one has to examine the ritual in close detail and from several standpoints. In the first place, the ritual is an aggregation of symbols. It is possible to make an inventory of these and against each to state its 'meaning'. How the meaning is to be ascertained we shall consider later. For the moment let us suppose that it is possible to record, in fairly complete form, what each symbol signifies to the average native informant and to the indigenous expert. We then have a quantum of information, which represents a set of 'messages' about a sector of socio-cultural life considered worth transmitting down the generations.

We next have to consider what kind of information it is that we have revealed. The occasions on which transmission occurs are hallowed occasions; the messages wrapped up in the ritual—and here, again, I agree with Leach that from our present viewpoint the distinction between verbalized and non-verbal symbolic communication is unimportant—are messages from or about the gods, and are charged with mystical efficacy. Our storehouse is also a powerhouse. In other words, we are dealing with information that is regarded as authoritative, even as ultimately valid, axiomatic. We are not dealing with information about a new agricultural technique or a better judicial procedure: we are concerned here with the crucial values of the believing community, whether it is a religious community, a nation, a tribe, a secret society, or any other type of group whose ultimate unity resides in its orientation towards transcendental and invisible powers. It is not only a question of values, but of the relationships between values— of an ideological 'structure', rather than a random assemblage. This aspect of 'structure' emerges perhaps most clearly when we examine the liturgical or procedural form of the ritual.

A ritual is segmented into 'phases' or 'stages' and into sub-units such as 'episodes', 'actions', and 'gestures'. To each of these units and sub-units corresponds a specific arrangement of symbols, of symbolic activities or objects. The nature of the relationship between two or more symbols is a valuable clue to the relationship between those of their *significata* which are contextually specified as important.

Underlying the observable structure of a ritual may be detected its 'telic structure', its design as a system of ends and means. Each phase and episode has its explicitly stated aim, and the end of one stage is normally a means to the fulfilment of the next, or of the ultimate end of the ritual. This aspect of ritual can very often be seen in the construction of a shrine, and in the deliberate fashioning of a symbolic object. Such a shrine or object is an entelechy, and a good deal of ritual activity consists of the manufacturing of certain key symbols, which represent, so to speak, the actualization of the work put into them. Unlike the Marxian labour theory of value, however, the value of the finished product (the Marxian 'commodity' or the completed symbol or arrangement of symbols) cannot here be measured in quantitative terms. The process of its manufacture is effected through a series of stylized acts and gestures, accompanied by verbal behaviour such as prayers and petitions to supernatural beings, words of consecration, blessing or warning, and each of these verbal, gestural, and kinaesthetic symbols contains a wealth of meaning. This wealth is stored up in the symbols and is a product of the cultural conventions of the ritual actors: it is a set of qualities expressed in sensorily perceptible form. But a ritual symbol shares this much with the Marxian 'commodity': it may frequently conceal beneath its integument a system of 'social relations'.

For the symbol is not just the product of purposive action-patterns (to use Nadel's phrase): it is the product of interaction between human actors of roles. Something of the character of this interaction may be said to adhere to the final symbolic form, or to be encapsulated in it. This holds true even when the construction of a symbol is the work of a single priest or ritual participant. For the role he or she occupies is always a representative one: in his ritual capacity he represents a social group or category, represents, indeed, the sum of its characteristic internal role-interactions. Furthermore, there is often present the notion that the symbol is made with reference to certain ultra-human entities or persons, the gods or ancestors of the group, who are believed to give power or 'grace' to the symbol. Generally, however, there is co-operation between role-players in the making of a symbol: one actor may collect the wood which another fashions into an image, others may bless or consecrate it, and others still may bow down before it, hold it aloft in triumph, or sacrifice before it. In a real sense the meaning of the symbol is bound up with all these interactions between actors in the ritual drama, for it would have no meaningful, cultural existence without this collaboration.

What is sociologically even more relevant here is the fact that the roles involved in one kind of ritual have connections both with those found in other kinds and with non-ritual roles. Thus, it may be culturally stipulated that a role found in one type of ritual should be played only by someone who has played a specific role in another type of ritual. A comparison of the two types in terms of symbolism and telic structure will then shed much light on the nature of both roles and of their interactions with yet other roles. It may also be sociologically illuminating to analyse a ritual role into components—using informants' statements and observations of the role in successive ritual contexts as the basis of such an analysis—and to investigate whether such components form part of different roles. Thus, one component of a male ritual officiant's role may also be found in the role of the father as culturally defined, while another may be identical with a component of a headman's role. A third again might even possess attributes of the role of the mother in that culture, thus crossing the sex division. But where ritual has become highly elaborate it is probable that an important component of the ritual expert's role will consist precisely in priestly expertise, knowledge of how to perform rites, interpret symbols, and pronounce prayers or formulae. Where this specialization is found in pre-literate societies, we have some measure of the degree to which religious relationships are becoming associational in character and detaching themselves from the matrix of the multifunctional kin-group.

It is clear from the above that any type of ritual forms a system of great complexity, having a symbolic structure, a value

structure, a telic structure, and a role structure. Furthermore,
it may itself constitute merely a part of a wider system of ritual,
which it is its purpose to maintain. For example, some symbols
recur throughout the different types of ritual forming the total
system: ritual roles are repeated, certain crucial values are
expressed in different parts of the system by different symbols,
and some of the aims of various types of rituals are often the
same. These multiple links combining the parts into a system
are reinforced by the constant repetition of symbolic acts
within single types of rituals. Leach (op. cit., p. 408) has commented on this repetitiveness, which he calls 'redundancy',
as follows: 'The ambiguity latent in the symbolic condensation
tends to be eliminated by the device of thematic repetition and
variation . . . this corresponds to the communication engineer's
technique of overcoming noisy interference by the use of
multiple redundancy.' The system as a whole is full of repetition, precisely because it contains images and meanings and
models for behaviour which constitute the cognitive and
ethical landmarks of the culture. Furthermore, it arrays these
in terms of relational patterns which are themselves regarded
as axiomatic for the religion's *Weltbild*.

Ritual in Social Dynamics

In the life of most communities, ancient and modern, there
appear to be interludes in historical time, periods of 'timeless'
time, that are devoted to the celebration of certain basic
postulates of human existence, biological and cultural. This
'moment in and out of time' (to quote T. S. Eliot) is the moment when ritual is being performed. In most known societies
it is a time for meditation upon, or veneration of, the transcendental, and behaviour regarded as appropriate during this
timeless time is both formalized and symbolic. It tends to be
rigid and patterned and the gestures, words, and objects that
compose it, and the myths and doctrines that explain it, represent, as we have noted earlier, far more than they appear
to do. Symbols are never simple; only signs, which by conven-
tion are restricted to a single referent, are simple. As we have
seen, many symbols are storehouses of information about the
major structural values of a culture. No doubt, much of
the rigidity and repetitiveness of ritual, like the chanting of the

multiplication table by children, is to instil into the minds of the participants certain axiomatic truths which form for them an appropriate evaluative framework.

Ritual activities, too, appear to be purposive; even if they do not seem to be directed to the achievement of any practical results, they nevertheless have effects upon the participants which influence their subsequent behaviour. As Hubert and Mauss remarked—and their words are applicable to most forms of religious ritual:

> These expiations and general purifications, communions and sacralizations of groups, these creations of the spirits of cities give —or renew periodically for the community, represented by its gods—that character, good, strong, grave, and terrible, which is one of the essential traits of any social entity. Moreover, individuals find their own advantage in this same act. They confer upon each other, upon themselves and upon those things they hold dear, the whole strength of society. They invest with the authority of society their vows, their oaths, their marriages. They surround, as with a protective sanctity, the fields they have ploughed and the houses they have built. At the same time they find in sacrifice the means of redressing equilibriums that have been upset: by expiation they redeem themselves from social obloquy, the consequence of error, and re-enter the community; by the apportionments they make of those things whose use society has reserved for itself, they acquire the right to enjoy them.[1]

Setting aside the mystical doctrine underlying Hubert's and Mauss's use of the term 'society'—a mysticism characteristic of the school of Durkheim—their formulation of the social function of sacrifice (and of ritual in general) indicates how important this activity is for the social process. Ritual is a periodic restatement of the terms in which men of a particular culture must interact if there is to be any kind of a coherent social life. This is clearly a far more 'practical' (in the sense of necessary and basic) goal than any type of specific practical activity. It has been more than once suggested that religious ritual is mainly 'expressive', that it portrays in symbolic form certain key values and cultural orientations. This is true as

[1] *Essay on Sacrifice*, Translated by W. D. Halls. London: Cohen and West (1964), pp. 102–3.

far as it goes, but it points to only one of many properties it possesses. More important is its creative function—it actually creates, or re-creates, the categories through which men perceive reality—the axioms underlying the structure of society and the laws of the natural and moral orders. It is not here a case of life being an imitation of art, but of social life being an attempted imitation of models portrayed and animated by ritual. This imitation is never fully successful, for a number of reasons. One is that self-interest cannot accept the self-limitations prescribed by a social model, with its altruistic implications. Another is that there is seldom a single internally consistent model, but several models, none of which is self-consistent. Ritual conserves models of public behaviour that might once have been consistent with such conditions as are provided by ecological, economic, or political factors, but which have now lost their efficacy. New models may incompletely reflect new conditions, but they coexist with older models and may contradict them.

Observable ritual behaviour taken by itself may not yield many clues to the understanding of what is going on. It may initially be meaningless to the alien investigator, or, worse still, he may think he finds meaning in it by drawing on his own experience, and proceed to totally erroneous interpretations of the rites he sees. Each society's ritual symbols constitute a unique code and each society provides a unique key to that code. I should say, rather, a 'bunch of keys', for some societies bring several systems of explanation to bear upon the symbols of ritual. These systems include: theology, dogma, doctrine, mythology, cosmology, allegory, parables, history or pseudo-history, and exegesis (or hermeneutics). Some religions stress one of these at the expense of the others; some have two or more interpretative systems; others have all. I do not believe that there exists anywhere a set of meaningless rites. Even when symbols are not explained in linguistic terms, they tend to appear in contexts which, to a person reared in the appropriate culture, abundantly elucidate them. Or where there are no positive hermeneutics, a material symbol, such as a species of tree or a statue, will appear in other contexts as a verbal symbol, as, for example, the name of a mythical deity. This name, which may itself derive from a stem the derivatives of which refer to basic physiological or cosmic processes, adequately explains its use in ritual, as a material symbol, for the indigenous participants. And that ritual usage will enhance the semantic wealth of the mythical entities. It is not necessary for a symbol to be verbally explained to be comprehended; its significance is often understood at preconscious, or even unconscious, levels.[1] The same verbal symbol can also be understood both verbally and non-verbally.

But the investigator must on no account make the cardinal error of attempting to go straight from the sensory appearance of the symbol to its 'social function'. He cannot evade the fact that symbols have meaning for the people he is studying which makes their ritual behaviour intelligible, not only to themselves, but also to their alien investigator. It is only after he has learned to crack the cultural code which explains the symbols of ritual that he is in any position to relate the semantic assemblage—which may be discovered to be a system—to the social system, and to the dynamics of that system. People only come together to perform ritual in terms of beliefs so powerfully held that they overcome all the forces that under other circumstances divide them from one another and set them at odds. If these beliefs lose their efficacy, the rituals and symbols that embody them will produce not cohesion but contention, or finally indifference. In this book we shall try to explain why it is that certain symbols do continue sufficiently to engage people in one particular society, the Ndembu of Zambia in Central Africa. First we shall use all the means at our disposal to 'crack the code' of Ndembu symbolism.

Ndembu Social Organization

As I have already written at considerable length on the social organization of the Ndembu,[2] I will here limit my remarks on this aspect of their culture, though my treatment of ritual throughout this book indicates that I believe social structure and process to be closely related to ritual structure and process.

The Ndembu, numbering about 17,000, today inhabit the

---

[1] See *Chihamba, The White Spirit*, Rhodes-Livingstone Paper No. 33, Manchester University Press (1962), p. 79.

[2] Mostly incorporated in *Schism and Continuity in an African Society*. For other publications on Ndembu social and economic organization, see Bibliography.

western portion of Mwinilunga District in the North-Western Province of Zambia, approximately between latitude 11° and 12° south. They claim to have come as invaders some three centuries ago from the Northern Lunda empire (Luunda) of

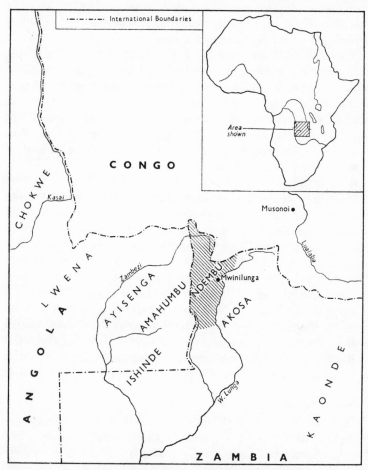

Fig. I. Map of the Ndembu and neighbouring tribes.

Mwantiyanvwa and to have conquered, or received the submission of, small scattered groups of indigenous Mbwela or Lukolwe.

On their well-wooded plateau the Ndembu practise a form of subsistence cultivation in which cassava growing is associated with hunting. In addition to cassava, finger millet is grown by small circle ash-planting methods mainly for beer-making, and maize is cultivated in stream-side gardens for both food and beer.

They are a matrilineal, virilocal people, with high personal mobility, and they inhabit small villages with cores of male matrikin of whom the oldest member of the senior genealogical generation is usually the headman.

The Ndembu did not have the high degree of political centralization enjoyed by their Northern Lunda ancestors. Villages in pre-European times possessed considerable political autonomy. Under British rule, however, a hierarchy was established consisting of a Chief (the 'Native Authority') and four Sub-Chiefs. Formerly, the Sub-Chiefs were drawn from a class of senior village headmen who held renowned historical titles but had little real power.

Among the Ndembu individuals and families have high rates of mobility. Men, of their own choice, and women, through marriage, divorce, widowhood, and remarriage—each of which normally entails a change in domicile—are constantly moving from one village to another. Men usually go where they have kin and this is possible since kin groups get widely dispersed over the region. The villages, too, move about and not infrequently tend to split in the course of time into several fragments. Individuals continually circulate through these moving villages. It is not surprising that many students of Central Africa, who work in areas characterized by much residential mobility, should have become interested in problems of social dynamics, and in processes of adjustment, adaptation and change.

Village Structure

Nevertheless, although the majority of local groups in Ndembu society are relatively transient and unstable, the organizational principles on which they are formed and re-formed are enduring. Particular villages break up or disperse, but the structural form of the Ndembu village remains. It is possible to assess from the comments of informants the degree of conformity between statistical and ideal norms of village structure. Most Ndembu villages are in fact much as informants thought they ought to be. Nevertheless, the principles on which they are built up are often incompatible, in the sense that they give rise to conflicts of loyalties. People who observe one set of norms find that they may transgress equally valid rules belonging to another set.

Two major principles influence the residential pattern: matrilineal descent and virilocal marriage. For men matriliny governs prior rights to residence, succession to office, and inheritance of property. A man has a right to reside with his matrilineal kin, primary or classificatory; he may reside in his father's village if his mother lives there; or, if she does not, as a privilege secured for him by his father, by virtue of that father's rights as a member of the village matrilineage. A man has the further right to be considered as a candidate for the headman-ship of his matrilineal village, and is entitled to share in the property of a deceased matrilineal kinsman. On the other hand, a man has the right to take his wife to reside in his own village. From this might arise the difficult situation in which women, on whom the continuity of villages depends, do not live in their own, but in their husbands' villages. This difficulty would be reduced if there was a clearly defined custom whereby boys went to live in their mothers' brothers' villages at a given age, say at puberty. But among Ndembu there is no such custom, and the outcome is left uncertain. The onus of choice is thrown on the individual. Men try to keep their sons with them as long as they can, and indeed the father-son relationship is highly ritualized, especially in the hunters' cults, and in the circumcision ceremony. There are thus strong patrifocal tendencies in a matrilineal society.

Matriliny and Virilocality: Some Implications

An overall picture emerges of groups of mobile male matri-lineal kinsmen, changing residential sites about twice every decade, in competition with one another for women and their children. For young children generally remain with their mothers, who are granted their custody after divorce. To obtain the allegiance of the children their maternal uncles must win over the children's mothers. A contradiction thus tends to arise between a man's roles as a husband and father who wishes to retain his wife and children with him, and his roles as uterine brother and uncle, whereby he seeks to win the residential allegiance of his sister and her children. This struggle, veiled though it often is and mitigated by customs enjoining friendship between in-laws of the same generations, is reflected in a divorce rate exceptionally high even for Central Africa. The importance of matriliny also appears in the custom by which widows return to the villages of their uterine or close matrilineal kin after their husbands' deaths. There is no levirate or widow-inheritance among free Ndembu. Thus, in practice, at any given time, the matrilineal structure of a village is made up of relationships, not only between male matrilineal kin, but also between these men and a variable number of matrilineal kinswomen who have returned to them after divorce or widowhood, bringing their children.

Let me put the matter in another way. In discussion with me, Ndembu emphasized the solidarity between two kinds of male kin; between fathers and sons, and between brothers. These are the relationships, for example, which receive ritual recognition in the boys' circumcision ceremony. Often, two or three full brothers are circumcised at the same lodge—and this is one reason for the wide age-range of the novices (between seven and seventeen). Alternatively, the oldest brother will act as 'shepherd' to his novice younger brothers, but not infrequently a father will play this part. The 'shepherd' attends to the needs of the novices, instructs them in various matters, and also chastises them for breaches of lodge discipline. The father's role in the ritual is important. He must refrain from sexual intercourse altogether until his sons' scars are healed. It is said that in the past a man would kill a circumciser who maimed his son. But the mother's brother/sister's son relationship is not ritualized at all circumcisions. Nor need the mother's brother practice sexual continence until the circumcision scars are healed.

Hunting rituals also emphasize the father-son bond, the patrifocal element in a basically matrilineal society. There is a masculine ideal of a community of male kin, consisting of full brothers, their wives, and sons. But matriliny, strongly ritualized in the girls' puberty ceremony and in many cults connected with female fertility, prevents the full realization of this ideal. Ndembu say that they trace descent through women, because 'the mother's blood is self-evident and manifest, whereas one can never be sure who is the begetter'. Matriliny provides a

more certain basis for tracing descent; one knows undeniably
just who are one's maternal kin. Thus matrilineal kinship
does provide a framework for persisting groups, and controls
succession and inheritance within such groups. But, given
matriliny, an Ndembu village can continue through time only
if sisters' sons come to live in it. Concomitantly, sons must
leave the village, to replenish the villages of their maternal
uncles. The village still remains essentially a structure of relationships between male kinsmen, but matriliny determines the
form of the majority of these relationships. The unity of brothers
is still stressed, but the brothers who live together are uterine
brothers, children of the same mother. They may, in addition,
be seminal brothers, sons of the same father, but the uterine link
is crucial for co-residence. Many adult sons reside with their
fathers, but after the death of the latter they must go where
they have matrilineal kin.

At any given time, sisters and adult sisters' daughters of the
senior male generation reside in the village. During their
reproductive period these women are residents only in the
intervals between successive marriages, but after the menopause they may stay there permanently. Sisters' sons and
sisters' daughters' sons tend to accumulate in each village,
sometimes along with their mothers, and sometimes remaining
behind after their mothers have married out again. As a result,
any actual village contains a number of adult persons related
by primary or classificatory matrilineal ties, and a smaller
number of persons linked to the village matrilineage through
their fathers. Male kin preponderate over female kin by more
than two to one. In other words, each real village tends in its
structure to represent a compromise between matriliny and
patrilocality (which I here take to mean residence with one's
own father). Patrilocality owes its importance to virilocal
marriage, and it is this aspect of marriage which enables uterine
brothers to reside together. If marriage were uxorilocal, uterine
brothers would be dispersed through the villages of their wives.

Some Features of Ndembu Religion

Probably because of their remoteness from urban centres and
the concomitant sparseness of European settlement, the
Ndembu have been able to preserve many features of their

traditional religious system at a time when most other Zambian tribes have been rapidly losing theirs. When I was working among them from 1950-4, great waves of change were sweeping over the lives of the Ndembu, for a motor road, cutting through the heart of the District, brought European traders into it, and took out many Ndembu as labour migrants. Nevertheless, the traditional religion was still sufficiently alive for me to observe many performances of ritual, and to find many informants willing to discuss its main features.

At the level of *belief*, Ndembu religion has four main components: (1) Belief in the existence of an otiose High God, *Nzambi*, who is said to have created the world and then left it to its own devices. He is never worshipped in prayer or rite; he is vaguely connected with the weather and with fertility, and some Ndembu say that ancestor spirits intercede with him on behalf of their living kin who have been smitten by misfortune. (2) The second component is belief in the existence of ancestor spirits or 'shades' who have power (*ng'ovu*) to bestow the good things of life on their living kinsfolk or to withhold them. This component is so important that Ndembu religion must be characterized as animistic or manistic rather than theistic. (3) Thirdly, Ndembu believe in the intrinsic efficacy of certain animal and vegetable substances, usually described in the literature as 'medicines', to work good or harm, provided that they are prepared and used by qualified practitioners in a ritual setting. Although medicines have an intrinsic power, this power remains latent until it is released by someone who has himself acquired ritual power. (4) Fourthly, there is belief in the anti-social, destructive power of female witches and male sorcerers (both called *aloji*; singular *muloji*, best translated by Fr. Tempel's phrase as 'perverted destroyer of life'). Both witches and sorcerers possess familiars which act partly as instruments of their owners' malevolent desires and ambitions, and partly, and frighteningly, on their own account, overriding their owners' wishes. Women inherit, willy-nilly, their familiars from deceased witch-kinswomen. These familiars, known as *andumba* or *tuyebela*, have the variable forms of stunted men with feet pointing backwards, jackals, owls, and rats. They kill primarily matrilineal kin and husbands of their owners, and are believed to be activated by gnawing jealousies and grudges.

es and familiars are thought to feast on the dis-
dies of their victims. Male sorcerers, on the other
not inherit, but manufacture their familiars or
aem from evil medicines. They manufacture wooden
activating them by pressing blood and medicines
3 in the heads, or grow creatures in pots at river-
Examples of such generated familiars include a huge
ake (*ilomba*) which has its owner's face, and a gigantic
fresh-water crab (*nkala*). These are invisible to all but
their owners and ritual specialists who combat them. A distinction worth making here is that female witches are believed to
inherit their dark power, in the sense that a woman is 'chosen'
by the familiars of a deceased witch as their new owner,
while male sorcerers become evil through ambition or envy.
Masculinity is thus associated with voluntariness, femininity
with necessity.

These simple and, indeed, naive beliefs stand in marked contrast to the complex practices of Ndembu religion. I shall call
such practices 'rites' or 'rituals', using these terms more or less
interchangeably. By 'rite' or 'ritual' I mean, when referring to
Ndembu culture, prescribed formal behaviour for occasions
not given over to technological routine, having reference to
beliefs in mystical (or non-empirical) beings or powers. But I
shall also define 'a ritual' or 'a kind of ritual' as a corpus
of beliefs and practices performed by a specific cult association.
Thus, there are in Ndembu culture many kinds of ritual which
may be termed collectively 'rituals of affliction' or 'drums of
affliction', for Ndembu often use the term 'drum' (*ng'oma*) as a
synonym both for a type and an actual performance of ritual.
These are performed by cult-associations on behalf of persons
believed to be afflicted with illness or misfortune by ancestor-
spirits, witches, or sorcerers. A person is, as Ndembu say,
'caught' for committing some misdemeanour by a spirit in a
particular 'mode of affliction'. The mode of affliction may be
revealed by the afflicted person's symptoms, such as twin birth
or periodic troubles in the case of women, or failing to find
game in the case of hunters. But in most cases the close kin of a
person smitten with misfortune consult a diviner, who uses
manipulative techniques to diagnose the particular mode of
affliction. The diviner then advises his clients to seek out a

senior practitioner or 'doctor' who knows the ritual procedures for propitiating a spirit which has 'emerged', as Ndembu say, in that mode. Such a practitioner then collects a band of adepts, consisting of persons who have themselves undergone as patients or novices, that kind of ritual, and allocates to each a ritual task according to the measure of his or her esoteric skill and experience. This cult-association then performs a ritual on behalf of the patient. If the patient is deemed to be cured, he or she may then assist at later performances as an adept. It is further believed that an afflicting ancestor spirit had been a member of the cult-association during life.

The sociological importance of the cult-associations is that they are recruited from many parts of the tribal territory, not from a particular clan, locality, or village. All who have suffered from ancestral wrath in the same mode of affliction, and have been treated by its curative cult, can qualify for membership, whatever their secular status may be. Since individuals move freely from one village to another, since villages themselves change sites often under shifting cultivation, and since there is no strong political centralization under a hierarchy of chiefs and officials, the system of cults helps to bond together the loosely organized Ndembu tribe. Most people belong to at least one cult, many to more than one.

But cults of affliction are not the only kinds of Ndembu ritual. There are also life-crisis rituals: circumcision for boys, puberty rites for girls. In a sense, the circumcision ritual introduces all males into a great cult-association, and the puberty ritual makes all women members of a single female community. In addition, there are male and female funerary associations which hold elaborate initiation rites for boys and girls when their members die. In all these life-crisis rituals is stressed the theme of suffering as a means of entry into a superior ritual and social status. The novices undergo symbolic death and real ordeal.

Each kind of Ndembu ritual contains a multitude of symbols. One might almost say that it consists of symbols or that it is a *system* of symbols. According to the Oxford Dictionary a symbol is a 'Thing regarded by general consent as naturally typifying or representing or recalling something by possession of analogous qualities or by association in fact or thought'. Ritual symbols fall into a special class of symbols. They are, for example, not *univocal*, having only one proper meaning, but *multivocal*, i.e. susceptible of many meanings. I shall examine this property later and then ask why such symbols have many meanings.

Meanwhile, I would like to raise the problem of what is involved in the 'meaning' of a ritual symbol. After attending a number of performances of different kinds of ritual and asking many informants, both during and after the performances, to interpret their symbolism, I began to realize that a symbol's meaning must include not only what was said about it but also how it was used: it had an *operational* meaning as well as an *interpretation*. It also became clear that a symbol's position with reference to other symbols influenced its meaning. It was important, for example, to determine whether a symbol was central and dominant, or whether it was peripheral and secondary. My exegetic data also suggested that the meaning of a symbol was modified or qualified by those adjacent to it in time and space in a configuration. Thus, there were at least three components or aspects of meaning: exegetic or interpretative; operational; and positional.

Here is an example. Full descriptive data for this ritual will be found in Chapter Seven. The dominant symbol of the girls' puberty ritual, *Nkang'a*, is a young sapling of a species of tree called *mudyi* (*Diplorrhyncus condylocarpon*). At its foot the girl novice is laid on the first day of *Nkang'a*. She has to lie there motionless for about eight hours covered with a blanket, while women from near and far dance around her singing and stamping. The site is known as the 'dying-place' (*ifwilu*) or 'place of suffering' (*chinung'u*), for it is there that she dies from childhood and enters the *passage* ritual which is aimed at making her a mature and fruitful woman. Birth and death are both represented by her attitude: it is the foetal position and the position in which corpses are buried.

But it is the tree itself in which we are interested at present. My wife and I collected dozens of texts from women and men about what they thought the *mudyi* stood for. Here I state their interpretations briefly. The *mudyi* tree when cut exudes a white, milky latex. From this natural feature, informants said that *mudyi* meant breast-milk and the maternal breast. Furthermore, they stated that it represents 'a mother and her child' (i.e. the mother-child bond), the novice's own matrilineal descent group, the principle of matriliny, and even Ndembu tribal custom itself. Other meanings given were 'life' (*wumi*), and 'the process of learning' (*ku-diza*). *Mudyi* wood is also used in many other ritual contexts. For example, in the *Musolu* ritual, performed to bring on delayed rains, a miniature bow of *mudyi* wood is said to represent 'the procreative power of women' (*lusemu lwawambanda*).

All these referents of *mudyi* are interlinked by their association with mother's milk. It is as though the Ndembu were saying that a person is nourished by the family, the matrilineage, and the tribe. Some of the referents are to organic or physiological phenomena; others, to components of the social system. Indeed, when Ndembu say that *mudyi* stands for 'tribal custom' or 'matriliny', they are using these terms as shorthands for complexes of rights and obligations governed by several principles of social organization, notably matrilineal descent. What is interesting is that there appear to be two distinct and opposed poles of reference. At one pole there is a cluster of referents to organic and physiological phenomena; at the other, a cluster of referents to the norms and values of society. The material in this book shows that it is the socially recognized organic pole of reference that appears to rouse feelings and impulses in the Ndembu ritual situation.

Not only *mudyi*, but several other Ndembu ritual symbols with this 'dominant' or 'focal' quality exhibit bi-polarity of reference. At one pole the referents are grossly, even blatantly, physiological; at the other, ideals and moral imperatives, as well as social rules, may be represented. How may this bi-polarity be explained? It is as though the whole strength of the emotion aroused by the ideas culturally associated with the organic referents of such symbols is borrowed, as it were, by the normative and ethical referents. At the same time, the emotions, which, as psycho-analysts have shown, may often be connected with illicit and socially reprobated impulses—especially, I have found, in Ndembu 'red' symbols representing blood—are purified by their association with morality and law. It is as though the 'energy' of virtue flowed from organic and primitive sources, though the original goals of the drives were altered. It is as though the infantile pleasure of breast-feeding were associated with the correct performance of one's duties as an Ndembu tribesman or member of a matrilineage. Conversely, the physical side of motherhood is elevated and purified by association with the values attached to the widest social continuity and cohesion. In this way the obligatory is made desirable, and the desirable allowed a legitimate outlet. Again it would seem that the needs of the individual biopsychical organism and the needs of society, in many respects opposed, come to terms with one another in the master-symbols of Ndembu society. An identity of interest and purpose is assumed at the level of exegesis. In the ritual moment of exaltation it is stated in the esoteric language of symbol: 'The mother's breast *is* matriliny, *is* the tribe', that 'the infant's tie to its mother *is* the crucial bond of adult society'. In the *mudyi* symbolism, the glowing and pleasurable feelings of infancy are reanimated and made to inform a normative order that might otherwise prove alien and oppressive. In other symbols and symbolic dramas of Ndembu religion, what can be shown to be infantile murderous and cannibalistic impulses are transmuted into zeal on behalf of certain moral imperatives and legal rules.[1]

But, even in the *mudyi* symbolism, aggressive impulses are given stereotyped expression. Ndembu do not admit these, stressing only its unitary and harmonious aspects. But, from the behaviour of the participants. it is abundantly clear that they are miming social conflict. For example, during the morning of the first day, the *mudyi* divides the women from the men. Only women may dance and sing round the recumbent novice, and they spend their time lampooning and ridiculing men in general and husbands in particular in a joyful dance. Later in the afternoon, men are gradually admitted to the dance, and at the finale the women in a group circle the men sitting in the village forum as a token of reconciliation and renewed interdependence. But at first the independence of the women from the men is stressed, and stressed, moreover, at the *mudyi* tree. The tree thus operationally becomes an emblem of womanhood versus manhood. Again, the tree divides a

[1] See my analysis of 'tooth' symbolism in *The Forest of Symbols*, Cornell University Press (1967), pp. 362-7, and in Chapter Six of this book.

3

mother from her daughter, for the novice's mother may not
attend the first stages of her daughter's ordeal. If she should
approach she is jeered at by the other women who are, in
sociological terms, the collectivity of adult tribeswomen who
are taking the novice into their ranks away from the mother.
Later, the mother will receive her back, not as a child, however,
but as a fellow member of a lineage. Furthermore, conflict is
mimed between the women of the novice's village and women
from outlying villages, who vie with one another for a spoon
of sacred food, representing the novice's wish for fertility.
Conflict is also expressed at *mudyi* between the bridegroom's
kin, who will take the novice to their village, and the novice's
matrilineage, who will lose her services. In brief, if we accept
that a symbol's meaning contains how it is used, and behaviour
closely associated with it, *mudyi* represents not only certain
salient principles of Ndembu social organization, but also the
sorts of social conflicts that habitually arise in connection with
those principles. Mother and daughter have a very close tie,
but nevertheless their interests diverge as the daughter grows
to maturity; men and women are united as tribal members and
as spouses in a great number of legitimate conjugal unions, but
nevertheless they are divided and opposed in many situations.
Women, while united by sex, are divided by village affiliation.
Yet despite these divisions of affiliation and interest, *mudyi*
presides over the total ritual and represents an ultimate unity.
Indeed, one might well argue that, just as at the level of
exegesis the pleasure-components of *mudyi's* meaning appear
to strengthen its normative side, so the aggressive and divisive
aspects of its operational meaning strengthen its socially
integrative side. Both as a set of stated referents, and as an
action system, *mudyi* is a unification of disparities, and even of
opposites. This is the strength of religious symbols.

Symbols of a similar type to *mudyi*, i.e. sacred trees, are found
throughout the ritual system, in rituals of affliction just as in
life-crisis rituals. Other symbols combine several symbolic
elements, each of which has its own set of referents. Examples
will be found in the rituals described later in the text. Here I
would like to point out that some of these dominant symbols
are at times actually *identified* with certain manifestations of
ancestor spirits, and not merely regarded as representing them.

Here the belief in the efficacy of certain substances and the belief in ancestor spirits appear to coincide. We find, in fact, a further unification of disparities. The natural order, represented by wild species of trees, is identified with the moral order, sanctioned by the ancestor spirits.

Ndembu ritual, in its original setting, with its rich multi-vocal (or 'polysemous') symbolism, may be regarded as a magnificent instrument for expressing, maintaining, and periodically cleansing a secular order of society without strong political centralization and all too full of social conflict. Through the wide range of reference possessed by a single symbol, almost all the things that matter can be concentrated into a small area of space and time, there to be re-endowed with value. Ritual is a *multum in parvo* of secular life, but when many elements are fused, the result may well be something altogether new. And the crucial question is, what is the nature of the unifying force? Why should men strive to unite under one rubric many things that reason would suppose are completely unrelated? Freud gives us his answer: 'Religion is an attempt to get control of the sensory world, in which we are placed, by means of the wish world, which we have developed inside us as a result of biological and psychological necessities.'[1] He would have argued, as I have myself heard analysts argue, that Ndembu wish that things and people, recognized in ordinary life as being irrevocably divided, should be brought into harmony, and that this wish engenders the belief that in ritual action there is some inherent efficacy that brings about this miracle of unification. He would also have doubtless argued that behind this wish stands the recognition of the need for social and economic security, and that in fact material interest is its prime mover. He might have said that people in such a precarious environment, with poor tools and little technological skill, unendowed with scientific knowledge, seek and find *emotional security* in ritual, and *pretend* while they perform it that reality does in fact conform to their wishes. But to my mind it seems just as feasible to argue that 'the wish to gain control of the sensory world' may proceed from something else—a deep intuition of a real and spiritual unity in all things. It may be a wish to overcome arbitrary and man-made

[1] *New Introductory Lectures on Psycho-Analysis*, London: Hogarth Press, p. 215.

divisions, to overcome for a moment—a 'moment in and out of time'—the material conditions that disunite men and set them at odds with nature.

This impulse among Ndembu may not be the product merely of wishful thinking and unscientific ignorance. We may find in it a groping attempt to use the esoteric language of symbols to say something significant about the nature and meaning of man. In the idiom of the rituals of affliction it is as though the Ndembu said: 'It is only when a person is reduced to misery by misfortune, and repents of the acts that caused him to be afflicted, that ritual expressing an underlying unity in diverse things may fittingly be enacted for him'. For the patient in rituals of affliction must sit, clad only in a waistcloth, in an attitude of penitent shame, and must not speak or do anything positive. He does not perform actions, but *passiones* in the ancient sense of that term. He is passive to the action of the ritual and receives the stamp of its meaning. It is as though he were stripped of all possessions, all status, all social connections, and *then* endowed with all the basic virtues and values of Ndembu society. *Pari passu*, the spirit which has been persecuting him is converted into a helpful tutelary. When a man ceases to *have*, then he can begin to *be*, the ritual idiom seems to suggest.

This is not to imply that Ndembu paganism is on an ethical or epistemological parity with the great world religions, but there is some satisfaction from a humanistic standpoint in finding similarities between men's modes of worship the world over. Ritual is not a contrivance of civilized men; it has roots deep in the human past.

What lessons may be drawn for those interested in liturgical problems from Ndembu ritual and symbolism? It would seem that ritual symbolism can only flourish where there is a thriving corporate life. The symbols are related to the process of adjusting the individual to the traditional social order into which he is born, and they imply some kind of general consent as to their meaning. Wherever our kind of Western individualism crops up in Central Africa, the tribal religions wilt and perish in a surprisingly short time, and with them vanish the ritual symbols. For men plunge into the struggle to earn and save cash for the new goods and prestige symbols that money can buy. To save money they must break the corporate kinship nexus; for in the old order of society, that which a man acquires, he must share out among his kin and neighbours. He cannot both save and distribute money. Thus, the crucial value attached to corporateness is rejected, and with it go many other values and obligations; frankness between group members, comradeship in adversity, mutual generosity and reciprocity. The symbols that represent these values in ritual disappear with them. Perhaps when a new social order becomes established in Africa, new symbols will express it; whether it will be the great traditional symbols of Christianity and Islam, or the newer ones of socialism and nationalism that take the place of the old is uncertain. But currently an aggressive individualism seems to be absorbing the energies of most people. New forms of social relationship are beginning to emerge, it is true, sometimes in revivalistic religious movements and separatist churches, but most of their nascent symbolism is secular and political. As one Ndembu put it to me, 'For Europeans, things are more important than people, for us, people are more important than things.' But Africans are rapidly becoming more 'European-ized' in this sense. And as 'people', or rather the customary ties between people, become less important, so does ritual symbolism lose its efficacy.

I once defined ritual custom as 'quintessential custom'. It is the concentration of custom, its refined extract as it were. In order to thrive, however, it seems to need a matrix made up of many long-standing customary ways of behaving, thinking, and feeling. It is distilled from custom, not directly from inter-actions. Where novelty and change characterize the life of a society, fewer people take part in public ritual. Only among those least influenced by technological change is ritual able to maintain its function. If the present rapid tempo of change in Africa, and the social mobility it is promoting, are ever slowed down and stabilized into a social order that will continue in much the same form over many years, then we may have a widespread revival of participation in ritual, and perhaps the social generation of new religious symbols, as well as the regeneration of many existing ones.

The chapters which follow are concerned with the function and meaning of Ndembu ritual activities not only with reference to traditional modes of social and political organization, but also to the effects of modern changes on the social system. As in my previous book, *Schism and Continuity in an African Society*, I have tried to bring into the analysis of what I there called 'social dramas' the changes in principles of organization and values which were in process of emerging out of British over-lordship. The social dramas considered in this book relate to crises that lead to the application of ritual means of redress (rather than legal machinery). But, in order to understand as fully as possible the issues involved in the ritual handling of the crises, it is necessary to scrutinize in close detail the antecedent chains of events in the ritual-performing community. Hence I have to discuss such non-traditional factors as the development of cash-cropping and wage earning, governmental restriction of the tribal political system, the growth of new forms of communication and transport, labour migration and the killing off of game—which has struck at the very basis of the tribally important hunting cults. In all, we see a field of social relations, in process of irreversible change, which viewed microscopically in terms of its day-to-day crises of living, exhibits a series of persistent, even desperate, attempts to retain its traditional regularities of structure.

II

DIVINATION AND ITS SYMBOLISM

INTRODUCTION

To give an adequate explanation of the meaning of ritual symbols, one has first to consider what kinds of circumstances tend to give rise to ritual performances, for these circumstances probably decide what sort of ritual is performed, and the goals of that ritual largely determine the meaning of the symbols used in it. The switchpoint between social crisis and performance of redressive ritual is the divinatory seance or consultation. I have already written a detailed account of Ndembu divination[1] and will here give only a brief summary of its role in the social process, in order to distinguish its symbolism from the symbolism of rituals of life-crisis and affliction.

Divination has certain affinities with the judicial process, for it is vitally concerned with the customs and interests of persons in complex social situations. But it also prepares the way for the more rigidly standardized processes of redressive ritual. It is this mediating function that determines the cognitive and flexible qualities of its symbolism. Clifford Geertz argues that 'sociological and cultural processes must be treated on equal terms—neither is a simple reflex, a mirror image of the other.'[2] His approach involves an analytical distinction between the cultural and sociological aspects of human life, which must be treated as independently variable yet interdependent factors: 'Though separable only conceptually, culture and social structure will then be seen to be capable of a wide range of modes of integration with one another, of which the simple isomorphic mode is but a limiting case—a case common only in societies which have been stable over such an extended time as to make possible a close adjustment between social and

[1] *Ndembu Divination: its Symbolism and Techniques*, Rhodes-Livingstone Institute Paper No. 31 (1961).
[2] 'Ritual and Social Change: a Javanese Example', *American Anthropologist*, lix (1957), pp. 32–54.

cultural aspects.' For Geertz, culture is 'the fabric of meaning in terms of which human beings interpret their experience and guide their action'. Social structure, in his view, is the form that action takes, the actually existing network of social relations. I am in agreement with this formulation which considers social action both in respect to its meaning for those who carry it out, and in terms of its contribution to the functioning of some social system. In this book, I am mainly intent upon examining these aspects in their interdependence, but I have tried in Chapters Four and Five to lay dominant stress on the social process, and in Chapters Seven and Eight on the cultural fabric of ritual. That is why in Chapters Four and Five I approach performances of rites in terms of such concepts as 'social field', 'process', 'situation', 'social drama', 'conflict', the difference between 'repetitive' and 'radical' change, etc., while in Chapters Seven and Eight I consider rites as concatenations of symbols and systems of values, beliefs, and 'meanings'. These two orders of things are not identical, and as Geertz says, 'the particular form one of them takes does not directly imply the form the other will take': there may be discrepancy, and even tension, between them in particular situations, notably in those dominated by rapid social change. Divination and redressive ritual are stages in a single process that is peculiarly sensitive to changes, and especially breakages, in the network of existing social relations. Since they are 'naturally' so closely involved with the micro-history of contemporary groups and personalities, they must be treated theoretically in conjunction with these. Life-crisis ritual, on the other hand, is less responsive to immediate social pressures and needs, since it is geared to the life-cycles of individuals, and therefore in its theoretical treatment the anthropologist may quite legitimately begin by analysing the cultural structure of these rites. This has many affinities with the social structure, but these are with social regularities which are deeply entrenched in custom, and not with those which are the product of transient alignments of economic and political interests. Such alignments are the very soul of the 'flow patterns' which form the basic data of Chapters Four and Five of this book, and it is with these chapters in mind that I discuss divination and rituals of affliction. It is true that this discussion centres on the morphological aspects of these institutions, but the key to their understanding lies in the extended-case studies presented in Chapters Four and Five. Such case studies do not form a necessary component in the analysis of life-crisis rituals, which are unaffected by the interplay of contemporary social forces. No recourse is made to divination to find a propitious place and time for life-crisis rites. But all rituals of affliction are preceded by some recourse to divination, however perfunctory, and it is in the divinatory process that quarrels, competition, and alignments among people are brought to light. We should therefore follow the Ndembu in giving precedence, in our analysis, to the symbolism and procedures of divination.

DIVINATION AND ITS SYMBOLISM

Among Ndembu, the diviner regards his task as the practical one of revealing the causes of misfortune or death. These are almost invariably 'mystical' or 'non-empirical' in character, although human wishes, desires, and feelings are involved.

The diviners disclose what has happened, and do not foretell future events. Unlike many Southern Bantu diviners, they are seldom oracular or mantic. Furthermore, they do not inaugurate the divinatory process, but wait until clients come to consult them. Modes of divination are regarded as instruments which both detect lies and discover truth, although, since they are operated by fallible men, their verdicts are not always accepted without question. For witches are credited with extraordinary powers of deception, and even great diviners fortify themselves with special medicines to combat the deceits and illusions sent by their secret antagonists to baffle them. One such medicine is used at the first stage of a consultation. A clearing is made in the bush about half a mile from the diviner's village. Two poles are inserted in the ground, and a third placed on them to make a frame resembling goalposts. On this are placed three head-pads (*mbung'a*), similar to those worn by women when they carry heavy loads. These are made of a special kind of grass called *kaswamang'wadyi*. Etymologically, this term is derived from *ku-swama*, 'to hide', and *ng'wadyi*, 'the bare-throated francolin', a bird like a partridge, much prized as a food, that loves to conceal itself in this long fine grass. In hunting cults the grass is used as a symbol for the desired invisibility of the hunter when he stalks game. Here it stands for the witch's attempts to conceal vital matters from the diviner. I translate a text given me by a diviner, explaining the meaning of the head-pad. 'The head-pad is a sign to the diviner not to forget anything, for he must not be ignorant of anything. A witch or sorcerer [*muloji* means both] could use medicine to deceive the diviner [*chitahu* or *mukwakuhong'a*], or hide things from him. The head-pad is medicine to prevent this, for it keeps the diviner wide awake, it is a reminder to him. The grass in it is twisted, like the witch's attempts to deceive.' Under the frame must pass the diviner's clients, who may unwittingly harbour a sorcerer or witch in their ranks. The medicine may expose him to the diviner.

Another medicine used by diviners, and kept by them in small calabashes (*malembu*) while they divine, is a nerve from the root of an elephant's tusk. In ritual contexts this is called *nsomu*. Because it resembles a limp penis, it often has the meaning of masculine impotence. In divination it has the further meaning of a sorcerer, for sorcerers are believed to be able to blast the fertility of their victims. They are also believed to be able to kill them. *Nsomu* is also a suitable symbol for death, since impotence is regarded as a kind of death. When an impotent man dies, a black line is drawn with charcoal from his navel downwards and over his genitals, indicating that his name, and with it certain vital elements of his personality, must never be inherited by the children of his kin. This is social death. Known sorcerers are treated in the same fashion.

As a divinatory medicine, *nsomu* was interpreted to me as follows by a diviner: 'Diviners use it to see secret things which crop up unexpectedly when they are divining, just as a hunter expects to come upon animals by chance when he is hunting. *Nsomu* is like a torch at night whereby he can see witches openly. This is because *nsomu* is a secret thing that has been brought into the open. Let me explain this to you further. A pregnant woman gave birth unexpectedly to a stillborn child. Some old women took that child to bury it in its grave. Before burying it, they cut off part of one of its fingers. These women were witches who eat human beings. They use the finger together with *nsomu* to kill people. The child was just like *nsomu*; it came suddenly and unfortunately died.'

I have cited these texts at length, for two reasons. The first is to demonstrate how readily and explicitly diviners are able to offer interpretations of their symbols. The second is to exhibit an important variation on a theme which pervades all Ndembu ritual, that of 'bringing into the open what is hidden or unknown'. This variation has the special sense of 'exposing deception and secret malice'. The main theme of 'revealing the hidden' is exemplified in all cults to cure persons afflicted by the shades[1] with disease, reproductive disorders, or bad luck at hunting. The cure is essentially a process of what Ndembu call 'making known and visible' (*ku-solola* or *ku-mwekesa*), albeit in symbolic guise, the unknown and invisible agents of affliction. This is brought about in various ways. One way is by mentioning the shade's name in prayer and invocation (*ku-tena ijina damukishi*). The belief is that the spirit is aggrieved because it has been forgotten, not only by the victim, but also by many of its other kin. It afflicts its living kinsman, sometimes in his personal capacity, but often in his capacity as representative of a kin-group. If, however, it is mentioned, and hence remembered, by many people, it will cease to afflict and will henceforward benefit its victim, who becomes a sort of living memorial to it. Another way is through representing the shade in some kind of material form, either as a figurine named after it, or as a contraption of branches covered with a blanket whitened with cassava meal. These representations are made at the end of protracted rituals, in sacred sites which only cult-adepts may enter, called *masoli* (from the verb *ku-solola*, 'to make visible' or 'reveal'). It is said that when the spirit is afflicting its victim, it is concealed in his or her body. This is thought especially to be the case where women suffer from some reproductive disorder. But when the spirit has been adequately represented in symbolic form, and frequently named, it is believed to emerge, reconciled with the victim and his whole kin-group.

The Ndembu term for 'symbol' itself contains the implication of a revelatory process. This term is *chinjikijilu*, and is derived from *ku-jikijila*, 'to blaze a trail' in the bush. When hunters set out on expeditions into the deep bush (perhaps into thick

expose, reveal

---

[1] Monica Wilson's term for 'ancestral spirits'. For Ndembu concepts of the shades and related entities, see Appendix A, pp. 284-90.

Cryptosepalum forest), they cut marks on trees, and also break
and bend over their lower branches to indicate the way back.
The blaze or landmark, in other words, leads from unknown,
and therefore in Ndembu experience as well as belief, from
dangerous territory to known and familiar surroundings, from
the lonely bush to the populated village. Ritual symbols have
a similar function, for they give a visible form to unknown
things; they express in concrete and familiar terms what is
hidden and unpredictable. They enable men to domesticate
and manipulate wild and wayward forces.

When the diviner confronts witchcraft, he seeks to expose
secret deceit and malice, to reveal the identity and the motives
of sorcerers and witches. This aim shapes much of the symbolism
of divination. Leaving aside the personal acuity of the diviner,
the symbols he uses reveal how Ndembu have come to stereo-
type certain forms of fraudulent and malevolent behaviour.
Ndembu have many types of divination. I have records of
ten, and C. M. N. White (1947) has written of others I did not
meet with. Here I am concerned with one mode of divination
only, since it brings out most clearly the stereotyping of hidden
malice, as well as certain other characteristics of divinatory
symbolism shortly to be discussed.

This is called by Ndembu *ng'ombu yakusekula*, literally
'divination by shaking up or tossing (objects in a basket)'.
The diviner keeps a set of anything from twenty to thirty
objects, of various shapes, sizes, and colours, in a round basket
with a lid. When he divines he places these objects in a round
flat open basket (*lwalu*), of the type used by women to winnow
millet, shakes them, and throws them up so that they form a
heap at the far side of the basket. He examines the top three
or four objects, individually, in combination, and with reference
to their relative height in the heap. Before throwing, he asks
his apparatus a question. Then he throws three times, after
each throw putting the top few objects under the rest of the
heap before shaking the basket again. After the third throw, he
asks his consultants a question, suggested to him, Ndembu say,
by the arrangement of the objects in his basket. If the same
object comes uppermost three successive times, one of its
various senses is reckoned to be certainly part of the answer the
diviner seeks. If a particular combination, stratified in a

particular way, comes to the top three times running, the diviner has the greater part of his answer. His skill as an individual lies in the way in which he adapts his general exegesis of the objects to the given circumstances. For he is usually confronted by a group of kin who wish to find out which particular ancestor, sorcerer, or witch is causing the sickness or misfortune of their relative. Ndembu believe that this group itself may contain sorcerers or witches. In reality, as the diviner well knows, it may contain rival factions, one of which may stand to benefit by the death of the sick person if the latter holds office or is wealthy. If his clients wish him to divine into the cause of a death, the situation is still more serious. In the past, before witchcraft and witch-finding were declared illegal by the British Administration, such consultations took place near the most important village in the neighbourhood cluster of villages where the deceased person lived. Everyone in the neighbourhood was expected to attend, and failure to do so was a cause of suspicion. The diviner had to make a sound appraisal of the balance of power between rival factions interested in the death who were present at the public gathering. If he did not, and gave an unpopular verdict, he was likely to be in some danger himself. Many diviners sought the protection of a chief and performed near his capital village. But I have been told of several diviners who, despite such protection, were speared to death by angry kin of the persons declared to be sorcerers.

The winnowing basket itself stands for the sifting of truth from falsehood. The diviner is believed to be possessed by the spirit of a diviner-ancestor, in a particular manifestation known as *Kayong'u*. *Kayong'u* is also said to be a 'man-slayer' (*kambanji*), because people may be slain as a result of a divining decision. It is the *Kayong'u* spirit which causes the diviner to tremble, and thus to shake the basket. Before becoming a diviner he must have been afflicted by this spirit, which causes asthmatic shortness of breath and makes him tremble violently while being washed with medicine. He is treated by a cult-group led by a famous diviner. Many of the symbols of the *Kayong'u* ritual stand for the 'sharpness' which he must display as a diviner. These include needles and razors, the former being embedded in the hearts of a sacrificed cock and goat. When the

diviner trembles and breathes heavily he is said to be feeling
the pricking of the needle, which itself symbolizes the *Kayong'u*
spirit, in his heart, lungs, and liver. After he has been treated,
the novice-diviner apprentices himself to an established
diviner, who teaches him the meanings of the objects in a
diviner's basket. The established diviner encourages the
novice to divine himself, criticizes his performance, and gives
him some of his own equipment. He enlists the aid of a professional wood-carver to make others. In Angola today, a
novice may pay forty yards of cloth or a cow for knowledge of
how to interpret divining objects. In the past, it is said that a
novice would give forty yards of cloth and a muzzle-loader, or
even a slave, for such knowledge.

I have information on twenty-eight divinatory symbols.
Their total range of meaning embraces the whole sorry story
of misfortune, loss, and death in Ndembu life, and of the mean,
selfish, revengeful motives believed to be responsible for
these afflictions.[1] Since so few objects represent so many things,
it is not surprising to find that each of them has many meanings.
Furthermore, the links between separate meanings of the same
symbol are often of the vaguest sort, indeed, in some instances
hardly perceptible to the European observer, unless he can set
the symbol in its specific context of Ndembu culture. It is
likely that some of the meanings have developed in the course
of time as the result of the recurrent appearance in configurations of the symbolic items. In a typical diviner's basket these
have come to possess the property of being easily combined in a
wide variety of such configurations.

The symbolic items are called by Ndembu, *tuponya* (singular:
kaponya). Some are further designated as *ankishi* (singular:
nkishi). These are figurines representing generalized human
beings in various postures. The root *-kishi* is found in the term
for ancestor spirit *mu-kishi*, and in the term for the masks and
costumes used at circumcision and funerary rituals, *makishi*
(singular: *i-kishi*). The general sense underlying these various

[1] Junod, H. (1927), p. 571. 'The diviner's basket [of the Mozambique Tsonga]
is a resumé of their whole social order, of all their institutions.' Ndembu divination
highlights the seamy side of social life, stresses *conflict* rather than regularity. Only
those aspects and institutions of society which consistently form part of the background of action-situations of conflict and disturbance are represented by the
symbols.

meanings seems to be some kind of mystical power associated with human beings, alive or dead. Here I will discuss three figurines or *ankishi*, and seven other divinatory objects or *tuponya*. Both classes have reference to human activity and purpose. Some represent structural features in human life, aspects of the cultural landscape, principles of social organization and social groups and categories, and dominant customs regulating economic, sexual, and social life. Others represent forces or dynamic entities, such as motives, wishes, desires, and feelings. Not infrequently the same symbol expresses both an established custom, and a set of stereotyped disputes and forms of competition that have developed around it. It is roughly true that the human figurines represent social and emotional stereotypes; while many of the other objects refer specifically to Ndembu structure and culture.

The same *tuponya* are used in different stages of a consultation, and the meaning of each symbolic item may change somewhat at each stage. Rather than follow a consultation through, stage by stage, I will present excerpts from texts about some *tuponya* and analyse those excerpts which exemplify their use at some stages and not at others. But something, I feel, should be said, by way of introduction, about the stages of a consultation. The diviner first invokes the aid of ancient chiefs, and of the spirit of a diviner-ancestor. Diviners claim that at this stage they already know everything about the case, but that their duty is to make everything clear to their clients. That is why they use the method of question and answer. The clients are expected to try to deceive the diviner by giving incorrect answers to his questions, feigning to agree with him when they really disagree, and vice versa. As their answers are of the 'yea and nay' variety, and as they must exhibit spontaneous unanimity before the diviner makes his next point, it is not too difficult for an experienced diviner to spot discrepancies. First of all, he ascertains why they have come: on account of death, or because of sickness or misfortune? If they have come 'about death', he finds out whether the deceased was a man or a woman. Next he discovers whether the death was caused by sickness or accident. If the death is by sickness, was the illness long or short, in what part of the body, and was it contracted during the day or at night? He finds out what kinds of bark rope were used for the stretcher to carry the corpse to the grave, also whether the body was buried wrapped up in mats or nailed up in a box. An experienced diviner will then ascertain the name given to the deceased at birth. He does this by classifying all Ndembu names under various rubrics (*nyichidi*, 'kinds') with an increasing specificity. Thus he will ask, 'Does the name belong to the ground, to trees, to water, to animals, to fish, where is it?' Step by step he proceeds until he identifies the right category. Under the rubric 'animals', for example, fall the subcategories *yikwa* ('hoof-marks') and *mafumbu* ('pad-marks'). *Chifulu* ('wildebeest') is a personal name belonging to the first of these sub-categories. Under 'water' (*menji*), fall the names *malowa* ('black mud'), *mulumbi* ('a torrent'), *chifu* (a small bush overhanging rivers), and so on. In all this, he is as logical as Linnaeus himself.

Then he finds out the precise relationship of each of his clients to the deceased person. Next he discovers the relationship to the dead, and the name of the sorcerer or witch who killed him. Finally, he finds out the exact nature of the enmity between witch and victim, its history and motivation. Often in the past the order of the last two enquiries was inverted. The consultation ended with the diviner's assistant putting red clay (*mukundu* or *nkung'u*) on the head of the sorcerer or witch as a sign of guilt. Meanwhile the diviner darted away into the bush to avoid being attacked by the latter's kin and friends.

If the person consulted about was sick, the enquiry would take a different course. The main trend of the divination would be to ascertain the relationship and name of the shade afflicting the patient, the grounds of its punitive action, its mode of manifestation, and the propitiatory cult ritual appropriate to that mode. Often, of course, sickness is also attributed to witchcraft. Both for death and sickness the divinatory process consists of first bringing to light matters hidden to the diviner, then matters hidden to the clients. Where sickness is concerned, the curative ritual completes this process of revelation, and, in the case of spirits, also of commemoration. Each pronouncement made by a diviner after questioning is called a *chidimbu*, 'a point' or 'statement.'

Bearing these phases of interrogation in mind, let us now examine the human figurines or *ankishi*. The most important

Shade affliction

of these is a group of three, clipped together in a band of horn, representing a man, a woman, and a child. These are called either simply *ankishi*, 'figurines' or *Akulumpi*, 'the Elders'. The prefix *A-* here implies that the figures are invested with some animate quality. They are 'Elders' in several senses. In the first place, they are the most important of the *tuponya*, the focal point of reference, so to speak, in the whole set. In the second place, they represent a chief and his kin. The male figurine is compared with *Mwantiyanvwa*, the title of the great Lunda king in the Congo, from whose kingdom the Ndembu, like many other Central African tribes, are said to have migrated about two hundred and fifty to three hundred years ago. If, when the diviner is trying to detect a sorcerer, a piece of red clay in a container of mongoose skin, representing 'enmity' or 'a grudge', comes persistently to the top of the set with 'the Elders', this means that the sorcerer belongs to the close kin of a chief, or might even be a chief himself. In the third place, 'the Elders' might represent a headman and his kin, depending upon the question asked. If a thin circlet of iron, called *Lukanu* and representing the bracelet worn among Ndembu only by Senior Chief Kanongesha, repeatedly comes to the top with 'the Elders', this means that either Kanongesha or his close kin played an important role in the situation divined into. Or if a lump of white clay (*mpemba* or *mpeza*) were to rise with them when sorcery was being investigated, this would mean that Kanongesha and his kin were innocent. Again, the diviner might himself specify that 'the Elders' stood for a particular matrilineage (*ivumu*), perhaps that descended from the dead person's own mother's mother. He might ask 'Did the enmity come from this lineage?' If then 'the Elders' came to the top three times, associated, for example, with red clay and another object called *Chanzang'ombi*, in the form of a wooden snake with a human face, representing a sorcery-familiar called *ilomba*, this would be proof that a male member of that lineage was the sorcerer, and had killed because he had a grudge against his victim.

In other contexts and phases 'the Elders' represent sorcerers or witches, in a general sense, without particularizing the mode of bewitching. Thus, if a random assortment of objects, consisting of 'the Elders', red clay, white clay, one called *Chimbu*, which represents a spotted hyaena and often stands for women's necrophagous witchcraft and a witch's familiar, and a piece of wood wrapped round with bark string, representing a corpse tied to a bier (called *Mufu*, 'a dead person'), rose to the top of the heap, the diviner might say, addressing his *tuponya*: 'Why have you appeared here, piece of white clay? Does this mean that there is no witchcraft here at all?' Then he might put the uppermost set under the other *tuponya* and shake his basket again. If all except the white clay appear again on top, and this combination is then repeated twice more, he would argue as follows: ' "the Elders" mean that someone has been bewitched—to death, for *Mufu* can mean a dead person (from *ku-fwa*, 'to die'). The red clay means that enmity or revengefulness (*chitela*) led to witchcraft. And *Chimbu* tells me that the killer was a woman, a necrophagous witch. Now I must find out where this woman came from. Perhaps from the mother's side, perhaps from the victim's father's? Or perhaps from a stranger residing in the village, or from a woman married into it (*kudi ambanda amasumbu*)?'

What is interesting in terms of social relations is that the man, woman, and child, comprising 'the Elders', are not primarily regarded as an elementary family, although they can be specified as such, but as co-members of a matrilineage—not necessarily brother, sister and sister's child, but interlinked in any way the diviner cares to designate. All kinds of groups, relationships, and differences of status can be expressed by this symbol doing all kinds of things. Divinatory symbols are multi-referential, and their referents are highly autonomous and readily detachable from one another. Ritual symbols proper are much more highly condensed; their meanings inter-penetrate and fuse, giving them greater emotional resonance.

The second figurine we shall consider is called *Chamutang'a*. It represents a man sitting huddled up with chin on hands and elbows on knees. *Chamutang'a* means an irresolute, changeable person. One informant told me a little tale to bring out the meaning of the term. 'Once upon a time a man became ill. One of his relatives said to the others, "Let's go to a diviner and find out why our relative is sick." The others answered, "We can't afford a diviner's fees." Later, the illness grew worse, and another relative said, "We really ought to consult a diviner." Again the others replied that they hadn't enough money. "Besides," they said, "we drank a lot of beer last night and got up early to work in the gardens, so we're tired out. But you're welcome to go to a diviner if you want to." Shortly afterwards some female relatives of those people came on a visit, and asked to see the sick man. "Oh, he is really sick now," they replied. "Perhaps we'd better have a look at him." They found him at his last gasp, but still just alive. "Oh, oh we think he's dead now. We can do no more for him now, poor fellow." A few days later the man died in good earnest. Eventually someone took the matter to a diviner. The diviner shook his *tuponya* and *Chamutang'a* kept coming up. He told the dead man's relatives, "This man has died because you could not make up your minds. Even if none of you are sorcerers, you have a share of the guilt." '

It is obvious that from one point of view diviners use *Chamutang'a* in their professional interest. They state firmly that, if someone falls ill, people should have speedy recourse to a diviner. Poverty is no excuse. On the other hand, the employment of this symbol asserts certain pervasive social values. People should put the care of their kin before all selfish considerations. Sins of omission in this respect are almost as bad as sins of commission, such as sorcery. Again, people should make up their minds quickly to do their duty; they should not equivocate.

Chamutang'a also means 'the man whom no one knows how to take'. His reactions are unnatural. Capriciously, informants say, he will at one time give presents to people, at another time he will act meanly. Sometimes he will laugh immoderately with others, sometimes he will keep silent for no apparent reason. No one can guess when he will be angry or when he will fail to show anger. Ndembu like a man whose behaviour is predictable.[1] They praise both openness and consistency, and a man whom they feel is not genuine may very likely be a sorcerer. The theme that what is hidden is probably dangerous and malevolent is once again exemplified.

Chamutang'a has the further meaning of 'a man who is all things to all men'. They put it in this way: 'Such a man is like beeswax. If it is taken to the fire, it melts; if it is taken into

---

[1] A high value is therefore attached to the man who observes custom.

the cold, it becomes hard.' In other words, a man of this sort doesn't ring true. He changes his behaviour with his company. The 'smooth' man, just as much as the awkward customer, is likely to be a sorcerer. Both are men whom, as Ndembu say, 'one fails to know'.

Diviners sometimes use *Chamutang'a* to withdraw from the awkward situation that may arise if they cannot enlist the unanimous agreement of their clients for their judgements. One client may deny the diviner's imputation that he is a sorcerer, others may support him, others, again, may say that they are not certain about it, and yet others may assert that the divination itself was false, perhaps because of the interference of a witch. In such situations, *Chamutang'a* is liable to come uppermost in the basket. The diviner asks *Chamutang'a*: 'What have you come here for? Does this mean that my divination is in error?' If it appears two or three times running, the diviner 'closes down' the divination (*wajika jing'ombu*), demanding from those who have come to consult him a couple of pieces of cloth for his trouble. The diviner tries to salve his reputation by blaming his clients for the failure, and tells them that the witch in their midst is trying to confuse his verdict. This is one of the sanctions against lack of unanimity in response to a diviner's queries and statements (*nyikunyi*).

The other figurine normally used by diviners is an effigy of a man in the traditional posture of grief with both hands clasped to his head. It is called *Katwambimbi* (from *ku-twa*, 'to pound' and *mbimbi*, 'weeping'). It means the 'one who inaugurates the mourning' when someone dies. *Kutwa* is used here with reference to the position of the two hands on the head, analogous to hands on a pounding pole. The primary sense is 'the one who brings news of death' to the relatives of the deceased. Here is an example of its use in divination. When a diviner is trying to ascertain the outcome of a serious illness, and *Katwambimbi* does not come uppermost, or, as Ndembu say, 'keeps on hiding itself',[1] then there is a very good chance that the patient will survive. If, again, 'the Elders' are thrown several times on top of the heap with *Katwambimbi* just below them, it is thought that if the patient is treated by a great doctor he might recover,

---

[1] Ndembu attribute personal qualities to *tuponya*, which are said to think and will.

though it will be touch-and-go. If, on the other hand, *Katwa-mbimbi* recurrently rests on 'the Elders', it is believed that the patient will die, whatever his relatives may do. Here 'the Elders' seem to have the meaning of 'life', and *Katwambimbi* of 'death'.

But *Katwambimbi* has another and, if anything, more sinister meaning. In the words of one informant: '*Katwambimbi* is a mischief-maker (*kakobukobu*) who carries tales from one person to another, claiming that each hates and is trying to bewitch the other. If one of them is induced to kill the other by witch-craft or sorcery, *Katwambimbi* is the one who weeps the loudest at the wake, although he is the one who has the greatest guilt.' This behaviour reminds one irresistibly of the double-dealing of Mord in the Icelandic saga of *Burnt Njal*. *Katwambimbi* differs from *Chamutang'a* in the realm of perfidy, in that his hypocrisy is cold-bloodedly deliberate, whereas *Chamutang'a*'s is rather the result of weakness and default. In Ndembu custom a person divined as a *Katwambimbi* receives the same punishment as a sorcerer or witch. In the past it was death by burning, or ostracism from Ndembu society with confiscation of property; today, banishment from village and neighbourhood.

In discussing these figurines, I have found it impossible to avoid mentioning several of the other *tuponya* or divinatory symbols, such as white and red clay, the Hyaena (*Chimbu*) and the Dead (*Mufu*). This is because the dominant unit of divination is not the individual symbol, but the symbolic configuration (*kudiwung'a hamu*). I shall now examine three other commonly used *tuponya*. The first consists of three or four oblong fragments of calabash strung together, called *Yipwepu*. The word means literally 'any part of a calabash used for domestic purposes'. One of its meanings is 'a matrilineage' (*ivumu*) and by extension 'the principle of matriliny'. My best informant on ritual explained this to me as follows: 'Before a calabash is used for drawing water, it contains many seeds; these seeds are members of the lineage [literally "womb"]. Those little seeds, when they are planted anywhere, will give rise to more and more calabashes. It is the same with men and women who come to a single lineage. Without a lineage [or, better, a reckoning of descent through the mother's side] a kindred would never become so many.' Just as the bits of calabash in the *kaponya* are threaded together, Ndembu would hold, so are matrilineal kin united in a group.[1]

Yipwepu also has the general sense of 'a collection of articles' (*kulong'eja*). One such collection is the set of utensils which a woman brings into a marriage with her; at her first marriage they are usually given to her by her mother and other female uterine kin. These include a calabash, a clay pot, a round basket, a plate, and a cup. She also brings assorted seeds for planting and cassava cuttings. All these together constitute her 'collection', called colloquially, and on the principle of *pars pro toto*, *Yipwepu*. From this usage, *Yipwepu* in divination has the further meaning of 'marriage', or even virilocal marriage, and, by extension, the vicissitudes of marriage. It can, for example, mean a severe marital quarrel and, indeed, divorce, since a woman takes her 'collection' of things with her when she 'goes off in a huff' (*ku-fundumuka*).

By a further extension, *Yipwepu* means 'travelling on visits', for a traveller takes a 'collection' of food with him, a man using a cloth bundle, a woman using a long openwork basket (*mutong'a*). Again, it can stand for any happening on such journeys, usually for misfortunes such as death, sickness, or violent accident.

Yipwepu also represents a collection of duiker horns (*nyiseng'u*) containing medicines. A collection of *yipwepu*, i.e. of broken calabashes containing medicine horns, is known as *yikuyung'ulu*. One term for a man with sorcery familiars is 'a man with *yikuyung'ulu*,' i.e. with a set of 'collections'.

Finally, *Yipwepu* represents the liquids water and beer, for these are contained in calabashes. It may also represent cassava mush, which is meal boiled in water. For example, if red clay rises to the top of the *tuponya* in association with *Yipwepu*, one interpretation might be that enmity between two women arose over the possession of a calabash. It might also mean that a calabash of beer or a plate of mush had been 'medicated' by a sorcerer. Which reading was correct would depend upon the juxtaposition of other *tuponya* as qualificatives.

Another *kaponya* is the large, hard stone of a species of tree called *mucha* (*Parinari mobola*). In divination, this is called

---

[1] The same principle applies in the girl's puberty ritual (*Nkang'a*) where a *string* of white beads represents the children of one womb.

Mwaka, which means literally 'a season', as in the expressions
'dry season' and 'rainy season'. It also stands for 'a long time',
and sometimes for 'long ago', 'in the distant past'. *Mucha*
fruits take a long time to mature, and the stones take an even
longer time to decay in the ground, considered by Ndembu to
be a remarkable phenomenon, with so many bird, animal,
and insect scavengers about.

In divination, one meaning of *Mwaka* is 'a long illness'.
This often has the implication of a long process of bewitching
or ensorcelling. For the *ilomba*, the human-faced snake-familiar
already mentioned, is believed gradually to swallow its victim,
beginning with the legs, and proceeding upwards. Only people
who have drunk a potion called *nsompu* can see this happening.
For others, the patient appears to be suffering from a protracted
illness.

Another meaning of *Mwaka* is 'long delay before consulting
a diviner'. It can also stand for 'a protracted sorcery duel'.
I have heard the following described as 'a case of *Mwaka*': a
man A had a younger brother B. Their mother lived virilocally
with her husband. B went to stay with her and married into
her husband's village. His wife had lovers there among her
village kin. It is alleged that some of them bewitched B, so that
he died. A afterwards came to the village, and, it is said, killed
two of its members in revenge by sorcery. He then fled from the
village. After many years he returned there to visit his mother.
Shortly afterwards he died. One of my diviner-informants told
me that he enquired into this case when A's relatives consulted
him. Clearly, he said, A had been bewitched by his mother's
affines. But the enmity between the parties had a long history.
This was first revealed to him by his *Mwaka*, which came to
the top 'four times in succession'. Then he searched out the
details of the case.

The last *kaponya* I will mention here is a tiny wooden carving
of a drum, known as *Ng'oma*, 'the Drum', or as *mufu wamwaka*,
'a dead person from long ago'. The appearance of *Ng'oma*
means that a spirit, and not a witch or sorcerer, has 'caught' or
'afflicted' the patient. The term 'drum' is frequently used for
a performance of ritual, and there are few kinds of ritual which
do not possess their own especial drum rhythm. Having ascertained that a curative and propitiatory ritual is required, the

diviner finds out which particular curative cult should perform it. He does this by mentioning the names of the cults in order. The diviner says to his *tuponya*, 'I am going to play the drum of the *Nkula* ritual, will you please let us know if this is correct?' If 'the Drum' then appears two or three times in succession on top of 'the Elders', he knows that he is right. The different kinds of ritual are not individually represented in the diviner's basket, although sometimes the *Kayong'u* shade-manifestation and the propitiatory ritual named after it are represented by a seed of the *mudidi* palm, from which palm wine is made, drunk by adepts at *Kayong'u* rituals. *Kayong'u*, it will be remembered, is the ritual men must undergo if they wish to become 'great diviners'.

On the face of it, divinatory symbols seem to reflect explicit human purposes. They are used to enable diviners to discover the causes of misfortune, and to suggest possible remedies. The diviner, as I have said, behaves in an astute and rational way, given his axiomatic beliefs in spirits, mystical forces, and witches. He is not above a certain low cunning at times, as we saw with regard to his manipulation of the figurine *Chamutang'a*. Nevertheless, the bases of his craft are rooted in mystical beliefs, and he is himself a believer. Without belief, I feel that he would not possess insight into Ndembu social life, which is governed by values with which he largely identifies himself. I say 'identifies' advisedly, since the diviner himself believes that he harbours in his body the *Kayong'u* shade-manifestation, which, more than any other manifestation, is believed to detect breach of norm, rebellion against, or deviation from, Ndembu moral prescriptions. The shade is using the diviner's sharp wits on behalf of Ndembu society. That is why a diviner must be in a fit moral condition before he undertakes a consultation. For example, he must be sexually continent for some time before and during the period in which he is divining. He must avoid many foods. He must not harbour malice in his heart against anyone, as this would bias his judgement. He must be a pure and empty vehicle for the *Kayong'u* shade. For instance, he may not eat two species of burrowing rodents which fill up the entrances to their tunnels. It is believed that if he eats these, they will 'stop up' his chest and liver, the parts of the body which *Kayong'u* occupies during the act of divination.

The diviner feels that he is not primarily operating on his own behalf, but on behalf of his society. At divinations, the physiological stimuli provided by drummings and singing, the use of archaic formulae in questions and responses, together with the concentration demanded by his divining technique, take him out of his everyday self and heighten his intuitive awareness: he is a man with a vocation. He also measures actual behaviour against ideals. As we have seen, several of the symbols he manipulates owe something of their meaning to values attached to openness, honesty and truthfulness. One of his avowed aims is to make known and intelligible in Ndembu terms what is unknown and unintelligible. Underlying his task is the presumption that unless people bring their grudges and rancours into the open, 'into the public eye', these will fester and poison the life of a group. Shades afflict the living with misfortune to bring such hidden struggles sharply to the attention of members of disturbed groups before it is too late. The diviner can then recommend that a cult-association be called in to perform ritual which will not only cure an individual patient, but also heal disturbances in the group. But where animosities have become deep and cankered, they become associated with the lethal power of witchcraft. The malignant individual himself becomes a social canker. At this point it is little use trying to cure the selfish or envious sorcerer or witch. He must be extirpated, rooted out of the group, at whatever cost to those of his kin who love him or depend on him. I am satisfied that some diviners, at any rate, are convinced that they are performing a public duty without fear or favour. It is a grave responsibility to be possessed by the *Kayong'u* shade and become a diviner. For henceforth one is not entirely one's own man. One belongs to society, and to society as a whole, and not to one or other of its structured sub-groups.

The diviner is a ratiocinating individual. But the premises from which he deduces consequences may be non-rational ones. He does not try to 'go behind' his beliefs in supernatural beings and forces. That is why divinatory objects are better classed with symbols than with signs, although they have some of the attributes of the latter. He treats as self-evident truths what social anthropologists and depth psychologists would try to reduce to rational terms. These scholars, in their professional role at any rate, do not concede that spirits and witches have existence. For most of them these entities are themselves 'symbols' for endopsychic or social drives and forces, which they set themselves the task of discovering.

Certain distinctions can be made between divinatory symbolism and the symbolism of rituals of life-crisis and affliction. In the former, the cognitive aspect is much more pronounced; in the latter, the orectic aspect, that concerned with feelings and desires, is clearly dominant. The diviner, granted his premises—which are shared by his consultants—is trying to grasp consciously and bring into the open the secret, and even unconscious, motives and aims of human actors in some situation of social disturbance. In the public ritual of the Ndembu, symbols may be said to stimulate emotions. Both kinds of symbols have multiple meanings, but in ritual symbols proper those *significata* which represent emotionally-charged phenomena and processes, such as blood, milk, semen, and faeces, are fused and condensed with *significata* which stand for aspects of social virtue, such as matriliny, marriage, chieftain-ship, etc., or virtues such as generosity, piety towards the ancestors, respect for the elders, manly uprightness, and so on. The emotional, mainly physiological, referents may well lend their qualities to the ethical and normative referents so as to make what is obligatory desirable. They seem, as Sapir wrote, to 'send roots down into the unconscious', and, I would add, to bring sap up to the conscious.

But the semantic structure of divinatory symbols shows that the senses possessed by a symbol are not so much 'fused' as sharply distinguished. Their semantic structure has 'brittle segmentation'. I mean by this that a divinatory symbol possesses a series of senses, only one of which is relevant at a time, i.e. at an inspection of a configuration of symbols. An important symbol in a ritual of affliction or of life-crisis is felt to represent *many things at once*; all its senses are simultaneously present. Divinatory symbols may, therefore, be called 'analytical', and ritual symbols 'synthetical'. The former are used to discriminate between items that have become confused and obscure; the latter represent fusions of many apparently disparate items. The brittle segmentation of divinatory symbols may be because the same symbols are used in a series of enquiries, each of which has its own specific aim—such as to discover a relationship between witch and victim, or to find a motive for ensorcelling, or to seek out the precise mode of shade-affliction, and so on. The meaning of each individual symbol is subordinated to the meaning of a configuration of symbols, and each configuration is a means to a clearly defined and conscious end. The system of meanings possessed by the ritual symbol proper derives both from some deep and universal human need or drive and from a universal human norm controlling that drive. A divinatory symbol, on the other hand, helps the diviner to decide what is right and wrong, to establish innocence or guilt in situations of misfortune, and to prescribe well-known remedies. His role falls between that of a judge and that of a ritual expert. But, whereas a judge enquires into conscious motives, a diviner often seeks to discover unconscious impulses behind anti-social behaviour. To discover these he uses intuition as much as reason. He 'feels after' the stresses and sore points in relationships, using his configurations of symbolic objects to help him concentrate on detecting the difficulties in configurations of real persons and relationships. Both he and they are governed by the axiomatic norms of Ndembu society. Thus the symbols he uses are not mere economical devices for purposes of reference, i.e. 'signs', but have something of the 'subliminal' quality of ritual symbols proper. With their aid he can say, for instance, that a shade is 'making her granddaughter ill because the people of such-and-such a village are not living well with one another', or that 'a man killed his brother by sorcery because he wanted to be headman'. With their aid he can prescribe remedial ritual measures. But he cannot diagnose the empirical causes of social 'divisiveness',[1] any more than of sickness or death. The diviner's conscious knowledge and control is limited by supra-conscious social and moral forces and by unconscious bio-physical forces. Yet divinatory symbols are as close to 'signs' as they are to Jung's 'symbols', pregnant with unknown meaning.

[1] 'Divisiveness' is defined by Beals and Siegel to describe 'those varieties of conflict which the membership of an organization regards as detrimental and as requiring remedial action' (Beals, A. R. and Siegel, B. J., *Divisiveness: Conflict within the Group*, Stanford University Press (1966), p. 1).

DIVINATION AS A PHASE IN A SOCIAL PROCESS

Divination is a phase in a social process which begins with a person's death or illness, or with reproductive trouble, or with misfortune at hunting. Informal or formal discussion in the kinship or local group of the victim leads to the decision to consult a diviner. The actual consultation or seance, attended by the victim's kin and/or neighbours, is the central episode in the process. It is followed by remedial action according to the diviner's verdict, action which may consist of the destruction or expulsion of a sorcerer/witch, or of the performance of ritual by cult specialists to propitiate or exorcise particular manifestations of shades, or of the application of medicines according to the diviner's prescription by a leech or medicine man.

Death, disease and misfortune are usually ascribed to tensions in the local kin group, expressed as personal grudges charged with the mystical power of sorcery or witchcraft, or as beliefs in the punitive action of ancestor spirits. Diviners try to elicit from their clients responses which give them clues to the current tensions in their groups of origin. Divination, therefore, becomes a form of social analysis, in the course of which hidden conflicts are revealed so that they may be dealt with by traditional and institutionalized procedures. It is in the light of this function of divination as a mechanism of social redress that we must consider its symbolism, the social composition of its consultative sessions, and its procedures of interrogation.

We must always remember that the standards against which social harmony and disharmony are assessed are those of Ndembu culture and not of Western social science. They are those of a society which, possessing only a rudimentary technology and limited empirical skills and knowledge, consequently has a low degree of control over its material environment. It is a society highly vulnerable to natural disasters, such as disease, infant mortality, and intermittent food shortages. Furthermore, its ethical yardsticks are those of a community composed of small residential groups of close kin. Since kinship guides co-residence and confers rights to succeed to office and inherit property, the major problems of Ndembu society bear on the maintenance of good relations between kin, and on the reduction of competition and rivalry between

them. Furthermore, since persons of incompatible tempera-
ments and characters are frequently forced into daily propinquity
by kinship norms which enjoin respect and co-operation
among them, inter-personal hostilities tend to develop that
are forbidden direct expression. Hidden grudges (*yitela*)
rankle and grow, as Ndembu are well aware. In the idiom of
Ndembu culture these grudges are associated with the mystical
power of sorcery/witchcraft.

Ndembu themselves list jealousy, envy, greed, pride, anger,
lust, and the desire to steal as causes of discord in group life,
and these vices are by no means unfamiliar to us. Nevertheless,
these symptoms of a disordered human nature spring from a
specific social structure. In their attempts to diminish the
disastrous consequences of these 'deadly sins' in social life,
Ndembu bring into operation institutionalized mechanisms of
redress that are ordered towards the maintenance of that social
structure. Divination, as we have seen, is one of those mechanisms, and in it we can observe many idiosyncratic features.

In the first place, the diviner clearly knows that he is investigating within a social context of a particular type. He first
establishes the location of the Senior Chief's area, then that of
the Sub-chief's, then the vicinage, and finally the village of the
victim. Each of these political units has its own social characteristics—its factional divisions, its inter-village rivalries, its
dominant personalities, its nucleated and dispersed groups of
kindred—each possessing a history of settlement or migration.
An experienced diviner will be familiar with the contemporary
state of these political systems from previous consultations and
from the voluminous gossip of wayfarers. Next he finds out the
relationship between the victim and those who have come to
consult him. He is assisted in this task by his knowledge of the
categories of persons who typically make up the personnel of a
village: the victim's matrilineal kin, his patrilateral kin, his
affines, and unrelated persons. He finds out the victim's relationship to the headman, and he then focuses his attention on
the headman's matrilineage, and discovers into how many
sub-lineages it may be segmented.

By the time he has finished his interrogation, he has a complete picture of the current structure of the village, and of the
position occupied in it by the victim and by those who came to

consult him. Since it is common for representatives of each of its important segments, as well as affines of members of its matrilineal nucleus, to visit a diviner in the event of an important man's death, and since these representatives may not make the same responses to key questions, the diviner does not have to look far for indications of structural cleavages in the village. Diviners are also aware that there is a general association between the kind of misfortune about which he is consulted, the sex of the victim, the composition of the group of clients, and the size and structure of the political or residential unit from which they come. Thus only a few close kin or affines will normally consult a diviner about a woman's barrenness or a hunter's bad luck. But a large party, representative of all segments of a Sub-chiefdom, will come to him when a Sub-chief dies. This association does not always hold true, however, for the death or even illness of a child may sometimes be taken as the occasion to bring into the open the dominant cleavage in a large village if the time is felt to be ripe. But diviners have learnt by experience—their own and their society's, incorporated in divinatory procedure and symbolism —to reduce their social system to a few basic principles and factors, and to juggle with these until they arrive at a decision that accords with the views of the majority of their clients at any given consultation.

They are guided, however, not by an objective analysis of the social structure, but rather by an intuition into what is just and fitting in terms both of Ndembu moral values and an ethical code which would be recognized as valid by all human groups. Just as Africans have been shown to operate in their judicial processes with the universally recognized concept of the 'reasonable man',[1] or 'man of sense', so do they operate in their divinatory processes with the universally recognized concept of the 'good man' or 'moral man', *muntu wamuwahi*. This is the man who bears no grudges, who is without jealousy, envy, pride, anger, covetousness, lust, greed, etc., and who honours his kinship obligations. Such a man is open, he has 'a white liver', he has nothing to conceal from anyone, he does

---

[1] See Gluckman, M. *The Judicial Process among the Barotse of Northern Rhodesia*, Manchester University Press (1955), p. 126. He argues that the Lozi concept of the 'upright man' embraces both 'sense' and 'uprightness'.

not curse his fellows, he respects and remembers his ancestors. The diviner looks for sorcerers and witches among those who do not measure up to this standard of morality. Indeed, he looks for them among the positive transgressors, among those whom his clients admit to be wrongdoers or 'slippery customers'. In the cases of illness, infertility, and bad luck at hunting, he applies the same measure of the 'moral man' to individuals, although he also applies the yardstick of the 'moral group', which lives in mutual amity and collectively reveres its ancestors and respects its political authorities. But here it would seem he is on the look out not so much for 'mortal sins' as for 'venial sins', for grudges that have not grown murderous, for offences that may yet be forgiven, for quarrels that have not yet split up a group.

A sinner (*mukwanshidi*) is defined by Ndembu as 'one who has ill feeling for other people (*mukwanshidi watiyang'a kutama nawakwawu antu*)'. *Kutama*, 'to be bad, evil, unpleasant, ugly', is linked with the symbolism of blackness, darkness, death, sterility, and night in Ndembu ritual. It is the opposite of *ku-waha*, 'to be good, morally upright, pleasant, beautiful'. It is also linked with witchcraft/sorcery, theft, adulterous lust, and murder. *Ku-tama* is associated with 'secret things' (*yiswamu*), with the concealment of thoughts or possessions from others. What is 'good', for Ndembu, is the open, the public, the unconcealed, the sincere. A man is said to be 'good' when he performs his duties from 'the liver', not from calculated policy with a show of outward politeness under which malice is concealed. A man is bad when there is a marked inconsistency, or disparity, between his public behaviour and his private thoughts and feelings. The former is outwardly correct, but it conceals malice and envy. Thus the hypocrite is the real sinner. We find in the diviner's basket a representation of the weeping hypocrite (*Katwambimbi*), and several references to the duplicity of 'bad' people, i.e. of the witches and sorcerers.

Thus the diviner has to take into account both the specific structure of Ndembu society and a set of moral values and norms. Both these referents are represented in the symbolism of divination. The symbols are mnemonics, reminders of certain general rubrics of Ndembu culture, within which the diviner can classify the specific instance of behaviour that he is considering. Moreover, they have to be of such a nature as to lend themselves to configurational analysis. It is the *constellation* of symbols rather than the individual symbol which forms the typical unit of interpretation. A symbol may appear as a substantive, and in this role it may possess, say, half a dozen basic senses. By noting the reactions of the clients and attenders, the diviner can make a guess, or 'formulate a hypothesis', which will enable him to establish the particular sense of the substantival symbol: he can then allocate senses to the modifiers. Here the vagueness and flexibility of the series of referents of each symbol leave him free to make a detailed interpretation of the configuration of symbols corresponding to the diagnosis he is making of the state of relationships between his clients and the deceased, and between the living kin concerned in the matter. And once he has established a *chidimbu*, a definite point of divination, and obtained agreement on its veracity or likelihood, he has a point of departure for further enquiry, something firm to go on. He may then deduce logical consequences from the *chidimbu*, regarded as a set of premises. Furthermore, he has established a certain psychological ascendancy over his audience, so that they tend to become less guarded in their replies, for with growing credulity in his divinatory powers they become more eager to give him the hard data he requires. I believe that this is one of the reasons why a basket-diviner tries to find the name of the deceased quite early in the seance. Diviners, as we have seen, have learnt that the vast majority of Ndembu names can be classified under relatively few main heads—'water', 'hoofed animals', 'chieftainship', etc., and after the manner of the English party game, 'Twenty Questions', they can quickly proceed from the general to the particular.[1] In a society not specially remarkable for its power of abstract thinking, the diviner's ability to do this must appear little short of miraculous. When the diviner names the deceased, therefore, he has won the credulity of his audience to such an extent that he can elicit key information without much difficulty. In other words, the logician is felt to be a magician.

It may be said in conclusion that the diviner occupies a central position with reference to several fields of social and

[1] See p. 34.

cultural relationships. He acts as a mechanism of redress and social adjustment in the field of local descent groups, since he locates areas and points of tension in their contemporary structures. Furthermore, he exonerates or accuses individuals in those groups in terms of a system of moral norms. Since he operates in emotionally charged situations, such norms are restated in a striking and memorable fashion. Thus he may be said to play a vital role in upholding tribal morality. Moral law is most vividly made known through its breach. Finally, the diviner's role is pivotal to the system of rituals of affliction and anti-witchcraft/sorcery rituals, since he decides what kind of ritual should be performed in a given instance, when it should be performed, and sometimes who should perform it. Since diviners are consulted on many occasions, it is clear that their role as upholders of tribal morality and rectifiers of disturbed social relationships—both structural and contingent—is a vital one in a society without centralized political institutions.

III

THE MORPHOLOGY OF RITUALS
OF AFFLICTION

THE single extended-case study presented in Chapter Four only becomes theoretically significant when it is placed in a series of contexts. One such context is the total system of Ndembu rituals of affliction.

Among the Ndembu, the ritual of affliction is the characteristic form of the ancestor cult. Radcliffe-Brown and other British anthropologists have pointed out that of all types of religion ancestor veneration seems most closely interconnected with social structure. This is true also of the Ndembu in a certain sense, but we must be careful not to conceptualize 'social structure' too rigidly. Ndembu society may be characterized as 'labile'; its parts are highly mobile, exhibit much independence, and are always entering into new, and generally transient combinations with one another.

Crises in the affairs of a social group often provoke ritual measures of redress. In most cases it is assumed that an unlucky or sick individual is afflicted by a shade; the whole matter speedily moves to a social plane and involves more or less everybody in the patient's local matrilineal descent group, the nuclear membership of a village.

Trouble, which may be man-made or a result of what we would call a 'natural disaster', may lead to a state of social relations in which feelings of anxiety, fear, and aggression become pervasive. Sentiments of mutual dependence are sooner or later mobilized by responsible persons; since the scale of action is public, this mobilization takes institutional forms, including recourse to divination to seek a ritual remedy. The ritual remedy thus invoked itself possesses a form similar to the whole process of crisis and redress. It originates in trouble, proceeds through the symbolization and mimesis of traditional causes of trouble and feelings associated with it, and concludes in an atmosphere of re-achieved amity and co-operativeness, with the hope of restored health, prosperity, and fertility. The rite reproduces the social situation, but in an orderly, formalized way. The quality of orderliness is connected with a belief in mystical beings which confer order on the universe as it is known to the Ndembu. Through their knowledge of the techniques of invoking such beings Ndembu periodically regain confidence in their capacity to cope with crises.

Ndembu ritual symbols represent universal values such as goodness, fertility, matrilineal kinship, generosity, elderhood, virility, contented polygyny, health, motherhood, etc. They do not represent specific corporate groups, such as moieties, clans, or lineage segments, for the Ndembu do not possess these permanent tribal divisions. Where social relationships are denoted by symbols, such relationships tend to be categorical rather than corporate. They are relationships of similarity, such as those between men, women, hunters, widows, the afflicted, and so forth, rather than relationships of commonness, which interconnect members of such corporate groups as families, villages, and political chiefdoms. Ndembu groupings are on the whole transient and unstable, and thus do not lend themselves to ritual stereotyping. What abides is not a stable system of matrilineages, but the principle of matriliny. There is not an age-set system to be ritually represented, but the principle of separation of adjacent generations. Such an assemblage of ritual symbols can the more readily be adapted to a variety of vicissitudes in the lives of small localized groups.

When we consider the social composition of ritual assemblies, we find a similar contrast between secular and ritual modes of relating roles. For rituals of affliction are performed *by* associations of the formerly afflicted, who now have the status of cult-adepts, *for* the presently afflicted and their corporate kin. The cult association transects villages and vicinages: to be a member one does not have to be another living member's kinsman. But to become a member one must be the kinsman of a deceased member. Kinship is with the dead and not necessarily with the living of a cult. Here one must advert to the distinction Ndembu make between a shade and its mode of manifestation, though many Ndembu use the same term, *mukishi*, for both aspects. It would appear, from the evidence of ritual songs and incantatory phrases, that the mode of manifestation was once distinguished by the term *ihamba*, a sense still possessed by the *lihamba* of the neighbouring Luvale; but, as we shall see, among the Ndembu *ihamba* is now restricted in its application to a specific manifestation of a hunter's shade. The mode of manifestation, in short, is common to all Ndembu of the appropriate sex and age, but the manifesting shade afflicts only its own close kin. Here we see how dependent the local community is upon the ritual associations, which together make up the widest community of adherents to Ndembu tribal religion. The multiple cult associations fulfil in some sort those social functions which, in more stable tribal societies, are fulfilled by segmentary lineage organization, by the ancestor cult, properly speaking, or by a centralized system of political and jural institutions. Social control in this labile society is to a much larger extent in the hands of specialized cult associations, uncentralized, not localized, and concerned with issues of a universal human character. Furthermore, nearly all Ndembu belong to at least one of these associations.

To convey some idea of the nature of the issues with which these cults are concerned, I present in tabular form, in Appendix C, pp. 300–302, a classified inventory of Ndembu cults of affliction known to me. This list (which I cannot claim to be complete, since Ndembu frequently adopt new rites from their neighbours) gives an impression of the exuberant development of rituals of affliction and the types of common misfortune that it is hoped they will remedy. I have described several of these rituals elsewhere,[1] and have analysed their main sociological characteristics in *Schism and Continuity*, Chapter Ten. I will now describe one of the most important rituals of affliction performed to propitiate a shade believed to cause reproductive disorders in women. My reasons for doing this are: (1) because I have myself been present at several performances of this ritual; (2) because it affords a detailed ethnographic account of a ritual which will probably soon be extinct; (3) because it provides fuller documentation for my hypothesis in a previous article[2] about the situational suppression of principles and norms from direct representation; and (4) because it is a typical cult of affliction.

---

[1] *Ndembu Divination*, op. cit.; *Chihamba, the White Spirit*, op. cit.; *Lunda Rites and Ceremonies*, op. cit.

[2] 'Symbols in Ndembu Ritual' in *The Forest of Symbols*, op. cit., pp. 39–43.

NKULA

SEQUENCE OF EPISODES

KU-LEMBEKA

Mythological charter—aims
1 Collection of Medicines
.2 Preparation of Medicines
  Nkula spirit hut
3 Treatment with Medicines
  Chaka chankula—nkula songs

KU-TUMBUKA

(*first day*)
4 Collection of Medicines
5 Preparation of Medicines
6 Dressing of Patients
7 Night Dance

(*second day*)
8 *Isoli* episode
9 Prayer at *Mukula*
10 Cutting of *Mukula*
11 Carving of Figurines
12 Medication of Figurines
13 *Ku-tumbuka* Dance
14 Payment
  Prohibitions

INTRODUCTION

Nkula is said by Ndembu to be of considerable antiquity—
'from Mwantiyanvwa', the king from whose realm in the
Congo they originally came. Its aim is to remove a ban imposed by the shade of a deceased relative on the patient's
fertility. The more obvious symptoms of affliction by a spirit
that has 'come out in (the mode of) *Nkula*' are menstrual disorders of various kinds. These include menorrhagia (excessive
flow of the menses), amenorrhoea (temporary cessation of flow),
and dysmenorrhoea (irregular periods). *Nkula* is also performed
for women who have undergone abnormal parturition, such

as breech-delivery, still-birth, and abortion. Other symptoms of *Nkula* affliction are marital frigidity and protracted incapacity to conceive, even after having borne children.

Nkula has three phases. The first is called *Ku-lembeka* or *Ilembi*, and consists of a short public ritual from sundown until about midnight. During this, a small hut called *katala kaNkula*, 'little hut of the *Nkula* (shade-manifestation)', is built immediately behind the patient's hut for the reception of a special pot containing medicines and other ritual objects. The second phase is one during which the patient is partly secluded from secular life. She and her husband must eat food from a special fire kindled at the *Ku-lembeka* rites. She has to observe certain food prohibitions. She must not come into contact with rivers or springs, and must wash herself every day with medicines in the pot in her *Nkula* hut. The third phase, called *Ku-tumbuka*, is a protracted ritual lasting from sundown on one day until midday the next. It has esoteric as well as public episodes, and the most important of these is called *kwisoli*, 'at the *isoli*', or 'place of revelation'. If a patient is believed to have been cured after *Ku-lembeka*, no *Ku-tumbuka* will be performed for her. On the other hand, if there has been no improvement in her condition for a considerable time after *Ku-tumbuka*, the ritual is believed to have failed or to have been wrongly prescribed, and a new diviner is consulted about her affliction.

Clearly, many of the beliefs connected with *Nkula* are concerned with blood. Consequently, much of its symbolism is red. Sometimes women are said to have dreams of dead female relatives who appear to them apparelled and equipped like hunters, wearing the red wing-feather of a lourie in their hair. Where such dreams occur there is no need to consult a diviner, for the dreamers can only have been caught by a shade manifesting as *Nkula*. Such a shade, in the idiom of Ndembu belief, wishes to be remembered by many people, and especially in the context of a performance of the *Nkula* cult ritual. For the afflicting shade was once, necessarily, a cult member herself, and she is also honouring the cult by providing the occasion for a performance of one of its rituals.

As in all other cults of affliction, the treatment is carried out by a group of doctor-adepts (*ayimbuki* or *ayimbanda*), the '*eniNkula*', who have themselves been closely associated with previous performances of *Nkula*. The women doctors must at one time have been patients (*ayeji*) themselves, and may not become practitioners unless they are generally regarded as having been cured after undergoing the ritual. The male practitioners must have previously acted in the capacity of *chaka chaNkula*, that is to say, male assistant of the principal *Nkula* patient, a role which will be explained below. A successfully treated patient is entitled to take part in future *Nkula* performances as a junior practitioner (*chimbuki wanyanya*, 'little doctor'), and her ritual status becomes higher the more she participates in rituals of this type, and the more she learns about its medicines and techniques. To whatever part of Ndembu tribal territory she may move afterwards—even if it is into other Lunda chiefdoms—she will still be entitled to take part in *Nkula* as an adept and practitioner. The shade which had once afflicted her is now believed to give her healing power as a practitioner, as well as fertility. It is 'her shade' (*mukishi windi*).[1] I tend to translate the terms *chimbuki* and *muyeji* as 'doctor' (or 'practitioner') and 'patient', rather than 'adept' and 'candidate', when discussing *Nkula*, as the directly therapeutic intention of this ritual is more strongly marked than in other rituals of affliction.

I have watched one performance of *Ku-lembeka* and two of *Ku-tumbuka*, one of these incompletely, but the other in all its detail, including the esoteric episodes. Sakutoha, one of my informants mentioned in *Chihamba, the White Spirit*, was a senior adept at that performance, and I was able to discuss it with him directly afterwards. The performance of *Ku-lembeka* took place at Mukanza Village, where I stayed for over a year, and again I was able to make detailed observations. In addition to this observational material, I collected descriptive accounts and interpretations of *Nkula* from several informants, the foremost of whom was Muchona,[2] Chief Kapenda (a prominent Government chief), an old hunter-doctor called Ihembi, and Sakutoha, a village headman.[3]

---

[1] See Appendix A, p. 284.

[2] See my article 'Muchona the Hornet' in *The Forest of Symbols*, op. cit.

[3] I was unable to take photographs at any of these performances, for on two occasions the rites were performed at night, and my camera was temporarily out of order when I had the opportunity of watching the *isoli* episode at one *Kutumbuka* held in daylight.

I will begin this account of *Nkula* by giving Muchona's version of *Ku-lembeka*, qualifying it whenever necessary from my own observations and from other informants' versions. The *Ku-lembeka* I saw was fragmentary and incomplete, largely because a crowd of youths, most of whom had recently been working on the Copperbelt, came with guitars and clinking bottles to enjoy themselves in modern style. Singing and dancing *nsabasaba*, and the local modern dance *chikinta*, they stole all the limelight and almost brought *Nkula* to a halt. A good deal of my note-taking concerned their activities, as the chance to study change in a ritual context was too good to miss. The circumstances did not lend themselves to recording traditional practices. But Muchona's account corresponded closely to what I did see of *Nkula*, and to the versions of others I questioned about *Ku-lembeka*.

THE MYTHOLOGICAL CHARTER

Nkula has a definite foundation myth which, as it happens, is rather literally connected with Mwantiyanvwa. Here is Muchona's version of it, corroborated by other adepts:

'A long time ago, Luweji Ankonde,[1] a woman chief Mwantiyanvwa and co-founder of the dynasty, went to her menstruation hut [*itala dikwawu*, literally 'other hut']. Her period lasted many days. Before she went in, she gave her *lukanu* bracelet [emblem of Lunda royalty] to her husband Chibinda Ilung'a, lest it should become impure [literally 'lack whiteness'] from contact with her menstrual blood [*mbayi*]. When the people found that Luweji did not come out quickly, they went to the bush and to the river to collect some medicine for her to cure her. Truly such medicine helped her. She came out quickly. This thing that happened to Chief Mwantiyanvwa, people called it "*Nkula*." *Nkula* means a long menstruation. From that time, she was given medicine, and then she gave birth perfectly well. The red feather of a grey parrot [*kalong'u*], used in *Kutumbuka*, stands for the menstruation of Luweji Ankonde.'

AIMS OF NKULA

According to Muchona, *Nkula* is performed 'to make children in a woman. It is performed when a woman has too much

[1] See my annotated translation of Carvalho's account of Luweji's love story in he *R.L.I. Journal*, XIX, Dec. 1955.

menstrual blood, or if she misses her periods but does not become pregnant. It is also performed if a woman has had no children for a long time. For example, my wife Màsonde had no children for some years, then I got *Nkula* medicine for her, and she bore my son Fanuel, who is a clerk for the Government. I made *Kulembeka* for her.'

Chief Kapenda said—I have collected the ritual histories of a number of women exemplifying this—that *Nkula* is also performed for women who have miscarriages or whose children die in early infancy. Since spirits emerging in other modes of manifestation cause the same calamities, Chief Kapenda said that diviners must be consulted to find out the specific mode and its treatment.

KU-LEMBEKA

Episode One: Collection of Medicines

'The patient', said Muchona, 'must stay in her village, while male and female doctors [a man becomes a doctor because a close woman relative or his wife passed through *Nkula* and showed him the medicines] go into the bush to collect medicines. They go an hour before sunset.

'In the bush they go first to a *mukula* tree,[1] which is the *ishikenu* medicine for *Nkula*, and means the menstrual blood [*kanyanda*] of women. Before invoking, they encircle the tree. This tree is now the senior or elder [*mukulumpi*]. When they go round, it means that from now on the patient must observe all the prohibitions of *Nkula*. Then the principal practitioner addresses the *mukula*. He says, "Come, O you *mukula, ishikenu* of women who give birth in order to rear children."[2] He takes beer, pours out a libation, and makes invocation with it, "Truly give us our procreative power."

'Then they dig up its root, take leaves and put them in the basket [*lwalu*]. After that they go to a *musoli* tree, dig up its root [*muzaji*], and take some leaves [*mafu*]. They do the same at the following trees: *kata wubwang'u, muhotuhotu, mukombukombu,*

---

[1] The *mukula* tree (*Pterocarpus angolensis*) secretes a red gum which speedily coagulates. It has the generic sense of 'blood' in many kinds of Ndembu ritual. In *Nkula* its property of coagulation is significant. The doctors want the patient's maternal blood to coagulate round the seed implanted by the husband and not to flow away 'uselessly'.

[2] *Twaya eyi mukula, ishikenu dawambanda wakusema nakulela.*

mututambululu, muntung'ulu. These are all collected in the bush. Now they go to the river and find in the *itu* [gallery forest], leaves and a root each of the following: *katochi, mujiwu, musojisoji, mudeng'udeng'u, kabwititeng'i,* and *katunya.*

'If *Nkula* is a "river" *Nkula,* called *chozu* or "wild duck"—but not *ng'uvu* or "hippo", for that is for the cult of *Chihamba* only— then the doctors go first to the streamside forest and pray at *katochi,* which is *ishikenu* for the river.'

Ihembi's list of medicines did not precisely correspond with Muchona's, for he included *museng'u* and *mucheki,* and omitted *kata wubwang'u* and *mudeng'udeng'u.* Sakutoha, again, thought that *mucha, museng'u,* and *mwang'ala* should be used, but not *kata wubwang'u.* At the *Ku-lembeka* at Mukanza Village, *kata wubwang'u* and *museng'u* were used but not *mudeng'udeng'u.* Muchona, in one of our discussions, explained that one of the reasons for such differences between *ayimbuki* was that sometimes one just could not find a particular sort of medicine. Another reason was 'plain forgetting' on the doctor's part. Yet another was that customs varied from chiefdom to chiefdom. For example, the Kosa of Musokantanda had slightly different customs from the Ndembu of Kanongesha, though both were Lunda. 'And those people who live near Luvale have taken Luvale customs here and there; so, too, those who live near Kaonde and Luba have borrowed Kaonde and Luba customs.' Muchona's criterion for skilled '*chimbuki*-ship' was always, 'did the ritual cure people?' The most important part of a doctor's work, he thought, was 'knowing how to address ancestor-shades, how to wake them up [*mwakuyitonesha*]'.

Exegesis

Muchona interpreted the symbolism of the medicine-plants as follows:

'*Mukula* is the tree of menstrual blood [*kanyanda*], of giving birth [*wakusema*].

'*Musoli* is used for speaking publicly. It can make things appear quickly. The patient can bear children presently.

'*Kata wubwang'u* is the *ishikenu* of the Twin Cult [*Wubwang'u*]. Its fruit is divided into two sections, representing twins [*ampamba*]. They use it because they hope for many children.

'If a person touches a *muhotuhotu* tree near the end of the dry season, all its leaves will fall. And so if a person has witchcraft-sorcery (*wuloji*), his familiars can go away quickly, and diseases can fall from the patient.'

The meanings Muchona attributed to *mukombukombu* and *mututambululu*, whose leafy twigs, together with *muhotuhotu*, are bound into a medicine-broom or sprinkler, were the same as those mentioned in *Chihamba, the White Spirit* (pp. 59–60).

According to him, '*muntung'ulu* has many spreading branching roots; in the same way a woman should have many children'. He mentioned, in passing, that he thought the verb, '*ku-tung'ula*', 'to spread gossip about a person', was connected with *muntung'ulu*. The 'ramifications' of gossip, in a context of anti-sorcery ritual, were the sickness and death of the victims brought about by envious sorcerers.

'If *katochi* roots are given to a woman', said Muchona, 'she can produce many children. It has many roots. Its gum coagulates [*ku-zemuka*], like the coagulation [*ku-konda*] of blood.

'*Mujiwu* has many roots, therefore many children.

'*Musojisoji* has many roots; its gum resembles blood.

'*Mudeng'udeng'u* has many fruits and roots. Its fruit is white. The skin of its root is black, but it is white inside.

'*Kabwititeng'i* has leaves that are used by women as calabash-stoppers. When women give birth they can do so as quickly as they throw away such leaves after use. The stopper is to keep insects [*tububu*] out of the calabash. Witches' familiars [*andumba*] are called *tububu*. So it also means to keep *andumba* away from the patients.

'*Katunya* has red gum like blood. A woman must show blood to other women when she gives birth to a child.'

Sakutoha made some illuminating comments on the general principles underlying the collection of these medicines. He pointed out that trees from which bark rope or bark string can be made are never used in ritual to make women fertile, as these would tie up (*ku-kasa*) their fertility. Many of the trees used, including *musoli*, *mucha*, and *mwang'ala* (the latter two did not figure in Muchona's *Ku-lembeka* repertoire), 'had many fruits', and 'so the doctors trusted that the patient would have many children'. Other trees[1] had honey-filled flowers attractive

---

[1] *Mukombukombu, mututambululu, muhotuhotu, museng'u, kabwititeng'i, musojisoji*, and *katochi*. Medicines used for drinking were: *mukombukombu, mututambululu, mukula, musoli*, and *mwang'ala*. The rest were used only for washing and sprinkling.

to bees. By using them, the doctors hoped to attract many children to the patient, and many people to the performance, 'to please the spirit'. *Katochi* had 'soft wood' (possibly saponaceous?) for washing the patient's body. *Museng'u* had 'a good name', for it came from *kuseng'ula*, to blow on food before and after eating in gratitude to the ancestors. Each of its flower-heads bears many little fruits; in the same way the patient will have many babies. *Mucheki* has a white wood, and this means good health and good luck.

I asked Sakutoha if roots, bark, and leaves had different meanings. He denied that they had, but said that the root of the *ishikenu* stood for the shade (*mukishi*). Otherwise, roots, bark, and leaves were the same; what mattered was the kind of tree used.

I then enquired whether there was any difference between medicine collected in the bush and medicine from the river-forest. He said that there was not. Both were to make the patient live (*nakumuhandisha*) and make her strong (*nakumu-kolisha*). The reason why medicines were collected both from bush and river was that when she passed through the former, bush-medicines 'of *Nkula*' would 'help' her, and when she crossed a river, *itu*-medicines would protect her from danger. Generally speaking, medicines helped the patient to remember the shade (*nakumwanuka mukishi*), and all those present would also remember the shade.

Episode Two: Preparation of Medicines

To return to Muchona's account: 'When the doctors return from the bush, they sing special *Nkula* songs. Having arrived at the village, they encircle the patient's hut (*ajing'amuka itala damuyeji*). And so the shade feels happy, for from that time the *Nkula* shade believes that they will play its drum. Then they put the medicine in the patient's hut. She stays there with the medicine. Just after sunset the principal doctor and other adepts enter and begin to cut up the roots collected. A big pot is brought in and the pieces of roots and leaves are put into it. Some medicine is kept aside for *nsompu*, to be washed on the patient's body. As they cut they sing.

'Now a small clay cooking pot (*kanung'u*) is brought up, bits of every kind of root are added, and cold water. This is placed near a special fire a few paces beyond the door of the patient's hut.'

Chief Kapenda told me that the patient's husband, if he was at home, helped to collect the wood for this fire.

Nkula Spirit Hut

Muchona then went on to tell me that 'the principal doctor that morning had made a little hut of grass just behind the patient's hut, before medicines were collected. A meal mortar is placed in this hut, called *katala kaNkula*, "little hut of the *Nkula* (shade)". Most of the leaves and some of the root parings are put in the mortar, and some cold water is added. Women do the pounding, and they sing as they do it. The patient sits by the mortar. After a while, the principal (male) doctor puts his hand in the mortar and gives the patient a little medicine to drink. Then he pours some on the top of her head, so that she will receive her shade (*mukishi windi*). He then washes her chest and shoulders so as to leave some pounded *nsompu* leaves visible on her body.'

Episode Three: Treatment with Medicine

'After washing her, the doctor catches the patient by her little finger, and says, "Will you please go to the fire to warm yourself?" He gives her a *muswayi* rattle, then takes it again and lifts her up with it in his right hand, still holding her little finger in his left hand. She must stand by means of the doctor's power, not by her own. He holds her little finger because she is taboo [*najili dehi*] or sacred.

'He leads her like this to the *Nkula* fire [*ijiku daNkula*]. All the adepts follow them there. First the patient must wash herself, then the doctor gives her a little pot containing root medicine taken from the big *izawu* pot. She is given this mixed with warm medicine from the small clay cooking pot. Then drums are beaten at the doctor's instructions. The patient must be warm so that bits of leaves from the *nsompu* washing medicine will dry and adhere to her body.

'After a while, the patient begins to tremble [*ku-zakuka*]. This is the first time she must shake during *Nkula*. The second is while the people are dancing. The third time is when the doctor gives the woman her shade by putting the red *ilembi*

/ Trembling
1-2-3

bead on her head. At that third time she must dance upright. Now she is sitting on a mat with her legs together in front of her. She is trembling because the shade has caught her. She moves her neck round and round. A woman adept can teach her friend to move her neck round, but not a male adept.'

Chaka chaNkula

'A male helper now squats behind the patient. He is called *chaka chaNkula*. Often her husband is *chaka*, but if he is absent she can choose a male relative of hers, even a young boy if he has been circumcised.

'The *chaka* puts his hands on her shoulders. Still squatting, they begin to go backwards to the little hut. The big doctor puts his medicine basket on the patient's head, while she keeps on turning her neck. At last, the *chaka* pulls the patient back through the entrance of the little grass hut, and there he drinks medicine from the meal-mortar, and washes his face and arms with it.

'In the course of the evening, as described, the patient and *chaka* go from the fire to the grass hut three times. The third time she enters the hut the big doctor gives her the *ilembi* bead to wear on her head just behind her brow. When the *ilembi* is on her head, the doctor offers her the *muswayi* rattle and she grasps it. Then he leads her backwards into her own hut to rest. She must go through the doorway backwards, like a girl novice [*kankang'a*] at the puberty ritual. She goes in at about midnight.

'The doctor instructs the patient to go on washing in the *izawu* pot at dawn and sunset. She is also to finish drinking the medicine in the small cooking pot. She must wash in the *katala kaNkula* grass hut.'

Exegesis

Muchona told me that the pieces of leaves adhering to the patient's body are a symbol of the *Nkula* shade. The *ilembi* bead, too, symbolizes the *Nkula* shade, for when the patient is given this red bead she is said to have been 'given *Nkula*'. Such a bead is given in no other ritual. It may be placed at the back of the head as well as at the front. When the patient goes to the menstruation hut, she must put it in a special calabash called *ilembu* which, as we shall see, plays an important role in *Ku-tumbuka*.

According to Muchona, the word *ilembi*, as applied to the first phase of a woman's ritual of affliction like *Chihamba*, came originally from *Nkula* and was then applied to other kinds of ritual, 'for *ilembi* only [i.e. properly] means the red bead of *Nkula*'. Various informants were inclined to derive the terms *ilembi*, *ilembu*, and *ku-lembeka* from *ku-lemba*, 'to express contrition'. But others, including Muchona, said that there was no connection between *ku-lemba* and the other terms cited.

There are two sorts of medicine, 'cold' and 'hot'. According to Muchona, cold medicine is used in order that a person may feel 'peaceful'. He went on to explain that the greeting '*Kwahola?*' (literally 'Is there cold?') means 'Are you free from the action of witchcraft?' If someone answers, '*Nehi, kwahola wanyi*', 'No, it isn't cold', it means that he is feeling 'hot in the liver' (*yiyena mumuchima*), i.e. that witchcraft is being used against him.

If cold medicine means benefiting the condition of the patient, hot medicine is used aggressively against witches, sorcerers, and their familiars. Thus Muchona says: 'Hot water medicine in *ku-kupula* [a rite occurring in several kinds of ritual involving violently sprinkling the patient alternately with hot and cold medicine by means of medicine-brooms, while an incantation is chanted] means killing the witchcraft (*wuloji*), the sprinkling of hot water catches familiars. Warm medicine for drinking is to kill *yipupu* (sicknesses that come quickly and unexpectedly) or *nyisong'u* (diseases) inside the patient.'

Nkula Songs

Songs are sung while the adepts are collecting medicine in the bush and during the preparation and application of medicines. As usual, three drums are brought to the site of the fire, one large *kayanda* drum and two small *mung'fuza* drums. They are played by men, while women do most of the singing. Interpretation of the songs, which are cryptic and elliptic in character like most Ndembu ritual songs, brings out several of the aims and values of the *Nkula* cult:

(1) '*Wavwala nshimba wayiwayi eyeyeye wayiwayi nyakasansa kanyonu.*'

'She wears [a skin] of the genet cat, [a] spotted [one], spotted; basket of lives.'

This refers to the fact that in *Ku-tumbuka*, as we shall see, the patient is dressed in a genet cat skin. *Nshimba*, the genet cat, is connected by Ndembu with *ku-dishimba*, 'to fornicate or commit adultery with [someone]'. The patient is spotted with white and red clay, like the spots of a genet cat. It is one of the assumptions of *Nkula* custom that the patient has been showing frigidity towards her husband or ex-husband—for *Nkula* is not infrequently performed for divorced women, or women living separately from their husbands.

Nyakasansa, the term used for the medicine-basket, means literally 'mother of sprinkling'. It is here applied to the sprinkling of *nsompu* on a patient. It means the sprinkling of life-giving (*ku-handisha*) medicines on the patient. Muchona said, perfectly explicitly, that *nyonu*, 'lives' (singular *mwonu*) means medicine (*yitumbu*).

(2) '*Wakisa nyilenji nkala chaku cheyochu chiwalekelang'a ama-yala*,

'You destroy stripes [or 'lines'] mongoose, that is your habit which causes you to refuse men,

Wakisa nyilenji nkala.'

You destroy lines, mongoose.'

According to Muchona this species of mongoose has 'red, black and white stripes down its back'. These lines, he said, are 'very important'. The song means that the woman patient 'is a bad woman, useless [*wamukunkulwayi*], she is powerless [*hawahetang'ovuku*]—you are destroying yourself, woman; you ought to have babies, by refusing men you will have no babies, you are an unworthy [*hawatelelaku*] woman, a guilty woman. You are a frigid [*wafwa mwitala*] woman. The genet cat has stripes, this woman, although she has been given her private part for men, has kept it useless, doing nothing with it.'

(3) '*Mwana moye mwanoye mwana wumu ikayi dakumwendu*

'One child, only one child, one child, a bracelet on the leg,

ileng'i wemana wamu.'

a split cane, it stands alone.'

Ihembi and Chief Kapenda said that this meant that 'a woman should have more than one child. You can't make a mat with a single cane. Although you can wear a bangle on one leg if you have borne one child, this is not enough.'

(4) *'Chawahi, tuhang'anenuhu chawahe, chawahe-e,*
'It is good [or 'better' in the sense of recovery from illness or misfortune], let us just dance, it is good, it is good,
Chawahi, ihamba daNkula, chawahi, chawahi munkondu,
It is good, *Nkula* manifestation, it is good, it is good, the position of clasping a baby in one's arms,
Mwila mwana eye chawahi chawahi.'
Having to do with a child, it is good, it is good.'

(5) *'Wabula chakoye e yeye wabula chaka cha Nkula wabula chaka,*
'She has no male helper, she lacks a male *Nkula* helper, she lacks a male helper,
wabaya eyeyeye akwenu niyaka yawu cha eyeyeye.'
She is guilty (or unsuccessful), your friends have their male helpers of equal size.'

Muchona derives the term *chaka*, 'male helper', from *kwaka*, 'to deliver a child' by catching it in one's hands. *Kwaka* is related to *kwakwila*, 'to catch with the hands anything in mid air', such as a ball. The *chaka* is, then, a sort of 'deliverer', to use the English word also in its double sense. His action of leading the patient backwards by the shoulders in and out of her shade-hut supports this interpretation.

Other songs speak of *Nkula* (the shade-manifestation) 'doing the dance with an axe in hand' (*ku-tomboka*) performed by Lunda war-leaders after victory, or by executioners after beheading their victims; and of 'walking on the verandah behind (the patient's) hut'—*'Nkula wenda hekeki'*. In the first place the reference is to menstruation, for the *Nkula* manifestation, according to Muchona, 'sheds the patient's blood'. In the second place, the reference is to the shade-hut, placed just behind the patient's hut of residence.

KU-TUMBUKA

Introduction

The *Ku-tumbuka* I observed was at Shika Village in Chief Sailung'a's area on 16 and 17 June 1953. There were two patients (see Fig. II). The first, Ediya, was the wife of a Government official's houseboy. She had been married several years without once conceiving, was sick 'with pains in her whole body and fever', and was reported to be frigid towards her husband. She had undergone *Ku-lembeka* about six months beforehand, and after the performance had lived in Shika Village with her matrilineal descent group, and not with her husband at the Boma. She was said to have been 'caught' by the shade of her mother's older uterine sister, Nyankinga, who had died more than five years previously. I did not know the village well enough to understand its internal divisions which would have given me clues as to why it was believed that Ediya had been afflicted by this particular shade. Her kin merely told me that she had 'forgotten' the shade, which was punishing her for this neglect by tying up her fertility. They said that immediately after the *Ku-tumbuka* ritual Ediya would go through the *ku-swanika ijina* ('causing to inherit a name') ritual, at which a *muyombu* tree would be planted to Nyankinga's memory, and Ediya would inherit her name. It was hoped that this would propitiate Nyankinga and end Ediya's sickness.

The other patient, Eni, was a recently divorced woman. She was a classificatory 'mother' of Ediya, but was only a few years older than her. She had one surviving child, but had been suffering from menstrual irregularities for some time. The diviner who had been consulted on her behalf had pronounced that her own mother Kalumbu was the afflicting spirit 'which had come out in *Nkula*'. Although Eni had never been to *Ku-lembeka*, the elders of Shika Village had decided to 'join' her *Nkula* to Ediya's. One reason for this, I was told, was that Eni had shown herself eager to become an *Nkula* doctor (*chimbuki*). She had said that she wanted to learn how to apply treatment to others for the troubles brought upon them by *Nkula* manifestations. It was thought that she would later undergo both *Ku-lembeka* and another *Ku-tumbuka*. She would not inherit her mother's name, since she was not 'sick' (*wakata*).

The principal practitioner was Sakutoha, Ediya's own father.

Episode Four: Collection of Medicines

Observations

Sakutoha and his fellow adepts collected the following medicines from the bush: *mukula, musoli, mukombukombu, mututambululu, muhotuhotu, museng'u, mucha, mwang'ala*; from the streamside forest: *katochi, kabwititeng'i, mucheki* and *musojisoji*. Portions of root and leaves were taken in each case, and, in addition, some bark-scrapings of *mukula* and *katochi*. These were the medicines of the *Katala matunga*, or 'bush' *Nkula*. The same medicines were used in *Ku-lembeka*. I have discussed indigenous interpretations concerning this phase on pp. 60–2.

Episode Five : Preparation of Medicines

Observations

The *ku-teta mazawu* episode is almost the same as Episode Two on p. 62. Medicines were pounded in a meal mortar and cut up in the spirit huts made for each of the patients. Drums were brought up near the entrance of each *katala* hut and *Nkula* songs sung to their rhythm by the adepts within. In Ediya's hut the ritual equipment of the doctors was laid on a mat, and four senior male doctors sat round it. Ediya herself was not present. On the mat were: a large *izawu* pot containing *nsompu* pounded medicine for washing, a smaller pot (*kanung'u* or *ndaba*) for drinking medicine, two bright red feathers of Livingstone's lourie (*nduwa*), a calabash containing oil, called *ilembu*, wrapped in a store towel stained with the patient's menstrual blood, a calabash containing red clay (*mukundu*), two genet skins, a bow and two arrows, a calabash containing white clay (*mpemba*), a *lwalu* medicine-basket, and Sakutoha's axe used only for cutting plants for medicines. Sakutoha prayed to the afflicting spirits and to other village ancestors, and anointed each of the ritual objects, starting with the big pot, with the white clay from the calabash, finally anointing himself and the other *ayimbuki* with it. Next he poured out a libation of 'white' maize beer around the objects. There followed a communal beer drink. Beer was given to the patients' relatives outside the grass hut, after the adepts and myself had been served.

A fence (*chipang'u*) had been erected around Ediya's grass spirit hut, the fence itself made of long coarse grass. All the female adepts were sitting within it when we emerged from the spirit hut. The patients were squatting in the middle of the group in an attitude of modesty (*nsonyi*), with downcast heads, covering their faces with both hands. They were now washed with medicine from the mortar and big pot. Then the senior women doctors, headed by Nyamanjombi, began to dress the patients for the coming rites.

Episode Six: Dressing the Patients

They were given short waistcloths to wear. Capes of genet skins were fastened around their shoulders. Each had a lourie feather inserted quill first into the hair over her brow. Then red clay (*mukundu*) was applied beside the outer orbits. Ediya was given a bow to carry, while Eni held an arrow.

Exegesis

According to Sakutoha and Muchona, the bow and arrows stand for '*iyala*', 'the man', more particularly the husband of the patient. Muchona commented, 'the husband must carry the bow and arrows, not the wife', rather as we might say, 'the man should wear the trousers'.

According to Sakutoha, the fence (*chipang'u*) was 'Mwanti-yanvwa's *chipang'u*, and was used because of Luweji Ankondi (see p. 58)'.

Muchona and Ihembi both said that 'the lourie feather stands for blood'.

Muchona's Account of Ku-teta Mazawu

Muchona described to me what he held was appropriate behaviour in the *katala kaNkula*:

'The doctor prays to the shade of his patient [i.e. the shade afflicting his patient]. Then he says: "Be strong, patient, do not be ill. If [a shade] catches you in the procreative power, be well that you may bear a child, so that people may praise me, the doctor [*chimbanda*]." He says: "Really I am one who has cured successfully." He puts powdered white clay in the pot, he puts maize beer in it. He divides various medicines among the other doctors. When they have sorted these out they put them one by one into the pot.'

Episode Seven: Night Dance

Observations

Three drums were set up in the middle of the village in an open space given over to dancing. A large fire was made near the drums. Ediya's husband, regarded as the greatest drummer in Mwinilunga District, played the large *kayanda* drum. The patients danced out of the *chipang'u* enclosure, in a sitting position with their backs to the drums and facing the enclosure. Women adepts and relatives of the patients danced around them. They danced in a special style called *ku-leng'a*, consisting of a lateral outward movement of the forearms, exposing the palms of the hands, as though in a gesture of acceptance. The patients were taken to the big fire, and the women danced round them in procession, singing *Nkula* songs.

Another circle had formed to dance the modern *Chikinta*. These were mostly women and young men; for the dance is unpopular among older men. Ndembu girls marry from five to eight years earlier on average than youths. Older polygynists with young wives feel extremely jealous of the gay young bachelors at *Chikinta*. In addition to quarrels between older and younger men, fights tend to break out between men from different villages. At this performance of *Nkula*, for example, young men from Mukanza Village became embroiled in a fight with Shika villagers. Trouble was avoided, however, by the portly headman of Shika Village, who bellowed jocularly that no quarrel (*ndombu*) had taken place, but only 'playing', since both parties were related by marriage and paternal ties.

Periodically, the patients were danced backwards to their spirit huts, and then to the drums again, where they were washed with medicines. Several times, hunters' dances and songs were played and sung, and the patients swayed in time with them. I saw no sign of any 'male helpers' at this dance. The patients 'trembled' (*ku-zakuka*), and 'danced moving their necks about (*ku-hang'ana nakucheka kunshing'u*)' as described on p. 64.

Episode Eight: The Isóli

Observations

About two hours after sunrise, a procession formed up in Ediya's enclosure. It consisted of male and female adepts. The two adepts headed the procession with their backs towards the entrance. At last, the whole crowd began to move. The two patients, in their short 'kilts', genet-skin capes, and carrying bows and arrows, looked like two ebony Dianas as they danced backwards to the heavy down-beat of the hunters' dance, followed by a clapping chanting throng of women, dancing in the *ku-leng'a* style. The adepts chose a path out of the village placed diametrically opposite to the one they had taken to collect medicines the previous day. After going through the bush for about a furlong, the principal practitioners, including Headman Shika, Sakutoha, Headman Machamba, and Nyamanjombi, pointed out a small *mukula* tree, and the whole crowd danced round it three or four times, to flatten the grass and consecrate it (the process of *ku-bola mutondu*).

Then the patients were led off to a hollow between two large termite-hills, about fifty yards away from the *mukula* tree, where they were made to sit down with extended legs, hands in laps, and bowed heads.

Episode Nine: Prayer at the Mukula Tree

All the *Nkula* equipment taken by the adepts, axe, basket, *ilembu* oil-flask, two small calabashes, lourie feathers, a red cock, a calabash of beer, some bark-string, and other things, were laid at the foot of the *mukula* tree. Then Sakutoha made a brief prayer, as follows:

'*Eyi mukula diyi mutondu wakanyanda wakusema, dichu*
'You *mukula* are the tree of [menstrual] blood, of giving birth, and so

tunakuwani dehi yeyi mukula ijina deyi yeyi Nkula chikupu
we have found you, *mukula* [is] your name, you [are] completely *Nkula*

muntu iwu lelu dinu kwakayayi akakoli ngu. Kamwinki kusema.
where today this person will go that she may get quite better. Give her fertility.

Neyi yeyi wamwinkang'a kanyanda wakama jokang'a kukayanda
When you give her menstruation, she goes on sleeping at menstruation

mafuku amavulu, lelu ketulaku kanyanda, mwinki mafuku antesha
for many days, today cut [short] menstruation, give her a few days

hohu, kumbidyi akawani mwana, lelu akoli.'
only, in future may she find a child, today may she be well.'

Episode Ten: The Cutting of the Mukula (ku-tema mukula)

After praying, Sakutoha poured out a libation (*kwichila*) of maize beer at the base of the tree, scraped away from soil, and put a few beans and maize grains in the hole thus made. He then proceeded to cut down the tree itself with his ritual axe.

While Sakutoha was cutting down the tree, drums were brought up and played and *Nkula* songs were sung. Beer from the calabash placed near the *mukula* was then drunk by all the adepts, the men first, in order of ritual seniority, beginning with Sakutoha, then the women. Next, Sakutoha cut the trunk of the *mukula* into roughly equal pegs. At the moment before it was cut, several adepts nudged me and told me, 'the tree is the shade (*mukishi*)' and 'that tree is *Nkula*'. This was afterwards corroborated by all my regular informants on *Nkula* ritual.

Episode Eleven: The Carving of the Figurines (ku-song'a wankishi)

Four adepts, including Shika but not Sakutoha, sat facing one another round the stump of the *mukula*. Musona, my assistant, tried to sit with them, but was jocularly chased off, 'because he did not know the mystery (*mpang'u*) of *Nkula*'. The adepts began to carve the pegs into figurines (*ankishi*). These were highly stylized representations of babies. Shika told me that they represented 'the shade' (*mukishi*). The adepts used hunters' small skinning knives to carve three figurines, one for each patient, and one for a female adept who had lost her own. The patients' figurines were named after the afflicting shades, i.e., 'Nyankinga' for Ediya, and 'Kalumbu' for Eni. If the patients bore children within a year or two of the performance, those children, regardless of their sex, would receive the names of the *Nkula* shades.

Much amusement was caused by the poor carving of one of the adepts. Shika took his knife away from him, and himself went to work on the *mukula* peg.

While the carving was going on, the red cock was decapitated in the bush nearby. A fire was lit, the cock was divided into portions and roasted over the flames, and each adept received a portion together with cassava mush cooked by Ediya's mother. The head, entrails, heart, liver, and many feathers were placed in the *lwalu* basket by the *mukula* stump, 'for the shade', as people said.

Episode Twelve: The Medication of the Figurines (ku-panda wankishi)

Each completed figurine had longitudinal lines for hair, crude marks for eyes and mouth, and 'arms' slightly crooked by the sides.

The next step was to cut two small round calabashes in half, and medicate them. The medication consisted of mixing a number of red substances in the *lwalu* basket ('of lives', it will be remembered in the song), then pressing most of the sticky mixture into half of each calabash, and a little of it into a small hole in the figurine's head.

The mixture contained:

The liver, heart, a portion of the intestine, the beak, and some blood of the red cock, with some of its red feathers.

The red lourie feathers worn by the patients.

A hair, a piece of finger-nail, and a paring from the big toe-nail of each patient.

Some body-residues (*mpelu* or *jipelu*) of an albino (*mwabi*).

Scrapings of *mukula* bark.

Powdered red clay (*ng'ula* or *mukundu*).

Some red feathers of the grey parrot (*kalong'u*).

Musona told me that some menstrual blood taken from the patients was also put in, but Muchona strongly asserted that this was 'a lie'.

All the adepts took part in preparing this thick glutinous red mixture. They did so with an appearance of animated pleasure, similar to that of villagers when the carcass of a goat or antelope is being divided up. The senior female adept, Nyamanjombi, poured oil into the 'medicine' (*yitumbu*, the name also given to vegetable medicines) to make it cohere better. The coagulation of the red mass (the term for the coagulation of blood, *ku-konda*, was used for it), according to some of the adepts present, made the blood cohere in the woman's womb, and not flow away in a long menstruation. Bark strings were now brought and medicated with the red mixture. After the figurines' heads had been medicated, more of the stuff was crammed into one half of the cut calabash. The figurine was put in the other half, and the first half was worked over it to form a lid. Holes were pierced in the 'lid' before it was put on, and the string, now adorned with red cock's feathers, was threaded through them. Like the oil flask, the completed calabash was called *ilembu*.

It was then put in a special basket, called *ikinda daNkula,* closely woven like the basket containing circumcision medicine (*nfunda*) at boys' circumcision rites (*Mukanda*). The name *ikinda* is derived from *ku-kinda,* a special dance in which the *Nkula* basket is brandished in the air 'just like the *nfunda* container at *Mukanda*', as all my informants said.

Exegesis

Muchona explained the *ilembu* medicines as follows:

'The heart of a cock does not rest from running after hens, so that a woman should have many children like a hen. A cock's beak is used for picking up food of all kinds, thus a woman should have as many children as pieces of food picked up. The intestines are the place where a cock gives semen [*matekela*].

'The hair means that the patient's body is also there with the figurine. The nails mean this also. An albino [*mwabi*] is very white and therefore gives luck. The lourie feather is menstrual blood [*kanyanda*]. The grey parrot's red feather stands for chief Mwantiyanvwa where everything came from, and for the menstruation of Luweji Ankonde. The blood of the cock is menstrual blood of procreation [*kanyanda kakusema*]. The *ilembu* must never be taken near a stream or touch water, for water weakens it and makes it flow [*ku-zokoka ilembu,* 'weakening of *ilembu*']'.

Of *isoli* he said: 'It is the place where the shade [*mukishi*] is. In *Nkula* this is the *mukula* tree.'

According to Sakutoha, the *ilembu* stands for *ivumu*; 'the womb'—which also means matrilineage in many contexts. The 'baby' is implanted in the 'womb' by male doctors. Discussion with Muchona, Sakutoha, Musona and Windson Kashinakaji produced the following comments, adding up to the Ndembu theory of procreation. I subsequently checked their account with other Ndembu, who agreed that it was in accordance with their own views.

'The father first gives blood to a woman. She keeps it in her body and makes it grow. Semen [*matekela*] is blood mixed with water. Semen comes from a man's power [*ng'ovu*]. Semen is quite white, it remains in the woman as a *kabubu kawumi* [which Windson rather poetically translated as 'a seed of life'; *kabubu* normally means an 'insect', a 'tiny living thing', an 'animated creature', sometimes it means a 'familiar of witchcraft'].

'The navel cord is also called *kabubu kawumi*, because if it is cut, the baby dies. It is semen that forms the child inside. It starts with a watery thing, a very soft one; it starts like *ibuji*, a seed, then it grows to a large ball [*iwundu*], then grows and grows till it forms legs, arms, fingers, head, and everything else. When it is ready, *Nzambi*, the High God, gives it life [*wumi*], then it begins to breathe [*ku-kona*] and move about inside the womb [*mwana wudinakwenda mwivumu*]. The child is kept in the placenta [*ng'oji*], a place in the mother's body. The same name is used for the cloth in which a mother carries her baby.'

Some Ndembu say that the spirit (*mukishi*) joins the semen and the mother's blood at the moment of conception.

Episode Thirteen: the Kutumbuka Dance

Muchona's and Sakutoha's Accounts

The *ikinda* basket containing the figurine is covered with the skin of a genet cat—the same one which the patient wore previously. It is said to represent 'her own body'. Its many spots stand for the many children desired for her.

Adepts and patients go back to the *chisela* dancing place in the village where the people danced the previous night. The patients dance in the midst of the people.

The word *Ku-tumbuka*, my informants agreed, means 'to jump in dancing' or 'to get up or start out' (*ku-nyamuka*). The patient is no longer in a sitting position; she 'stands up' to dance.

During the dance the patient carries a mat on her head. In it are wrapped the *ikinda* basket and its medicated contents. She has now been given her own, and her best, clothes to wear. She and the principal practitioner dance with the *ikinda*, just as circumcisers dance at *Mukanda*, holding the basket aloft.

When the dance is over, the practitioner tells the patient to take the mat into her grass spirit-hut. When she is in the doorway, he takes the mat from her and puts it on the *izawu* medicine-pot which stands in the hut. Then he unties the mat and puts it between two rafters in the roof. In addition to the *ilembu* calabash containing the figurine, the basket now contains the *ilembi* bead, from *Ku-lembeka*. He instructs the patient to sleep that night in the enclosure (*chipang'u*).

Episode Fourteen: Payment

Next day the senior practitioner returns to claim his payment which in *Nkula* is known as 'the tribute of Mwantiyanvwa' (*mulambu waMwantiyanvwa*). At Shika Village, Ediya paid Sakutoha one calabash of beer, one *mutong'a* (a long open basket) of soaked cassava roots, some *ibanda* salt on a bark platter, some meat and fish, and four yards of cloth. When these things were collected, Sakutoha, the senior practitioner, had them taken down the path about a hundred paces from the village. There he divided them among the other adepts according to the work they had done. 'All the female adepts were paid something' said Sakutoha.

Nkula Prohibitions

According to Muchona and Sakutoha, 'the patient must not touch water (i.e. carry it from a spring, well, or river) until some seeds of maize and beans planted round the big *izawu* begin to grow. People who enter the patient's own hut must come in backwards. Until the seeds grow she must not greet people with her hands. She has a young girl to draw water for her, although she can carry calabashes in a *mutong'a* basket. Similarly with cassava roots.

'She must sleep in the enclosure. Her husband may sleep there also.

'She is not allowed to eat *mukung'a* and *mbing'a* fish, because they have sharp teeth, nor *musonji* cat-fish, because it is too slippery, and might make her child slip out too soon.

'Similarly she is not to eat [slippery] spinach leaves as relishes, such as *wusi*, *mwilembu*, and *kalembwila*.

'She must at all times walk slowly because she is with something [i.e. is pregnant].'

Exegesis

'Water is forbidden because it leaks and is a soft thing (*chuma chachovu*). If she touches water her medicines will not stay strong.

'Maize and beans stand for the bearing of children.'

These prohibitions continue until she is better, or has a live baby. The same prohibitions apply between *Ku-lembeka* and *Ku-tumbuka*.

Finally, I asked the two doctors why different medicines were used by different doctors, a question I had previously asked Muchona alone. Looking at each other warily, both agreed that all doctors should use the same trees for *Nkula* medicines. Where difference occurred, they said, was not in the medicines, but in 'the style of applying treatment', *mwakuukila*. This was expressed in ways of praying, in ways of dancing, and in the kinds of gestures used.

COMMENTARY ON NKULA

Nkula as a Cult of Affliction

Nkula exemplifies most of the typical features of Ndembu cults of affliction. The afflicting shade is a known and named deceased relative of the afflicted person or patient '*muyeji*'. The patient is, at the same time, a candidate for initiation into the curative cult; the doctor (*chimbuki*) is an adept in the cult. The mode of affliction refers to certain characteristics of this shade which are correlated with outstanding features of the sufferer's misfortune or illness. The name of the mode of affliction is also the name of the ritual performed to treat the afflicted person. Treatment is carried out by a number of 'doctors' or 'adepts' (*ayimbuki* or *ayimbanda*), both male and female, who have themselves been closely associated with previous performances of this kind of ritual, either as patients, or as near kin or affines of patients. They form a sort of *ad hoc* and transient cult group. The doctor-adepts, or 'practitioners', are arranged in a loose hierarchy of ritual prestige, and each is assigned a different task. Between doctors and patients there need not necessarily exist any ties of kinship or affinity. Generally speaking, the afflicting shade is a relative of the same sex as the patient, though there are exceptions to this, notably in the case of Ihamba.

Each cult has both exoteric and esoteric phases, the former attended by anyone who can come, and the latter by initiates and initiands only. Esoteric phases take place either in the privacy of a patient's hut or in the bush behind a sacred fence or screen. In the past doctors drove away the uninitiated (*antondu*) from such sacred areas.

Most cults have the classical *rite de passage* form, involving the performance of two successive rituals, separated by a period during which the patient undergoes partial seclusion from secular life. The first of these rituals, in women's cults and certain generic hunters' cults, is called *Ku-lembeka* or *Ilembi*, and the second, and more elaborate and important, *Ku-tumbuka*.

The Typical Pattern of Shade Affliction

Nkula, as we have seen, has all these features of affliction ritual. Nor does it differ from other women's cults in its typical pattern of affliction. Tables 2 and 3, pp. 303–06 and the genealogy on page 309, indicate what kind of pattern is involved. In the first place, shades very rarely afflict classificatory kinswomen, but principally their direct uterine descendants. This pattern is consistent with the structure of a society without deep localized lineages organized into a lineage system. It is also consistent with the dispersal of women among their husbands' villages for the greater part of their reproductive cycle. Under this system of virilocality, mothers and daughters are often separated, and yet the mother-daughter tie constitutes the crucial jural bond in this matrilineal society. It is in this relationship, therefore, that we might expect to find a high degree of tension, with strongly ambivalent feelings in both partners. There is also a strong emotional bond between a woman and her maternal grandmother, for it is often in the grandmother's hut that she is reared from the age of three or four until a few years before puberty. And it is precisely these relatives, mother and grandmother, who return as shades most often, first to afflict, and then to assist, their living kinswomen. The shades of paternal kinswomen afflict very rarely. This pattern of affliction by close matrilineal kin often affecting the reproductive capacities, is consistent with Meyer Fortes's hypothesis that the ancestor cult is mainly concerned with the transmission of jurality *per se* from one generation to another, and that this partly accounts for the harshness and punitiveness of ancestral intervention in the affairs of their descendants. For even gentle and amiable persons are credited after their death with the ability to bring disease, barrenness, and other trouble upon their kin. It is the 'hardness' of law, the obligatoriness involved in performing a social role, that are symbolized by the punitive actions of the shades, and the character traits of the person when alive simply do not enter into the reckoning. Similarly, it is the power of organized society that is symbolized by the benevolence of the shades—once they have been publicly recognized and propitiated.

Some Comments on the Symbolism of Nkula

Nkula has what may be called a 'telic structure', i.e. it may be regarded as a sequence of culturally standardized ends and means. The chief end of *Nkula* is to make a barren woman fertile. A variety of means are employed to attain that end. Since a shade has brought the affliction, that shade must be propitiated, and there are a number of standardized procedures for doing this. Since the woman's barren state is here connected with menstrual disorder, much of the therapy is devoted to treating menstrual irregularities. According to the Ndembu theory of procreation, a relationship exists between menstruation and procreation, so that a shade may prevent the 'mother's blood' from 'coagulating' around the 'seed of life' implanted by a man; the blood may then run away in menorrhagia, or the shade may dry it up altogether in dysmenorrhea. But, although these aims are bound together in a single process, they affect different aspects of the rites, and dominate different episodes. Furthermore, they are associated with ancillary aims, such as that of initiating candidates into cult-adepthood, and training new adepts in cult esoterica. And beneath this manifest telic structure there is a latent structure concerned with the 'social function' of the rites in overcoming divisions and restoring solidarity in the local community.

The Semantic Paradigm of the Dominant Ritual Symbol

The ritual symbol is a positive force in social action. Its semantic structure is articulated by culturally standardized ends and means. Each dominant symbol may be said to represent a crystallization of the flow pattern of the rituals over which it presides. With this in mind, I would like to consider some further properties of dominant symbols, in addition to those we have already discussed, e.g. multivocality, polarity, and condensation.

In any given instance of a symbol's use, we have to take into account at least three orders of reference: 1) its *manifest* sense, of which the subject is fully conscious, and which is related to the explicit aims of the ritual (to remove sterility, bring on rain, extract an *ihamba*, etc.); 2) its *latent* sense, of which the subject is only marginally aware but could become fully aware, and which is related to other ritual and pragmatic contexts of social action (thus *mukula* denotes maternal blood in the *Nkula* ritual, but also marginally aspects of male circumcision); 3) its *hidden* sense, of which the subject is completely unconscious, and which is related to infantile (and possibly pre-natal) experiences shared with most other members of the society, and perhaps with most other human beings (the cutting down of the *mukula* tree in *Nkula* may be connected with unconscious feelings of aggression against the mother).

Now let us consider the relationship between these orders of reference and the analytical frames discussed in Chapter One. These frames, or 'levels of meaning', were respectively: 1) exegetical, 2) operational, and 3) positional or contextual. Clearly, the manifest order of reference is directly correlated with the exegetical level of meaning, for people are always willing to explain what they know. But exegesis also provides data which can be examined in terms of the latent senses. Here the investigator has only to compare his exegetical reports on the significance of the same symbols when they recur in different rituals. Certain senses of a dominant symbol may be manifest in one ritual, but others are latent, for different senses are assigned to that symbol in native interpretations of other rituals. The investigator may then test out his hypothesis by enquiring whether in the first ritual there is further evidence of symbolic or semantic connections with other rituals. Thus there is not only the presence of *mukula* both in *Nkula* and in *Mukanda* (Boys' Circumcision) as a clue to affinities between these rites, but also the wearing of lourie feathers by important participants in each, and the presence in both of the *ku-kinda* dance. Further interrogation of informants may bring to light more and deeper interconnections. It is in analysing the data in the positional-contextual frame that traces of a symbol's hidden senses are exposed, for the juxtaposition of certain symbols may defy indigenous explanation. For example, the regular association of

the forked *chishing'a* pole, representing huntsmanship and virility, with a ring of twisted grass which encircles it below the
fork, may well represent an Ndembu belief, repressed in the
unconscious, in basic human bisexuality. But the possiblity that
a symbol has hidden senses is sometimes disclosed at the operational level. The exchange of clothing by mother and daughter
at the *Kwing'ija* is a case in point.[1] The operational level often
reveals a symbol's latent senses, as in the case of the behaviour
enacted with reference to the *mudyi* at *Nkang'a*.[2]

It is in the relationship between these orders of reference, and
on these three levels of analysis, that we see most clearly how
Ndembu interpret their social experience. We see, for example,
how, in order to focus attention on certain structural principles
and cultural aims, the Ndembu have to suppress other principles and aims, which then find disguised representation in
marginal symbols and behaviour. When matriliny and female
sexuality are strongly stressed in ritual symbolism, as in those
episodes pivoted on *mudyi* and *mukula* symbols, then symbolic
articles and actions indicative of virilocality or masculinity
simultaneously make their appearance. The arrow thrust in the
mudyi tree and the struggle for the porridge of *chipwampilu* pro-
claim the aggressive thrust of virilocality in woman's 'sovran
shrine' at *Nkang'a*. The chopping down of the *mukula* tree, and
the carving of baby dolls by male practitioners demonstrate
how men assert their importance in the procreative process.

The Semantic Structure of Mukula

In *Chihamba, the White Spirit*[3] I pointed out that analogy and
association are the main principles 'upon which are constructed
the chains of *denotata* and *connotata* making up the "meaning"
of most kinds of symbols.' In the particular case of Ndembu
ritual symbols there are three main points of departure for
analogy and association. The first of these is the *name* of the
symbol; the second is its *substance* or essential character, including its physical and biological character—a particular species
of tree which wholly or in part becomes a symbol would, for
example, be an aspect of its 'substance'; and the third is its

---

[1] See p. 210.
[2] See pp. 32–38.
[3] P. 73.

appearance as an *artifact*, as the product of human fashioning, in short, as an object of *culture*. Thus, it is possible to distinguish 1) *nominal*, 2) *substantial*, and 3) *artifactual* sources of significance.[1] Now let us consider the actual example of the *mukula* tree as it is used in *Nkula*.

The Name. Ndembu themselves derive *mukula* from *ku-kula*, 'to mature'. *Ku-kula* is used to describe several stages of biological or social status. A woman 'matures' at her first menstruation; she 'matures' at her first pregnancy. She 'matures' at her first parturition; she 'matures' yet again when she has borne several healthy children, and she 'matures' finally when she has passed the menopause and become, in many respects, sociologically a man. The same term is applied to masculine changes of status, but it is universally conceded that the archetype of all such changes is a girl's first menstruation. This primary usage is again reflected in the fact that the noun *nkula* frequently has the sense of 'menstruation'. Thus, *mukula* most intimately stands for 'the tree of menstruation', and secondarily for the tree of 'status changing'.

The Substance. The botanical term for *mukula* is *Pterocarpus angolensis*, the 'Rhodesian teak' of commerce, a handsome hardwood. In common with many other species of this genus it secretes a dusky reddish gum that coagulates rapidly into a scablike lump. These properties are likened by Ndembu to the flow of blood at menstruation and in childbirth. The coagulation of the gum is regarded as an auspicious property in ritual contexts, for it is thought to represent the formation of a placenta. When nominal and substantial meanings are combined, we have the picture of a magical substance which may be employed to ease and expedite the process of maturation in situations where the shedding of blood and formation of scabs or red solids are prominent. At this level of generality, *mukula* can be seen to be an apt symbol in gynaecological and circumcision ritual. In both instances there is a flow of blood which ritual aims to check, by the formation, in the one case, of a placenta and foetus, and, in the other, of a scab. The common symbol also cloaks many subtle interconnections between these kinds of

[1] In 'Themes in the Symbolism of Ndembu Hunting Ritual', *The Forest of Symbols*, op. cit. pp. 285–98. I have analysed the symbol '*chishing'a*', a forked branch used as a shrine in hunting ritual and *Ihamba*, in these terms.

7

ritual, for the first menses and first pregnancy are thereby compared and, indeed, identified with the bloody induction into manhood. Conversely, boys' circumcision becomes the analogue of female menstruation and parturition. The Ndembu intuition of human bisexuality is again given a visible, if disguised, form in this symbolic identification.[1]

In *Nkula* itself, as we have seen, *mukula* specifically represents: 1) 'the menstrual blood [*kanyanda*] of women'; 2) 'the tree of giving birth', *wakusema*; and 3) 'coagulation of blood', *ku-konda*. These manifest senses are consistent with the avowed aims of the ritual, to cure menstrual disorders and restore female fertility.

The Artifact. Both in the *Ilembi* and *Ku-tumbuka* the *mukula* tree becomes an object of purposive human manipulation. In the first of these phases *mukula* is the *ishikenu* ('dominant' or 'inaugural') medicine, and is consecrated by the group of adepts, both male and female, who encircle it in order to bring it within the sacred milieu of the rites (see p. 72). Then the principal practitioner addresses the tree itself, asking it to give those present procreative power, and its root and some of its leaves are taken as ingredients of the medicine to be drunk by the patient. One of my informants, it will be remembered, said that the *mukula* root symbolized the shade. At all events, when the senior practitioner poured some medicine, which included root parings of *mukula*, on top of the patient's head, it was said that in this way she would 'receive her shade' (p. 63). The leaf fragments adhering to her body after the medicine has dried on it are also a sign (*chinjikijilu*) of the shade.

These manipulations of *mukula* suggest that: 1) the tree is a special emblem of cult membership, distinguishing *Nkula* adepts from all other Ndembu: 2) it has, when consecrated in the cult ritual, mystical power and even something akin to a personality of its own (the species, not the individual tree); 3) *mukula* is sometimes regarded as a symbol, sometimes as a repository, and sometimes as a direct manifestation of a shade who is a former cult member (since Ndembu often apply the term *mukishi* indiscriminately to an invididual shade and to the mode of its mani-

---

[1] See Bettelheim, B., *Symbolic Wounds*, Glencoe, Ill.: The Free Press (1954), *passim*, and my article, 'Three Symbols of Passage in Ndembu Circumcision Ritual' in Gluckman, M. (ed.), *Essays in the Ritual of Social Relations*, M.U.P. (1962) for an analysis of *mukula* symbolism in circumcision rites.

festation—*Nkula, Chihamba, Ntambu*, etc.,—it is impossible to say
whether the individual shade is here thought of as merged in
a collective cult entity, or as personally present); 4) *mukula* is
represented as an ambivalent power or entity that can confer
not only troubles but boons, the greatest of which is fertility;
5) the Ndembu concept of medicine (*yitumbu*) is a complex one,
since *mukula*, regarded as a medicine, is at the same time a shade
manifestation and a mystical power. Part of its mystical power
derives from the 'mystery of the red river, or river of blood',
which is taught to Ndembu novices during circumcision and
funerary rites. Redness, like whiteness and blackness, is conceived by Ndembu as a primary and eternal power, issuing from
the supreme being, *Nzambi* himself, and pervading the pheno-
menal world with its quality. It is impossible to draw the line
here between animism and dynamism. All one can say is that
Ndembu try to tap many sources of 'power' (*ng'ovu*), treating
their dominant symbols as power-accumulators.

But the most dramatic and significant manipulations of
mukula take place during the esoteric episode of the *Ku-tumbuka*
phase. When the tree is explicitly identified with the shade and
with '*Nkula*', i.e. the mode of manifestation. In cutting down
the tree and simultaneously decapitating the red cock, the
shade-manifestation is ritually slain, only to be regenerated as
an infant in the womb, as the figurine in the symbolic calabash.
Perhaps it would be more exact to say that the shades' mode
of being has been altered. In any case, the themes of death and
rebirth, familiar in many systems of ritual, are clearly represented here. Sociologically, the identification between shade,
patient (who drinks and is anointed with 'medicines' representing the shade), and the patient's child (represented by the
figurine) is most significant. For it lays stress on directly uterine
ties, and not on those between members of a wide matrilineage.
It also seems to be a device which compensates in some measure
for the dominance of patrilaterality in the assignment of birth-
names (*majina akusemuka*). For normally it is the father's privilege
to divine for his child's name, and he assumes that this will be
bestowed by one of his own shades, either from the father's or
mother's side. In a sense the infant's character is thought to be
inherited from the father, and its first tutelary shade is a paternal one. But, in the case of a child born to a recent *Nkula* patient,

the birth-name is always that of the afflicting shade, whether the child be male or female. Thus, the birth-name of one of the main characters of this book, Kamahasanyi, was Mbayi (literally, 'menstrual blood'), and this was an *Nkula* name. Men with such names are expected to display certain female character traits, and I knew one who regularly enacted the ritual role of *Nyakayowa*, 'generic womanhood', in the boys' circumcision rites. For the child in some sense is felt to be a reincarnation of the shade, or at least of some of her physical and mental characteristics. Such a child, if a boy, is regarded as an adept in *Nkula*, and is entitled to receive training in its medicines and esoterica when he is sufficiently mature.

It might be plausibly argued that a woman's 'masculine protest', expressed in frigidity, periodic disorders, and barrenness, is what is being cut away and destroyed, when the tree is felled and the cock slaughtered. Ndembu society, through its *Nkula*

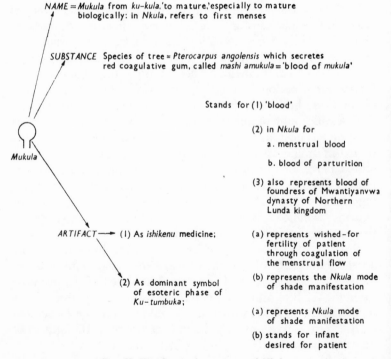

NAME = Mukula from *ku-kula*, 'to mature,' especially to mature biologically: in *Nkula*, refers to first menses

SUBSTANCE Species of tree = *Pterocarpus angolensis* which secretes red coagulative gum, called *mashi amukula* = 'blood of *mukula*'

Stands for (1) 'blood'

(2) in *Nkula* for

   a. menstrual blood

   b. blood of parturition

(3) also represents blood of foundress of Mwantiyanvwa dynasty of Northern Lunda kingdom

Mukula

ARTIFACT ⟶ (1) As *ishikenu* medicine;

   (a) represents wished-for fertility of patient through coagulation of the menstrual flow

   (b) represents the *Nkula* mode of shade manifestation

(2) As dominant symbol of esoteric phase of *Ku-tumbuka*;

   (a) represents *Nkula* mode of shade manifestation

   (b) stands for infant desired for patient

FIG. II. The Semantic structure of *Nkula*.

doctors, is transforming the woman from a would-be masculine shedder of blood into a normal wife and mother. In a sense *Nkula* complements *Nkang'a*. *Nkang'a* or girl's puberty, as we shall see, emphasizes lactation and nutrition and those aspects of matrilineal relationship which are unitary, harmonious, and mutually beneficial, The symbolism of menstruation and, indeed, of other 'red' aspects of the world, seems almost to be deliberately suppressed. It is as though the 'red' aspects of life, implying discontinuity, strife, aggressive feelings, bloodshed, and impurity, burst out to plague most women in the first few years after their puberty rites. For a very high percentage of women undergo *Nkula*, and most of these undergo at least *Ilembi* during their first decade of married life. The *mudyi* tree represents matriliny as an unblemished ideal; the *mukula* tree represents actual matriliny, blemished by human passions and resentments.

Unpretentious in outward form as these arboreal symbols are, nevertheless, each is rich in meaning. I have attempted, in the case of *mukula*, to express this semantic wealth diagrammatically, not indeed in the context of the total Ndembu ritual system, but merely in that of *Nkula*. See Fig. II, p. 86.

Conclusion

In this chapter we have subjected to close study the elaborate cultural apparatus that Ndembu deploy when they wish to deal with serious personal and communal misfortune. We have also made a microscopic analysis of a single ritual belonging to this genre. This ritual, *Nkula*, was chosen not only on account of its typicality, but also because its symbolic idiom is governed by the theme of redness or 'blood'. It therefore provides an appropriate introduction to the single performance of ritual that forms the core of the first section of this book. For this ritual, *Ihamba*, is also pervaded by the theme of blood. Our next task is to make an analysis of the social field setting of this performance, so that it may be analysed in the social-structural, as well as in the cultural, dimension. Rituals of affliction must be understood in close relation to the contemporaneous structure of the social field for which they are events. In this they differ from life-crisis rituals, which take no account of the actual balance of power between persons and groups, but dogmatically stress the key values and concepts of Ndembu society, in virtual independence of the concrete historical situation.

We now know something about the cultural tools of ritual redress: the next step is to consider the nature of a social field in which such tools are used, and the relationship between the two.

IV

FIELD CONTEXT AND SOCIAL DRAMA

THE cases now to be examined may, in one respect, be considered instances of what Llewellyn and Hoebel have called 'trouble-cases'.[1] In the trouble-case the individual and his society or his sub-group 'appear in dramatic relation at a moment of maximum pressure, each upon the other'. In another respect, these cases may be regarded as components of 'social dramas'. I have used this term elsewhere to distinguish a four-phased unit of social process that begins with a breach between persons and probably leads to a breaking off of relations up to the limit that the group can permit. Various adjustive or redressive mechanisms are then deployed to heal the breach, and these lead either to a re-establishment of relations or the social recognition of an irreparable breach between the contesting parties. Among the 'redressive mechanisms', which constitute the third phase, are divinatory and ritual procedures. These tend to be invoked in the face of what we would call a 'natural' disaster, for which mystical causes are sought, but in many instances the divination may bring to light secret cleavages in the structure of the group. Sometimes, indeed, mounting tension in the group is itself the precipitating cause of redressive ritual. When a group feels that it is in conflict with itself even a relatively minor misfortune tends to be regarded as the work of mystical beings or forces. Where norms conflict; where values are discrepant, and respectable persons find themselves compelled by circumstances to become rule-breakers; where the very axioms of society appear to be ineffective in preventing the outbreak of bitter disputes—then people experience a sharp sense of insecurity, even panic. In this social atmosphere charges of witchcraft and fears of ancestral wrath are generated and proliferate.

The cases I now wish to discuss represent the phase of ritual redress repeated over and over again. For the outcome of this stage is never certain, and regression to a state of unresolved

---

[1] *The Cheyenne Way*, University of Oklahoma Press (1941), p. 21.

crisis is always possible. This is particularly so when the conflict in a group has reached a point at which individuals, who would normally be expected to live in amity together, are being increasingly driven asunder. For example, as I have shown in *Schism and Continuity*, ecological and structural pressures may force villages to split, but a high value is attached to keeping them intact. Rituals, whose dominant symbols represent values which all Ndembu share and which therefore have a unifying character, are then performed; their latent function is clearly to reanimate the sentiment of loyalty to the group. But where cleavages are deep, such performances can seldom bind the members together again, though they may well reduce considerably their mutual animosities, and make the split, when it comes, a friendly and acceptable one.

Most Ndembu are today experiencing a silent but severe revolution in their social life, and an insidious restructuring of social relationships at many levels. At the same time, many values and beliefs still hold good, and it is common to find that some natural misfortune is not merely associated with one set of social conflicts, but with many. As different kinds of ritual stress different aspects of Ndembu culture and structure, a protracted state of illness or ill luck may give rise to performances of several kinds of ritual. Redressive ritual here becomes a treadmill, vainly turning without making progress, but revealing as it does so numerous sectors of the traditional culture. I was fortunate enough to come across such a ritual sequence during field-work. It was centred on a single individual, whose neurotic condition both resulted from and made visible traditional conflicts that had been exacerbated by modern political developments. This individual, for temperamental and biographical reasons had become peculiarly vulnerable to the forces that were reconstituting his society.

To analyse satisfactorily even a single social drama, it is necessary to place it firmly in what may be called its field context. My method is frankly along *Gestalt* lines. As mentioned earlier, a ritual performance should be viewed, in the words of Lewin, 'as occurring in, and being interpenetrated by, a totality of coexisting social entities such as various kinds of groups, sub-groups, categories, or personalities, and also barriers between them, and modes of interconnection'.[1] These form the field context. But I would go further than Lewin, whose assumptions here are structuralist-functionalist, and give a preliminary account, wherever possible, of the *history* of the field context, of how the kinds of groups and sub-groups came to be what they are, and of what accounted for their present modes of relationship. And when one speaks of 'history', one often speaks of personalities. If, therefore, we possess adequate, or even meagre, biographical information about our actors, we should not scruple to use it. For among the relevant dimensions of our field context we should include not only social structure and culture (which often vary independently in times of change), but also personality (the causative importance of which increases with change).

Another factor not always sufficiently recognized as having a formative influence on the field context is the role of the investigator himself. His enquiries and actions necessarily modify the behaviour of those he studies. In my attempt, therefore, to characterize the field context, I shall include as far as possible an account of my own relationships with the principal actors.

The Social Field of Mukang'ala Chiefdom

When I began my field work among the Mwinilunga Ndembu in 1951, my first base was a 'Holiday-House' for missionaries on local leave, close to a waterfall of the Lwakela River, a sub-tributary of the Zambezi. Between the Lwakela and the Kaseki stream about a dozen miles away, there straggled along the Government motor road about a dozen Ndembu villages in various stages of decrepitude. These villages together constituted the vicinage of Chief Mukang'ala (see Fig. III, p. 92). Until 1947 Mukang'ala was a Sub-chief under Senior Chief Kanongesha, the Ndembu 'Native Authority'. In the interests of centralization, recognition was then withdrawn from him by the British Government of the time, and his area was amalgamated with that of Kanongesha.

It soon became evident that Mukang'ala's chiefdom had

---

[1] Lewin, K., *Field Theory and Social Science*, London: Tavistock Publications, p. 200.

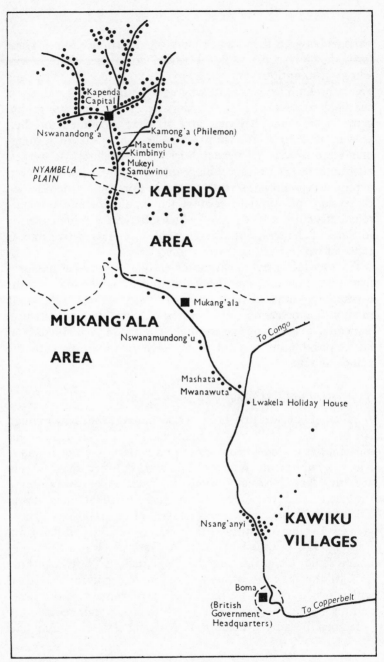

Fig. III. Map of Mukang'ala area.

become a depressed area. Symptoms of decline were everywhere visible in the cultural landscape. The Mission Outschool near the chief's capital village had been closed down. The capital village itself had shrunk in size from over thirty to a dozen huts. The disused court-house had begun to crumble beneath its rotting thatch. The school had been closed not only because the capital had been abandoned by many of its inhabitants, but also because villages formerly adjacent to it had moved further off, some even into different chiefdoms. Numerous individuals had gone to live permanently in more prosperous areas, and the villages that remained presented a seedy, unkempt appearance. Huts were in disrepair, their surrounds unswept, and the bush made deep salients into the inhabited clearings.

If it were not for the outward signs of modern development that had failed to take firm hold, one might have characterized Mukang'ala's area as 'primitive', compared with other Ndembu chiefdoms. But its primitiveness was reversionary. Regression had taken place, not to a former state of Ndembu tribal society, but in the sense, rather, of a breakdown of modern organization. Concomitant with this visible 'dedifferentiation' (to use Kurt Lewin's term) had occurred certain reversionary changes in the behaviour of the inhabitants. The former Court Clerk and the former *Kapasu* (Native Authority Messenger) had become Village Headmen. But neither fulfilled the traditional functions of headmen. The former spent most of his time in the bush, hunting and honey-gathering, and seldom appeared in the village to offer hospitality to visitors. The latter abandoned himself to drinking illicitly distilled spirits, and was hardly ever seen sober. Both retreated from contemporary reality, but neither reproduced the behaviour of a bygone time. It was as though the whole community was in recoil from a sharp blow to its self-esteem.

But among its inhabitants there were some who fought hard to restore the area's former prosperity. The ex-chief himself, for example, attempted to persuade a succession of District Commissioners to reinstate him. His appeal was almost invariably couched in terms of traditional political values. He had been deposed principally because his area contained relatively few people, even before 1947. After 1947 its population had further diminished. By contrast, the population in adjacent government chiefdoms had risen. The only claim that Mukang'ala could make to have his position reviewed, therefore, rested on traditional criteria. These were twofold. The first Mukang'ala had been the son of the second Kanongesha, who had come from the empire of Mwantiayanvwa in the Congo with an invading force over two centuries ago. This Mukang'ala had been entrusted with the task of subduing the indigenous Mbwela, and, as a reward for conquering them, Kanongesha had given his son a senior headmanship, and conferred on him the title of *Mwanawuta* (literally 'son of the bow'). Succession to the office of Kanongesha was then patrilineal, and the appellation *Mwanawuta* indicated that a Mukang'ala could no longer take part in that succession, although he remained a senior headman in his own right. The first Mukang'ala also held, through the maternal line, the office of *Lupang'u* (steward) to Kanongesha. It was a *Lupang'u's* duty to manage the supplies of a Lunda army on the march, and the first Kanongesha's *Lupang'u* had been appointed by the Lunda emperor, Mwantiyanvwa himself. The deposed Mukang'ala claimed that he was an important traditional functionary; for in addition to his title as a senior headman he held two other titles—*Mwanawuta* and *Lupang'u*. The title 'Mukang'ala', which took precedence over the other titles, was the nickname of the first incumbent. It means 'he who ties on the laths of a hut', and refers to an incident in his life, and was afterwards inherited as a title by successive incumbents. The ex-chief[1] claimed and in this case his claim was supported by elders belonging to other chiefdoms—that in the pre-European past, it was Mukang'ala's task to collect tribute from the other Ndembu senior headmen to give to Chief Kanongesha, whenever the latter decided to send a caravan to Mwantiyanvwa. The ex-chief held that this clearly indicated that the status of his office was higher than that of any other Ndembu senior headman under the chief.

It was not altogether unrealistic of the ex-chief, Kambung'u, to seek support from these traditions. A few years before his deposition the Government had withdrawn recognition from

---

[1] I use the terms 'chief' and 'ex-chief' to refer to an officeholder under the British Administration; and 'senior headman' to refer to an officeholder under the single 'chief', Kanongesha, under the traditional system.

another sub-chief, Nyakaseya, whose area lay within the north-western corner of Mwinilunga District. Nyakaseya had prompt-ly paid a visit to Mwantiyanvwa's *Musumba*, or state capital, on the Lulua River, where in return for tribute he had been awarded a crown of office (*chibang'ula*) and other insignia by the sacred head of all the Lunda. Mwantiyanvwa also sent a letter to the Provincial Commissioner of the Kaonde-Lunda Province of what was then Northern Rhodesia, recommending that Nyakaseya should be restored to office in view of the traditional importance of his headmanship. The first Nyaka-seya, a chieftainess, had been the principal wife (*mwadyi*) of the first Kanongesha to leave the Lunda homeland, and was, indeed, related to an important noble matrilineage at Mwanti-yanvwa's capital. In view of the fact that Nyakaseya was restored to his Government chieftainship, it was widely believed among Ndembu that Mwantiyanvwa's letter had turned the scales in his favour. But it is likely that without the presence of other important factors, such as the large population of Nyakaseya's area, and its proximity to the Mission station that gave employment to many Africans and ran a hospital and a school, Mwantiyanvwa's influence would not by itself have been enough. And it was just its lack of population and its distance from any centre of European settlement that rendered Mukang'ala's area 'redundant' as an administrative unit from the Government's point of view. It was true that a number of villages under Mukang'ala's traditional surveillance were clustered together in a small vicinage some five miles from the Mwinilunga Boma (District Office), but the vicinage where most of the chiefly lineage and their patrilateral kin lived was more than twenty miles from the Boma. The villages near the Boma were inhabited either by descendants of the conquered Mbwela, called Kawiku, or by Ndembu who came originally from other sub-chiefdoms. The heartland of Mukang'ala's area, between the Chitunta Plain and the Kaseki river, contained no Kawiku—apart from spouses of village hut owners—and lay at an approximately equal distance from the Boma and the European mission and farm in the Northern Pedicle. In terms of the modern cash economy and political system, this inner strip along the motor road was just 'for passing through' (*nakupandakana hohu*).

When the aged Mwantiyanvwa Kawumba died in 1951, the Belgian authorities recognized a District Chief entitled Mbaka as his successor. Mbaka immediately sent invitations to all chiefs of Lunda origin in the Belgian Congo, Angola, and Northern Rhodesia, to visit him at his capital. He was known to favour the Ndembu of Kanongesha and of Ishindi, who were, like himself, descended from the ancient Lunda line of Luweji Ankonde, and not from the Luba line of her husband Chibinda Ilung'a[1], as all previous Mwantiyanvwas had been. Among the Ndembu chiefs and senior headmen to visit him was Mukang'-ala Kambung'u. According to Kambung'u's account, Mwanti-yanvwa entertained him lavishly (a sure sign among African peoples of royal favour), made him accept a crown (for which he had to pay a considerable sum), and gave him a letter for the Provincial Commissioner. In this letter Mwantiyanvwa was said by Kambung'u to have confirmed that the Mukang'ala lineage originated in the Lunda homeland, and that he was, indeed, both *Mwanawuta* and *Lupang'u* of Kanongesha. Mwanti-yanvwa concluded by stating that in Lunda custom Mukang'ala should be the last Sub-chief 'to lose his chair', and recommen-ded his reappointment. The Provincial Administration ap-parently was unimpressed, and Mukang'ala Kambung'u was still a mere village headman in 1954 when I left the field for the last time. He made an attempt to go to Lusaka to see the Governor of Northern Rhodesia personally in October 1953, with a view to being re-instated, but was refused permission to leave Mwinilunga District for such a purpose by the District Commissioner. It was said by those close to him that Kambung'u used to brood continually over his loss of office, that 'he never slept, but lay all night thinking, thinking', and that he suspected other Ndembu chiefs, notably Kanongesha, who had 'swallowed up his area', and Kapenda, a young English-speaking chief, trained at Chalimbana School of Local Government, of having intrigued together to bring him into disfavour with the Government. My own impression of him was that he was a proud, aloof figure, doomed by history and geography to the role of a misfit, and tragically incapable of comprehending the causes of his downfall.

[1] See my article 'A Lunda Love Story and its Consequences' in *R.L.I. Journal*, xix, pp. 1–26.

But even before Kambung'u's deposition the people of his area had never fully acquiesced in European rule. Mukang'ala Ibala,[1] 'the bald', a fierce old warrior, according to Ṇdembu accounts and those of the pioneer missionaries in the District, had resisted the attempts of the British South Africa Company to impose its authority on the Ndembu. When taxation was first introduced in 1913, he had at first fled with his people to the Belgian Congo, and had afterwards built a large stockaded village at Kalene Hill, fifty miles from the Boma. He had then been ordered to return to his own area so that the Native Commissioner could 'keep an eye on him', in the words of an entry in the Mwinilunga District Notebook. Even in the 1920's, according to the evidence of village genealogies, he had taken part in feuds. I recorded, for example, that in Chikang'a Village, situated on the borders of Mukang'ala's area, two men had been killed by Ibala during this period, *'hanjita'* ('in a raid'). But Ibala had been recognized by the Administration in 1929, when the term Native Authority was introduced, as a Government Sub-chief. Two years after this he died, and a member of another branch of the office-holding matrilineage succeeded him. I shall discuss in some detail the struggles between various branches of the Mukang'ala lineage in the next chapter. Here it is sufficient to state that it was during the incumbency of Ibala's successor Mundong'u Kabong'u (D10) that the modern development of the area may be said to have begun. Under the Native Authority system a number of paid officials were appointed. These included councillors, assessors, a clerk, unarmed police, a postman, a school attendance officer, and foremen of road and building gangs. During Mundong'u Kabong'u's time, the Mission Out-school was built, and the schoolmaster held religious services for the few Christians in the area. I mention these facts because they help to explain the conflict between the two main branches of the Mukang'ala lineage within the field of modern political relations. For it was during the incumbency of Mundong'u Kabong'u's successor, Kambung'u (E13), that the Administration withdrew recognition from the Mukang'ala chieftainship. As a result of this disaster many

[1] See Fig. IX. Here Kambung'u is marked E13 (the letter E refers to his generation level). Ibala (C4) is his mother's mother's brother.

people lost paid employment and social status. Mutual recrimi-
nations were many and imaginative.

The senior men of Mundong'u Kabong'u's lineage used to
argue that if one of their number had succeeded instead of a
close matrilineal relative of Ibala (C4), who had been noted
for his hostility towards the Europeans, the Administration
would never have 'destroyed the chieftainship'. They complained that Kambung'u was old-fashioned and uneducated,
that he had never been to an urban area to work or had even
been locally employed under Europeans—which would have
given him an insight into their manners and customs—and
that he was 'shy' or 'ashamed' (*nsonyi*) in the presence of the
District Officers. Thus he could not make out a good case on
behalf of his people. They said that, unlike Chief Kapenda,
he did not put on a smiling face in the presence of Government
officials and missionaries, who would consequently have been
more ready to praise and less apt to censure their efforts in the
sphere of local government. But they, too, were anxious that
the chieftainship should be reinstated and supported Kambung'u's efforts to this end. When he made his trip to Mwantiyanvwa, for example, most of them contributed money
towards his travelling expenses and the tribute he had to give
as a mark of respect. That the tribute was not inconsiderable
may, I think, be gathered from the warmth of his reception by
Mwantiyanvwa. Moreover, the matrilineal kin of Mundong'u
were firmly in support of Kambung'u when he criticized
Government Chief Kapenda. By contrast with Mukang'ala
Ibala, the father's mother's brother of Chief Kapenda had
strongly supported British rule, and his people had remained
in the District when taxation was introduced. It seems likely
that this difference in response to British administration was
influenced by a long tradition of feuding between the two
neighbouring senior headmen. At any rate one of the 'excuses'
made by all members of the Mukang'ala matrilineage for the
abolition of their office was that the present Kapenda had mis-
informed the District Commissioner about the traditional
importance of Mukang'ala. He had done this, they alleged, in
order to extend the boundaries of his own chiefdom at Mukang'-
ala's expense. It is quite certain that much of Kapenda's
present territory to the south was formerly under the authority

of Mukang'ala, and that a further tract of Mukang'ala's land was added to it in 1954.

It was into this both embittered and discouraged social atmosphere that I plunged in the first innocence of my field-work. My earliest impression, as I have said, was of the physical decrepitude and primitiveness of Mukang'ala's area, after the neatness and order I saw at the Boma. But it was only gradu-ally that the tensions in the social structure of the broken chieftainship and the undercurrents of intrigue within it became detectable. My eyes began to open to the true state of affairs towards the end of my two months' stay at the 'Holiday House'. I had paid several visits by vanette to Kapenda's area, and had been most favourably impressed by the possibilities that existed there for a detailed study of social and economic change. The Government Chief himself was a frank informant and charming host, extremely intelligent, and apparently anxious to provide facilities to further my work. In his area the people were making rapid progress in assimilating the modern cash economy, and I had already met half a dozen African traders involved in it. I decided to set up a temporary camp at Kapenda's capital village, and study the social consequences of the introduction of a cash economy.

When I informed the people of Mukang'ala's area of my proposed move, however, there was an immediate and lively response. I was warned that Kapenda was not what he seemed, that he had gained his chair by witchcraft, that he was deceitful and dangerous 'like a snake' (*neyi kapela*), and that he would try to turn me against my friends in Mukang'ala's area. They said that if I really liked them, as they had been led to believe from my words and behaviour, I should build a permanent camp among them. One of the Mundong'u Kabong'u faction (E12), a man regarded as a likely successor to the present Mukang'ala, went so far as to offer the free services of all the people in his village to build me a house at the source of the Zambezi, in the north of Mukang'ala's area. He said that they would do this without pay, if only I would remain. Kapenda (E14, see Fig. X, p. 312) had been 'raised up', he went on, because of the presence of Europeans in his area. His great-grandfather, Kapenda Kambolu (B5), had given Mr. Smithers (the son of an earlier missionary in the District) a large piece

8

of land on which to make a farm, in exchange for some bales of cloth. Today, Mr. Smithers had grown rich and powerful (he was 'stronger than the District Commissioner'), and he employed many Ndembu as labourers, herdsmen for his cattle, storekeepers, clerks, carpenters, domestic servants, fitters for his lorries, and builders. He had opened a store where he bought local products such as baskets, mats, knives, and even 'medicines'. He bought cassava meal from the villagers for re-sale to the Boma. He ran a transport service to the Copperbelt. Furthermore, he sold a wide range of store goods, including clothing, cloth, utensils, gunpowder, and tools and imple-ments. Many Africans had settled permanently in Kapenda's area to be near Mr. Smithers's farm at Dellwood where they could make use of the facilities he provided. Kapenda had many people in his area, my informant continued, because Europeans lived on his land. And in his turn, Mr. Smithers wanted a strong chieftainship near him. When I objected that a few years previously Mr. Smithers had urged the District Commissioner to arrest Chief Kapenda for abducting a car-penter's wife on his farm, and that at the death of the previous chief he had opposed the nomination of another member of the Kapenda matrilineage on the grounds that the man had been imprisoned for theft, my informant had his answer pat. 'Mr. Smithers', he replied, 'likes a strong chieftainship (*wanta wakola*), but a pliant chief (*mwanta wawovu*)'. He had not attacked the chieftainship, in other words, but its incumbent. Certainly, Mr. Smithers had never been known to suggest that the chieftainship itself should be abolished. On the con-trary, his anxiety to see that the incumbent was beyond re-proach in terms of values stressed by the Mission suggested that he set great store by the maintenance of the chieftainship itself.

I pointed out to my informant that Chief Kapenda had not shown himself particularly 'pliant' at the time of the abduction. He had been arrested, I had been reliably informed both by Europeans and Africans, at the instigation of Mr. Smithers, and had promptly appealed to the Provincial Commissioner's Court against his arrest, on the grounds that it had been customary for Ndembu chiefs in the past to take in marriage any women they favoured, whether these were already married or not. Kapenda had been acquitted by the Provincial Commissioner, although he had been ordered to restore the woman to her husband and pay him damages. My informant replied that since his release Chief Kapenda had done his best to ingratiate himself with Mr. Smithers. For example, he attended religious meetings twice a week at the farm. Besides, he had the support of the Administration, to which he owed his chieftainship. Here my informant complained that Kapenda did not have the interests of his people at heart, but only his own interests, and that to further them he did what the Europeans told him to do. It did not matter, from this point of view, whether the Europeans in question were the missionaries, the Administration, or traders from the Copperbelt who came to buy rice grown by Kapenda's people. Kapenda wooed them all, my informant said, to make himself wealthy and his position strong.

My informant failed to realize that Kapenda was an astute and flexible politician who played each set of Europeans off against the others, not only for his private ends but also on behalf of his Ndembu followers. Taking advantage of the divisions in the ranks of the European ruling group, he was able to prevent Mr. Smithers from obtaining a trade monopoly over his area. He sponsored the opening of another European store at his capital, and thus smoothed the way for the trader to obtain a permit from the District Administration. The abduction case had led to considerable coolness in the relationship between Mr. Smithers and the Administration. Chief Kapenda took advantage of this to advance the economic prosperity of his Ndembu subjects. He invited the Boma to buy supplies of cassava meal directly from African traders in his area and not through Mr. Smithers. He obtained seed rice in quantities from the Government, and persuaded many of his people to grow it. Through his 'pull' with the Government he made contacts with European traders from the Copperbelt, who sent lorries to his area to buy rice at prices far in excess of those paid for comparable amounts of cassava. Like all politicians Kapenda could only further his own interests by advancing those of the people he relied upon for support. Although he was in many ways a calculating and opportunistic man, impelled by ambition, his energy and diplomatic flair nevertheless made him a spearhead of the new money economy, and a formidable agent of rural Africa's current transition from tribalism to peasant individualism.

But Mukang'ala and his people could see only selfishness and treachery against the traditional order in Kapenda's actions. In their view all Europeans were alike. They were capricious and terrible beings, who, unfortunately, held the reins of power in their hands. It was necessary in public to treat them with polite reserve, but to have as little to do with them as possible. They felt, nevertheless, that it would be an advantage to have a European settler in their area. He would give them a measure of local employment so that all the young men would not have to leave the area to find work. In one way or another he would enable them to earn money, that modern necessity. He might follow Mr. Smithers's example, and open a store where they could buy the goods all had learnt to appreciate. Less people would leave their villages, and others would settle in the area if he dwelt there. If many Ndembu immigrants came, there was a chance that the chieftainship would be restored, for a much increased population could not be effectively administered from the remote capital village of Chief Kanongesha. But these conservative Ndembu believed that their dealings with him should be impersonal and confined to the minimum necessary to satisfy their needs. In the villages life could go on much as it had always done. But it was rank treachery for a Ndembu authority to enforce Government-inspired legislation, as Kapenda was doing. Kapenda actually fined headmen for not making latrines in their villages. He arrested people for distilling spirits. He insisted that villages were kept free from weeds and rubbish. He not only agreed verbally with the District Commissioner's orders and suggestions, but acted on them, as though he believed they were right and beneficial! This was too much for the stalwarts of the old order to stomach, even the 'moderates', who appreciated the benefits of European material culture, without accepting European values.

I remarked to Mukang'ala's people that if I made a base camp among them I could not greatly assist them, since I could only remain in the District for a comparatively short time to write down the customs and present social conditions of the Ndembu. They replied emphatically that they would make it worth my while to stay in their area 'forever' (*hayan-yaka*), by building a farm-house for me and clearing the bush, so that I could grow crops and raise cattle. They could not, at this early phase of my field-work, assign me to any category of European with which they were familiar, administrator, missionary, trader, or farmer. I am sure that they felt that my real, undivulged motive for living among them was to seek out a suitable piece of land on which to commence farming and trading. Indeed, I was afterwards told by Ndembu I had come to know well that stories to this effect then circulated widely in the District. It is interesting to note that Ndembu, unlike many other Northern Rhodesian peoples in the period immediately before the African protest against the Central African Federation, were not all uncompromisingly opposed to the acquisition of Native Trust Land by a European. Mukang'ala's people, at any rate, finding that I was friendly towards them, were emboldened to feel that as a settler I would be their spokesman and defender. This book is not an account of my personal moral dilemmas, but I am sure that I speak for many field anthropologists when I say that I experienced pangs of conscience on more than one occasion of this kind. If a field worker endeavours to understand a group of human beings, however much their culture may differ from his own, he is bound to feel sympathy with their miseries and aspirations. Through this sympathy, he tends to become their partisan, especially when he becomes aware of the objective, and quite often remediable, causes of their misfortunes and frustrations. But as a scientist, as a person seeking to describe and analyse facts without bias, he cannot commit himself emotionally to the interests of any single section or faction in the social field he is studying.

I mention my own motives and inner deliberations not to justify my behaviour, but as a set of factors that had effects in the field of action I was studying. As a social scientist, I felt that I could not identify myself completely with Kambung'u's factional struggles against other chiefs, or with his drive to regain the recognition of the Administration. And, indeed, I could not in any way delude his people that I had come, as a sort of *deus ex machina*, to lift them out of the depression into which they had sunk. I had to argue to them that I had come to study the customs and present ways of *all* the Ndembu, and not to settle in Mukang'ala's area for its own especial benefit: I was not leaving their area because I disliked them personally, but solely to further my work. I promised to pay them frequent visits by vanette from my new camp, and to present their case as fairly as I could when I came to write my book about the Ndembu. So I left the area, not without qualms of guilt induced by the social skills of Mukang'ala's people in an already divided mind, and made my base camp in Kapenda's area.

I have now roughly sketched in the main outlines of the social field within which the secular and ritual events I wish to consider became relevant. In this field several sets of relationships already appear to be significant. It may be said that the set of White-Black relationships is dominant among these, although observable interactions between members of the colour-categories were few in number. The Government had the power to make and break senior headmen by granting recognition to them, or by withholding or withdrawing it. Since the Government, in the interests of administrative neatness, did not recognize all traditional authorities, senior headmen competed with one another to obtain and maintain recognition. Such competition often followed the lines of traditional cleavages. Competition between traditionally opposed senior headmen was strongly influenced at that time by the presence or absence of European settlers in their areas. If settlers were present, many Ndembu would build near them, and swell a senior headman's following. Since the Administration tended to recognize as chiefs and sub-chiefs mainly senior headmen with large followings, the presence of *a few* Europeans was to their advantage. *Large-scale* settlement of Europeans, on the other hand, was universally feared by Ndembu, who believed that this would mean the loss of their Native Trust Land and its conversion into Crown Land that could be purchased by Europeans. In fact, when the Administration sent spokesmen to argue in favour of Central African Federation in August 1951, great numbers of Ndembu assembled at the Boma to declare their opposition to Federation on these very grounds. Sub-chiefs, who in the normal course of affairs competed against one another to secure the favour of the Administration, made common cause against Federation. All spoke of their fears that the land would be taken from them and parcelled out among Whites. For once, the cleavage between Blacks and Whites took precedence over local cleavages between Blacks who recognized White supremacy. However, in the situation I am about to describe, the set of relationships between Blacks and Whites was characterized by a general acceptance of the reality of White political control and of the benefits of limited White settlement.

Government chiefs also sought to play off the Administration against the other kinds of Europeans, missionaries, farmers, and traders. Chiefs would complain to the District Commissioner, for example, that the missionaries were neglecting the schools, or that European farmers had killed more game on Native Authority Land than their licences entitled them to do. On the other hand, they might connive at the illicit activities of European traders in selling such items as gunpowder to African hunters whose licences to buy it had expired. Presents from traders to chiefs were said to have resulted in the turning of many a blind eye to officially forbidden transactions.

In the widest relevant system of social relations we have to examine, a system that almost coincides geographically with Mukang'ala's and Kapenda's chiefdoms, the latter chief was adroit and the former maladroit in dealing with the Whites. This was partly due, as we have explained, to the different histories of the two senior headmanships before their elevation to the status of Government chieftainships. The Kapendas had co-operated with the Boma from the beginning, the Mukang'ala's had opposed it. It was partly due to the presence of missionaries and farmers in Kapenda's area, and not in Mukang'ala's. There also appears to have been a difference in soil fertility favouring Kapenda's area. But one of the major differences was in the social composition of the two areas. Kapenda's contained a heterogeneous population, including members of several tribes other than Ndembu. Some of them were Luvale who had followed the missionary, Dr. Smithers, from his previous station in Luvale territory. Kinsmen had joined them later from time to time, until there was an appreciable Luvale population in Kapenda's area. In 1921 a group of Ovimbundu entered the area with another missionary and settled on the Sakeji River. The Ovimbundu, who were advanced agriculturalists and craftsmen, at first came into conflict with the local Ndembu, but were afterwards accepted by them as valuable members of the community. In addition to these relatively advanced aliens, many Ndembu from other chiefdoms migrated to Kapenda's area to seek work at Mr. Smithers's farm and to grow crops for sale to Europeans. The present Chief Kapenda, Kalombu England (E14) had, before he became chief, made friends with influential members of the Luvale, Ovimbundu, and immigrant Ndembu groups. This proved to be far-sighted policy, for later a Government chief in Mwinilunga District came to be elected by a meeting of the headmen of his area in consultation with the District Commissioner. Kalombu England was opposed by most members of the chiefly lineage (see Fig. X, p. 312), ostensibly on the grounds that, although his father Samuheha (D19) had been chief, his mother had been a slave of Senior Headman (now Government Chief) Nyakaseya. A more cogent reason for their opposition, however, had been because he was too friendly with the immigrant stranger element. At the time of his candidature, too, he was known to have been recommended to the D.C. by Mr. Smithers, and this fact did not commend him to the traditionalist party. Their candidate, Philemon Chonyi (E15), had incurred the disfavour of Mr. Smithers by stealing a consignment of beeswax from the farm store, and had been imprisoned for this theft. When the village headmen were summoned by the District Commissioner to elect a new Kapenda in 1942, the votes of the immigrant headmen turned the scale in Kalombu England's favour. Before the late chief's death many members of his lineage lived at his capital village. When Kalombu England became chief, most of them refused to join his new village (after the death of a chief or a senior headman it is customary for Ndembu to abandon his village), and scattered to found their own villages at varying distances from the new capital.

Thus Kapenda Kalombu England tended to rely on immigrants for support, and found himself faced with the covert hostility of many members of his own lineage. The same situation prevailed even in his domestic life. His first, or ritual, wife was Ndembu. She still performed ritual functions, had borne Kapenda several children, but had long ceased to have a place in the chief's affections. His second wife was a Luvale and his third wife a Mbundu. But 'the wife of his heart' (*ng'oda yamuchimawindi*), his fourth, was a half-caste Portuguese-Luvale woman. She had previously been married to a Portuguese, and then to a Greek trader. From them she had acquired such items of wealth as a bicycle, a sewing machine, and a wireless set. She put to account her knowledge of 'European customs' by acting as hostess for Kapenda when he entertained European visitors at his large house of sunbaked brick. Kapenda's wives were drawn from each important social component of his chiefdom. He used to joke about this to me and say that he had 'married all his people'. The attraction exerted on him by the European style of life was mirrored in the attentions he paid to his half-caste wife, but the careful respect with which he treated his first wife on formal and ritual occasions reflected his general attitude towards the more traditional Ndembu whom he was careful not to offend too openly. Nonetheless, his first wife was known to be bitterly jealous of the half-caste wife, and a song popular during the period of my field-work pithily commented on the fact.

Mukang'ala Kambung'u, on the other hand, was supported by the more traditional inhabitants of his area. Although its population could be called 'homogeneous' in the sense that there had been little immigration into it from surrounding areas for many decades, there existed a deep division within the traditional group itself, between the matrilineal descendants of the original Lunda invaders and the matrilineal descendants of the autochthonous Mbwela. These people of Mbwela origin called themselves Kawiku after the name of the plain near which their first settlement had been made. The senior Kawiku headman, Nsang'anyi, had indeed tried to persuade the Administration to make him a Government chief, but the District Commissioner, in consultation with the Senior Chief Kanong'esha and Mukang'ala Ibala (C4), had rejected his claim. But Kawiku supported Mukang'ala against Kapenda, and shared the bitterness of Mukang'ala's followers of Lunda descent when their chief lost his office.

Another group which supported Mukang'ala Kambung'u (E13) in his efforts to be reinstated, but which opposed him within the framework of traditional Ndembu politics, was the

Mundong'u Kambung'u (D10) branch of the Mukang'ala chiefly lineage. It was this branch which particularly urged me to make my home in Mukang'ala's area. It was in their interest to have the chieftainship restored, for they hoped to provide the next chief from their ranks. They acted as though they felt that if they were on close terms with me, and if through my help the chieftainship were to be restored, one of them might conceivably be appointed as chief. Perhaps they hoped that the deposed Kambung'u (E13) would not be re-appointed by the Administration, and that a member of their own branch would succeed. Nevertheless, in their relations with the Administration they supported Kambung'u publicly, for he represented the chieftainship, even though they privately opposed him as members of a rival branch of the chiefly lineage.

Several structural cleavages, then, run through the system of social relations we are investigating. There is the local expression of the Black-White cleavage, which, indeed, dominates social relationships throughout Central and Southern Africa. Next, there is the Mukang'ala-Kapenda dichotomy. There is, too, the division between 'progressives', who are successfully adapting themselves to modern politico-economic conditions, and the 'traditionalists'.[1] Then within each chiefdom there is a sharp split between the office-holding branch of the chiefly lineage and the other branches. These cleavages sometimes, but by no means invariably, coincide, and different cleavages are stressed in different situations.

The social system we are studying has two focal points, the capital villages of Mukang'ala and Kapenda. Mukang'ala's chieftainship is the focus of traditionalist, anti-European sentiments; Kapenda's of progressive, pro-European sentiments. But within each chiefdom one finds an opposition to the chief, which tends to stress attitudes and goals antithetical to his. Thus, certain branches of the chiefly lineage that do not possess office in Kapenda's area tend to present themselves as traditionalists and sticklers for customary ways. Like Mukang'-ala's people they affect to despise what they consider Kapenda's

---

[1] This difference is also reflected in the frequency and type of rituals performed in the different areas. See, Table 2, 'Experience of Ritual Performances, Classified by Area and Sex', p. 303, and Table 3, 'Incidence of Shade Affliction, Classified by Area and Sex', p. 304-6.

'truckling' to Europeans. On the other hand, rival factions in Mukang'ala's lineage claim that they are more progressive than the deposed chief, and that they would have encouraged the economic development of the area if one of their senior members had been chief. The tumbledown air of their villages and their reversionary social and economic practices are due, they maintain, solely to the action of the Government, which 'destroyed' the chieftainship. The similar structural position of out-of-office factions in each of the two adjacent chieftainships has had the effect of drawing them together as allies in various situations. I give a few examples of these temporary alliances and their after-effects, for the tendency of dissident branches to unite across local divisions is an important factor underlying the cohesion of the Ndembu people as a whole. Furthermore, instances of this kind of alliance influence the rituals I analyse later on.

The best example I have of alliance between out-of-office factions in adjacent chieftainships is the relationship between Philemon Chonyi (E15), mentioned above, of the Kapenda matrilineage, and Kimbinyi (D3), of the Mukang'ala matrilineage. When Kambung'u became Mukang'ala, a number of members of a rival branch of the Mukang'ala lineage left the area and settled in that of Kapenda. Among these dissident folk was Kimbinyi. He was a cripple, a man of sharp intelligence and equally sharp tongue. He was feared and admired for his mordant wit. Now Kimbinyi settled in Kamong'a Village, where Philemon Chonyi (E15), classificatory sister's son of the late Chief Kapenda, was headman. The two men struck up a firm friendship. When the chief, Kapenda Samuheha (D19), died, a whispering campaign, probably begun by Philemon's rivals, developed, which finally gave rise to the following myth. It was said that Kimbinyi, strongly suspected as a sorcerer, had gone to Philemon, and had offered to help him kill the chief by magic when he was out hunting. In return he sought Philemon's aid to kill Mukang'ala Kambung'u by the black art. As a result of this evil collaboration both would become Government chiefs. When Kapenda died, it was said that half the compact had been fulfilled. But Kalombu England, who, it will be remembered, in fact became Kapenda, appears to have taken advantage of this tale to discredit his rival and thus to further his own claim. In a parallel fashion Mukang'ala Kambung'u seems to have exploited the same tale to blacken still more Kimbinyi's reputation, and so reduce the possibility of his eventually succeeding to the Mukang'ala chieftainship. Certainly, the effect of the tale was to prevent Kimbinyi's recruiting a following in Mukang'ala's area, where even the members of the Kabong'u Mundong'u branch, a family genealogically close to that of Kimbinyi, accepted the story as authentic.

The grain of truth in it is that both Philemon and Kimbinyi were capable and politically ambitious men, who sought what at the time (1942) was the supreme position of local influence, that of Government Chief. Their subsequent careers afford an interesting glimpse into the process of social change consistent with the spreading money economy. Blocked—it would seem permanently—on the traditional route to politico-economic power, they turned, especially in the post-war years, to trading as a means of wealth and influence. When I knew Kimbinyi first, in 1951, he was toying with the idea of buying a vanette out of his trading profits to carry commodities and fare-paying passengers to the railway. And Philemon was beyond question the richest African trader in the north-western pedicle. In addition to buying large quantities of cassava from the villagers for re-sale to the Boma, he ran a store where he sold a wide range of goods of European manufacture. But as Philemon and Kimbinyi became ever more deeply involved in the cash economy, so they tended to become trade rivals. Eventually Kimbinyi left Kamong'a Village, and founded a small village (or 'farm' in the argot of the developing black state) of his own, about a quarter of a mile from Kamong'a. Both Philemon's and Kimbinyi's settlements were roughly equidistant from Kapenda's capital village and Mr. Smithers's farm, some three miles from both. In fact, they were situated in a thickly populated quarter where conditions were propitious for their business activities. Kapenda's and Mukang'ala's capital villages were connected by a motor road, called locally 'the Boma road'. Along a short stretch of this road, beginning about a mile or so from Kapenda's village and ending about three miles further on in the direction of Mukang'ala's village, a number of settlements extended in a ribbon to the margin of the Nyambela Plain. This grassy plain had once been part of Mukang'ala's area but at this time came well within Kapenda's domains. In this populated strip, villages founded by dissident members of Mukang'ala's lineage were closely interspersed with villages occupied by rival kin of Kapenda. The structural forces that had repelled each group of dissidents from the opposite poles of the Mukang'ala-Kapenda field now brought them into spatial juxtaposition and social alliance. That this juxtaposition should have occurred within Kapenda's area, and not on the boundary between the areas, is due, I think, to the pull exerted by the European settlement in Kapenda's area. The dissident factions of the Kapenda lineage did not quit the field of conflict in which they had been defeated, because around Mr. Smithers's farm was concentrated a large population deeply committed to the cash economy. Their leader, Philemon Chonyi, could regain influence by acquiring wealth through the exploitation of that population. Those who opposed Mukang'ala tended to leave their home area because it was much more difficult to obtain cash there. Few of them went to build near the Boma, the administrative headquarters on the opposite side of Mukang'ala's area, principally because many Kawiku, their ancient foes, lived there. These Kawiku, and neighbouring Ndembu villages linked to them by a complex network of marital and patrilateral ties, had established a virtual monopoly over the local jobs available to Africans in domestic service and road maintenance at the Boma. One section of the Mukang'ala lineage lived in the Kawiku area, mainly because its senior member was patrilaterally related to the headman of the largest Kawiku village. But members of the Mukang'ala lineage who were not closely connected with Kawiku by kinship and affinity were not welcomed in the cluster of villages near the Boma, probably on account of the traditional hostility between Mukang'ala's Ndembu and Nsang'anyi's Kawiku. Another factor that may explain why Mukang'ala's Ndembu and Kawiku tended to inhabit different parts of the area is that the senior headman of the Kawiku held a ritual office in connection with the installation of a Mukang'ala. It was a common practice among peoples of Lunda affinities for the senior political and ritual functionaries within a chiefdom or a senior headman's area to build at a distance from one another.

Thus, it might be said that there existed a social barrier against movement towards the Boma by members of Mukang'-ala's lineage. No such barrier prevented them from migrating in the opposite direction. In fact, as we have seen, Mukang'ala Ibala had once built his village on the north-western boundary of Kapenda's area. More importantly, the same attraction that held the dissident factions of Kapenda's lineage *within* Kapanda's area drew not only Mukang'ala's people but many other Ndembu *away from* their own areas. This social 'magnet' was Mr. Smithers's farm, the economic (though not geographical) centre of the entire Ndembu region. The visible end-product of these various, and often conflicting, tendencies is the spatial distribution of the dissentient groupings well within the Kapenda area, but at a significant distance from the capital village. The dominant trend is the rapidly expanding cash-economy which is realized by most Ndembu to be working strongly in favour of the incumbent of the Kapenda Government chieftainship. For this reason, many of Mukang'ala's people are to be found today in Kapenda's area, while few of Kapenda's people are to be found in Mukang'ala's area. This fact gives additional grounds for resentment to those who continue to hope for the restoration of Mukang'ala's former position against Kapenda and all that he seems to them to stand for.

The Ritual Specialists

My own intention in forsaking Mukang'ala's area for Kapenda's was to make a detailed study of the economic and social changes taking place in the latter. I collected material relevant to such an enquiry, and for a time forgot my promise to revisit Mukang'ala's area. In the course of research I became extremely interested in the Ndembu system of ritual, of which I saw much evidence. I tried to strike up an acquaintance with ritual experts or 'doctors' (*ayimbuki*; sing. *chimbuki*), to discuss with them the symbolism of the different kinds of ritual. Possibly the friendliest, and certainly the most astute, of these was an old man named Ihembi, who will play an important part in this account. Ihembi (D16) was a member of the Kapenda chiefly matrilineage, but he was no supporter of the present chief. He lived in the village of Matembu, and was the classificatory 'older brother' of its headman (see Fig. X, p. 312). The core-membership of Matembu Village belonged to the chiefly lineage, but had a special relationship with it. In the early days of the Ndembu penetration, and/or several generations afterwards, it was customary for the headman of Matembu Village to succeed to the office of Kapenda, after the death of each incumbent. A similar mode of succession is found today in the Senior Chief's area, where each Kanongesha is succeeded by a Chibwika, appointed from the chiefly lineage during the lifetime of the Kanongesha. According to the present Kapenda, one of the incumbents of the Kapenda headmanship in the nineteenth century was attacked by a Matembu and his followers. Kapenda defeated Matembu and slew him. He then appointed a new Matembu, and decreed that from that time the Matembu lineage would not enter into the Kapenda succession. Instead, the office of Matembu would become a ritual one, that of *chivwikankanu*, a function of anyone who installs a headman among the Ndembu and purifies his medicines. This office corresponds to the one held by Nsang'anyi, the Kawiku senior headman, in Mukang'-ala's area. The offices of Kapenda and Matembu are interdependent, since only a Matembu can install a Kapenda, and since a Matembu's position depends on the maintenance of Kapenda's role in the total politico-ritual system of the Ndembu. The present headman of Matembu Village had lent his support to Philemon Chonyi's claim to succeed as Kapenda, and had vigorously opposed Kalombu England. But when Kalombu had been appointed, Matembu had consented to perform the traditional installation ritual on his behalf. Matembu himself was rather conservative in disposition and manners, and though he disapproved personally of Kalombu England, he did not feel able to refuse to perform his customary role. Nevertheless, he made his disapproval felt in a number of ways, opposing Kapenda almost as a matter of principle, whenever the latter summoned his headmen to discuss an important issue. Matembu's village was sited between Philemon's and Kimbinyi's, and its occupants, like those of the other two villages, were forever grumbling about Kapenda's behaviour.

The old ritual specialist Ihembi belonged, then, to the anti-Kapenda party, and had made his home in the village of the traditionalist Matembu. Ihembi had been a famous gun-hunter (*chiyang'a*) in his youth, and like many such hunters had led a nomadic life which had taken him at various times to the Belgian Congo, to Angola, and to Balovale District in Northern Rhodesia, where he had stayed for many years. He claimed to have practised as a diviner but to have given up this profession after he had been heavily fined by the British Administration, which had made the divining of witches a punishable offence. But Ihembi was everywhere regarded as a great expert in two kinds of curative ritual, and was in constant demand. These kinds of ritual were called *Ihamba* and *Kaneng'a*. Since a large part of this book will be taken up with an analysis of the sociology and symbolic structure of these rituals and of others related to them, I will do no more here than briefly relate some of their principal characteristics.

Both rituals are performed to cure sickness. When either is invoked it is believed that the patient is being afflicted by a mystical agency. *Ihamba* is the name not only of the ritual but also of the afflicting agency, in this case the shade of a dead hunter, which is thought to inhere in one of the two upper front incisors of the dead man. These teeth are also called *mahamba* (pl. of *ihamba*). Under the influence of the shade, the tooth is believed to fly about invisibly and to fix itself in the body of a living relative of the dead hunter. In this way it punishes a person who has failed to pour out a libation of blood or beer to the shade of the deceased, who has 'forgotten the shade in his heart', or who has offended the shade by quarrelling with his kinsfolk. In some cases the *ihamba* may afflict someone as a representative of a kin group that has collectively offended the dead hunter. The ritual of *Ihamba* (*chidyika chehamba* or *ng'oma yehamba*, literally 'the drum of *Ihamba*') consists in washing the patient's body with 'medicines' (*yitumbu*), i.e. pounded leaves, roots, and bark scrapings, giving him medicines to drink, and applying cupping horns (*tusumu*) to his body to 'suck out' (*ku-sumwena*) the hunter's tooth. The tooth, it is believed, tries to avoid capture as long as possible, and travels about beneath the skin of the victim, dodging the cupping-horns. Much depends on the moral condition of the patient and of his group in determining whether the hunter's shade will allow the tooth to be removed. The *Ihamba* ritual is of immense interest to the social anthropologist, since it throws into clear relief many of the current antagonisms in the patient's group. Sometimes, indeed, in the course of an *Ihamba* ritual, performed for a person occupying a significant position in the social structure of a wider system than the village, the investigator is able to collect material, in the form of prayers, invocations, confessions, comments, and asides, which shows him precisely where the main areas of tension and conflict lie within that system.

Kaneng'a is performed to cure persons bewitched by the living. A male sorcerer or a female witch causes severe illness by sending familiars against his or her kin. The *Kaneng'a* specialist aims either to drive away these familiars from the patients, or to force their owners to call them off by the threat of public exposure. Both the *Ihamba* and the *Kaneng'a* rituals are said by Ndembu to have been introduced into the Ndembu region, although many of the symbols used in both occur with the same meanings in demonstrably traditional Ndembu rituals. Most of the West-Central Bantu tribes, including Lunda, Luvale, Luchazi, and Chokwe, have a common fund of symbols, though the tribes differ in the degree of importance they attach to certain symbols and in the particular combinations of symbols used in cognate rituals. *Ihamba*, said to have been introduced from the Luvale or Chokwe, has been grafted on, as it were, to the main stock of the Ndembu gun-hunters' cult (*Wuyang'a*), with which it has many symbols in common. *Kaneng'a* is reputed to be of Mbwela origin, but has the same symbolic idiom as traditional Ndembu rituals, notably those connected with divination. If these rituals are borrowed, they were probably borrowed a long time ago, for they have been completely incorporated into the Ndembu ritual system.

Ihembi allowed me to attend a number of performances of *Ihamba* at which he was the senior doctor (*chimbuki*). He had two assistants, both of whom at that time lived at Matembu Village, and were his classificatory sister's sons. The first was called Mundoyi. He belonged to the matrilineage of the headman of Matembu. The other was Mundoyi's paternal half-brother Mukeyi. Their father had been chief of Konkoto, a Lunda area in the southern Belgian Congo. It will be found that Ndembu with patrilateral connections with Konkoto play leading parts in this account. Mukeyi had strengthened his tie

with Matembu Village by marrying the headman's classificatory sister. This woman, Nyasapatu (D18, see Fig. X,
p. 312), was Mundoyi's classificatory mother, and, indeed,
before he married her, Mukeyi, in his role as brother to
Mundoyi, called Nyasapatu his 'mother'. Although Mukeyi
and Nyasapatu were only extremely distantly related, there
was a faint tinge of incest about their marriage, which roused
public disapproval and led eventually to the departure of
Mukeyi and his wife from Matembu Village to found a 'farm'
nearby. Both Mukeyi and Mundoyi were members of the
hunters' cult: indeed, if they had not been, Ihembi would
not have accepted them as apprentice-doctors in the *Ihamba*
techniques. Mukeyi and Mundoyi were usually intimate for
paternal half-brothers. When Mukeyi, resentful of the scandal-
mongering about his marriage to Nyasapatu, left Matembu,
Mundoyi wanted to join him there, and, when I left the area,
was busy manufacturing witchcraft accusations against Headman Matembu, to provide himself with a generally acceptable
excuse for leaving his matrilineal village. Like Ihembi, who
had spent most of his adult life outside Mwinilunga District,
neither of the brothers really 'fitted in' at Matembu Village;
for they had spent many years with their father at his village
in the Congo. Indeed, several of the noted practitioners in
curative ritual that I have known are men who simultaneously
belong to an Ndembu local group (usually by matrilineal
descent) and do not 'belong' in it (often because they have
resided outside it patrilocally or uxorically for many years).
Their ambiguous position is epitomized in the proverb: 'The
flying squirrel said "I am a bird-squirrel; I am a bird, I am an
animal." ' A folk-tale (*kaheka*) explains this proverb: 'The
flying squirrel tried to live with the birds, but they rejected
him because he had a tail, teeth, and fur, like an animal. Then
he tried to live with the animals, but they rejected him because
he flew like a bird.' In a society such as that of the Ndembu,
which is characterized by an exceptionally high mobility of
individuals and groups, and in which local units themselves
tend to be unstable, one finds a fairly high proportion of
'flying-squirrels', men who are always changing their mind,
mode of action, or residence. It is from their ranks that great
ritual specialists are often recruited. Village heads, on the

other hand, are usually men who have lived more or less continually with the same sets of kin. Such men are able in time to attach to themselves a stable following of kinsfolk who may support them in factional struggles for village headmanship. Or, if they found new villages, they have a nuclear group of kin to build with them. Thus, to our list of cleavages between social categories we can add the cleavage between the relatively stable and the relatively mobile. We can also state with some confidence that the heads of local politico-kinship units are dominantly drawn from the former category, while the leading ritual specialists tend to belong to the latter. We shall see, to anticipate a little, that the widest interests and values not only of the Ndembu, but also of the whole complex of peoples of similar culture whose ruling elements claim to come from Mwantiyanvwa's Lunda empire, are maintained by these mobile, nomadic ritual specialists. Headmen, on the other hand, represent the values and norms of local kinship units, of the structured sub-groups of Ndembu society.

How the Ritual Sequence Began

My observations of the sequence of rituals studied here began when I at last fulfilled my promise to return to Mukang'ala's area. I had decided to collect data on hunting, beecraft, and fishing, and it was impossible to collect adequate material on these pursuits in Kapenda's area where they had become marginal to cash-cropping and wage-employment. In any case, most of the game in that area had been shot or chased away by Europeans, or by Africans with muzzle-loading guns, whereas in Mukang'ala's area with the reduction of population wild life had become relatively plentiful again. Moreover, most of the people had tended to revert to traditional economic pursuits, especially hunting.

I went to the village of Nswanamundong'u, founded by Mukang'ala Mundong'u Kabong'u before he became Government chief, to make enquiries. I had previously made a census of the village population, taken genealogies there, and drawn a diagram of the siting of the huts. When I had stayed at the Mission Holiday House I had frequently visited Nswanamundong'u to discuss Ndembu customs with its inhabitants and collect linguistic data. My wife and I had observed a girl's puberty ritual there. As a result of these contacts we had struck up more than a casual acquaintanceship with several of the villagers. Indeed, it had been the people of Nswanamundong'u who had pressed us hardest to remain in Mukang'ala's area.

I had with me my cook, Musona, a Kawiku from the southeast of Mukang'ala's area, who had worked at Bulawayo and on the Copperbelt. He had also worked as a road foreman in Mwinilunga District, and had been employed in various capacities by a succession of District Officers. He was thus widely travelled and experienced. But, most valuable to me, he had innumerable acquaintances within the District. A man of considerable charm as well as of much ambition, he aspired to the position of local notability. He made it his business to find out the social and economic background of every person he met whom he considered influential enough to be of potential use to him. In this way he acquired a formidable store of knowledge about many of the people and events in the District. As he keenly enjoyed weighing up the strengths and weaknesses of people, and as he found me a ready listener, he kept me well informed about our mutual contacts.

In Nswanamundong'u Village he met an old friend called Jim, who had been at Bulawayo with him in the early 40's. A close bond usually exists between Ndembu who have been work-mates or neighbours in the urban areas of Central Africa. They joke freely together, offer each other hospitality, and confide in one another. Jim was an intelligent man, and was generally regarded as a strong candidate for the office of Mukang'ala when it should fall vacant again. It was largely through his friendship with Musona that I was able swiftly to get on good terms with his fellow-villagers.

In spite of my 'desertion' of their area, I was well received by the people of Nswanamundong'u, and one of them, a man called Kamahasanyi, who will play the central role in this narrative, volunteered at once to show me how he made snares to catch duiker, a woodland species of antelope whose meat is greatly relished by Ndembu.

The Sequence of Ritual Performances

Kamahasanyi (F2) was an own sister's son of the headman of Nswanamundong'u Village (see Fig. IX, p. 311). The

latter, Kachimba by name (E8), was also his father-in-law, for
Kamahasanyi had married his daughter Maria (F6). Like
Mundoyi and Mukeyi, Kamahasanyi had spent nearly all his
adult life in Konkoto, in the Belgian Congo. Like them also he
had lived for the most part in his father's village. He had been
deeply attached to his father (E3), was always talking about
him—his prowess in the chase, his skill in debate, and his close
relationship to Senior Headman Konkoto (D7). Konkoto area
appears to have been strongly influenced by Luba culture, and
adjoins Luba territory. It is possible that the emphasis placed
on patrilateral ties by Ndembu with Konkoto fathers may be
reinforced by Luba values—for many Luba groups are patrilineal, according to Verhulpen[1] and others.

Kamahasanyi was in his forties and had been previously
married three times, twice to patrilateral cross-cousins. He had
left his paternal village because he feared witchcraft from some
of its members. When his third wife (F5) died, he attributed
her death to the witchcraft of her mother, who wished to 'eat
the *mpepi*', or traditional death-payment made by a surviving
spouse to the matrilineal kin of the deceased. The old woman,
Nyamusana (E6), was married to an Ndembu of the Kapenda
matrilineage called Kalusambu. When we made our permanent
camp in Kapenda's area, Kalusambu had recently built a hut
in the nearest village to us. He was suffering from severe
tuberculosis, and died within a few weeks of our arrival. His
death was attributed to his wife's witchcraft, according to local
gossip. This was also the view of the ritual specialist Ihembi,
who maintained that Kalusambu had consulted three diviners
about the case of his wasting illness. The first two diviners had
told him that his wife was bewitching him. But he refused to
believe them, and went to a third diviner who attributed his
illness to the punitive action of an ancestor shade. He had
performed the ritual that the third diviner had prescribed to
propitiate the shade, thus notifying the world that he believed
in his wife's innocence. Later, just before he died, my wife and
I attended a 'modern' ritual, called *Tukuka*, performed for
this incredibly thin victim of tuberculosis. In the beliefs
associated with *Tukuka* the afflicting agents are said to be the
spirits of living Europeans that fly about at night 'troubling

---

[1] *Baluba et Balubaises de Katanga*, Anvers: L'Avenir Belge (1936), *passim*.

Africans'. Among the other ills they are believed to cause, tuberculosis is prominent. In short, Kalusambu believed in his wife's innocence to the very last. I mention this case as an instance of the general opinion that Kamahasanyi's former mother-in-law was a witch, whom Kamahasanyi hated and feared.

But despite these arguments which Ndembu found cogent reasons for Kamahasanyi's departure from his late father's village, Kamahasanyi himself felt extremely uneasy about taking such a step. This reaction is decidedly unusual for Ndembu, since it is customary for a man to leave his father's village almost immediately after the latter has died, and to settle among his maternal kin. But Kamahansanyi was an unusual person in many respects, as we shall see.

The first indication I came across that all was not well with Kamahasanyi, and, indeed, with his village, was when I noticed that at each junction of the paths leading to the village from the bush and from the motor road there was a forked branch covered with white clay. Such forked branches, peeled of bark and inserted in the ground, are symbolic objects belonging to the hunters' cult. They are called *ayishin'ga* (sing. *chishing'a*) or *nyichanka* (sing. *muchanka*), and constitute the pivotal symbols at shrines for hunters' shades. They are also planted on hunters' bush graves. I asked Kamahasanyi what these *ayishing'a* were for, and he answered briefly, 'For *Mukala*.' Now *Mukala*, or *Kaluwi*, is the name of a certain manifestation of a hunter's shade in which the deceased appears in his victim's dreams as a man clad in a kilt of skins or grass—the traditional garb of hunters in the past. *Mukala* is a mischievous manifestation. He is seldom seen except in dreams, but makes his presence felt in no uncertain manner in waking life. He is said to drive game away from an approaching hunter, by riding on the back of the leading animal of a herd of antelope or wild pig and urging them swiftly away. He also scares them away from traps and snares, or whistles warningly when a hunter is stalking them. At other times he leads hunters into swamps at night by showing them a light like a torch, which makes them believe they have seen another hunter. His low eerie whistle, it is said, can be heard in the deep bush, and men have told me, with every evidence of fear, how they have heard his whistling far from human haunts. *Mukala*, then, possesses the more malevolent attributes of Robin Goodfellow and the Will o' the Wisp in British folklore. To rid oneself of the afflicting tendencies of *Mukala* it is necessary to perform a complicated ritual, also called *Mukala*, which can be regarded as a phase in the complete cycle of hunters' ritual. If *Mukala* is placated by the performance, he becomes a helpful being who drives game towards, and no longer away from, the hunter. Nearly every hunter, it is said, has at some time been persecuted by one of his deceased hunter relatives in the form of *Mukala*.

When we reached Kamahasanyi's duiker snares, sited in a semi-circle within a few hundred yards of the village—for duiker are inquisitive animals who like to come close to inhabited sites to their undoing—he suddenly told us that he had not trapped a single duiker for a long time. This was due to *Mukala*, he said, who had been persecuting him.

On the way back to the village by another path, I chanced to look up at the top of a large termite-hill. Its crown had been cleared of bush, and at least half a dozen *ayishing'a* had been planted on it. Each of them had recently been smeared with white clay, and pieces of meat had been impaled on the forks. There were also traces of dried blood on the *ayishing'a*. Kamahasanyi noticed my interest, and whispered, 'That is *Mukala* too.' He then told us to whisper, for '*Mukala* does not like people to talk aloud.' I asked in a low voice whether I could take a photograph of this shrine—where, it turned out, the main part of the propitiatory ritual had been performed—but Kamahasanyi firmly refused my request. This in itself was interesting, since I had already taken a number of photographs of ritual and had never as yet met with any objection. And later on I was to take a number of photographs of Kamahasanyi himself undergoing ritual. Kamahasanyi then explained that *Mukala* was a very powerful shade (*mukishi*) who could kill people, and that he was still very dangerous.

As though to make amends for his refusal, Kamahasanyi invited Musona and myself to take some beer with him at his hut in the village. To the right of the doorway we saw further evidence of the recent ritual to propitiate *Mukala*. A moulding, in the form of the letter 'm' in relief, had been made in red termite earth. In one compartment of this 'm' was a mortar for pounding cassava meal, in the other was a pounding pole. The mortar was striped with alternate bands of red and white clay. Kamahasanyi told us that the 'medicines' used in the ritual had been pounded in it. He said it protected him from dreaming of *Mukala*. The *ayishing'a* at the forks of the village paths, he said, protected the whole village against bad dreams of *Mukala*. This was the first hint I had received that not only Kamahasanyi but the whole Nswanamundong'u group were under supernatural attack. It was as though the village itself was in a state of spiritual siege. A mystical force, capricious and dangerous, associated with the wild bush, seemed to be beleaguering its ritual defences. Kamahasanyi had activated this force, but he was by no means its only target. Everyone in the village feared *Mukala*. I learnt subsequently that the particular shade 'who had come through [or emerged] (*kwidyikila*) in *Mukala*' had been divined to be Kamahasanyi's classificatory mother's mother's brother, the late Mukang'ala Mundong'u Kabong'u himself (D10). Not only had he been persecuting poor Kamahasanyi in this form, but also he had been afflicting him as an *ihamba*. In fact, a Luvale expert in the removal of *mahamba* upper central incisors had been engaged to perform the appropriate ritual the very next day. I then mentioned that I had seen Ihembi at work as an *Ihamba* doctor in Kapenda's area. The men of Nswanamundong'u who had collected around the beer calabash immediately begged me to bring Ihembi along to the ritual. They said that they were not at all sure whether the Luvale doctor really 'knew the medicines of *Ihamba*', and, in any case, Ihembi could help him to collect medicines and prepare the shrine. Ihembi, they all agreed, was a 'great doctor' (*chimbuki weneni*) who had 'helped many people'. Moreover, the father of Mukeyi and Mundoyi had been a close relative of Kamahasanyi's father. Some believed that 'the *ihamba* had come from Mudyigita, Kamahasanyi's father', and not from Mundong'u Kabong'u. If this were so, the afflicting shade might listen to the exhortations of his relatives from Konkoto (see p. 119). Usually, *Ihamba* contains its own set of divinatory techniques. It is a sufficient indication of an *ihamba* for a person to suffer from sharp pains in the body. A specialist is called in, and he divines at the beginning of the ritual whether the afflicting agent is an *ihamba* or not. If it is divined to be an *ihamba*, further means are employed to find out its name and its relationship to the patient. But before a performance of *Ihamba* there is much speculation about the identity of the *ihamba* and about why it has afflicted the patient.

It was highly significant that Mundong'u Kabong'u should have been regarded as a possible agent of affliction, for he had been successively founder-headman of the village and Government chief of the area. It was said by the villagers that his spirit was troubled because 'there was no proper headman in the village'. When Kambung'u had succeeded Mundong'u Kabong'u, Kabong'u's youngest brother Samuwinu (D13) had fled from the village and the area for fear of the new chief's jealousy and sorcery. He was the last member of the generation that had held authority in the village; for both Mundong'u Kabong'u (D10) and his brother Nswanamundong'u ('successor of Mundong'u', D11) had held the village headmanship before Samuwinu. Samuwinu had settled in Kapenda's area, close to members of other dissident factions of the Mukang'ala chiefly lineage. A temporary headman, Kachimba (E8), had been appointed by the villagers. Kachimba belonged to the junior adjacent generation to Samuwinu, and also to a different segment of the village matrilineage. It was held that the shade of Mundong'u Kabong'u was angry that 'a younger man' had become headman while a member of his own generation remained alive. His anger was manifested in several strange incidents. Once, there had been a whirlwind which had ripped the thatch from Kachimba's hut, and people had seen flames leaping above it. Several people had dreamt that Mundong'u Kabong'u had come to reproach them.

It was also said that the spirit of the dead chief was aggrieved because the office of Mukang'ala had lost its former importance. He blamed the people of the area, and particularly those of his own village, for this fall from grace.

Thus the persecution of Kamahasanyi was not so much in his personal as in his representative capacity. When I asked Musona why the dead Mukang'ala did not persecute Kachimba, the acting headman, he replied that the shade wanted to shame everyone by 'catching' (i.e. afflicting) one of

Kachimba's people. If he had attacked Kachimba it would have been thought that he was angry with Kachimba himself. In fact, it was the village group as a whole that had behaved irresponsibly. They should have made Samuwinu headman, and Samuwinu himself should have remained in the area. Indeed, Kachimba asked me earnestly to bring Samuwinu to the *Ihamba* ritual, as well as Ihembi and his team of apprentice doctors, so that Samuwinu could invoke the shade on behalf of his afflicted relative. The shade, he said, would listen to Samuwinu, his brother, but would not take any notice of his sister's son Kachimba, whom he did not recognize as 'full headman' (*ntung'i yachikupu*). I later found out that Samuwinu had not received the wholehearted support of his close maternal kin when he claimed the office of Mukang'ala. Some of them had even supported Kambung'u (E13), on the grounds that he was an abler man than Samuwinu. Samuwinu was notorious for his garrulity and love of scandal. He was the butt of many unkindly jokes; not least on account of the influence wielded over him by his plump and querulous wife, Nyasondoyi, from Kapenda's area. She was forever complaining of imaginary ailments and pressing her husband to pay for ritual treatments. Wherever he went visiting she went with him. This atypical uxoriousness obtained for him the reputation of having a weak and indecisive character. It was said by many Ndembu that if he had been 'a real man' (*iyala walala*) he would have pressed his claim for the chieftainship with vigour, and would not have fled from the area when Kambung'u succeeded. Notwithstanding his personal deficiencies, however, the flight of Samuwinu was regarded by the villagers of Nswanamundong'u as a source of shame (*nsonyi*) for them. They openly admitted to me their dissatisfaction with the present state of affairs, and attributed it to their implicit rejection of Samuwinu's cause. The villagers were suffering from several kinds of misfortune, bad luck in hunting and trapping, loss of crops to wild pigs, and internal quarrels. Their ancestors, notably Mundong'u Kabong'u and his brother Nswanamundong'u, were angry at their behaviour during the critical period when the succession had been in doubt, and afterwards when they had made Kachimba acting headman and had failed to beg Samuwinu earnestly to return.

But, as I have argued elsewhere,[1] when misfortune is attributed to mystical causes in Ndembu society more than one set of social conflicts is considered as precipitating factors by those involved. In the present case, for example, while it was thought highly probable that Mundong'u Kabong'u had afflicted Kamahasanyi 'in *Ihamba*', the action of other spirits was not ruled out. Indeed, some believed, and even whispered to Musona, that Kamahasanyi was being bewitched by someone in his village. It was also suggested that the spirits of living Europeans were troubling him.

I have mentioned that some believed that Kamahasanyi's father Mudyigita (E3), and not Mundong'u Kabong'u, was afflicting him in the mode of *Ihamba*. Kamahasanyi lent strength to this view by telling his kin that his father had come to him in repeated dreams to blame him for accusing his father's matrilineal kin of having bewitched his wife. He also said that his father was angry with him for having left his village in the Congo. Since it is Ndembu custom to leave a father's village on his death, it is hard to understand Kamahasanyi's attitude, unless, indeed, his mother had been his father's slave. When I visited Nswanamundong'u Village for the first time, to collect genealogies, Musona had, in fact, told me that Kamahasanyi was an '*ndungu*' ('slave'), but I had discounted this remark as being merely malicious, for Kamahasanyi was a full sister's son of headman Kachimba. But the slave status adheres to a person unless he or she has been redeemed by payment. This is true even of slaves who have returned to their own villages of birth or rearing. I was never able to find out any more information on this point, but it seems very likely that Kamahasanyi had at one time been the slave of his father's matrilineal kin. If this were so, it would account for the fact that Kamahasanyi and other Ndembu found it possible to believe that his father's sister—who had also been his mother-in-law—might bewitch him. Free Ndembu are not usually thought to be in danger from the witchcraft of patrilateral kin, but only of matrilineal kin or wives. But slaves can be killed by the witchcraft of their owners.

Thus, two shades were regarded as possible agents of affliction, Kamahasanyi's 'grandfather' (D10) and his father. Each

---

[1] *Schism and Continuity in a Central African Society*, op. cit., pp. 127–8.

represented a conflict in a different set of social relations. The 'grandfather', Mundong'u Kabong'u, symbolized the troubled political situation of the village and the area. The father epitomized a conflict in the relations between Kamahasanyi and his patrilateral kin. At a deeper level of social structure, the belief that his father was persecuting him in his mother's village of origin reflected the irresoluble contradiction between the principles of matrilineal and patrilateral affiliation in Ndembu society.

Two performances of the *Ihamba* ritual rapidly followed one another, both of which I was able to observe. The first began under the control of the Luvale doctor, but was completed by Ihembi and his apprentices. I brought Samuwinu, as requested. Ihembi feigned to remove an *ihamba* tooth from Kamahasanyi's body. He said that the tooth belonged to Mundong'u Kabong'u, but that another tooth, that of Kamahasanyi's father, still remained inside. Furthermore, he told Kamahasanyi that one of his kinsmen had cursed him by raising a ghost to afflict him. Before he could perform a second *Ihamba* ritual, he said, he would have to perform 'a small *Kaneng'a*' (*Kaneng'a kanyanya*) or *Lukupu* ritual, to rid him of the malevolent ghost (*musalu*). Ihembi told me confidentially that he had made a divination into the cause of Kamahasanyi's affliction in a pounding mortar filled with liquid medicines, and had seen the *'mwevulu'* ('shadow' or 'reflection') of one of Kamahasanyi's fellow-villagers, Wilson (E11), the son of the late headman Nswanamundong'u, on the surface of the medicated water. Before he could perform *Ihamba*, he said, it was necessary that he should free Kamahasanyi from the sorcery of his kinsman. Ihembi told me that he had mentioned the name of Wilson to no-one except myself, for he did not want to be said to have caused trouble in the village.

I attended both the *Lukupu* and the *Ihamba* rituals performed by Ihembi. Ihembi removed a tooth at the second *Ihamba* which he claimed was Mudyigita's. He then told me that he had been mistaken as to the identity of the person who was bewitching Kamahasanyi. The real culprit was a female witch, and was none other than Kamahasanyi's wife Maria, egged on and abetted by her mother Ndona (E9), Kachimba's senior wife. Ndona, by her arts, had substituted the appearance of

Wilson for her own in the medicine. But Ihembi had made another divination before the *Ihamba* ritual proper, and had seen the two witches in his medicine. Without mentioning precisely who were the culprits, he had strongly advised Kamahasanyi to undergo the 'big *Kaneng'a*', the full anti-witchcraft ritual, always performed at night—in contrast to *Lukupu*, which is performed in the daytime. He had then told Kamahasanyi to leave Nswanamundong'u Village and settle elsewhere, preferably with a close relative in Kapenda's area.

Two further rituals were performed for Kamahasanyi, neither of which I was able to attend. The first was *Tukuka*, mentioned above in connection with Kalusambu's illness, a ritual said to have been introduced from the Luvale and Ovimbundu peoples. The second was *Kaneng'a*, performed for Kamahasanyi just after I left Mwinilunga District at the end of my first tour. I am unable, therefore, to place these two performances in their social setting as adequately as the performances that I attended of *Ihamba* and *Lukupu*.

V

THE SOCIAL SETTING OF THE
RITUAL SEQUENCE AT
NSWANAMUNDONG'U VILLAGE

INTRODUCTION: CONTINUITY AND CHANGE
IN MODERN NDEMBU SOCIETY

A ritual that assists in the consolidation of village unity may place that village in active opposition to rival villages in the same chiefdom, and so diminish the over-all cohesion. But ultimately a tendency towards restoring the dynamic equilibrium of the whole would seem to exist, and this tendency finds expression in certain critical ritual symbols and the values contained in them. Nevertheless, processes of social change, of a self-sustaining character, are breaking up traditional relationships and calling into question the values and norms that support them. These processes, which were gathering rapid momentum during the period of my field-work, had by no means reached the point at which a new dynamic equilibrium based on a money economy with White political control could emerge. Their immediate effect was to promote instability in most social relationships and perpetually to thwart attempts to restore social cohesion in terms of traditional values. The trend of the ritual sequence I observed, when looked at from one point of view, exemplifies this increasing failure to restore cohesion. There was first a traditional hunting ritual. Ndembu believed that it failed to relieve Kamahasanyi's ill luck at hunting. The next two performances were of a kind of ritual which had been assimilated into the Ndembu system. After this, a thoroughly modern ritual, *Tukuka*, clearly associated with current tensions in Black-White relations, was tried and found wanting. Finally, the cause of Kamahasanyi's bodily pains became attributed to witchcraft. It is becoming increasingly common nowadays for people to attribute the cause of illness, and not only—as in the past—of death, to witchcraft or sorcery. For, under modern conditions of change, conflict in inter-personal relations is becoming exacerbated, as traditional corporate ties lose their effectiveness and economic individualism grows stronger. Belief in the moral power of the ancestors weakens, as belief in the maleficent power of the living increases. The ritual placation of ancestors gives way to the ritual exorcism of witchcraft. Where misfortune formerly tended to bind a group together in joint veneration of the shades who sanctioned the moral order, it now tends to break a group up by precipitating inter-personal accusations of witchcraft and sorcery.

Redressive ritual of the *Ihamba* and *Mukala* types handles breaches in customary relationships, and corrects deviation from traditional norms of behaviour. Many new relationships between persons and groups are developing that have no precedent in the traditional social structure. To the conservative Ndembu these appear to represent deviations from custom rather than nascent custom of a new kind; they fail to realize that their society is being restructured, and that its traditional relationships are breaking up irreparably. They cannot patch rotten cloth, even with the new patches of recently introduced rituals, such as *Tukuka*. Deviation no longer represents extreme variation from a commonly accepted norm; the old norm has itself deviated radically from the current, and still hardly recognized, practice. Kapenda and the new class of traders had perhaps seen this, but Mukang'ala and the majority of his villagers had not.

It is an extremely difficult matter to isolate traditional from new social tendencies in contemporary Ndembu behaviour. Both kinds of tendencies influence behaviour in the same field of action. One finds attempts to resolve new conflicts by traditional redressive machinery, while processes controlled by ancient custom are deflected from their expected course by changes in the system of social relationships. At the same time, in particular situations, conflicts between persons and groups, arising from discrepant traditional principles of social organization, are still handled by customary institutions. Ndembu society is in transition, but the rate of change varies from area to area and within each area, dependent on the kind and extent of European influence, and the degree to which each is penetrated by the modern cash economy. Here one finds customary social regularities dominant; there one finds old custom without force.

Everywhere one comes across hybridization between old and new, as in the *Tukuka* ritual which contains traditional ritual symbols interspersed with symbols of contemporary life, such as representations of aeroplanes, the use of knives and forks at ritual meals, and so forth. The members of any kind of social field attempt to stabilize their relational structure, in order that each may live his or her life with the minimum of uncertainty. They try to slow down the rate of change by many devices, in order that they may carry on their daily lives within a framework of routine. One of the ways in which they attempt to do this is by domesticating the new, and subjectively menacing, forces in the service of the traditional order, so that for a time, for example, cash is accumulated in order to acquire traditional symbols of prestige or build up a clientele of followers to bid for long-established positions of authority. But ultimately the contradiction between the basic assumptions of the new order and those of the traditional order distorts and then disrupts the social structure. The new order smashes the old, and the traditional set of conflicts is supplanted by a different one.

During the process of transition, traditional kinds of conflict that were formerly not merely controlled by customary machinery of redress, legal and ritual, but were also converted by them into social energy which sustained the system, can no longer be so controlled, for the redressive machinery is breaking down. The result is that such conflicts accelerate the destruction of the traditional order. On the other hand, new kinds of conflict, which are part of the dynamic maintenance of the new system, do not impede the growing dominance of that system, but further weaken the traditional system by underlining the inadequacy of traditional redressive machinery to resolve them.

It is no longer a question, in contemporary African studies, of isolating what is ancient from what is modern. Processes of change, repetitive processes, and processes of disintegration, co-exist in the same field of action, and at all points influence the behaviour of each individual. It would be impossible to analyse the social setting of these rituals, and indeed many of their material elements and symbols, without taking all these processes seriously into account.

It is now necessary to examine in some detail the social setting of the rituals performed for Kamahasanyi at Nswanamundong'u Village. Since the supernatural agent of affliction was thought to be the shade of a former Mukang'ala who had been enraged by the present conduct of affairs in his area, it is also necessary to consider certain episodes in the history of the Mukang'ala lineage which bear directly on the present crisis.

The Mukang'ala Chiefs

Fig. IX (p. 312) shows that in the last three generations the office of Mukang'ala has been held alternately by segments of the chiefly matrilineage descended from two sisters, Nyakanjata (B2) being the elder and Kawang'u (B4) the younger. The segment descended from their elder sister, Mbuiya Nyawichila (B1), has failed to provide an office-holder, although as we have seen, Kimbinyi (D3), the trader who settled in Kapenda's area, once aspired to the succession. Today, then, for all practical purposes the succession may be said to lie between members of Nyakanjata lineage and of Kawang'u lineage.

It is impossible to obtain accurate genealogical information about the senior headmen who preceded Mukang'ala Chinseli (B3), though there is wide agreement about their order of succession. I begin, therefore, with some comments on the incumbency of Chinseli.

Chief Mukang'ala Chinseli

Mukang'ala Chinseli (B3) had made his capital village in the area of Kang'ombe, an Mbwela senior headman in the far south of Mwinilunga District. He had fled to the south to escape from the Chokwe and Luvale marauders, who harassed the Ndembu in the last two decades of the nineteenth century.

Chief Mukang'ala Mwashelinyama

Munkang'ala Chinseli was succeeded, as sometimes happens among Ndembu, by his son Mwashelinyama (C3). The latter, who married his father's sister's daughter, thus ensuring that his children would belong to the Mukang'ala matrilineage, moved across the Lunga River into the Lunda-Kosa area of senior headman Kanyama.

Chief Mukang'ala Ibala

Mwashelinyama was succeeded by a full sister's son of Chin-seli, Ibala Kabanda (C4), mentioned above, who returned to the traditional area of the Mukang'alas, and built his village at the Mpalapala Stream, about a dozen miles from the Boma in the direction of Kapenda's present village. Ibala had a very large village, which included in its membership most of the matrilineal descendants of Mbuiya Nyawechila (B1), Nyakan-jata (B2), and Kawang'u (B4). When the British South Africa Company introduced taxation in 1913, it will be recalled that Ibala and his followers fled to the Belgian Congo for a time, and then returned to the District to build a large village at Kalene Hill. The spatial mobility of the Mukang'ala matri-lineage had thus been very considerable as the result of external pressures ever since the early 1880s. It was during their stay in the Congo, in the area of Nyamwana, an important Lunda-Kosa chief, that I believe they first entered into relations with the people of the Lunda-Luba chiefdom of Konkoto. A signifi-cant amount of intermarriage took place between the Mukang'-ala matrilineage and inhabitants of these two areas in the Belgian Congo. It would even seem as though Ibala had taken several slaves from Konkoto and had lost several of his own people as slaves to Chief Konkoto (D7), including Kamahas-anyi's mother (E7). Ibala, 'the bald one', is still spoken of as the strong man of the area. According to many Ndembu, he was killed by the sorcery of Mundong'u Kabong'u (D10), who was also a great gun-hunter (*chiyang'a*).

Chief Mukang'ala Mundong'u

Mundong'u (D10) was mother's sister's daughter's son of Ibala (C4), in other words, a classificatory sister's son who belonged to a different segment of the Mukang'ala matrilineage. Mundong'u made a new capital village, the core membership of which consisted of the descendants of Nyakanjata (B2), and their spouses and children. But the majority of the members of Mbuiya Nyawechila and Kawang'u lineages would not reside with them. Most of the former went to Kapenda's area, and the latter made an independent village under the headship of Kambung'u (E13), who later became Mukang'ala. Ibala's children by several wives founded a new village in the area, today called Samuheha. Other children founded the village of Samuhima. It is a common practice among Ndembu for the children of a chief or senior headman to remain in their father's area after his death, rather than to return to their mother's natal areas. A chief's children usually support their father's primary matrilineal kin in disputes within the area, and endeavour to obtain the election of a primary patrilateral cross-cousin to office. My informants told me that Mundong'u (D10) owed his election mainly to the Kawiku villages and to other villages that had been raided by Ibala in the past. The senior Kawiku headman, Nsang'anyi, it will be remembered, had been frustrated in his claim for a Government chieftainship by Ibala, and he and his Kawiku would not support a close relative of Ibala at that time. Although Ibala's many children supported Kambung'u (E13), Ibala's own sister's daughter's son, they could not obtain success for him in face of the united opposition of Mundong'u's primary kin, the Kawiku, and other important headmen in the area.

Mundong'u's tenure of office, however, soon came to an untimely end. The best version I heard of his last days was given me by an English-speaking Mission teacher, Windson Kashinakaji, who was reared in Mukang'ala's area. Windson's father, Kashinakaji, went to visit Mundong'u Kabong'u, but on his arrival at the capital village (*ng'anda*), was informed by the chief's two wives that Mundong'u had gone into the bush to hunt two days previously. Kashinakaji waited for the next two days at the capital, but still Mundong'u did not return. He then upbraided Mundong'u's relatives, saying, 'Why did you let Mundong'u go into the bush alone? Don't you know that there are many dangerous things in the bush?' He told two young men to accompany him in search of Mundong'u. After a time they came upon a recently built shelter of leaves (*chimba*) such as is used by hunters. The door was shut. They opened it and found Mukang'ala lying on a rough improvised bed. He had a severe flesh wound in the calf of his leg. They carried him back to his village where he thanked Kashinakaji for sending help, 'otherwise he would have died alone in his *chimba*; for who would have given him food and drink or fetched firewood in the bush?' He told them that he had seen some guinea-fowl, and had begun to remove the large charge of gunpowder in his

muzzle-loader reserved for firing at big game. But he had forgotten to remove the firing-cap (*musumu*), and the gun had gone
off, implanting a bullet in the fleshy part of his leg. At the capital
he was treated with Ndembu medicines—various kinds of leaves
pounded, mixed with water, and applied as a poultice. But
Mundong'u's leg became gangrenous, and as a last resort the
chief was carried on a stretcher of poles to the Mission Hospital.
He committed suicide there in 1936, or 1937 as other informants
claim.

I give this straightforward record of events, almost in Windson's own words, to show how Ndembu habitually take care
to present the facts of an important situation as clearly and
objectively as they can. Much experience in village courts
underlies this skill in realistic description. For Ndembu, however, the chief's misfortunes did not result from accident but
from the maleficent action of sorcery. Windson told me that as
a good Christian he did not believe in sorcery as an adequate
explanation of Mundong'u's self-wounding, but he presented
the currently accepted Ndembu view that sorcery was its cause,
as though he, too, shared that belief. Mundong'u, he said, was
considered by many to have been attacked by the sorcery of
Katoyi (D15), son of Ibala's older brother Chinseli. Katoyi
had sought to avenge (*ku-tenda*) the death of his 'younger father'
(*tatayindi wakansi*), Ibala, who had been slain by the sorcery of
Mundong'u. He had, it was said, gone into the bush with
Kambung'u (E13), who aspired to succeed Mundong'u, and
with Dikashi, Kambung'u's uterine brother, to shoot what
Frazer might have called the 'external soul' of Mundong'u. According to Ndembu belief, a chief or a titled senior headman at
his accession acquires from the ritual officiant (*chivwikankanu*)
who installs him—as a Kapenda is installed by a Matembu,
and a Mukang'ala by a Nsang'anyi—certain medicines that enable him to form or develop a magical creature or familiar[1] in
the shape of an elephant, hippopotamus, a huge snake with the
face of its owner (called *ilomba*), or a giant fresh water crab
(called *nkalajobu*). This creature, which is invisible to all who

---

[1] Commoners, or members of a chiefly matrilineage who have not succeeded to
office, may also acquire medicines to make a *chiswamu*, but a chief's *chiswamu* is
thought to be exceptionally powerful.

have not drunk and washed their eyes with a special medicine called by the generic name of *nsompu*—there are many different species of *nsompu*—is called *chiswamu chawanyanta* (literally, 'a place to hide in of chiefs'). Windson translated *chiswamu* to mean 'a medicine-body'. A chief's *chiswamu* is said to contain both his *wumi*, or 'life-principle', and his *ng'ovu*, or 'power', a concept which includes both mystical and physical power. Katoyi was said to have shot Mundong'u *munzovu*, literally 'in elephant', i.e. to have shot Mundong'u's external soul in the form of an elephant. To shoot an external soul, or 'medicine-body', a special kind of weapon is required. This is the *wuta-wawufuku* (literally 'gun of night'). The 'night-gun' is supposed to consist of a portion of human tibia carved into the shape of a gun, and loaded with pellets compounded out of decomposing human flesh, powdered human bone, graveyard earth, and other substances connected with the dissolution of the human body.

The 'medicine-body', however, is no mere receptacle of its owner's life and power. It is thought to be possessed of an active and autonomous malignity of its own, and to press its owner repeatedly to point out victims for it. It is thus a creature or familiar of sorcery as well as an external soul. Most 'medicine-bodies', or *yiswamu*, are said to kill their victims by devouring their 'shadows' (sing. *mwevulu*), which may be said to be their personal, unique life-principles, in contrast to *wumi* which is 'life-in-general', the quality of 'being alive'. The power of the 'medicine-body' is augmented by each victim, and as its power wanes, so does that of its owner.

Katoyi did not succeed in killing Mundong'u's 'medicine-body' outright, according to Windson's story. He shot it through the hind leg, at the same moment that Mundong'u's accident occurred. The 'medicine' that 'was given' to Mundong'u was part of the treatment he underwent during the ritual of *Kaneng'a* that was performed for him on his return to the village. If the owner of a *chiswamu* is wounded 'in *chiswamu* form', as Windson put it, it is believed by Ndembu that there is only one effective remedy. The *Kaneng'a* specialist advises the patient to obtain a portion of the skin of a child to make a patch for the wound. Thus, it is necessary to secretly catch and kill a child, preferably from a distant village, at nightfall. Such a child is called euphemistically 'a black goat' (*mpembi yayila*). I do not know whether ritual infanticide for this purpose is actually carried out today, but it forms an important element in the complex of beliefs about sorcery and witchcraft and the defensive measures against these black arts. I was told by several Ndembu —but not by Windson—that Mundong'u was 'perhaps' treated in this way. With more assurance they told me that Mundong'u made clairvoyant by drinking *nsompu*, had seen that Katoyi was trying to kill him, and had shot Katoyi's *ilomba*, or snake-familiar, so that Katoyi fell ill from a wasting disease.

I asked Windson why Mundong'u had taken his own life at the Mission Hospital. He replied that the chief had been told that his leg would have to be amputated, and he could not bear to face life as a cripple. But others had told him, he went on, that Mundong'u thought that 'much of his body had been stolen by sorcerers'. He thought, for example, that his *'muchima'*, a term applied both to the liver and heart, had been removed by sorcery, and that as a result he was doomed to an unpleasant death. Shortly after his death Katoyi died also, and this was regarded as proof that a contest between them in sorcery had taken place.

I have heard of several Ndembu who committed suicide because they believed they were being bewitched. This is because some (unspecified) part of the psychophysical nature of a victim of witchcraft or sorcery is thought to be converted into a familiar, or into a portion of a familiar, of the witch or sorcerer. Thus, the late Chief Kapenda Samuheha used to threaten people when he was drunk that 'he would make them *tulala* or *tulama* [a term formerly used for messengers or un-armed police] of his *chitakachi* tree'. The *chitakachi* tree has large spreading branches, and sorcerers are thought to keep their familiars concealed in it. This meant that he would kill them by sorcery and in some way transform them into animated wooden figurines—*katotoji* and *nzoji* are two types of such figurines believed to guard their owner against black magic and kill his enemies. It is likely that the animating principle of such figurines is thought to be the *wumi* or *ng'ovu* of a victim of sorcery. But a person may by killing himself avoid this ignominious fate.

A Royal Sorcery Contest

I give another example of a sorcery contest between a chief and his would-be successor because of the additional light it throws both on rivalry between matrilineal kin for office and on Ndembu sorcery beliefs. This case concerns succession to the Kanongesha chieftainship. My informant was Muchona, perhaps my best source of information on ritual matters. He had spent many years in Angola, and had acquired a large stock of tales about the Kanongeshas who had reigned there. Towards the end of the nineteenth century, Chababa was Kanongesha. His sister's daughter's son (classificatory 'grandson', or *mwijikulu*) Izemba, was his favourite relative. Here is a literal translation of Muchona's account, to give something of the flavour of the original:

'When Chababa succeeded, he told his grandson Izemba to have a private medicine-body (*chiswamu*) somewhere near his own. Each made a separate *chiswamu*. Each *chiswamu* was *nkalajobu*, a big crab. Chababa put his on the top of a hill, but Izemba put his at the side of the same hill. So they knew each other. Izemba's crab made sounds like the sound of rain (hissing?) to show that it was growing strong. Chababa's made the same sounds. Those *yiswamu* made deep burrows that joined together, so that they saw each other. Izemba's crab was very clever, Chababa's was not. Izemba and his crab said, "This chieftainship which is my grandfather's must be given to me, because Chababa is no longer clever. One day I shall try to kill him to be given the chieftainship." So the *yiswamu* crabs met and fought. They fought and fought and fought. Chababa's grew tired of fighting. They left their holes and came to the surface of the hill. They came out and climbed down fighting, and much water came with them. They came down to Mukwita Village at the foot of the hill. People heard their sounds in the village. People were swept before them. Such people died. They reached the Lubula river still fighting. When they reached the river Chababa was killed by Izemba, for Chababa died in the river in his *chiswamu*. He was buried. Later Izemba came and wished to succeed. Everyone agreed that he had wanted to be chief. They brought him presents. Mwininyilamba, Makang'a, and Kafwana were called to install him for that is their work.'

It is difficult not to glimpse, behind the myth of the grappling crabs, the real tragedy of the ageing chief trying to hold his own with his ambitious and able rival. For long the struggle

had been concealed. Each had carved out his own area of influence, his 'burrow in the hill'. Finally they recognized that it
was to be a battle to the death between them—'they saw one
another'. The situation is rendered not less poignant by the fact
that Chababa had been fond of Izemba, and had recognized
in him a worthy successor. He had wanted him for an ally,
symbolized by the tale that each kept his *chiswamu* in the same
hill. But Izemba's *chiswamu* forced Chababa's from the top of
that hill (the chieftainship?) to the river, and there killed it. A
long time ago, it is said, and in some chiefdoms until quite recently, chiefs of Lunda origin were buried in the beds of temporarily dammed rivers. The supposed death of Chababa's
crab in the river may well refer to that custom. Izemba had at
any rate brought him low.

Ndembu regularly associate the death of an important per-
sonage with some dramatic or disastrous natural event, such as
a fierce storm or a flood. Thus, after Headman Mashata died
during my stay at the Lwakela Holiday House, the villagers
said that his *ilomba* snake-familiar and external soul had been
shot by a 'night-gun' at the very moment that my mud-brick
garage had subsided under the battering of torrential rain the
previous week. The *ilomba* had been coaxed from the Lwakela
river in that night of furious thunder and lightning, and fatally
wounded by his nephew and sorcerer accomplice. Mashata had
fallen ill, and died within the week.

Chief Mukang'ala Kambung'u

After Mundong'u's death Kambung'u (E13) was elected to
office. This time he was supported by the majority of the
Kawiku, and by the Ndembu villages in the Kawiku area. One
of Kambung'u's wives came from Ng'ombi, a Ndembu village
near the District Headquarters. The people of Ng'ombi Village
and of Chibwakata Village, from which Ng'ombi had hived off,
gave Kambung'u firm backing. So also did the village of Mwanawuta, a true Kawiku village. Its headman's father belonged
to the Mukang'ala matrilineage, and he stressed this relationship at the time of the election to justify his support of Kambung'u. Kambung'u received more support than he might
otherwise have done, because there was no effective candidate
available in the other local segment of the chiefly lineage, that

of Kawang'u. At the time of Mundong'u's accession, Kam-bung'u had been considered rather too young to succeed. Mundong'u had acted as regent (*Mwambailung'a*) during the interregnum before a new chief had been chosen. Ordinarily, a regent does not succeed in Ndembu society, but Mundong'u, as we saw, had received strong support from those who had suffered at the hands of Ibala, or who had considered that Ibala's close kin were too inveterately opposed to the British authorities to adapt to the new order of things. Certainly, Mundong'u's accession had met with the bitter opposition of Ibala's primary matrilineal kin and his children. It is possible that, if the Administration had not withdrawn recognition from the chieftainship, a custom might have become established whereby each of the two important segments of the Mukang'ala lineage would have supplied chiefs in turn. A similar custom prevails today in the Kanongesha chieftainship, where successive chiefs are chosen from different branches of the chiefly matrilineage. Such rapprochements between contending segments of a chiefly lineage are not uncommon in Central Africa, in chiefdoms where every male member of the widest recognized lineage is a potential candidate for office.[1]

When Kambung'u (E13) succeeded, Samuwinu (D13), the only surviving brother of Mundong'u, fled from Mukang'ala's area, as has been stated. He feared that Kambung'u would be-witch him as the new chief had bewitched his brother with the aid of Katoyi. In the contest for office between the sub-lineages of Nyakanjata and Kawang'u, the reigning incumbent tended to fear the revenge by sorcery of the senior male member of the rival lineage. Correspondingly, the latter dreaded the enhanced mystical power of the chief. Nevertheless, Ndembu feel that it is the duty of a powerful disappointed candidate to remain in the chiefdom as a focus of the loyalties of his kinship faction. Since Samuwinu had recently succeeded his brother Nswana-mundong'u (D11) as village headman, his retreat to Kapenda's area was regarded as a cowardly act. His kin were left leader-less, and his village had no effective headman, since Samuwinu retained that position while he lived.

[1] See, for example, my article 'A Lunda Love Story and its Consequences', *R.L.I. Journal*, xix (1955), for information on the Bangala mode of succession (pp. 20-21).

It is in this context of struggle between factions linked to opposed segments of the Mukang'ala lineage that the role of Mundong'u's shade as an agent of mystical affliction begins to be meaningful. He had come 'in *Mukala*' and 'in *Ihamba*' to a member of his village and matrilineage. The people were being punished through a scapegoat for their collective responsibility in Samuwinu's defection. At this early stage in the ritual sequence, strong feelings of collective guilt, associated with political conflicts, are involved. Later the emphasis shifts to inter-personal tensions within the village as precipitating factors for mystical intervention. There is a narrowing-down of the range, as well as a change in the kind of social relationships made visible in the ritual situation.

Conflicts in Nswanamundong'u Village

If the performance of the first *Ihamba* at Nswanamundong'u was closely associated with conflicts in the political system of Mukang'ala's chieftainship, the performance of the second *Ihamba* manifested hidden conflicts within the village itself, between its two main sections. As the sequence proceeds, we shall see how the kind and range of social relations regarded as relevant narrows until it is hardly possible any longer to avoid giving public recognition to covert, and potentially disruptive, hostilities within the local group. From one point of view it is possible to see the whole sequence as an elaborate, but unconscious, attempt by Kamahasanyi to obtain his own way in village affairs—to silence those whom he felt were critical of him, and to win the sympathy of those who might be useful to him. Kamahasanyi is, in fact, using accepted ritual beliefs and practices to put pressure on others to give him the security and attention for which he yearns. But this persistent, unconscious drive sets in motion certain custom-governed processes that bring to light hidden conflict in a number of sets of social relations.

If readers consult the hut plan of Nswanamundong'u Village, they will observe that the village is divided into two hut circles. (See also the genealogy on p. 311.) The larger circle contains the huts of acting headman Kachimba (E8), his adult children, several of his matrilineal kin (D14 and E12) in Nyakanjata lineage, and the son of the late headman, Nswanamundong'u (E11). The smaller circle, sometimes called 'Makayi Farm' by the members of the village, contains the huts of Makayi (E1), his son Jackson (F1), and his classificatory mother's brother, Kapansonyi (D4). Makayi and Kapansonyi are the immigrants from the chiefdom of Konkoto in the Belgian Congo. Both are classificatory matrilineal relatives of Kamahasanyi's late father (E3), a village headman in Konkoto. Makayi (E1) had married a woman called Hangayika (E2), who called Kachimba (E8), *manakwetu*, 'our brother'. According to Hangayika, both her mother and father came from Konkoto. In fact, she claimed that her father, Chibala (D7), had been chief of that area. Now Kamahasanyi told me that his father's father had been Chief Konkoto, by name, Chiyamasang'i Chibala (D7). Makayi's

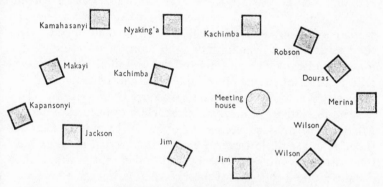

Fig. IV. Hut plan of Nswanamundong'u village.

mother (D5) was a classificatory sister of Hangayika's father Chibala, so that Makayi and his wife were 'cross-cousins'. Makayi called Kamahasanyi's father (E3), his 'cross-cousin' (*musonyi*), and called Kamahasanyi (F2), his 'sister's son' (*mwihwa*); for, according to the ideal logic of the Ndembu system of kinship nomenclature, which assumes continuous cross-cousin marriage, Kamahasanyi could have been the son of Makayi's sister. Kamahasanyi called Hangayika (E2), 'mother' (*mama*), because a mother's brother's wife is always thus termed. If Hangayika had not been married to Makayi he would have called her, 'father's sister' (*tata wamumbanda* or *tatankaji*), because she was his father's seminal sister. Hangayika called Kachimba (E8), Kamahasanyi's own mother's brother, her 'brother', because she stressed her role as Kamahasanyi's 'mother'. On account of this stress, Makayi (E1) and Kachimba (E8) called each other by the self-reciprocal term for 'brother-in-law' (*ishaku*). Whatever the precise nature of the connection between them, it is certain that Makayi and the other members of his 'farm' were called the *akwaKonkoto*, 'the Konkoto group', by the rest of the village.

It will be noted that Kamahasanyi's hut is situated outside the main circle of Kachimba's kinship group. It is, in fact, in an intermediate position between the two village hut circles. This siting reflected Kamahasanyi's intercalary position between the Konkoto group, to which he was patrilaterally attached, and the local segment of the Mukang'ala matrilineage, of which he was a member. This position was an uncomfortable one, for a state of tension existed between the two sections of the village. Makayi and his kin had hoped, when they settled at Nswanamundong'u, that they would derive material advantages from their affinal and filial links with certain of its members. Before Kambung'u had been deposed, for example, Kachimba had been his Court Clerk, an important post in all Native Authority centres. He had been expected by Makayi and his son Jackson to obtain paid employment for them. The group, however, had been interested in more than immediate advantages; for they had hoped that in the not too distant future a member of the Nyakanjata lineage would succeed Kambung'u as Government Chief. If this were to happen, they might legitimately expect that some of the spoils of office would come their way as a reward for their fidelity. For example, Jackson, Makayi's son, told me that he had once hoped to become Court Clerk, for he had passed Standard Four at the Mission School. Since the Administration now demands a higher level of education than this, he would have sought a place as a boarder in Mutanda Upper School near Solwezi, if he had thought the effort to raise boarding fees would have helped him to gain his end. But with the abolition of the chieftainship itself, and realizing that it might never be restored, Jackson lost heart and just sat around the village all day. The Konkoto group began to seek relief for their thwarted ambitions by criticizing the Nyakanjata lineage for their lack of initiative and drive. These criticisms irritated the latter, and quarrels between the sections increased in frequency. Kamahasanyi

entered this troubled situation early in 1951, when he returned
from his paternal village of Kanema and built a hut in Nswanamundong'u with the intention of remaining there for good. He
may well have had hopes of succeeding at some future date to
the village headmanship, for he was a full sister's son, as well
as a son-in-law, of acting headman Kachimba. In the village
he was immediately subjected to pressure by each section to
take its part against the other. Kamahasanyi often tried to solve
his dilemma by 'leaving the field'. On my visits to the village I
could usually see several of the men of Nyakanjata lineage chatting in the men's forum (*chota*) of their section, and Makayi,
Jackson, and Kapansonyi in theirs. But if I wanted to talk to
Kamahasanyi I usually had to call him from his hut, where he
sat alone. He was by no means an unsociable person, but he
appeared to be constitutionally incapable of tolerating a large
amount of tension in his social relations. Some men, like Sandombu of Mukanza Village, whose career I discussed at length
in an earlier book, seem to thrive in the hurly-burly of Ndembu
village politics. But Kamahasanyi, in many respects occupying
a similar social position to Sandombu, reacted very differently,
turning his aggressiveness against himself and not against others.

At the time I knew him Kamahasanyi seems to have been
peculiarly a victim of the conflict, never altogether absent from
Ndembu social life, between matrilineal and patrilateral allegiance. He had spent most of his life, before settling in his
maternal village, in the village of Kanema in Konkoto, of which
his father was headman. His marital history suggests that,
either by parental arrangement or of his own free will, he had
tried to attach himself permanently to Kanema Village through
marital ties. His first marriage, when he was still in his late
teens, had been to a patrilateral cross-cousin, Manyunsa (F3).
He had soon divorced her, and had then married a woman
from a nearby village. After her death he had married Safi (F5),
another patrilateral cross-cousin, and her death he attributed
to the witchcraft of her mother Nyamusana (E6), who, he
claimed, wanted to receive the bulk of the substantial death-
payment (*mpepi*) he had made—four sheep, and 300 francs in
Belgian Congo currency. He had quarrelled with his paternal
kin over the death-payment, and had insinuated that at least
one of them had bewitched his wife. Not long afterwards he had

paid a protracted visit to Nswanamundong'u, where he had married Maria (F6), Kachimba's daughter.

Despite the bad feeling that existed between Kamahasanyi and his patrilateral kin, he had returned to Kanema Village with Maria. As far as I can gather, his father was still alive on his return, though he must have died soon afterwards. Certainly, he was alive when Safi died, for Kamahasanyi told me, and the matter was mentioned during an invocation to his father's shade during the second *Ihamba* ritual, that the old man, Mud-yigita, had rebuked him angrily for quarrelling with his relatives. But, even after Mudyigita's death, Kamahasanyi remained in Kanema Village. This was partly because he and Maria, an exceedingly hard worker, had made large gardens of cassava, for which the Belgian authorities paid higher prices than were obtainable in Mwinilunga District. But Maria, so Jim (E12) told Musona, was always urging her husband to return to Nswanamundong'u, where her mother and father were. She had a young daughter by a previous husband and a baby in arms, and, like many Ndembu mothers, she no doubt felt that the matrilineal kin of her children would look after them better than their step-father's kin. Since Nswanamundong'u was Kamahasanyi's own matrilineal village, and since he stood a good chance of succeeding to the headmanship, it was by no means unreasonable that she should incite him to settle there. At all events, Kamahasanyi and his wife, a matrilateral cross-cousin, were not made welcome in Kanema, where the quarrel over Safi's death payment had not been forgotten. Early in 1951 Kamahasanyi came to Nswanamundong'u with the intention of settling there permanently.

It is true that in many respects he was in a difficult position in his new village. He had few intimates among his matrilineal kin, apart from an elderly woman called Nyakinga (D14), his classificatory mother's mother. Nyakinga had been Maria's ritual instructress (*nkong'u*) at her puberty ritual. She it was who had offered Kamahasanyi hospitality when he had visited Nswanamundong'u in the past. Kamahasanyi built his hut next to hers, a little way outside the main village hut circle. A few paces to the right of his hut was situated Makayi's 'farm'. Kamahasanyi had, indeed, closer ties of friendship with Makayi's group than with Kachimba's for he had known them well in Konkoto. It was perhaps bad luck that Kamahasanyi found himself confronted in his maternal village with the same conflict of loyalties between matrilineal and patrilateral affiliation that had led him to leave his father's village. This reduplication of a conflict that in the past must have caused him much anxiety may well have contributed to the state of mental imbalance in which I found him when I visited Nswanamundong'u during the ritual sequence performed on his behalf. During the first *Ihamba*, Kachimba invoked the shade of Mundong'u (D10), and mentioned that the latter had been angry with Kamahasanyi because he had remained in his father's village and had not returned to his matrilineage. No doubt it was hoped that by placating the shade and removing the malignant tooth of the dead hunter, Kamahasanyi would feel himself accepted by his matrilineal kin. During the same performance Kamahasanyi had publicly reproached Kachimba and Jim (E12) for not seeking speedy recourse to a diviner after he had become too ill to work in his gardens.

Among the inhabitants of Nswanamundong'u, Wilson (E11), the son of Mundong'u's younger brother, Nswanamundong'u (D11), meaning 'successor of Mundong'u' (i.e. as village headman), disliked Kamahasanyi most, and had quarrelled with him on a number of occasions. Ihembi, the *Ihamba* doctor, had noticed this, and had told me, it will be remembered, that Wilson had been bewitching Kamahasanyi. He had done this, said Ihembi, by cursing him in a moment of anger, a fact he had found out from other members of the village. This kind of curse (*ku-shing'ana*) is thought to involve 'the mentioning of a dead person's name'. The dead person is then said to 'come out in *musalu*', that is, to rise from the grave as a malevolent ghost who causes illness, and even death, to the person cursed. This belief acts as a restraint in Ndembu society on the expression of ill-feeling, since the consequence of anger may be the death of those it is directed against. Later Ihembi reconsidered his verdict, and claimed that he had been deceived by the witchcraft of Kamahasanyi's wife Maria (F6) and mother-in-law Ndona (E9).

Ritual and mystical beliefs often make explicit what is in the ordinary course of affairs either sensed but not said, or else what is said only in whispers between close friends, such as Jim

and Musona. It is clear from what has been stated that Kamahasanyi's matrilineal kin did not readily accept him as a full
village member, and that subjectively he tended to exaggerate
their hostility.

But Kamahasanyi also came into conflict with Makayi's kin,
the Konkoto group. Shortly after his arrival, Maria began an
affair with Jackson, Makayi's son, and when I first visited the
village to make a hut plan I found that Maria had left Kamahasanyi's hut and was apparently living alone in Nyakinga's
kitchen. That the liaison was known to several people I found
out in dramatic fashion a few weeks afterwards. My wife and I
had been invited by Kachimba to the induction phase (*kwing'ija*)
of a girl's puberty ritual at Nswanamundong'u Village. Jackson,
who had been 'fishing' for a job as my clerk, took it upon himself to usher me into the village. At one point I turned round to
ask him a question and found that he had disappeared. Then
I saw him skulking on the other side of the village behind
Wilson's hut. I went over to him with Musona and asked him
why he had fled. He told Musona with a shame-faced grin that
he had been avoiding 'his mother-in-law'. The lady in question
was Ndona, Maria's mother. Musona then whispered to me
that it was usual for Ndembu to avoid their mistresses' mothers,
just as if they were really mothers-in-law. He added, rather
sanctimoniously, 'This is a useless village.' Musona, it will be
remembered, was a Kawiku, one of the autochthonous inhabitants of Mwinilunga District whose ancestors had been
conquered by the first Mukang'ala, and he neglected no opportunity to comment critically in private on members of Mukang'-
ala's lineage—except on his friend Jim. Later Jackson and
Maria visited me together on several occasions at the Lwakela
House. But when I returned to Nswanamundong'u eight
months later from Kapenda's area, Kamahasanyi and Maria
were living together again, and Jackson had gone away to
Chingola on the 'line-of-rail' to find work. According to
Musona, Kachimba and Jim had put pressure on Maria to
return to her husband who after all, was their matrilineal
kinsman, and to leave Jackson who belonged to the Konkoto
group. I discuss the structural implications of this marital
conflict in greater detail later.

It must be stressed that despite their differences, at the time of which I am writing the two village sections still attached a value to residing together. All hope had not been abandoned that the chieftainship might be restored, with the possibility of a better time for all. If the chieftainship were restored, many people in Mukang'ala's area, including most Kawiku, were prepared to support Jim (E12), of Nswanamundong'u Village, as Kambung'u's successor. Jim, an adept village politician, always did his best, to my knowledge, to keep on good terms with Makayi and Jackson, and never publicly criticized Kamahasanyi. Indeed, at both *Ihamba* rituals Jim undertook the by no means pleasant task of applying the cupping horns to Kamahasanyi's body. This involved slitting the latter's skin with a razor blade, sucking the blood out through the horn, and sealing the filed-off tip with beeswax. Jim, too, confessed his remissness in failing to seek out a diviner quickly when Kamahasanyi's illness seemingly incapacitated him from working in his gardens. Towards the end of my stay in Kapenda's area, a diviner from Angola paid a surreptitious visit to a village near my camp, and Jim, getting to hear of it, walked the twenty miles from Nswanamundong'u to consult him about Kamahasanyi's continuing illness. At the same time, he remained on a friendly footing with Jackson, and even contemplated a trip with him to the Copperbelt. I believe that it was partly due to his tactful handling of the situation that Maria and Kamahasanyi were reconciled without serious conflict between Jackson and the man he had cuckolded.

Moreover, it was Jim who, more than anyone else, strove to compensate for the deficiencies of Kachimba as a headman. Kachimba, since he had lost his job as Court Clerk, had become very timid and reserved. When strangers visited his village, Kachimba, instead of greeting them in the men's forum and seeing that they were offered hospitality or accommodation, remained in his hut or slunk off into the bush, with the excuse that he was going hunting. He seemed oppressed by the knowledge that he was not the rightful headman of the village. Many Ndembu, in different parts of the District, commented critically on his inhospitable and evasive manner. But Jim was always anxious to please and assist the frequent passers-by, who came to rest in his village after tedious hours of tramping along the 'Boma road' on visits to relatives, or, not infrequently, in search of work at the distant 'line-of-rail'. In his role of *de facto* headman, Jim used to seek out Makayi's advice, and never neglected to pour him out a good measure of beer when a calabash was broached. His friendliness, however, was not altogether disinterested, for like all men with political ambitions, he found it necessary to build up a following and establish a wide range of favourable contacts.

Kachimba and Makayi, on the contrary, were always at loggerheads. At an early stage of my field-work, before I became well acquainted with the rules of Ndembu etiquette, I committed a social gaffe, which brought to light the tension between them. Makayi gave me a duiker he had trapped as a present. I took this to be a present from the whole village, and after a week had passed, I returned to Nswanamundong'u to make a cash present in return. Makayi was away on a visit and I gave the money to Kachimba, asking him to divide it among his people whilst giving Makayi the largest share. Not long afterwards an irate Makayi arrived at the Lwakela Holiday House, and demanded to speak privately with Musona and myself. He told me that he had heard that Kachimba had received a gift from me in return for Makayi's duiker. Kachimba had kept the whole sum for himself, and had not given him a single penny. Then he told me that, according to Ndembu custom, a return gift should go to the original giver only, who could then divide it as he thought fit. But Kachimba had taken advantage of my ignorance, he went on, to deceive me about Ndembu custom, and to deprive Makayi of his rightful present. Kachimba 'had a black liver', was selfish (*wudi nachifwa*), and did not look after his people. After this incident, I noticed that Kachimba and Makayi never addressed one another in the men's forum, and never sent out invitations to one another when they offered beer.

Kamahasanyi was at the point of stress between the conflicting sections of the village, and the conflict had penetrated his own domestic life. How he reacted to the invidious situation in which he found himself depended to a considerable extent on his own temperament and cast of character. In view of his central role in the ritual sequence, I began to observe his behaviour very closely and to collect biographical information about him, both from himself and from others who knew him well, such as Jim, and Mundoyi (E5) who knew his kin in Konkoto.

In the first place, it was apparent that Kamahasanyi was in no sense a masterful personality. Although he was aware of the liaison between Jackson and his wife, he did not come to blows with the adulterer, as most Ndembu husbands would have done. Nor, I am told, did he ever beat Maria. In fact, the whole matter was regarded as rather a joke by most Ndembu who knew of it. Musona in particular, who took stern action when his own junior wife was unfaithful to him, scaring her lover into emigrating to Chingola, regarded Kamahasanyi's complaisance with amused contempt. In the second place, Kamahasanyi had markedly effeminate behavioural traits. He braided his hair in the long parallel plaits of a fashionable feminine hair-style called *lumba*. He delighted in anointing his body with castor-oil (*imonu*), and spent long hours on his toilette. At girls' puberty rituals he used to lead the singing in the circle of women who danced all day round the blanket-covered novice. Other men would do this for short periods, but Kamahasanyi would sing and clap among the women for a whole afternoon. Again, it was usual to find Kamahasanyi chatting with the village women in their kitchens, while the menfolk debated or argued in the men's forum. But it was explicitly denied by my close informants that Kamahasanyi was a homosexual. He was just 'without strength' (*ng'ovu kwosi*).

Nevertheless, Kamahasanyi had a strong sense of his own importance. In a society whose members liked to stress their connections with chiefs and senior headmen, Kamahasanyi was more snobbish than most. Whenever I discussed the traditions of the Mukang'ala lineage, for instance, Kamahasanyi brushed aside or interrupted such senior men as Kachimba, Jim, and Wilson, and told me tales of the dead Mukang'-alas such as Chinseli (B3) and Ibala. He was the only man who remembered the clan-formula of the Saluseki clan to which the Mukang'ala matrilineage belonged—the clan, or *munyachi*, has ceased to have any political importance among Ndembu today, and its social importance is small. Again, he was exceptionally proud of his paternal connection with the Konkoto chieftainship.

Musona told me that Kamahasanyi was reckoned to be

impotent. His marital history showed that at any rate he was sterile. He had married four times without issue. Two of his wives (F3 and F5) had been patrilateral cross-cousins of his, members of his father's village; and certainly Kamahasanyi had been dominated, practically and morally, by his headman father, who had arranged those marriages. His father had been a hunter, and, like most hunters with muzzle-loading guns, an aggressive and self-willed old fellow, a 'real man' (*iyala wachikupu*). The weak, feminine, conceited Kamahasanyi seems to have leaned heavily on his strength and to have yielded to his authority in crucial matters. It will be remembered that Kamahasanyi, just before the second performance of *Ihamba*, had been dreaming of his father, usually in minatory form, and had said that the old man had disapproved of his quarrel with the people of Kanema. It had been Maria, Kamahasanyi's wife, also a strong, ruthless, and capable personality, who had urged him to leave Kanema Village. In surrendering to her demands, Kamahasanyi may well have felt guilty of disloyalty to the dead man. On the face of it, his break with the village in which he had been reared, but in which he could not obtain office, was an adult decision. For in his matrilineal village he had claims to succeed to the headmanship, and, moreover, by matrilineal descent he was a potential candidate for the office of Mukang'ala. Leaving Kanema, he left behind him the vestiges of his unnaturally protracted dependence on his father. But since Maria had been the active agency of change, and he had only passively acquiesced in it, he had merely exchanged a male for a female despot.

Jim told Musona that Kamahasanyi, since he had come to Nswanamundong'u, had done little but complain that his village kin were neglecting and despising him. In actual fact, they had helped him by giving him part of their standing crops of cassava to feed him until he could make his own garden. After a few months he developed the following symptoms of illness: he had rapid palpitations of the heart, he had severe pains in his back, limbs, and chest, and he became easily fatigued after a short spell of work. It was at this time that he took to shutting himself up in his hut for most of the day— normally Ndembu men only use their huts to sleep in—where he lay in his bed or braided his hair. It was at this time, too, that Maria began to commit adultery with Jackson: perhaps the affair began, as Ndembu affairs often do, in the bush near the gardens where the women go to hoe from dawn until the sun becomes unpleasantly hot. According to Kamahasanyi, the villagers took little notice of his sufferings, and no-one consulted a diviner to see what was wrong with him. I cannot say with complete certainty whether Kamahasanyi's symptoms were real or imaginary, or whether they were what Western Europeans might call 'neurotic'. What I do know is that towards the end of my first tour and throughout my second tour, from about a year to two years after the ritual sequence, Kamahasanyi was well able to cultivate rather more than the average amount of gardening land, and that he was able to travel considerable distances on visits to kin and friends. To all appearances there was nothing the matter with him—he looked healthy and could dance untiringly all night long. I suspect that Kamahasanyi's illness was psychosomatic, and was partly an unconscious attempt to attract the sympathetic attention of his village kin.

For a fairly long period there appears to have been a state of deadlock in the village. Kamahasanyi groaned and preened in his hut: the villagers stubbornly refused to regard his troubles as serious. Indeed, the general irritation felt against him erupted in Wilson's display of temper. It was only when Kamahasanyi began to announce that shades were afflicting him in dreams that social action was taken to resolve the deadlock. The whole matter was immediately raised to the level of public importance. Ancestors do not afflict casually or capriciously in Ndembu society: they make their presence felt when something is basically wrong. And we have seen that many sources of tension could be found in the village and in the chiefdom.

Kamahasanyi became the channel through which a number of distinct, but co-existing, and even related, conflicts became publicly recognized, and hence to some extent accessible to redressive measures. In the course of integrating Kamahasanyi into his new social environment, ritual behaviour involved a close collective scrutiny of the principal factors making for his partial exclusion. These factors may be divided into two main categories: (1) conflicts in the social relationships of the village, and (2) conflicts of loyalties within Kamahasanyi's psyche arising from the demands of competing social principles. The resolution of the conflicts within proceeded *pari passu* with the resolution of the conflicts without. For, in the idiom of *Ihamba* ritual, the process of bringing to light the causes of a shade's anger against an individual is accompanied by a series of confessions by his village kin of ill feeling in relationships that ideally should be free from it. The tooth of the dead hunter, it is believed, will not submit to being captured until all those with grudges against the patient have publicly admitted to holding them. The complexity and long duration of the sequence of rituals for Kamahasanyi may perhaps be accounted for by the coincidence that a psyche deeply divided inwardly confronted a deeply divided social system.

To recapitulate: Central Africa was at the time of my research parcelled out between several European powers. Each colonial nation recognized certain indigenous authorities as agencies of local government, and withheld or withdrew recognition from others. When recognition was withdrawn from Mukang'ala on demographic grounds, his area tended to revert to a pre-colonial economic and social set of conditions, but its inhabitants were unable and unwilling to attempt to reduplicate the antecedent order, for they had come to value highly cash and European goods, education, and paid, high-status occupations in the new political system. Reversion was reluctant, and took the form of depression and degradation rather than renaissance. Cleavages between branches of the chiefly lineage were sharpened, although these were to some extent reduced by the intensification of hostility felt by all inhabitants of Mukang'ala's area against Chief Kapenda, the modern darling of the Administration. Dissatisfaction with the contemporary state of affairs was exceptionally severe in Nswanamundong'u Village, the nucleus of which consisted of members of a dissident branch of the chiefly lineage. These members felt that if one of their number had held the chieftainship, the Government would have continued to recognize it. They had let down their senior member at the time of the late chief's death, and had in turn been abandoned by him. At the same time, at the level of internal village relations, they had been left without a traditionally acceptable headman, who might have rallied them as a coherent faction in the future struggle for succession, and within the village established a conflict-free *modus vivendi* between the nuclear lineage and Konkoto sections. The general breakdown in morale and cohesion within the chiefdom was reflected with an additional intensity within the village. The prevailing social atmosphere was one of mutual mistrust and petty jealousy. Against this, a man like Jim, who had a vested interest in the restoration of the chieftainship and who sought to build up a confident following, struggled in vain. Kamahasanyi, a man of weak character and strong emotions, entered this field of conflict, with its atmosphere of despair mingled with unrealistic hope, at a most inopportune moment. He had deferred until early middle age making the adult decision that would have placed him among his matrilineal kin. Among them he would have had to take a fully responsible part in the jural and administrative life of his village, helping to decide on such matters as the return of marriage-payments, the payment of *mpepi*, the adjudication of adultery cases, and so forth. Instead, he had remained under the authority of his father, a man of strong character. When he had at last been jostled by his energetic wife into quitting his paternal village, he had arrived among his maternal kin as a querulous source of irritation rather than as a capable ally in coping with their difficulties. Moreover, through his position in the kinship structure of his new village he found that he had not resolved the dilemma of matrilineal versus patrilateral affiliation. For in Nswana-mundong'u itself his matrilineal kin, his jural group, were sharply critical of his patrilateral kin from Konkoto.

Kamahasanyi, passive in disposition, appeared to find the strain of living in these conditions intolerable, and sought sanctuary in his hut, pleading ill-health. He wanted to be liked by his new group, who would not accept him on the evidence of his behaviour. He seems to have been for a time virtually boycotted by all, including his wife, who made no secret of her adultery with Jackson. But Kamahasanyi, with the obstinacy often found in weak characters, persisted in claiming that he was ill, and played upon the powerful sentiments of matrilineal kinship to force his kin to pay attention to him. Among Ndembu, it is axiomatic that a kinsman, even if he is a wastrel and a lazy good-for-nothing, has the right to shelter and gardening land while he resides with his matrilineal relatives. He cannot be turned out of the village, unless he is divined as a sorcerer, and it is not the weakling and the ne'er-do-well, but the aggressive and ambitious man who is most often suspected of using the black art. In a sense, the idle man who takes much and gives little provides the acid test of the strength of kinship sentiments. He is the greatest challenge to a socio-political order based fundamentally on kinship axioms. If he is rejected, the social and moral order itself is radically challenged. Certainly, all the devices which normally secure conformity to reasonable standards of industry and decency are brought to bear against him—ridicule, reproach, contempt, occasionally 'sending him to Coventry'—but if he can brazen these out, actual force will not be used to drive him away from his village. And he can claim his share of beer and gifts when these are distributed. Usually, too, he can find a wife who will garden for him and brew beer. Kamahasanyi was not a ne'er-do-well by nature. His gardens were of quite a respectable size. He set many snares for game. But for a time he found himself unable to cope with a difficult social situation, and sought to obtain what the psychoanalysts might call 'passive mastery' over his environment, rather than actively attempt to change it in his favour. He felt that it was up to his relatives to give him the respect and attention for which he craved, without being himself prepared to earn it by industrious and mature behaviour. He wanted them to feel that he was peculiarly the victim of circumstances and so deserved their sympathy.

But he was unable to compel their attention by minor illness—what Ndembu call *musong'u hohu*, 'just illness'. Such complaints can be treated by herbalists or leeches without recourse being sought to mystical notions. It was only when he claimed that his misfortunes and ailments were caused by ancestor shades that Kamahasanyi's kin were constrained to take notice. Just as the values of kinship are felt to have axiomatic force, so the belief that misfortune or illness—if sufficiently severe—is inflicted by ancestors for a breach of kinship norms, falls beyond the scope of legitimate scepticism. By invoking this belief Kamahasanyi could appeal to the basic sentiments of Ndembu society. It was no longer a question of coping with an awkward individual: now the major faults in the contemporary structure of social relations would have to be brought to light and, if possible, remedied. Much 'perilous stuff' would have to be purged from the collective bosom.

In the next chapter I discuss the cultural form of the *Ihamba* ritual, its symbols and practices. Readers will then be able to judge for themselves whether it is a mechanism of redress appropriate to the kinds of conflict that typically arise in Ndembu society. I interpolate this cultural study in the sociological analysis at this point because it is impossible to examine the social content of the particular performances I witnessed without a prior knowledge of the general form of this ritual. But I shall stick to my sociological last in this chapter by citing in Appendix B a number of instances of *Ihamba* I saw performed in villages beset by different kinds of conflict from those which form the central material of this book.

VI

A PERFORMANCE OF IHAMBA ANALYSED

KAMAHASANYI and most of his fellow villagers were active participants in at least seven performances of ritual. I personally attended only three of these, though I had accounts of the others. But, since all centre on the same social situation, it will be enough to record a single performance. In order not to break the continuity of the narrative I will set down my observations almost as I first recorded them. These refer to the second performance of *Ihamba* for Kamahasanyi, presided over by Ihembi, who was assisted by Mundoyi and Mukeyi.

The previous day, these three practitioners had performed a short rite, called *Lukupu* or *Kukupula*, for Kamahasanyi. *Lukupu*, sometimes known as 'the *Kaneng'a* of the day' to distinguish it from 'the true *Kaneng'a*', or 'the *Kaneng'a* of the night', is performed before a ritual to propitiate the shades. The rites of *Kaneng'a* constitute an exorcism of witchcraft and sorcery. In Kamahasanyi's case, Ihembi prescribed *Lukupu* before *Ihamba*, because he suspected, so he told everyone, that Kamahasanyi was the victim not only of ancestral wrath but also of a witch or sorcerer, whose identity Ihembi would not publicly disclose, among the members of Nswanamundong'u Village. Privately he revealed that his suspects included Wilson (E11), son of a former headman of the village, and Kamahasanyi's present wife Maria and her mother Ndona (E9). But *Lukupu* tends to be directed not against specific named evil-doers, but against witches and sorcerers anonymous. Ihembi asserted that he would not be able to withdraw the *ihamba* tooth from Kamahasanyi's body unless the patient's hidden foes refrained from bewitching him. Furthermore, in the course of the *Ihamba* rites all who had cherished grudges against Kamahasanyi, for whatever reason, would have to confess them before the shrine erected during the rites to the hunter shade.

THE IHAMBA BEGINS

On the morning of 6 November 1951 I arrived at Nswanamundong'u Village at about 8 o'clock, to find that its members and the three visiting practitioners were already heavily involved in preparations for the performance. Villagers had no hesitation in telling me that when Kamahasanyi went to Angola to consult a diviner, the latter diagnosed that Kamahasanyi's own father, Mudyigita (E3), had come out to him in *Ihamba*, and they reiterated that Mudyigita's shade was angry over the death of Safi (F5), Kamahasanyi's wife and patrilateral cross-cousin from Kanema Village in Konkoto Chiefdom. Safi's matrilineal kin had alleged that Kamahasanyi had failed to make the traditional *mpepi* payment, and they also hinted that Safi's death was due to Kamahasanyi's sorcery. The shade of Mudyigita had characteristically, in terms of Ndembu thinking, taken the side of his matrilineal relatives against his own son. For men, according to the beliefs of the hunting cult—in which *Ihamba* is included—may be afflicted by patrilateral, as well as matrilineal, shades.[1] This is a reflection of the relationship frequently obtaining between men and their sons in the economic sphere. For men often train their sons to follow them in such specialized pursuits as hunting, blacksmithing, and woodcarving, and teach them the magic which, while it does not replace, reinforces technical skill. Mudyigita had been a great hunter; his son, though not a great hunter, had been trained by him in hunting lore. The bonds of *Wubinda*, though not perhaps as strong as those of matriliny, have a special mystical efficacy which may raise fatherhood to the plane of the ancestor cult.

Some of the villagers also conjectured that Mudyigita's shade resented Kamahasanyi's departure from Konkoto Chiefdom to stay with his matrilineal kin. The two theories explaining the anger of Mudyigita's shade seem contradictory, but they both express the resentment of Kamahasanyi's father's matrikin against him in his new residence. Such theories, exempting as they did the matrikin from blame for Kamahasanyi's condition, might be expected to find a ready acceptance among them and to prepare the way for Kamahasanyi's fuller incorporation

---

[1] See Table 3, p. 304.

in their ranks. For it meant, in effect, that the last traces of
Kamahasanyi's alien quality, of his Congolese, Konkoto, and
paternal origins, might be physically removed from him in the
form of his father's 'biting tooth'.

Ihembi's strategy at this point in the affairs of the Nswanamundong'u group is quite clear: impress upon the villagers
that they must feel well disposed towards Kamahasanyi, who
must not harbour grudges against them, and above all that they
must not tolerate active witchcraft in their midst; make them
feel that they must provide sanctuary and protection for him
against strangers from another territory and chiefdom; rein-
force their sentiments in favour of matriliny and use its binding
power to cement Kamahasanyi firmly into the village life.

Soon after my arrival Kamahasanyi himself told me he had
dreamed a few hours before that he had seen his father standing
between the forked-branch shrines (*yishing'a*) set up in front of
his hut to placate the hunters' shades which had affected him
in various manifestations on previous occasions. On the strength
of this information Ihembi had decided that *Ihamba* rites should
be performed just there.

I then inspected these *yishing'a*, and found that several other
sacred and symbolic articles had recently been placed on and
near them. The *chishing'a* at the extreme left, looking from the
door of Kamahasanyi's hut, the centre of ritual orientation,
was of *kapwipu* wood.[1] In its fork was inserted, on Ihembi's
advice, a small plate which would later be used for the rites.
On this was placed a wad of *kapakamenena* grass, later to be
pounded in the mortar as a constituent of a potion to be drunk
by the patient. Between the lower and upper branches on the
left was a bundle of grass in which were concealed two tiny
calabashes plugged with wild rubber (*ndunda*), containing
mahamba said to have been previously extracted from Kamahasanyi. On its immediate right a wand of the *mukula* was
planted in the ground. On its right was a *chishing'a* of *kapepi*
wood with a single fork. At its base was a square piece of small
termitary (*ifwamfwa*), on which were placed, to the right, a
lump of white clay (*mpemba*), and to the left, a lump of red clay
(*nkundu*). On its right fork was hung an enamel cup of the sort
sold in European-owned stores. Just in front of the termitary

[1] See pp. 183–5 for a discussion of *Yishing'a* symbolism.

a red feather of the Livingstone's loury (*nduwa*) was inserted upright in the ground. This *chishing'a* had clearly been cut for the present performance. A twist of braided *kaswamang'wadyi* grass was tied near its base just above the termitary. On the right of the *chishing'a* was planted a quickset rod of the *musuwa* tree. Behind the composite shrine, parallel with its base, was laid a portion of rolled bark recently used for carrying home a duiker trapped in the bush by Jim, Kamahasanyi's classificatory mother's brother.

Collection of Medicines

When I had inspected the shrine I was invited to go into the bush with a small party of practitioners to collect the medicines of *Ihamba*. We proceeded in single file led by Kachilewa, an initiated hunter from the neighbouring village of Mangameli. He carried his gun, leather wallet and belt, and axe, as a proper hunter should. Ihembi followed, carrying a wooden friction bar, or 'stridulator' (*ndamba*), which he rubbed rapidly with a peeled stick, making a sound that is sometimes compared with the shrill noise of cicadas. Behind him walked Mukeyi carrying a hoe and the flat winnowing basket (*lwalu*) in which practitioners put their vegetable medicines. His brother, Mundoyi, followed him playing another stridulator, while I brought up the rear. We all sang the mournful air (*mukoke-e*) that is sung by a hunter returning with his kill, to a friction bar accompaniment. We walked briskly along the path connecting the village to its cassava gardens. Suddenly Mundoyi stopped and pointed at a sapling of the *musoli* tree. This tree is the *ishikenu*, 'the tree of greeting', or *mukulumpi*, 'the elder' of *Ihamba*. In other words it is the dominant symbol of the medicine complex. Ihembi then felt in the pocket of his old American army greatcoat and pulled out a small pouch of galago- or mongoose-skin, and stood before the *musoli* tree. Mundoyi took both stridulators and touched the tree with them in turn. Then Ihembi unfastened the strings of his purse and laid it at the foot of the tree. Next he put Kachilewa's gun in a fork of the tree. He took out white clay and placed it beside the purse. Then he asked me to pay '*nyishing'a*', a small token payment for the privilege of observing sacred objects or actions, and began to invoke the *musoli* tree itself. He did not at this point petition any of the shades, but simply pleaded with the tree 'that its root might be found quickly'.[1] After this he picked up the lump of *mpemba*, and drew a white line on the ground from the base of the tree towards himself. Mundoyi now hoed out a long white runner, possibly the tap root of the *musoli*, put it in the winnowing basket, and took a handful of its leaves for the medicine. At this point Wilson, whom Ihembi had suspected of working sorcery against the patient, joined the party.

We now moved on, and to the friction music of the *andamba* we collected the following medicines,[2] but without making any further invocations:

1) Roots and leaves of *mwang'alala*
2)   „   „   „   „ *museng'u*
3)   „   „   „   „ *mututambululu*
4)   „   „   „   „ *kabalabala*
5) A root only of *kasasenji* (for drinking)
6) Roots and leaves of *mukombukombu*
7)   „   „   „   „ *muneku*
8) Leaves only of *ikunyi*
9) Roots and leaves of *mufung'u*.

Now we left the path and entered the bush. There we collected:

10) Roots and leaves of *mutata*.

In the meantime Ihembi had slipped off quietly to collect some secret, but to his mind essential, medicine. Mundoyi now collected:

11) Root and leaves of *mutuhu* (a small shrub with leaves like grass).

Here Ihembi returned and we all crossed the path at a right angle to it, to collect:

12) Root and leaves of *munjimbi*.

Whenever roots were dug up the resulting cavities were always carefully filled in again.

Mundoyi now cut three pegs of equal length from branches of a *mukula* tree to use as a stand or a container at the performance. Mukeyi cut a portion from the thick root of *muchikachika* which appeared above the surface of the path.[3] This was done, he said, as a precaution against a certain type of sorcery which

---

[1] See Notes on Narrative, No. 1, p. 173, for fuller version of this invocation.
[2] See Notes on Narrative, No. 2, p. 174.
[3] See Notes on Narrative, No. 3, p. 174.

involved concealing bad medicine in frequently used paths. For the same reason Mukeyi cut a small chip from a branch of *mutalu* which crossed the path at about breast height. Musona told me that the cutting of these plants was also a protection against the pollution of sacralized persons and articles by those who had had intercourse with their spouses or lovers in the village the previous night. He said that unless all the villagers refrained from intercourse that night[1] it would be very difficult for Ihembi to remove the troublesome *ihamba*.

As we were about to enter the village on our return Mundoyi procured the root of a small herb called *musong'usong'u* (also called *muvulama* and *mujimbi*). When we reached the shrine again we circled it three times singing hunting songs and playing the stridulators. Mukeyi, legs apart, several times held up the medicine basket dramatically before the new *chishing'a*.

The Scene is Set to Catch the Ihamba

The skin of a duiker killed by Jim was now laid on a grass mat before the shrine and the medicine basket placed on it. The gun was propped on the *chishing'a* of *kapepi* wood. Mukeyi inserted a *mukula* peg at each end of the cube of termitary and laid the other peg across them. Kachilewa's hunter's pouch was deposited under the *chishing'a* of *kapwipu* wood, while the stridulators were placed on a mat. Wilson went to his hut, brought his gun, and stacked it over Kachilewa's. In fact, it was noticeable that Wilson was doing his best to further the ritual action. It may have been hinted to him that he had been suspected of using sorcery, and he was taking the opportunity of showing everyone that his intentions towards Kamahasanyi were good.

Mukeyi now scraped the roots we had collected, in no set order, depositing the scrapings (*nyemba*) in the *lwalu* basket. As they were peeled the roots were placed at the base of the *musuwa* wand. Mundoyi went off alone into the bush, and returned with a sprig of *chikochikochi* grass which he added to the *lwalu*. Meanwhile Kamahasanyi was walking about near his hut with every appearance of enjoyment, smiling and making comments to the older women. The *lwalu* was placed for a moment on top of a meal-mortar. The leaves of the castor oil plant (*imonu*) were brought in and placed near the gun butts,

---

[1] See Notes on Narrative, No. 4, p. 174.

top side down. Ihembi's knife lay on the mat. Dry wood was brought for kindling the ritual fire, and Mukeyi chopped it into faggots with his practitioner's axe, then laid it behind the meal-mortar, which stood on the right of the *musuwa* wand. Makayi, the head of the Konkoto section of Nswanamundong'u Village, had not yet put in an appearance, but Mafuta, the acting headman of nearby Mashata Village, arrived and greeted everyone. Mukeyi took a handful of grass from the thatch of Kamahasanyi's hut, set light to it and kindled the ritual fire with it. Then Nyaking'a (D14), a matrilineal 'grandmother' of Kamahasanyi's, and the only surviving female member of the late headman's genealogical generation, brought in a calabash of water. Ihembi took it and poured out some water beside the meal mortar, poured some into it, and put some more in a broken calabash, in a potsherd, and in a bowl placed beside the piece of termitary. This bowl was taken by Kachilewa and placed between the *kapwipu chishing'a* and the *mukula* wand, and covered with the leaves of the castor oil plant. A calabash of honey beer, sacralized for the occasion, was brought up, and a cupful of it was poured into all the receptacles mentioned, on the termitary, and on the axe. Mukeyi briefly put the broken calabash on the fire—after putting bark scrapings and some leaves into the water and beer it contained. Mukeyi removed the grass mat and placed the duiker hide, skin-side uppermost, before the composite shrine. Meanwhile Kamahasanyi had stripped to the waist, around which he held a blanket. Some maize stalks were placed before the termitary, and the bowl, still covered with castor oil leaves, was placed on them. Kamahasanyi himself now brought in the cupping horns (*tusumu*) and two small blue duiker horns. All present were offered beer. Then Ihembi pounded medicine leaves in the mortar, using only his right hand, 'the hand of power', to do so. He took the cup from the *kapepi chishing'a* and gave it to Kamahasanyi to hold. Then he took the sprig of *kapakamenena* grass and put it in the meal-mortar along with the leaves Mukeyi had been giving him. Mukeyi gave the root scrapings to Mundoyi, who put them in a leaf-funnel. Ihembi mixed the pounded leaves in the cup and returned them to the mortar. Then he put the empty cup on the right of the termitary. More broken leaves were given to Ihembi, who appeared to reject them and returned them to the *lwalu* basket. The leaf-funnel was placed in the *lwalu*. Mukeyi took over the pounding for a while, and all four practitioners—Mukeyi near the shrines on the right, Ihembi behind him, Mundoyi on Ihembi's left, and Kachilewa opposite Mukeyi to the left of the shrine—sat down around the duiker skin. The medicine hoe was laid before the shrine. Mundoyi, but none of the other doctors, had anointed himself with red clay on the temples, just beside the eyes—as is customary for adepts in the hunting cults.[1]

The Singing Begins

While all this had been going on, Kamahasanyi had been standing near his hut, but now he sat down on the duiker skin at a right angle to the shrine, with his feet outstretched towards the mortar and broken calabash. The bowl was returned to its original position between the *kapwipu chishing'a* and the *mukula* wand. Kachimba, the acting headman of Nswanamundong'u Village, seated himself behind the shrine and apart from the other villagers. Nearest to him, and on his right, was Samuwinu (D13), the 'real' headman of the village, who, as we have seen, had fled to Chief Kapenda's area when Kambung'u succeeded to the Mukang'ala chieftainship. Since he was a close rival for the chiefly stool, he had feared the chief's jealousy and possible sorcery. At the last moment Maria, Kamahasanyi's wife, placed something I could not recognize in the *lwalu*, possibly an article intimately connected with their marital life.

Ihembi now began to sing a song, taken from the repertoire of the hunting cults, and all present joined in the refrain: '*ikombela kombela, kombelenu kombela*' (from *ku-kombela*, to invoke a shade). As other *Ihamba* songs were sung Ihembi opened his mongoose-skin purse, put some white and red clay from it among the pounded leaf medicines floating in the mortar, and studied the patterns formed by the grains of coloured matter. He cried out '*Twaya washi!*' (which means 'come quickly' in the Luvale language), and repeated this several times. Mundoyi and Kachilewa joined him in peering sagely into the mortar. This was a form of divination, similar to one I have described in *Ndembu Divination* (1961), p. 80. Ihembi began to sing with his familiar sad smile, then he took medicine from his purse

[1] See Notes on Narrative, No. 5, p. 175.

and spat it into the mortar and the *lwalu*. He exhorted Mudyi-gita's shade 'to come quickly and leave off troubling his son'. By these words he appeared to have confirmed the Angolan diviner's diagnosis: that Kamahasanyi's father's was the shade afflicting him in '*Ihamba*'.

Cupping Horns are Applied

Kachilewa now took medicine in both his hands from the broken calabash and the potsherd, and splashed it over Kamahasanyi's whole body and face, while the hunting song with the refrain '*Mukoke-ye, mukoke nambwa*' was sung by all present. Ihembi took powdered red clay (*mukundu*) from a purse, and drew two parallel lines with it on Kamahasanyi from the dorsal vertebrae parallel with the curve of his shoulders, and also just in front of his ears. He then took white clay (*mpemba*) from an empty packet of 'Belga' cigarettes I had once given him, and drew white lines just above the red lines. Meanwhile Kachilewa prepared the cupping horns—goats' horns with the tips cut off—by perforating the beeswax plugs inserted in their narrower ends. The cigarette packet had been brought by Kamahasanyi when he came with the cupping horns, presumably from his hut, where Ihembi may have performed private rites for him. The practitioners now occupied the following positions: Mukeyi sat by the fire, Mundoyi sat in front of the shrine, Kachilewa sat beside Kamahasanyi, Ihembi stood by the mortar. Kachilewa put medicine from the *lwalu* basket in the cup, bowl, broken calabash, and potsherd. The last two containers were now to the left of the *kapwipu chishing'a* and each contained two cupping horns. Ihembi then gave Kamahasanyi medicine to drink (see Plate 1*a*). After that Kachilewa took a store-bought razor blade, made two small parallel incisions in Kamahasanyi's back near his left shoulder blade, and sucked a cupping horn over them, plugging it with beeswax when he had finished (see Plates 2*b* and 3*a*). He then applied the other three cupping horns on Kamahasanyi's back to form a rough square. While this cupping operation was taking place many of the villagers and their neighbours stood about gossiping and laughing and paid no heed to Kamahasanyi. Mundoyi brought a big '*kayanda*' drum from Kamahasanyi's hut. The meal-mortar was taken round behind Kamahasanyi. Then Mundoyi

PLATE 1

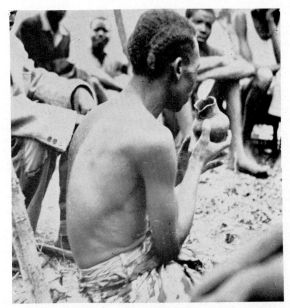

a. Kamahasanyi drinks medicine to fortify himself for his ordeal. Note his feminine hair-style.

b. The Luvale doctor inserts medicated duiker horns between Kamahasanyi's toes. Ethnographer in background.

PLATE 2

a. Kamahasanyi: Practitioner spits medicine into cupping horn.

b. Jim places a cupping-horn in position on Kamahasanyi's back. Note the fragments of medicine leaves adhering to the patient's back— symbolizing the hunter-shade.

put the *kayanda* drum beside Ihembi, who picked up his *ndamba* stridulator, made of *mudyidyi* wood, and began to play it. He had beside him a small clay pot. Mafuta, of Mashata Village, had by this time anointed his outer orbits with red clay and was playing the other stridulator. Mundoyi beat the *kayanda* drum; Kachilewa, Wilson, and others clinked axe heads (an action known as *ku-kenkumwina*)[1] in time with the drumming. At a sharp word from Mundoyi all gathered more closely round Kamahasanyi. One horn dropped off his back. Then Kachilewa filled the leaf funnel with water, and more pounded root medicine. Ihembi called a halt to the drumming, and warmed an old tin containing medicine. He soaked a piece of bark fibre in the medicine, and applied it to the scar on Kamahasanyi's back left by the fallen cupping horn.[2] Wilson then put some white *mpemba* on the *kapepi chishing'a*, a token, no doubt, of his good intentions towards the patient. Next Ihembi picked up a duiker horn striped with *mpemba*, filled it with medicine, gave it to Kamahasanyi to drink twice, and sprinkled what was left on his back and forehead.[3] Then he inserted it tip foremost into Kamahasanyi's front hair so that it projected over his brow. He repeated this process with a blue duiker horn, which he finally inserted in Kamahasanyi's back hair. He then placed the red feather mentioned earlier quill first beside the duiker horn over the patient's brow. After this he took the tin that had contained the medicine, and replaced it among the pile of peeled roots. Then he gave the signal for drumming and singing to begin again, and the mournful theme song of *Wubinda*, the generic hunters' song, rang out: '*Iyajinayi ewo*', approximately, 'the animals have gone away'. Since the afflicting shade was a hunter the practitioners held that hunters' songs should be sung.

The broken pot near the mortar was now transferred behind the broken calabash. Mundoyi fetched more medicine leaves and put them before the *lwalu* basket. Maria, Kamahasanyi's wife, went into the bush to get *mudyi* leaves.[4] On her return she went straight to her hut, and brought out a hand rattle (*nzenzi*).

[1] See Notes on Narrative, No. 6, p. 175.
[2] See Notes on Narrative, No. 7, p. 175.
[3] See Notes on Narrative, No. 8, p. 175.
[4] See Notes on Narrative, No. 9, p. 175.

She chewed her leaves and spat the juice on her husband's feet, temples, and hands, finally tapping him smartly on the back and head with her rattle. The congregation appeared to rejoice in the aesthetic aspects of the rites, the singing, dancing, and ritual movements. When the drum rhythm and the song proper to *Ihamba* were played, Kamahasanyi began to sway and tremble in time with the music. This trembling is known as *kuzakuka*, and is thought to be caused by the arousal of a shade in the patient's body. The drums were suddenly stilled, while Kachilewa removed the remaining cupping horns amid general silence. Ihembi dried off Kamahasanyi's back with mongoose-skin purses. He then took out some secret ingredients from one purse, and added them to the bowl, calabash, and potsherd. Kachilewa thoroughly washed out the blood from the cupping horns into the bowl, and placed two in the calabash and two in the potsherd. He covered the bowl again with castor oil plant leaves. To Kachilewa had been delegated the responsibility of cupping and washing.[1] He next applied the cupping horns on Kamahasanyi's back in the same places as before.

By this time the women of Nswanamundong'u and others from neighbouring villages were seated in a body on mats just beside Kamahasanyi's hut, at some distance from the men. Kachilewa squirted medicine from the leaf funnel round the bases of the horns. Another hunting song began. Ihembi went over to the women and exhorted them to come closer to the men and sing loudly, even though they might thus approach their sons-in-law and fathers-in-law. 'It was important', he said, 'that they should give their power to help Kamahasanyi'. The patient's quivering shook off a cupping horn, and Kachilewa then removed the others. At that moment Mukeyi stalked in solemnly with a pounding pole, and walked round the shrine beating the pole rhythmically before him on the ground, before dropping it outside the circle of attenders. Kachilewa, having washed out the four horns as before, re-affixed the two horns from the broken calabash in their former situations, and made new incisions lower down and sucked on the other two. Ihembi then gave Kamahasanyi medicine to drink from a small clay pot. Jim now took over the big *kayanda* drum while

[1] See Notes on Narrative, No. 10, p. 175.

Kachimba brought in a new red toy rattle of tin purchased by a labour migrant on the Northern Rhodesian Copperbelt. A woman came with a live fowl trussed at the feet, and laid it near the shrine. Kamahasanyi soon began to tremble and writhe again, this time violently; three horns flew off. The singing stopped, and Kamahasanyi abruptly stopped trembling.

Mukeyi brought in more leaves, again of the *mudyi* tree. Jim took one and chewed it. Ihembi, Headman Mangameli, and Mundoyi each placed a leaf on his left fist, and brought down his flat right hand upon it with a sharp smacking movement, breathing heavily and chanting '*Maheza!*' Mundoyi then made a brief invocation to 'the shade who has come in *Ihamba*'. As he spoke, Jim (E12) punctuated his words with drum taps, while Kachilewa applied the cupping horns again. At intervals the men chanted '*Maheza ngambu yafwa*'. Mundoyi said: 'You are my brother Mudyigita, the same father begat us. My brother, our son Kamahasanyi was not brought to the village of his mother first, but to the village of his father. After he married there his wife died, and her relatives think that he should also die. If we were not born of the same father, remain in Kamahasanyi's body; if we were so born, come out of our son quickly.'

After the invocation the fowl was dipped in medicine both in the broken calabash and small clay pot, then thrown roughly away. Drumming and singing began again, Kamahasanyi trembled and a cupping horn was shaken off (see Plate 3b). Every time this happened, I noticed, Kachilewa carefully collected in the fallen horn any blood spilt on the ground, and transferred it to the bowl. At one point, however, Ihembi stopped the performance and angrily told Kachilewa not to put the blood in the bowl, but in the small calabash so that it could be properly covered and concealed. Otherwise, he said, 'The *ihamba* will not be caught.'

A little later Kachilewa danced in the traditional hunters' style, pointed with his gun at Kamahasanyi's back, 'to shoot *Ihamba*'. Meanwhile Mukeyi cut and scraped out a small calabash to contain the blood, according to Ihembi's instructions. I observed that out of the fourteen men present, seven were at that time playing musical instruments of one kind or another.

Kachilewa took a purse, put medicine from it into the new calabash, carefully poured the contents of the bowl into it—both blood and medicine—and then covered it with castor oil plant leaves.

Ihembi, who had apparently been cogitating, suddenly roused himself, took a gun in his right hand and a *lwalu* medicine basket in his left, and danced before Kamahasanyi. Then he danced round to Samuwinu and myself, and extended the *lwalu* for *nyishing'a* ritual payments. We paid up and he went to the acting headman, Kachimba, who did not. Kamahasanyi was now in a very ecstasy of quivering. Ihembi next went to Kamahasanyi's hut carrying a medicine purse, sprinkled medicine on the right of the threshold and roof, circled the hut once, and put more medicine on the left of the threshold. He then went into Kamahasanyi's kitchen and remained there for about a minute, but I was unable to see what he was doing. From there he went to the bush on the outskirts of the village, collected some leaves and, still dancing, went in turn to three cross-paths, at each of which he gathered some dust and rubbed it into the medicine. He also collected some dust from Nyaking'a's threshold, and swept in a wide circle round the whole assembly. He circled the shrine, and made his return just behind Kamahasanyi, who was still trembling and writhing. Ihembi rubbed the new medicine he had collected on Kamahasanyi's body, and, while he did this, Mundoyi commanded the women to stand up. They all rose and some men with them. Ihembi applied medicine from a purse to Kamahasanyi's back. The drumming stopped abruptly. Ihembi sat beside Kamahasanyi, groping about in his purses. Eventually he took from them a fine powder and dabbed it on the weals left by the fallen cupping horns, and on the chest and stomach. He invoked the shade as follows: 'If you are indeed Chitampakasa[1], you should not make Kamahasanyi stand up [for Kamahasanyi had half risen while trembling], you should not raise him up. If you want a small 'ground hut' [*katunda ka heseki*], one will be built for you after the rite is over.' Then from each of the two mongoose skin purses he added medicines to the new calabash. He took a purse of worn cloth from the tin, and dropped powder from it into the calabash. Then he took powdered white clay from

[1] See Notes on Narrative, No. 11, p. 175.

PLATE 3

a. Jim sucks a cupping-horn on to Kamahasanyi's back. His assistant holds the store-bought Gillette razor blade with which he has made the incisions.

b. Ihembi's assistant plunges a cupping-horn just removed from Kamahasanyi's back in a cut calabash of medicines. It is in this that the *ihamba* tooth will be 'found'.

PLATE 4

a. Ihembi divines in a medicated meal-mortar. Note the hunter's shrine on the right. It is a forked stick, peeled to show the whiteness of the wood (which has a symbolic value). At its base is a fragment of termitary—believed to be the temporary 'hut' of the hunters' shades.

b. Scene at an *Ihamba* rite performed for Nyasapatu by Ihembi. He has cut the feet of a chicken and is allowing the blood to drip into medicines in a meal-mortar. Note the cupping-horns on the patient's back and the duiker-horn in her hair. In the round flat winnowing basket behind the hunter-shade's shrine are vegetable medicines recently gathered in the bush.

the 'Belga' cigarette packet, sprinkled some in the calabash and anointed Kamahasanyi by the orbits.

The bundle of grass, mentioned earlier, on the *kapwipu chishing'a* is classed by adepts in the hunting cult as 'a small hut of the sky', or 'of the above' (*katunda ka hewulu*). These huts 'of the below' or 'of the above' are regarded as occasional dwelling places of hunters' shades or repositories of *mahamba*. A *katunda ka heseki* may sometimes be much larger, about six feet in height. Only initiated hunters are allowed to look inside it, for it contains secret and powerful hunting medicines.

After invoking the shades Ihembi scoured out the calabash with his knife, and cut up a root, dropping some portions in the meal-mortar, some in the broken calabash, and some in the potsherd. Finally he put some portions of the root (probably of the *musoli* tree) in the calabash containing drained blood.

He then sat on the stool and patiently surveyed Kamahasanyi's back, to which only a single cupping horn now adhered. He motioned to Kachilewa not to add any other horn, and ordered the drummer to play the thematic rhythm of *Ihamba*. Kamahasanyi, apparently in an agony, clasped his neck with both hands. Ihembi crouched close to Kamahasanyi and dusted his back with a purse. For some time he held the purse close to the cupping horn. I expected him to pounce, but no: although Kamahasanyi leaned back towards him, Ihembi stopped the singing and went into the bush, whence he swiftly returned holding both hands behind his back. He then put the leaves he held in them into his mouth, chewed them, and spat the juice above Kamahasanyi's ears, on the back of his arms and on his knees.

The 'real' headman, Samuwinu, now spoke in the tone Ndembu reserve for ceremonial utterances, but so quickly that I could only catch a few words. Among them were the phrases, 'these slaves of Nyakapakata' and 'older brother of Nyaking'a'. Nyakapakata (C1) was the mother's mother's mother of Kamahasanyi, and the brother of Nyaking'a referred to was the late Chief Mukang'ala Mundong'u, whose *ihamba* had been extracted from Kamahasanyi a short time before. Samuwinu concluded with the traditional formula of the hunters' cult: '*mangameza mafwa*'.

Thereupon Kachilewa splashed white clay mixed with water

over Kamahasanyi, and applied three more cupping horns lower down on his back. The cigarette packet and other medicines were put in the tin, and Mundoyi led the hunting song '*mwana kang'ombi*'. The pounding pole was now placed beside him. Kamahasanyi began to twitch again, and Kachimba, quickly followed by all present, broke into the *Ihamba* song. A cupping horn fell, open end first, spilling all its blood on the earth. Kachilewa rushed to it, meticulously collected every spot of blood, and poured it into the new calabash (see Plate 3*b*). Ihembi went on his knees, and, like a hunter stalking his prey, closed in on Kamahasanyi, holding two purses in his right hand. He shook his head and withdrew, saying that '*Ihamba* has moved away'. But the people sang louder than ever. Ihembi went to the *katunda ka hewulu* mentioned above, and took from it two small calabashes containing *mahamba* previously 'extracted' from Kamahasanyi. When he put them in the *lwalu* basket the singing died down. Ihembi said 'It has gone away'. I got the impression that Ihembi was now doing what I had seen him do at the first performance of *Ihamba* for Kamahasanyi, i.e. he was building up suspense. More *mudyi* leaves were brought, and once again hands were smacked on them and '*Maheza!*' chanted. This time Kachimba spoke a *kupandula* address to the shades: 'Dead brother-in-law [*ishaku wafwa dehi*], we have killed many goats and chickens for you, so that our sister's son might be strong, but you are still dodging about. This is no good at all. Please come quickly.' Ihembi now instructed Kachilewa to suck a cupping horn on the right of Kamahasanyi's neck[1]. Jim brought a new calabash of beer, and we drank from it. The former servant of the missionary, Mr. Smithers, looked in for a moment, and after he had gone Jim wondered a little concernedly whether he would inform the missionaries that pagan rites were being performed at the village.

Now the drumming and singing began again. Ihembi brought the meal mortar close to Kamahasanyi, and repeatedly splashed the whole of his body with medicine from it. Three horns fell off from the violence of Kamahasanyi's shaking. Only the one on the neck remained. It was noticeable that Wilson's wife sat at a distance from the other women (whose young children were allowed to watch with them). When the cupping horns fell

[1] See Notes on Narrative, No. 12, p. 175.

the women all rose to their feet, and when the last horn then fell off Ihembi shouted out 'Pour much medicine over him!' This, he explained, had to be done because Kamahasanyi was sweating profusely; he and Kachilewa splashed the patient copiously from the meal-mortar. Ihembi now announced: '*Ihamba* will not come out, but is still dodging about; this can be seen from the fact that Kamahasanyi keeps looking at the sun.' Mundoyi then took out two whistles and blew each twice. '*Twaya washi!*' he shouted excitedly, urging the shade to 'come quickly'.

Once more, cupping horns were applied, and drumming and singing began. Kamahasanyi immediately started to tremble and sway about. The *Ihamba* song began. Two horns dropped off. Samuwinu stood up and danced behind Kachimba as the excitement grew to fever pitch. Many singers massed behind Mundoyi to form a kind of vocal battery of power. Ihembi prepared for 'the kill', again with a purse in either hand. He made passes in the air behind a cupping horn on Kamahasanyi's neck, and then blew in his purses. He picked up the cup and threw medicine over Kamahasanyi. The drums beat strongly, and a repetitive, exciting song was sung. Ihembi went off, and returned with two leaves, one of which he inserted in the front of Kamahasanyi's waist cloth and one at the back. Then he blew in Kamahasanyi's ears and round the remaining horns on his neck, and spat on his head. The drumming stopped as a cupping horn was attached to the other side of Kamahasanyi's neck. Ihembi then gave Kachilewa a bunch of grass from Kamahasanyi's hut. Kachilewa lit it from the fire and described a circle with it round Kamahasanyi, finally letting it burn out between his feet. Another cupping horn was affixed to Kamahasanyi's right temple. The practitioners said that the *ihamba* had been located in Kamahasanyi's head. Mukeyi sealed the weals on Kamahasanyi's back with large blobs of white clay.

Kamahasanyi himself now broke rather unexpectedly into vehement speech, and complained that Kachimba and his other matrilineal relatives (*akumama*) never gave him any assistance when he was feeling very ill. They should have gone to Angola and consulted a diviner to find out what had been troubling him. In the end he and his wife Maria had to go themselves, although he was not at all well. True, his kin had cultivated his gardens for him while he was away, but this was not important. Kachimba and Jim made faintly demurring sounds, but in this ritual situation Kamahasanyi was privileged to speak without contradiction. He then went on to say that if he was being troubled by the shade they all thought it was, it would surely come out, since Mundoyi and Mukeyi were his 'fathers'. Now that he had told his grudge to everyone, he said, all would be well. His hard thoughts had been keeping back his cure.

Mundoyi now took the duiker horn out of Kamahasanyi's front hair,[1] washed it, filled it with medicine, and replaced it at the back. He did the same with the blue duiker horn, replacing it at the front. He blew his whistle twice. Kamahasanyi started to quiver again, and the horn on the left of his neck fell off, unpleasantly spilling what appeared to be a small chunk of flesh. Next the horn on his temple fell off. Ihembi sat very quietly, not registering any emotion at all. I felt at the time that what was being drawn out of this man was, in fact, the hidden animosities of the village. To all appearances Kamahasanyi appeared to be quite dissociated. Now Ihembi fitted a long thin duiker horn on the little finger of his right hand, took a purse in his left hand, and pointed the horn at a cupping horn, wiping Kamahasanyi's skin above it with the purse as he did so. All rose as one to their feet again, and Ihembi fastened on the twitching Kamahasanyi, who fell on his side, writhing convulsively. Kamahasanyi cried out and sobbed as with pain when Ihembi removed the blood-dripping horn in a large skin purse. Mundoyi and Kachilewa threw large quantities of medicine over Kamahasanyi. Ihembi rushed to the small calabash, and threw the cupping horn now concealed by the purse into it. He then spat *mpemba* on the really ugly bulge on Kamahasanyi's neck where the horn had been. Kachilewa held his hand poised over the leaf-concealed calabash while all waited intently. He removed the leaves and delved and dredged in the bloody mixture. After a while he shook his head and said, '*Mwosi*' (There's nothing in here). Ihembi with a smile took over. He plunged his fingers into the gruesome liquid and I saw a flash of white. He rushed with what was in his fingers out of the circle of onlookers. From the edge of the village he beckoned to the elders

[1] See Notes on Narrative, No. 13, p. 175.

PLATE 5

a. Nyasapatu. An apprentice applies medicine from a leaf poke to the patient's scars.

b. Tightening the drum-skin for Nyamukola's *Ihamba*.

PLATE 6

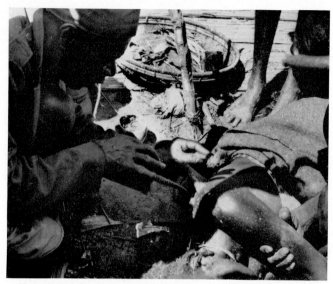

a. Ihembi 'catching' an *ihamba* tooth. See description in text. He has drawn a duiker-horn on to the little finger of his right hand. The patient is quite dissociated.

b. Nyamukola. The patient has a violent fit of shaking, and tension mounts.

and to me. Led by Samuwinu, Kachimba, and me, we went one at a time to Ihembi to confirm that it was indeed a human tooth. He had not deceived us, he said, for it was not a monkey's tooth or a pig's tooth. When we expressed our assent the women all trilled with joy.

Mundoyi with his ritual hoe excavated a small hole just behind the shrine on the side away from Kamahasanyi's hut, and buried what was left of the medicines there. At the same time Jim pounded some maize grains to make fresh flour for putting into a small calabash, the container of the recently removed *ihamba*. The white flour is said to 'cool' the *ihamba*, i.e. prevent it from flying away and venting its ire on one of its living kin. Kachilewa plugged the calabash with beeswax, while Wilson made a sling of bark string for it. Ihembi sat with Kamahasanyi just by the hut, amiably talking and smoking. Kamahasanyi pointed to his neck and head several times, while Ihembi nodded understandingly. After the *ihamba* of the late Chief Mundong'u had been extracted at the previous ritual, there had been a spontaneous outburst of friendly feeling, embracing the entire village membership. Persons whose relationship had been hostile had shaken one another warmly by the hand. The atmosphere now was less dramatically amiable, but a mood of quiet satisfaction seemed to emanate from the villagers.

To conclude with financial details: Kamahasanyi had agreed to stand the whole cost of the treatment, about 15s. od. The chicken was given to me. It should have been eaten by the senior practitioner, but Ihembi insisted that as I had brought his team of adepts by car all the way from Chief Kapenda's area, I was the 'true *chimbuki*' who had ensured the success of the rites!

NOTES ON THE NARRATIVE

1. I will not describe in any detail the first performance of *Ihamba* I attended at Nswanamundong'u Village; for it was less elaborate in form than the second, and involved a smaller congregation. It is sufficient to mention that at the beginning of the first performance the leading officiant was a Luvale hunter and that he was superseded about half-way through the performance by Ihembi and his assistants. The transfer of control was brought about without any overt friction between the two

specialists. First the Luvale, then Ihembi, made statements to the effect that there was no jealousy between them, for they were both gun-hunters and *Ihamba*-doctors. The Luvale doctor stressed that he would help Ihembi in any way that he could; for did not both of them wish earnestly to cure the patient? Ihembi said that though he had come along later and intruded (*wunashinki*) on the work of the Luvale, this did not mean that he was a better doctor. But his assistants, Mukeyi and Mundoyi, were patrilateral kin of the patient from Konkoto. He said that although divination and dreams had shown that Chief Mukang'ala Kabong'u's shade had come 'in *Ihamba*' to afflict the patient who was his sister's daughter's son, it was probable that there was yet another *ihamba* in Kamahasanyi—his father's. If this were so, the shade of that dead hunter Mudyigita might listen to the clinking (*ku-kenkumwina*) of his seminal brothers' axe-blades and come out quickly from his son's body. For Mudyigita's father Chibala was also father of Mundoyi and Mukeyi, who were thus classificatory fathers of the patient (see Fig. IX, p. 310). The Luvale doctor agreed that Ihembi had put forward cogent reasons for taking over control of the ritual. At the end of the performance, Kamahasanyi paid Ihembi, who 'removed' a tooth from the former's body, 10s. for his services, and Ihembi gave 5s. to the Luvale doctor.

2. According to Mundoyi and Mukeyi, in a discussion I had with them several days after the performance, the medicine actually drunk by the patient at *Ihamba* was prepared from the root parings of:

    1) *kasasenji*—dug out of the side of a large termitary.
    2) *muhang'andumba*—from *ku-hang'a*, 'to chase'; and *andumba*, 'witches' familiars'.
    3) *mushilambulu*.

3. The root collected from the village path was used for washing Kamahasanyi's body.

4. According to Mundoyi and Mukeyi, in contradiction to the views of many other Ndembu, only the practitioners (*ayimbanda* or *ayimbuki*) and the patient (*muyeji*) must refrain from sexual intercourse on the night before *Ihamba* is performed. The patient must also abstain from eating *musonji* (a variety of catfish). He and his wife must also cook their food on a separate fire that night.

5. A *mulundu* bird, I was informed later, was hung on a near-by tree. Kamahasanyi said that 'its blood had been given to *Ihamba*'.

6. The *kukenkumwina* sound of clinking axe-heads, said Mundoyi, is 'to call *Ihamba* quickly'.

7. Ihembi told me that the medicine applied by a practitioner to the razor cuts is kept ready always in his mongoose-skin purse.

8. Kamahasanyi, said Mukeyi, must continue to drink medicine 'of a different kind' some time after *Ihamba* is over.

9. According to Ihembi, Kamahasanyi's wife brought and chewed leaves of the *tukuka* plant, and not, as others told me, the *mudyi* plant. This was done to prevent him from shaking (*ku-zakuka*, the stem of which is related to that of *tukuka*) too violently.

10. An *Ihamba* practitioner must be an initiated hunter, a *chiyang'a*. Kachilewa was a *chiyang'a*, not a *chimbuki*.

11. Mundoyi and Mukeyi told me that '*Chitampakasa*' was the mode of manifestation in which his shade had previously afflicted Kamahasanyi. They said that the medicines of *Chitampakasa* are the same as those of *Ihamba*, but the patient washed himself with them. The shade which comes out in *Chitampakasa* gives his victim bad luck in hunting. If he is still angry after the rites of *Chitampakasa* he catches the patient in *Ihamba*.

12. Ihembi said that cupping horns were placed on Kamahasanyi's neck, not by his instructions, but because everyone thought that the *ihamba* was there when Kamahasanyi clutched at his neck. At the beginning, he went on, the *ihamba* was near the patient's liver, even though the horns were fixed on his back.

13. When the practitioner shouts '*Pia!*' in the duiker horn inserted in the patient's front hair, said Mundoyi and Mukeyi, '*Ihamba* can hear and come out'.

THE CULTURAL STRUCTURE OF IHAMBA

A. *Beliefs Connected with the Ihamba Tooth*

Although several informants have told me that *Ihamba* is not a traditional ritual (i.e. was not brought by Ndembu when they came from Mwantiyanvwa's empire in the Belgian Congo), it appears, nevertheless, to be of considerable antiquity, and is perhaps as old as the gun-hunters' cult of *Wuyang'a*, which is said to have been introduced by Luvale and Ovimbundu slave-traders about the middle of the nineteenth century. A prayer always made during the gun-hunters' ritual of bestowing a special hunter-name on a candidate includes the following sentences: '*Twenjili kuMwantiyanvwa. Wuyang'a wenjili naKasanji Kamalundu. Diyi wenjili namata yakesi ninfundang'a.*' 'We came from Mwantiyanvwa. The gun-hunters' cult came with Kasanji Kamalundu [said to be an Ovimbundu chief]. He is the one who came with fire-arms and with gunpowder.' Since *mahamba* teeth play an important part in the gun-hunters' cult, as we shall see presently, it is probable that the *Ihamba* cult is nearly coeval with it. Nevertheless, the possibility should not be excluded that the *Ihamba* ritual was introduced later than *Wuyang'a* by members of other tribes who practise closely similar hunters' rituals.

Among the Luvale and Luchazi the term *lihamba*, cognate with *ihamba*, stands for a particular manifestation of a shade. The shade appears to rouse the *lihamba* from its domicile under the ground for this purpose. An echo of this Luvale usage is found in the ritual of *Kayong'u*, frequently performed by Ndembu today. *Kayong'u* has two functions. The first is to cure persons who have been afflicted by ancestor spirits with disorders of the chest or lungs. The second is to initiate candidates into the cult of diviners. A man who has passed through *Kayong'u* successfully—and if he has proclaimed his intention of becoming a diviner he is subjected to a number of exacting tests to see whether he can discover hidden objects—is entitled to apprentice himself to a recognized diviner, who will teach him his divinatory techniques for a large payment in cash or kind. The *Kayong'u* spirit is said to enter a man's body and aid him in reaching a correct decision. This shade is referred to as an '*ihamba*', the *ihamba* of divination (*ihamba dakuhong'a*).

But among Ndembu the term *ihamba* usually refers either to an upper central incisor of a dead hunter or to the ritual employed to remove such a tooth from the body of a patient afflicted by the hunter's spirit.[1] The *ihamba* tooth is an element

---

[1] I write *Ihamba* for the ritual and shade-manifestation, and *ihamba* for the tooth. The term *ihamba* refers to the incisor of a *dead* hunter. The incisor of a living hunter, like any tooth of any person, is called *izewu*.

in a whole complex of beliefs associated with the gun-hunters' cult. It is believed that the two upper central incisors of a gun-hunter (*chiyang'a*) contain much of his power to kill animals. If one of these teeth is knocked out, or drops out as the result of pyorrhoea—a common gum disease among Ndembu—the hunter must preserve it. He keeps it in a square leather wallet (*ngonga*) sewn on to a leather belt. The wallet is worn at the small of his back. In it is a curious assortment of objects, some of practical use in his profession, others thought to possess magical efficacy. The top layer consists of strips of bark wadding for his muzzle-loader. Beneath this are several bullets of indigenous manufacture to shoot 'were-lions', human beings who can transform themselves into man-eating lions by medicine. In the same layer is a small triangular tang of iron (*mukalula*), a flake of flint (*ilola dambanji*, 'the stone of killing'), and some fluffy dried moss (*mfufu*) as tinder. With these a hunter can make a fire. Beside these he places cartridges and a bag of gunpowder (*nfundang'a*). Underneath these layers he carries three or four skin bags containing powdered red clay (*mukundu* or *ng'ula*). Redness among Ndembu stands primarily for blood (*mashi*), more particularly for blood that is shed and 'can be seen' (*mashi alumbuluka achimwekeshi chejima*, 'blood that is self-evident and is made visible to all'). In the hunting-cult it represents the power (*ng'ovu*) that hunters obtain from shedding blood. For the same reason the hunter smears the flap of his wallet with the blood of his kills. At the bottom of his wallet the hunter keeps his *mpelu*, a term which denotes a special category of magical substances. *Mpelu*, or the alternative plural form *jipelu*, are organic residues,[1] which by contagious magic[2] impart to the hunter certain desired qualities possessed by the creatures or objects from which they have been taken. Thus, the wing-case of the Goliath beetle gives him strength, while the purple wings of a species of wood-wasp 'make him sting', i.e. shoot accurately and lethally. The hair and nail-parings of Europeans and chiefs impart strength. The hair of an albino (*mwabi*) gives luck, for whiteness (*wutooka*) is lucky. And so on. The hunter's

---

[1] See also White, C. M. N. *Elements in Luvale Beliefs and Rituals*, Rhodes–Livingstone Paper No. 32 (1961), p. 35.

[2] Ndembu say that *mpelu* has power in itself (*mpelu jikweti ng'ovu jaju*); i.e. it is not given power by ritual practices.

incisor is placed among these objects of sympathetic magic, at the bottom of his wallet. It is not described as *mpelu*, but is felt to 'resemble' it: like *mpelu* it gives him 'strength and good luck'.

When a gun-hunter dies, his upper central incisors are knocked out. The left incisor belongs to his mother's side, the right to his father's side. They must be inherited by relatives who are also gun-hunters with names bestowed on them by senior members of the cult at a special ritual called *Ku-telekesha*, 'causing to cook'. In theory the person who inherits the *ihamba* should dream of his dead relative, and then inform the senior members of the cult in his neighbourhood that the hunter's spirit requires him to inherit his *ihamba*. But in practice an informal meeting of cult-members in the neighbourhood decides who will be a worthy successor of the deceased.

An inherited *ihamba* is carried in a pouch with a long strap of white or coloured cloth. The pouch itself (called *mukata*) is made of white cloth. The *ihamba*, concealed beneath a long flap, is embedded in a paste of corn meal mixed with the blood of slaughtered game. Above it are inserted two cowrie-shells (*mpashi*), which are known as 'the eyes' (*mesu*). With these the hunter's spirit is said to 'see animals' in the bush. The *ihamba*-inheritor, known as the *nswana-ihamba* (from *ku-swana*, 'to succeed, or inherit') carries the *mukata* pouch into the bush with him when he goes hunting. Within the carrying strap are folded strips of clothing from the dead hunter. When it is not in use, it is hung up in a shrine dedicated to hunters' spirits. This shrine, called *katunda kaWuyang'a*, is set up a few yards in front of its owner's hut. Some *tutunda* (the plural form of *katunda*) resemble small thatched hen-houses on stilts. A famous hunter, however, may build quite a large *katunda*, usually tubular in shape, the walls consisting of reed mats. The *katunda* on stilts is referred to as *katunda kahewulu*, 'the spirit-hut of the above', and the larger hut as *katunda kaheseki*, 'the spirit-hut of the below [or 'on the ground']'. Sometimes a *katunda kahewulu* is no more than a bundle of grass tied round the middle with bark-string and containing an *ihamba*-receptacle. This receptacle is a small stoppered calabash, and contains an *ihamba* which has been 'extracted' from a patient's body. The *katunda kaheseki*, on the other hand, contains, in addition to an inherited *ihamba*, certain powerful hunting medicines, and no one but their owner may look inside it, on pain of bleeding to death when next cut. Women are forbidden to approach closely to a *katunda* of either sort. Should they do so inadvertently, they are believed to develop menstrual disorders or to bleed to death after giving birth. This prohibition derives from a basic principle of Ndembu ritual that 'the blood of huntsmanship' (*mashi aWubinda*, from *Wubinda*, which means all kinds of hunting, including trapping and snaring, other than hunting with firearms) or 'the blood of animals' (*mashi atunyama*) must not be brought into contact with the 'blood of motherhood' (*mashi amama*) or 'blood of procreation' (*mashi alusemu*). Thus, for example, when a hunter's wife is about to give birth, he must remove all his hunting gear from his hut and its vicinity, lest it lose its efficacy. Behind this principle lies the notion that for a child to be born the maternal blood must coagulate around the foetus. Hunters shed blood and make it flow. Again, women give life, hunters take it. The two functions are radically opposed. At a deeper level of sociological analysis, dichotomy between the sexes is expressed in this ritual idiom. As Professor Gluckman[1] has pointed out, custom in African society frequently accentuates biological distinctions between men and women, and exaggerates the different, complementary roles of spouses. Such estrangements, between the sex categories and within marriage, are, he considers, 'part of the cohesion of the larger society'[2]; for these customary forms first divide and then reunite the members of society in wider ranges of relationships. I shall have occasion to discuss the sex dichotomy in its ritual aspect and social significance later. Here it is sufficient to state that *Wubinda* is in many ritual contexts equivalent to *wuyala*, 'manliness' or 'masculinity'.

It is necessary to discriminate between two ritual usages in connection with *mahamba* (the plural of *ihamba*). An *ihamba* tooth may be inherited by a renowned hunter, and may then be used as a kind of charm or amulet to bring luck in hunting and increase the power and skill of its possessor. On the other hand, it will be recalled, some *mahamba* are believed to afflict the living by burying themselves in their bodies. In the latter case, the afflicting *mahamba* are said to be of two kinds: some of them are

---

[1] Gluckman, M. *Custom and Conflict in African Society*, Oxford: Blackwell (1955), pp. 60–61.

[2] Ibid, p. 78.

13

from the corpses of hunters whose upper central incisors were lost before burial; others are 'escapes' from *mukata* pouches, or from calabash containers in which they had been placed after a previous 'extraction' by an *Ihamba* doctor. It is extremely rare for an *ihamba* to leave its inheritor's *mukata* pouch, but instances have been mentioned in my hearing where this is said to have happened. Here the exasperation of the shade with the living was said to have been very great. In reality, of course, the dead man's tooth must have been stolen from its inheritor's pouch as it hung inside the *katunda*, a mystically dangerous feat for any-one who was not himself a member of the hunters' cult. But *mahamba* do disappear fairly frequently from their calabash con-tainers. I attended a performance of *Ihamba*, for example, at which Ihembi presided, for the wife of Mukeyi, his assistant. After the drumming, singing, and treatment had gone on for a long time, Ihembi called a halt to the proceedings and said: 'Previously, this *ihamba* (named Mpoku—the patient's mother's brother) was taken from another woman and sealed in a small calabash. But it escaped, for I know that the calabash is now empty. Now it has entered Nyasapatu (Mukeyi's wife). Mpoku is annoyed because no one inherited his name.[1] If this *ihamba* is removed, his name should be given to someone. Otherwise it will fly away again.' I asked Ihembi afterwards whether this often happened, and he answered strongly in the affirmative, then shook his head sadly over the wayward behaviour of *mahamba* in general.

Ihamba represents an aggressive, usually but not invariably, masculine power which, when socially controlled, works for the benefit of its possessor and the community. To be brought under control it must be properly inherited, and fixed firmly in a ritually prescribed manner in its *mukata* pouch. Thereafter, it must be propitiated with offerings of blood whenever a kill is made, and during all performances of the *Wuyang'a* cult. In this way a potentially dangerous power is domesticated into the service of society. On the other hand, if a hunter loses his in-cisor, it becomes a dangerous *ihamba* after his death, as does an

---

[1] This does not refer to the *Wuyang'a* cult, but to the custom of naming a new-born child after one of its deceased relatives. Although the name is found by divi-nation, it sometimes happens that a given name is not submitted to the diviner. If a person was mean (*waheta chifwa*), sterile (*nsomu*), or a mischief-maker (*chip-wapwoki*), his name will not be revived in this manner.

unremoved *ihamba*. And even after extraction, when an *ihamba* has been sealed up in 'cool' meal, in a small calabash stoppered by a maize-cob, it is liable to escape and 'bite' people.

What are the symptoms of affliction by an *ihamba*? Let me quote from comments made by various informants at different times. Nyamuvwila, the aged wife of a headman, told my wife that she had once been 'eaten' (*ku-dya*) in the chest, neck, and shoulders by an *ihamba* which had 'fallen' (*ku-holoka*) into her body. At the time we knew her she was suffering from leprosy. The first time she had been 'caught' (*ku-kwata*) by an *ihamba* was in 1940, and the ritual had been performed for her three times afterwards. The last performance I witnessed. The *ihamba* came from her uterine brother, a hunter whose *ihamba* tooth had not been removed before burial. After his death it 'wandered about and went after meat'. Another woman from the same village 'had become sick' (*wakata*) 'in the back' (*munyima*), because an *ihamba* had started 'to bite' (*ku-suma*) her. My best informant on ritual matters, Muchona, in describing to me the circumstances surrounding a particular case of *ihamba* affliction, said: 'Chain [the patient] comes from the village of Makumela, his mother's village. That is where the shade of *ihamba* [*mukishi wehamba*] has come from. His grandfather is the spirit, the mother's brother of his mother. He is the one who has fallen on his grandson Chain Mbunji [*Diyi wunaholokeli mwijikulwindi Icheni Mbunji*], to obtain blood from his grandson. He has come that he may be known [i.e. remembered]. People will say: "This is his grandfather who has fallen on him that he may be well known." When they have sucked him out [i.e. as an *ihamba*] in order to give him the blood of animals [as offerings to the tooth], if it is well [i.e. if the *ihamba* is removed], they should give him the blood of an animal, so that they may stay well [i.e. live in health, accord, and prosperity], and that the patient who used to be sick, may stay well. They pray to him that they may put him in a pouch of cloth and sing and dance with drums for him.' An *ihamba*, then, 'falls' on its victim, 'bites', or 'eats' him. It can be seen moving about under his skin, like 'the movements of an insect' (*nyisesa yakabubu*). It is said 'to catch him with its teeth', the plural form *mazewu* being sometimes used for the single tooth that has been extracted. It can afflict any part of the head and body, and can move from one part to the other when it is 'chased' by the doctors. I myself have seen *mahamba* 'extracted' from the neck, back, limbs, and buttocks. It 'flies in the air' (*watukang'a mumpepela*) to reach its victim. It demands its victim's blood. The blood sucked out through the cupping horns (*tusumu*) is carefully collected in a calabash cup, covered with a leaf of the castor oil plant, and buried behind the temporary shrine erected for the performance of an *Ihamba* ritual, for the spirit to drink.

The nature of an *ihamba* is ambiguously conceived by Ndembu. It has some of the qualities of an object of contagious magic (*mpelu*), in that it contains the power to kill and 'stab' (*ku-tapa*) of the hunter from whom it was taken or from whose corpse it comes. At other times it is identified with the hunter's shade (*mukishi*), and seems to be regarded as a special manifestation of that shade. When it is 'flying', moving about in the body, or 'wandering' in the air seeking its victim, it seems to be thought of in the latter sense. When it is placed in a container, either a hunter's wallet, a *mukata* pouch, or a small calabash—when, in Ndembu idiom, it is 'quiet' (*ku-fomoka*), it has something of the character of a charm or a talisman, helpful to the interests of its possessor and, indirectly, of his kin.

If one considers its alleged attributes carefully, it is difficult to avoid coming to the conclusion that the *ihamba* epitomizes the aggressive drives in human nature. Such drives can be given aims and objects beneficial to society—e.g. hunting game, and punishing law-breakers and evildoers. But, if they are not given a legitimate form and direction, they may become socially disruptive. *Ihamba* may be said to represent the turning of aggression against oneself instead of against others. A person often becomes sick in this way because he feels violent hatred against others and knows that he ought not do so. His symptoms are partly self-punishment, but they are also an expression of his concealed aggression against others. Like Kamahasanyi and other *Ihamba* patients I have known, the sick person makes himself a nuisance to those he hates, who, he believes, reciprocate his ill feeling. In a society living at bare subsistence level, anybody who does not pull his or her weight in food-production, the running of village affairs, or the care of their children, and who diverts others from such activities, causes a much greater disturbance than would be the case in

European urban society. But, since the whole bias of the value-system of his society, supported by its ritual beliefs and practices, runs counter to such deliberate withdrawal from social and economic life, the person who hates his kin and retreats from social intercourse feels guilty, and may well believe that his minor ailments are signs of punitive affliction by shades.

B. *The Semantic Morphology of Chishing'a*[1]

Although the *chishing'a* forked branch shrine is an important element of Ndembu hunting ritual, there are hundreds of other symbols in the system, some of which are full or partial expressions of the same basic themes, while others represent different themes. Each of the *Wubinda* rites, for example, has its own ritual 'plot' and idiosyncratic character. But *chishing'a* may fairly be said to typify the hunting symbol, since it is found in every hunting rite.

Starkly simple in outward form, a mere forked stick bare of bark, it is, as we have seen, rich in meaning. Let me try to express this semantic wealth diagrammatically, so as to bring out the semantic structure of the symbol.

The following may be said to comprise part of the 'meaning' of a *chishing'a*:

(1) Social Relationships
    (a) Between hunters and non-hunters
    (b) Between hunter's elementary family and matrilineal kin
    (c) Between full and classificatory matrikin of hunter
    (d) Between hunter and 'his' hunter shade (most frequently of the mother's brother or father)
    (e) Between hunter and his instructor in 'huntsmanship'
    (f) Between fellow members of the hunters' cults.
(2) Values
    (a) Toughness of mind and body
    (b) Efficiency in providing meat
    (c) Piety towards the hunter ancestors
    (d) Making known or visible what is unknown and hidden

[1] This section is taken from my article 'Themes in the Symbolism of Ndembu Hunting Ritual', in *The Forest of Symbols*, op. cit., pp. 299–301.

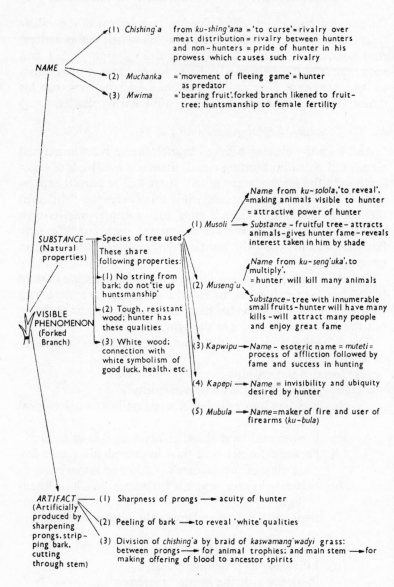

NAME

(1) *Chishing'a* — from *ku-shing'ana* = 'to curse' = rivalry over meat distribution = rivalry between hunters and non-hunters = pride of hunter in his prowess which causes such rivalry

(2) *Muchanka* = 'movement of fleeing game' = hunter as predator

(3) *Mwima* = 'bearing fruit', forked branch likened to fruit-tree; huntsmanship to female fertility

SUBSTANCE (Natural properties) → Species of tree used

These share following properties:

(1) No string from bark; do not 'tie up huntsmanship'

(2) Tough, resistant wood; hunter has these qualities

(3) White wood; connection with white symbolism of good luck, health, etc.

VISIBLE PHENOMENON (Forked Branch)

(1) *Musoli*
- Name from *ku-solola*, 'to reveal', = making animals visible to hunter = attractive power of hunter
- Substance – fruitful tree – attracts animals – gives hunter fame – reveals interest taken in him by shade

(2) *Museng'u*
- Name from *ku-seng'uka*, to multiply', = hunter will kill many animals
- Substance – tree with innumerable small fruits – hunter will have many kills – will attract many people and enjoy great fame

(3) *Kapwipu* → Name – esoteric name = *muteti* = process of affliction followed by fame and success in hunting

(4) *Kapepi* → Name = invisibility and ubiquity desired by hunter

(5) *Mubula* → Name = maker of fire and user of firearms (*ku-bula*)

ARTIFACT (Artificially produced by sharpening prongs, stripping bark, cutting through stem)

(1) Sharpness of prongs → acuity of hunter

(2) Peeling of bark → to reveal 'white' qualities

(3) Division of *chishing'a* by braid of *kaswamang'wadyi* grass: between prongs → for animal trophies; and main stem → for making offering of blood to ancestor spirits

FIG. V. The Semantic structure of *Chishing'a*.

(e) Fertility (multiplicity, fruitfulness)
(f) Hunters' skill in concealing themselves from animals
(g) Fairness in meat distribution
(h) The sacredness of age and sex distinctions (taboos against eating of *yijila* by women and uncircumcised boys)
(i) Suffering that good may come of it
(j) Acuity of hunter's responses
(k) Skill in the use of weapons.

(3) Topographical Features
(a) Forest
(b) Plains
(c) Termite hills and nests
(d) Burial sites.

All these referents[1], merely at the level of Ndembu exegesis, are possessed by a piece of stick, a bit of grass and a fragment of termitary. This is but a single example of the mighty synthesizing and focusing capacity of ritual symbolism. It might almost be said that the greater the symbol, the simpler its form. For a simple form is capable of supplying associative links of a very generalized character; it displays a feature, or features, which it shares, literally or analogically, with a wide variety of phenomena and ideas. Thus, the whiteness of *mpemba* clay recalls the whiteness of milk and cassava meal and, more than these, such abstract ideas as freedom from impurity, goodness 'without spot', etc.

Finally, it must be stressed that the *chishing'a* is regarded by Ndembu not so much as an object of cognition, a mere set of referents to known phenomena, but rather as a unitary power, conflating all the powers inherent in the activities, objects, relationships, and ideas it represents. What Ndembu see in a *chishing'a*, made visible for them in its forked and awe-inspiring nakedness, is the slaughterous power of *Wubinda* itself.

C. The Medicines of Ihamba

The *musoli* tree is called the *ishikenu* or *mukulumpi* (the 'elder' or 'senior') of the trees from which medicines are taken. Ihembi

---

[1] And others—implicit in those aspects of the symbolism which connect it with such sectors of the ritual system as life-crisis ritual, gynaecological ritual, veneration of village ancestors, anti-witchcraft ritual, divination procedures, etc.

addressed the tree itself, not the afflicting spirit. This is the usual practice when medicine is about to be taken from the *ishikenu* tree of any kind of ritual. He said: 'You *musoli* tree, of animals [i.e. of huntsmanship], come quickly [*twaya washi*: the Luvale term for 'quickly', *washi*, is used in *Ihamba*], may this *ihamba* come out quickly, so that the patient may become well soon.' Ihembi meant that he wanted the main root of the tree to be found quickly by his assistant. If this happened, it would be an augury that the tooth would be caught soon. I think, however, it would be an error to call these addresses to trees 'dendrolatry'; rather they are injunctions to the particular species to lend their unique qualities to the total set of medicines that collectively represent the manifestation of the punitive spirit and also the process of propitiation. What is worshipped is the shade, not the tree. Nor is there any suggestion that there are tree-spirits. Each species of tree has its own kind of power, which is put at the service of society when portions of it are collected by a ritual specialist who has been initiated into its occult meanings and the appropriate ritual techniques. In each kind of ritual the *ishikenu*, the dominant medicine-tree, is, in a sense, the representative of all the other species from which medicines are taken. To address this tree is to 'awaken' (*kutonisha*) its specific power (*ng'ovu*) to cure people.

My informants agreed in deriving *mwang'alala* from *kumwang'ala*, 'to be scattered'. The leaves of this tree, it is said, are blown away in a few days in the July winds. In the same way, it is hoped that the affliction of the patient will promptly leave him as a result of the treatment.

Museng'u is a tree frequently used as a forked-branch shrine or as a source of medicine in the hunters' cults. I have discussed the meanings attributed to it by informants on page 62.

Mutututambululu (*Xylopia antunesii*) is derived from *ambululu*, a species of small bee that nests in the ground or in disused termitaries. Such bees come in swarms to the *mutututambululu* tree to gather its pollen and nectar. One of my informants, Nswanandong'a, argued from this that, if it were used in a hunters' ritual, those treated by it would attract many animals towards them, so that they could be shot. He stated also that many people would come like many bees to a performance of ritual where it was used. The punitive shade which had sent misfortune on a hunter 'because it had been forgotten' would then be pleased because it would be named in the presence of many people, and thus remembered. It would, therefore, help the hunter, instead of afflicting him. Muchona gave me an additional meaning. He said that the bees 'came from time to time' to the flowers. In the same way a hunter, who had drunk, or been washed with, the medicine, would kill a steady succession of animals—'from time to time' (*mpindyi hampindyi*). In many rituals, *mutututambululu* leaves form part of a broom (*musampu*) for sweeping a patient's body with medicine. There are usually leaves from two other kinds of tree in such a broom. One is *mukombukombu* (*Tricalysia niamniamensis*), collected at *Ihamba*, and the other, *muhotuhotu*. In *Ihamba* a medicine-broom is not used, and *muhotuhotu* is not collected. The term, *mukombukombu*, is derived by all my informants from *ku-komba*, 'to sweep', and refers to its use as a component of a medicine-broom.

Mukombukombu, like *musoli* and *museng'u*, expresses a dominant ritual theme. From *ku-komba* is derived *ku-kombela*, 'to invoke' shades. Before they make invocation at a *muyombu* village shrine, a *chishing'a* hunting shrine, or the temporary shrine erected for any other ritual of affliction, Ndembu sweep away any dust or debris lying at its foot. This is to make it 'white' or 'pure' (*ku-tookisha*). In the same way, a patient's hut is swept out before the performance of a curative ritual, 'to sweep away' or 'chase' (*ku-hang'a*) 'bad things' (*yuma yatama*) or 'things of witchcraft or sorcery' (*yuma yawuloji*). According to Nswanandong'a, a person treated with *mukombukombu* or brushed by it, will become white and clean (*-tooka* has both meanings). If he is clean, animals will not be able to see him when he goes hunting, and he will kill them easily. A clean person is *wawuwahi*, which may be translated as 'good', if one is referring to moral qualities, and 'fair', 'handsome' or 'attractive', if physical appearance is stressed. *Ku-waha*, the infinitival substantive, summarizes all that is regarded as worthwhile and desirable in life, that has what Lewin would call a 'positive valence'. Its antonym, *ku-tama*, epitomizes everything with a 'negative valence'. *Ku-waha* is most comprehensively symbolized by powdered white clay (*mpemba*). What it implies is the manifest order of the universe, the open expression of harmony in individuals, society, and nature. It also means legitimate pleasure, as in the phrase *natiya kuwaha*, 'I am pleased'—with the beauty of a woman, at a fine piece of conduct, with a well-ordered village or a healthy stand of cassava, and so forth. *Ku-tama*, 'to be bad', 'wicked', implies disorder or breach of order. It also stands for displeasure, as in the phrase *natiya kutama*, 'I am displeased', usually because something has been done inappropriately or illicitly. Witchcraft, dirt, sickness (*yikatu*), disease (*musong'u*), death (*ku-fwa*), madness, deception, thieving, adultery, incest are all *ku-tama*. In ritual, black objects often stand for witchcraft and the death and sickness it produces. 'Sweeping', and prayer after sweeping, mean in ritual 'to dispel evil influences', such as grudge-bearing or sorcery. It may also mean 'to free from ritual impurities', such as result from the presence of un-circumcised boys or menstruating women. Each of these categories is called *wunabulakutooka*, 'one who lacks cleanness or whiteness'. Other impure persons include those who have just had sexual intercourse and those who have broken a ritual taboo, such as eating foods prohibited to them for a period after they have undergone a curative ritual.

The theme of *ku-komba*, 'to sweep', is related to that of *ku-solola*, 'to reveal', and both are included in the concept of *ku-tooka*, 'whiteness', 'good luck', 'health', 'friendship', etc. The main difference between them consists in the notion that *ku-komba* is to rid of external impurity, that which hides from without, while *ku-solola* is to bring to light what is hidden within. *Ku-komba* is to get rid of inimical influences in the social and natural environment that threaten the ritual subject and impede the ritual process. *Ku-solola* is to reveal what is concealed within the patient, his grudges, the punitive or malevolent beings and forces inside his body, and what is concealed within the minds of his kin and neighbours—the secret resentments of the village.

Kabalabala is a tree from which *chishing'a* forked-branch hunting shrines are sometimes made. It is a fruit-bearing tree; string cannot be made from its bark, and its wood is very hard. In *Ihamba* it is a symbol for huntsmanship (*wuyang'a*), and is used 'to make the patient strong' (*ku-kolesha muyeji*).

Kasasenji, sometimes called *ikunyi*, is used in the boys' circumcision ritual as sacred firewood. Like *kabalabala*, it seems to mean little more in *Ihamba* than 'to give strength'. It was one of Ihembi's special medicines, and was not used by other doctors I saw perform *Ihamba*. It is just possible that the term *ikunyi* is connected with *mukunyi*, an address made to the *Ihamba* shade. (See page 297.)

Muneku is a tree whose leaves and roots appear frequently as medicines in ritual concerned with death and sorcery or witchcraft. The *muneku* tree has black inedible fruits, and their blackness is said to represent *ku-fwa*, 'death', *ku-tama*, 'badness', *ku-bula kutooka*, 'impurity', *yihung'u*, 'misfortunes', *malwa*, 'trouble'. Muchona and Windson Kashinakaji derived *muneku* from *kunekuka*, 'to change', as in the phrase '*kumuchima kunanekuki*', 'one's mind has changed' (literally, 'at one's liver'). Windson thought that it was also connected with *ku-nekama*, 'to sink down'. He speculated that *muneku* meant that the *mufu*, or ghost raised by a sorcerer, should change its mind about afflicting the victim, and sink down into the grave again.

Whatever truth there may be in Windson's speculation, *muneku* does seem to represent a death-dealing force, or being, in a number of situations. For instance, when a man goes on a long journey or fishing trip, he often puts a leaf of *muneku* in the fork of a tree and covers it with a small termitary. All my informants agree that this is to keep under the familiars of sorcery sent by his enemies to attack him while the traveller is on lonely bush paths.

The other medicines used in *Ihamba* are less important than the ones already discussed. Most of them exemplify themes with which we are now familiar. *Mufung'u*, for instance, is a tree which bears fruits closely resembling British wild plums. In September these fruits strew the ground thickly beneath the *mufung'u* trees. In women's ritual, such as *Isoma*, *mufung'u* medicine is used because it has many fruits to bestow fertility on the patient. But in *Ihamba* the term is said to be derived from *ku-fung'a*, 'to gather together' a herd of animals. *Mutata* means *ku-tatisha wubinda*, 'to heat huntsmanship'. *Mutuhu* is from *ku-tuhula*, and means 'to bring animals quickly to the spot where the hunter is hiding'. *Munjimbi* is from *ku-jimbala*, 'to forget, be lost', and signifies that the animals 'forget' to keep a careful watch for the hunter. All these medicines are symbols of huntsmanship, and portray that the afflicting agent is a hunter's spirit. But *munjimbi* (also known as *muvulama*, from *ku-vulama*, 'to forget', and *musong'asong'a*), also means that witches and sorcerers 'must forget' the patient, i.e. cease to bewitch him.

The root collected from the village path is another protective medicine against sorcery. Ndembu believe that sorcerers conceal destructive medicines beside or beneath paths, to injure or destroy their personal enemies.

It is thought that witches and sorcerers may be among those present at a ritual assembly, and may, indeed, be the cause of the patient's troubles, which, by means of hoodwinking magic, they have caused to be divined as due to affliction by a shade. The root across the path means that the doctors are aware that a sorcerer or witch may be at work, and can, if necessary, counter the malignant magic. It belongs to the same class of protective medicines as *muneku*, mentioned above, a class organized around the theme, 'to make visible or expose the secret action of witchcraft or sorcery'.

Ihembi, the *Ihamba* doctor, told me that the branch of *mutalu* that crossed the path at face level was to protect the patient against persons who had recently had sexual intercourse. Sexual desire (*wuvumbi*) makes a person for a time ritually impure (*wunabula kutooka*), and the presence of such a person 'spoils the medicines' (*ku-kisang'ana yitumbu*). Thus at *Ihamba*, the patient, the senior doctor, and his assistants are prohibited from having sexual relations during the day and night before the performance and on the night following it. Contact with '*wuvumbi*' renders the medicines inefficacious and destroys their 'power' (*ng'ovu*). In the boys' circumcision ritual (*Mukanda*), medicines are kept permanently in the vicinity of the seclusion lodge, to protect the novices against the uncleanness of visitors who might have recently slept with their wives or lovers. The impurity of such visitors, it is thought, will undo the influence of medicines to heal the boys' circumcision scars.

Mutalu was derived by Ihembi from *ku-tala*, 'to look at', and means that the medicine 'looks at', or 'detects', those made impure by sexual intercourse. Once they are 'known' by the medicine, they can no longer harm the patient. *Mutalu*, in fact, is yet another expression of the theme of 'revelation or exposure of the hidden', or 'the making public of what has been private'.

Since Ihembi suspected that Kamahasanyi was being bewitched by a kinsman, as well as afflicted by an ancestor, he collected in addition to the above medicines, most of which are in the general repertoire of *Ihamba* doctoring, the root of a *muhang'andumba* tree. The name of this plant is self-explanatory, for it is derived from *ku-hang'a*, 'to chase', and *andumba*, a term for the familiars of witches, otherwise known as *tuyebela* or *tushipa*.

Parings of the roots of *muhang'andumba* and *kasasenji* were mixed with water in a clay pot, and given to Kamahasanyi to drink as a potion. The *kasasenji* root was hoed out from the side of a termitary, said by Ihembi to stand for a hunter's grave. In this way the doctor made contact with two suspected sources of Kamahasanyi's bodily pains, witch's familiars and a hunter's shade. All the other medicines were used as ingredients in a lotion for washing his body.

Sociological Commentary and Analysis

In Nswanamundong'u Village we have been observing a social drama of considerable scope and intensity. It involved the breach not merely of a single relationship but of several interconnected relationships, as well as conflicts of principle and value at different structural levels. There was the endemic conflict (discussed in Chapter Four), implicit throughout the action but of decisive importance, between British and Ndembu political values. The withdrawal of recognition from the Mukang'ala Sub-chieftainship was connected with the impoverishment and low public morale of the community; resentment of the administration was partly expressed in complaints against the authorities, and partly by a reversion to traditional ways. There was thus a favourable climate for the sharpening of disputes between the two major local branches of the chiefly lineage. This quarrel, followed by the failure of the Nswanamundong'u branch to obtain office, was ultimately responsible for Headman Samuwinu's flight to a rival chiefdom. His flight was a major cause of the pervasive sense of failure and guilt among villagers now left without a proper traditional head. The tension over leadership was not unconnected with the exacerbated tensions between its matrilineal members and the Konkoto group with whom they had several patrilateral ties. It seemed almost fated that Kamahasanyi should undergo some kind of breakdown, since he was not only the headman's sister's son and son-in-law, but was also patrilaterally affiliated to the Konkoto group. His biography showed that he had had unusually close relations and bonds of sentiment with his patrilateral kin, among whom he had dwelt for many years in Konkoto Chiefdom itself. It would seem, too, that a temperamental factor exaggerated the conflict of loyalties between matrilineal and patrifilial norms. For Kamahasanyi appeared to have passive homosexual tendencies, which suggested that there might be a conflict between masculine and feminine strivings in his unconscious psyche. It is not perhaps too surprising that he had undergone several performances of *Ihamba*, a ritual which might be considered to provide masochistic gratifications, and to imitate, in its emissions of blood, agonized writhings, and final expulsion of an object from within the body, certain of the features of parturition.[1] I have suggested that Kamahasanyi had become, in a sense, the scapegoat for all the ills of the villagers. He occupied the social position under the greatest strain in the network of actually existing social relations. And though his behaviour was obviously a nuisance and an irritant to others, he was also an object of mutual concern and responsibility. And if he were an irritant, he also managed to build up through successive ritual accretions the pearl of matrilineal unity. The main source of tension, of course, could not be removed by these rituals. For it depended on factors beyond the control of the villagers, such as white administrative policy and population shifts brought about by the post-war cash economy. At this macro-social level, crisis might be said to be chronic and redress a mere temporary palliative. But at the level of village relations, the result of the ritual series was a strengthening of matrilineal relationships at the expense of patrilateral and other cognatic ties. When I visited the village eighteen months later, the Konkoto group had all gone elsewhere, and Kachimba's sons, Douras (F8) and Robson (F9), had made 'farms' in other parts of the chiefdom.

---

[1] It should, perhaps, be mentioned that Kamahasanyi was very sensitive to comments on his lack of children. In making a census of Nswanamundong'u Village, I found him most reluctant to admit that he had no children.

But Kamahasanyi and Maria still lived in the village, to all appearances on good terms with their kin. The village itself had shrunk in size, in consonance with the general trend towards smaller residential groups. But what is significant is the tenacity of the matrilineal bond in areas less heavily exposed to the influence of European cash incentives.

To return to the situation in Nswanamundong'u Village before the *Ihamba*, it is worth considering the particular relations between acting Headman Kachimba, Makayi (E1), head of the Konkoto group, Jackson (F1), Makayi's son, Kamahasanyi, and Maria. Kachimba, as we have seen, had for long failed to behave as Ndembu expect headmen to behave, and other village members grumbled continually about his faults of omission. Makayi was possibly Kachimba's severest critic. It is in this context that Maria's infidelity with Jackson must be examined; for Maria was Kachimba's daughter, and Jackson, Makayi's son. A few moments' reflection, given a knowledge of the nature of the social field, will show the reader how difficult it would be for Kamahasanyi to divorce Maria, and for Maria to marry Jackson. Jackson, of Standard IV education, intended to migrate to the Copperbelt at the earliest opportunity, to cash in on his literacy. If he had married Maria, she and her small daughter by a previous marriage would have gone with him, thus further depleting the membership of a village where both her parents resided. In any case it hardly ever happens that a woman's husband and ex-husband continue to reside in the same village, for such situations have been known to give rise to *crimes passionnels*. Thus, if Maria had married Jackson and stayed, Kamahasanyi would have been forced to move. This he would have been extremely reluctant to do, for he had just been virtually expelled from the village of his patrilateral kin. He might indeed have gone to live with his aged mother and younger brother in Chief Kapenda's area. His mother had remarried and was living with her present husband's matrilineal kin. Kamahasanyi did not want to live with his stepfather, and when Ihembi advised him to go and reside with his mother, he refused to do so. Ihembi, it will be remembered, had suspected Maria, in collusion with her mother Ndona, of bewitching Kamahasanyi. He claimed that when he had divined before officiating at *Ihamba*, they had imposed on the medicated water an image or reflection (*mwe-vulu*). This led him erroneously to suppose that Wilson was a sorcerer, but when he divined later in private, his apparatus pointed to female witchcraft as the cause of Kamahasanyi's weakness. I do not know whether Ihembi communicated these suspicions directly to Kamahasanyi, but he did advise him to live with his mother. Kamahasanyi determined to remain, however, and, indeed, it was greatly in the interests of village matrikin to retain him. For example, Jim, as we have seen, had reasonable expectations of becoming the next Mukang'ala, and needed all the support he could get. He it was who vehemently urged Jackson to abandon his affair with Maria, but as long as Jackson remained in the village, so long, I was told, would Kamahasanyi remain a cuckold. One of the two men, in short, has to go. It is easy to be wise after the event, but in the ordinary course of things there were clearly strong pressures on Jackson to move. For one thing, it would have been easier for him than for Kamahasanyi to find paid employment in a British territory, for he had been born, bred, and educated in Northern Rhodesia, and knew more than a smattering of English. The very factors that made his position in village life insecure favoured his incorporation in the modern urban situation. He had no matrilineal or marital ties to a village. Indeed, his link to Nswanamundong'u Village was primarily through his father Makayi, whose own residence there was on a temporary basis. Jackson did not 'belong' to the village as both Maria and Kamahasanyi did. As it happened he went to Chingola, the northernmost Copperbelt town. I met him there once by chance in the shopping centre, on my second visit to the field. I asked him whether he would soon return to Nswanamundong'u. He shook his head decisively, and said that he would always stay in town, even though at the moment he had no permanent job. Jackson was one of the *deraciné* of modern Africa, with no assured place in tribal society. We see in him the microcosmogony of a large-scale process. Those Africans who become permanently 'urbanized' may, in many cases, have been forced out of the tribal milieu by structural pressures.

Jackson's departure before the performance of the *Ihamba* did not markedly relieve the tensions of the village. For Makayi (E1) several times blamed Kachimba and some of his matrikin for the loss of his son's company and support, and Kamahasanyi was maintaining a cold demeanour towards Maria in revenge for his loss of face. On the other hand, Jackson had been popular with everyone, and many, notably Wilson, grumbled that Kamahasanyi 'spoilt' the village. His peculiarities, such as adopting a feminine hairstyle, were sarcastically commented on in the *chota*, and it was hinted that he was conceited and idle. He evidently felt himself generally disliked, withdrew more and more from public conversation and began to complain of illness. It was at this point that the cycle of ritual performances we have been considering began.

Yet, personal considerations apart, all were aware that Jackson had broken a social norm by committing adultery, and in a brazen way, with a fellow villager's wife. Moreover, the marriage he was jeopardizing was one that was firmly maintained by a plurality of social forces, as we have seen. There was a partial resolution of the marital crisis. Jackson went into 'exile'—a result analogous to 'resignation' in many of our own institutions. He was, after all, a norm-breaker. But the deeper conflicts, arising from discrepant structural principles, could not be redressed by rational or jural measures. In circumstances where schism threatens an Ndembu village, mystical causes are frequently alleged for village troubles, divination is resorted to, and rituals are performed according to the diviner's diagnosis. In this situation Makayi threatened repeatedly to leave the village, taking his wife, his remaining children, and Kapansonyi (D4) away with him, to found his own farm. Jim as often pleaded with him to remain. Kamahasanyi withdrew from this crisis, clearly divided in mind between his attachment to his patrilateral kin of Konkoto and his matrikin. His dreams about his wrathful father suggest that he felt guilty about being the occasion of distress among his paternal relatives. At the same time Kamahasanyi did not want to be estranged from his maternal kin. Maria, on the other hand, remained her old brassy, confident self, and, according to gossip continued to take lovers from among the wayfarers through Mukang'ala's realm. But she was not lacking in good nature—indeed, in this she resembled her formidable mother, Ndona—and continued to garden and cook for Kamahasanyi, with a sort of cheerful contempt.

It will have been noted that during *Ihamba*, Maria, acting under Ihembi's instructions, had been instrumental in fetching and applying medicines to Kamahasanyi to ease his violent tremors. Among these were *mudyi* leaves, the arch symbol, or meta-symbol, of matrilineal continuity in Ndembu society. Although this is a generic treatment, and not something prescribed for the individual case, on many occasions when *Ihamba* is performed, this symbol of matriliny, introduced during dramatic episodes, must refresh and revive in the patient and attenders sentiments of loyalty to their matrilineal groups. The fact that it was Kamahasanyi's *wife*, and not, as in other performances I have seen, a different category of relative, who came with the symbol of matriliny, must have suggested to those present that the continuity of the marriage was bound up with that of the matrilineal nucleus of the village. Here, in my view, we have an example of the skilled manipulation of symbols, under the authority of a professional healer, to bring about the restoration of broken or jeopardized social relationships.

It must have been clear to everyone, including Kamahasanyi, that he would not himself beget any children. After four marriages he had not begotten a single child. But for the matrilineage, it was not of the first importance that Kamahasanyi should be the genitor of any children that might be born to Maria in the future. For all her children would be theirs. But, since Kamahasanyi was their own matrilineal kinsman, they had duties towards him more deeply binding than merely jural ones; duties deriving their force from the mystique of unity through blood. In the idiom of matrilineal thinking, Kamahasanyi was 'of their womb', while Maria was 'their child, whom they had begotten'. The pair were united in primary cross-cousin marriage, a form which evoked the interest of a village matrilineage in both partners. Moreover, when a headman's own sister's son marries that headman's own daughter, this often indicates that the sister's son is considered to be his likely successor to office. Thus, if Jim were to become chief, and so be removed from the village system, there would be a strong likelihood that Kamahasanyi would succeed Kachimba as village headman. Although sterile men are not favoured as headmen, they do sometimes obtain that office, as my genealogies indicate. Sterility is less of a curse in a matrilineal than in a patrilineal society. Under matriliny a man requires a fruitful sister. That is probably why among Ndembu the shades are believed to concern themselves so intensely with female fertility, and hardly at all with male reproduction. Thus, Kamahasanyi, sterile though he was, weak, effeminate, formerly suspected of sorcery, slightly paranoid, could still hope to become a headman one day. And even if this route to status were denied him, he could turn his disabilities to account by eventually becoming a senior practitioner in one, or several, of the cults into which he had been initiated. Perhaps we have here the clue to the heavy ritualization of Ndembu society itself, for Kamahasanyi's case is only an extreme example of the conflicts inherent in that society. In the absence of satisfactory secular adjustments between male and female roles, matriliny and virilocality, and in view of the former power and present weakness of the Lunda Ndembu, the poverty of status and greatness of ambition, we might expect to find compensatory forms of unification and the displacement of ambitious strivings in the ritual sphere. We might expect to find adversity and empirical weakness exalted into qualifications for, and tokens of, ritual eminence. Over the centuries the Ndembu had been at first isolated from the main streams of Central African culture, and later harassed and persecuted by better armed and organized slave traders. Is it any wonder, then, that they so readily took flight into a world of symbolic compensations? Furthermore, relations between Lunda invaders and the indigenous Mbwela never seem to have been compounded in a stable structure. Ritual, in this society, represented a symbolic overcoming of empirical cleavages, rather than an expression or reflection of an underlying and axiomatic unity. It was an ever-reiterated aim, only partly and ephemerally realized, rather than a celebration of a constant state of affairs. Thus, Ndembu would say to me at one time: 'We Ndembu are great "doctors" (ayimbuki)'; and at another, with sour humour: 'We Ndembu are a very jealous people.' There was no notion of a permanent 'conversion' of those undergoing ritual into compassionate and charitable people; only that of a temporary victory of local unity over a besetting mutual jealousy. A battle might be won, but never the war.

VII
NKANG'A: PART ONE

INTRODUCTION

IN the foregoing analysis of the complex extended-case history of Kamahasanyi and his kin, affines, neighbours and fellow citizens, stress was laid on the organizational principles of matriliny and virilocal marriage. These principles are regarded as possessing the highest possible legitimacy, in the sense that they are positively evaluated, and accepted as valid and binding by all Ndembu. They are axioms of action in a wide variety of situations—domestic, local, kinship-dominated, economic, jural, political and recreational. What we have to enquire into in the present chapter is the principle or source of their validity.

This leads us into the major watershed division between rituals of affliction and life-crisis rituals. While the former are *ad hoc* and unpredictable in their origin and represent responses to unprecedented events, the latter accompany the passage of an individual, or a set of similarly circumstanced individuals, from one social status to another. It is on such occasions of life-crisis, when fairly elaborate *rites de passage* are performed, that the legitimacy of certain crucial principles of Ndembu society is most fully and publicly endorsed. In the rituals of affliction we see these principles under challenge; in the life-crisis rituals we see them being renewed and replenished.

The importance that matriliny, virilocality, seniority, masculinity, femininity, affinity, village solidarity and other principles quite clearly held for Kamahasanyi, Jim, Kachimba, and the rest can only be fully understood after we have closely examined the symbolism and role structure of an important life-crisis ritual. Among such rituals the attainment of adult status by a woman is of the utmost significance in a matrilineal society. I propose, therefore, to make a close examination of the Ndembu girl's puberty ritual, known as *Nkang'a*, in order to give us some understanding of the emotional power of matriliny, and the concrete symbols in which this principle is expressed.

Such an understanding will make more fully intelligible many of the relationships between persons and between ideas that we encountered in the Kamahasanyi case. It will also help us to understand the emotional impact on personalities and groups of breaches of matrilineal norms.

In making this study of *Nkang'a* our point of departure will no longer be the historical event, the breach of custom; on the contrary it will be the customary form of the ritual. The maintenance of the performance of this form has long been considered indispensable to the maintenance of the image of the Ndembu as a distinctive people. Thus in *Ihamba* we went from the particular to the general form; in *Nkang'a* we proceed from the general form to particular instances.

My wife and I attended a dozen performances of *Nkang'a* during our two periods of field-work. These took place in residential units of every type and size, from chief's capital villages to small 'farms' of four to six huts. We saw both the first and third phases, and my wife visited many novices in their seclusion huts and talked with the women who were training them. In addition I collected some numerical data about other performances I was unable to visit, and about women who gave me their ritual histories. Such data included the interrelations between the main participants, amounts of bridewealth and who gave and received it, and the like. No ritual of affliction is performed nearly as frequently as *Nkang'a*. The extreme accessibility of *Nkang'a* made it possible to establish to some extent what was normative and invariant, and the degree of variance. My own impression was that there was less variation in the ritual details than in other kinds of ritual, probably because it was performed frequently and publicly.

A prominent feature that distinguishes it from the puberty rituals of most Central African peoples is that it is regularly performed *before* the first onset of the menses.[1] Its main

[1] In this respect Ndembu differ from the neighbouring Luvale, where the onset of the menses is taken as a sign that a girl is ready for the *wali* puberty rites (White, C. M. N., *Tradition and Change in Luvale Marriage*, Rhodes–Livingstone Paper No. 34 (1962), p. 2). The importance of first menstruation as an indication of a girl's readiness to undergo puberty rites is also stressed for the Ngulu of Tanzania by Beidelman in 'Pig (Guluwe): an Essay on Ngulu Sexual Symbolism and Ceremony', *Southwestern Journal of Anthropology*, Vol. 20, No. 4 (Winter, 1964). Here the 'wild dangerous' aspects of femininity are stressed in connection with dangerous, unclean, and lethal aspects of blood, especially menstrual blood. The

biological referent is the development of the breasts, and not menstruation. In Ndembu ritual idiom Nkang'a is a 'white', not a 'red' ritual, and, furthermore, a ritual of 'milk', rather than 'blood'. This is demonstrated also in the symbolism. It is when a girl's breasts are beginning to ripen that her parents think of 'passing her through' Nkang'a. Until fairly recently Nkang'a continued into the marriage ritual; its last episodes overlapped with the beginning of marriage. This meant that girls tended to marry rather earlier than in tribes where puberty rites followed first menstruation. Betrothal, as in many other Central African tribes, often took place early, when the girl was seven or eight. But she did not live with her husband until she had passed Nkang'a, although he might visit her frequently, and even have intercrural. intercourse with her. But if he made her pregnant before Nkang'a, her parents could take legal action against him and obtain substantial damages. On the other hand, no severe supernatural penalty was believed to be incurred by a woman who married without having undergone Nkang'a. Among the Nyakyusa, for example, it was said than an uninitiated woman would become mad, contract diseases, or remain infertile, if she slept with her husband before undergoing her puberty rites. I knew several women, most of them brought up as orphans by missionaries, who had not undergone Nkang'a. They were said to 'feel ashamed' because of this, but all were married and had at least one child. They were said to be 'not fully Lunda'. Nkang'a is regarded as giving a girl a better chance of becoming fertile, but Ndembu recognize that it does not guarantee fertility. They say that the shades are pleased if a girl has Nkang'a, and may be angry if she has not passed through the rites, rendering her temporarily sterile. Yet the Ndembu recognize, in their practical way, that though some have not been initiated, they have still had children. Others again have undergone Nkang'a and have remained barren. This may be modern scepticism, but I have the impression that even in the past the Ndembu possessed an

---

Bemba cisungu rites, too, are performed following a girl's first period (A. I. Richards, Chisungu, London: Faber and Faber (1956), p. 54). This is also the case among the patrilineal Nyakyusa of Tanzania (Monica Wilson, Rituals of Kinship among the Nyakyusa, London: Oxford University Press, for the International African Institute (1957), p. 87), and many other Bantu-speaking peoples.

earthy common sense, regarding ritual (much as we regard medical treatment) as benefiting, but not ensuring, health.

Nkang'a brings to light a contradiction between fundamental principles of Ndembu social organization; the contradiction between matrilineal descent and virilocal marriage as determinants of residential affiliation. A young woman at puberty, who is at once the 'growing tip of a matrilineage', to paraphrase Professor Fortes, and the potential nucleus of a matricentric family living virilocally, is indeed a point of stress in the social structure, the 'sorest point' of all (see Fig. VI, p. 206). But both principles of social organization have, in fact, coexisted in Ndembu society from the remote past, and customs have been elaborated to mitigate and exclude their conflicts in many sectors of social life. A girl's first marriage, however, brings out their open incompatibility. Now, whenever one finds the danger of manifest discrepancy between social processes, one tends to find ritualization. The paramount values of the society are symbolically asserted against the dividing tendencies inherent in its structure.

Nkang'a has three phases: (1) *Kwing'ija*, or 'causing to enter'; (2) *kunkunka*, or seclusion in a grass hut (*nkunka*); and (3) *kwidisha*, or 'bringing out'.

KWING'IJA: THE RITE OF SEPARATION

The first phase may conveniently be regarded as falling into fourteen successive episodes. Before *Nkang'a* begins, beer is taken to the local chief or sub-chief, as in the boys' circumcision ritual, and his permission to hold the rites is obtained.

Episode One: The Exchange of Arrows

On the eve of *kwing'ija* proper, the bridegroom (*kalemba*) and the novice's mother (*nyakankang'a*) exchange arrows. The bridegroom gives another arrow to the novice's instructress (*nkong'u*), together with a calabash of beer. The instructress that night keeps the arrow in her sleeping quarters. Alternatively, the parents of the couple (who call one another reciprocally *nkulanami*) exchange arrows when the marriage has first been arranged. These arrows are used in the ritual.

The bridegroom's arrow, called *nsewu*, stands for the bridewealth he will pay when his bride comes out of seclusion. This bridewealth is also called *nsewu*. In the symbolism of Ndembu ritual an arrow stands for masculinity, while the curved bow stands for femininity. The arrow is held in the right hand, which also stands for masculinity, while the bow is usually held in the left hand, which represents femininity. We shall meet with several instances of the bow-femininity equation during the seclusion phase of *Nkang'a*.

In passing over this arrow the bridegroom signifies to the instructress that he is empowered by the novice's mother to ask her to prepare the girl ritually and physically for her new role as wife and mother.

Episode Two: Village Headman's Invocation to the Ancestral Shades

Not long after sunset that night, the headman of the village at which the novice (*kankang'a*) is to be initiated goes to the village *nyiyombu* tree-shrines with the novice and her mother. The novice kneels with her open hands on the ground facing the shrines. The headman sits on a stool facing the shrines. He takes a tiny piece of cassava root, places it at the foot of a *muyombu* tree, and invokes the shades.[1] Here is a prayer I recorded at Mukanza Village:

'*Eyi Kahali Webala mukwashuku iwu muntu ashakami chachiwahi, bayi*

'O you Kahali Webala [a former headman of the village] help this person, that she may remain well, not

wakata nehi-chatama. Enu akishi twinki mbiji twendi chachiwahi

be ill—that is bad. O ye shades, give us meat that we may walk well

mwisang'a twani mbiji. Tunalembi tutiyi kuwaha. Iwu mwana

in the bush and find meat. We are contrite that we may be happy. This child

ashakami kunkunka watoha kanda wakediki wakosaku. Tunasakwili. Twinka mbiji mwani.'

may she stay fat in the seclusion hut, not come out thin. We offer thanks. Please give us meat.'

---

[1] Audrey Richards records that in the first rite of the Bemba girls' puberty ceremony, known as *cisungu*, the headman of the village 'called the blessing of his ancestral spirits'. *Chisungu*, op. cit., p. 63.

Indigenous Exegesis

In other villages we frequently heard the phrase: '*Twinki mbiji yatunyama bayi mbiji yawantuku*', 'Give us the meat of animals, not the meat of human beings.' This means: 'Protect the village from necrophagous sorcery and witchcraft.' Ndembu believe that whenever many people are gathered together, sorcerers, witches, and their familiars mingle with them, ready to profit from quarrels and fights which activate their power to do harm.

One prayer I heard, asked for the specific protection of the shades against sorcerers who might want to kill the novice 'to make *nyalumaya*' (*nakupanda nyalumaya*). *Nyalumaya*[1] is a figurine representing a novice with nascent breasts, and is called by the name of a young girl, killed by 'medicine' to activate it. It is also known sometimes as *kankang'a*, 'the novice'. The girl's blood is smeared on the figurine, and mixed with medicine pressed into a hole in its head. The medicine makes it 'walk about'. *Nyalumaya* is equipped by its owner with a knife, and sent out to kill his personal enemies. It is believed to be the most dangerous kind of sorcery-figurine. Sandombu gave me another version of how it is made. '*Nyalumaya*', he said, 'is made in a *muyombu* tree, perhaps it is carved from one. A figurine is made; it is given the blood and milk of three or five goats. When it is finished, medicine is put in it to make it move. It is set free in the village, that it may catch a person in his hut. If anyone sees it he will die, he will not live, that is certain! Every day you must take *mukula* gum[2] which causes nose-bleed, so that people will think that that person has died of "bleeding by day" [*musong'u wamwana*, literally, 'disease of the day or the sun']. But he is not really dead.[3] Nyalumaya herself has taken him to be killed.' Other villagers told me that by 'three or five goats', Sandombu (himself suspected of being a sorcerer) was speaking in innuendo of a girl novice (*kankang'a*), just as the term 'black goat' means a child slain to provide a patch of skin to heal a man 'shot in *ilomba* [form]'. The *ilomba*, as I have

---

[1] See also Melland, F., *In Witchbound Africa*, London: Seely Service & Co. (1923) for an account of *nyalumaya* sorcery.

[2] Probably smeared on the figurine.

[3] i.e., the body men see is not the victim's real body, but its simulacrum, manufactured by sorcery and substituted to deceive people. The real body will be eaten by witches, sorcerers, and their familiars.

mentioned, is a human-faced snake familiar. If it is wounded or killed by magical means, its owner suffers a like fate. But magical wounds can be healed as described.

The invocation I heard asks for ancestral protection against (male) sorcerers who want to kill the novice to make a new *Nyalumaya* familiar. Invocations of this sort are not uncommon. Indeed, the *Kaneng'a* ritual is devoted to the exorcism of witchcraft-sorcery familiars. Witchcraft beliefs and ritual directed against witchcraft are, in fact, an integral part of the religious system.

After invoking, the headman picks up the piece of cassava and places it in the mouth of the novice, who swallows it. This ends the episode. Sometimes the cassava root is omitted, and white clay is used in the orthodox way. The headman, after invoking, with the powdered clay draws three lines from the base of the *muyombu* tree—one towards the novice's mother. Then he first anoints himself with the clay by the orbits and above the navel, and then anoints the novice by the orbits.

Comments

All informants agree that only men can invoke the shades at this episode. Usually it is the village headman who prays, whatever may be his relationship to the novice. But sometimes the novice's father may invoke his own matrilineal shades, either after the headman or by himself if the headman is absent. He can even invoke them at a *muyombu* tree planted on behalf of one of the novice's mother's matrilineal ancestors.

The invocation at *Nkang'a* is similar in form to that made before the boys' circumcision rites, when the sponsoring village headman and lodge officials invoke their shades for the protection of all persons entrusted to their care during the course of the whole ritual.

But in *Nkang'a* the novice is felt to be not only in personal danger but also dangerous to her kin; for if she breaks one of her taboos, a kinsman is thought to fall sick, or even to die. In his address the headman begs the shades to protect his villagers. If some are offended—for example, because he has failed to mention their names while invoking them—they may not give their mystical protection, and wicked persons will have full scope to wreak destruction. Tensions and hidden conflicts are disclosed by this address, since the witches and sorcerers are thought usually to be kinsfolk of those most closely concerned with the ritual, and to be able to utilize the situation to pay off old scores. There is in this invocation, then, a tacit recognition that social life in a village is full of hidden jealousies and struggles. I believe that there is also the implication that a ritual subject, such as a young girl on the verge of sexual life and made physically passive by ritual custom, stimulates, in the words of Freud, 'both desire and aggression by her special helplessness'. She is a danger to the cohesion of the group, since she arouses temptation. This is partly why she is tabooed and has to keep taboos. The invocation, too, suggests ambivalence in the attitude of the living towards the dead, who stand for traditional authority. The dead may bestow benefits, in the way of game-meat, an appropriate symbol for all good things in a hunting society; but they may also allow inauspicious things to happen, such as the death of village members. Piety and resentment are thus present in equal proportions in this address.

White clay and cassava (usually cassava meal) may be used interchangeably in situations of prayer. An important role is played by cassava in the rite of *Chihamba*.[1] Both symbols, of course, refer to the basic theme of 'whiteness' that pervades Ndembu ritual and, indeed, their whole cosmology.

Episode Three: Sacralizing the Mudyi Tree (Ku-bola Mudyi)

After the invocation, the novice's mother leads her by the hand into the bush. The instructress (*nkong'u*) follows them. The novice walks humbly and modestly, holding her hands before her eyes so that she may not see the *mudyi* tree. They go to a short *mudyi* sapling, previously selected by the instructress, usually a short distance outside the village. They circle the bush in single file three times, singing in a high soft tone, the novice between her mother and the instructress, and then return to the village. That night the novice must fast, or at least eat only very sparingly. There is no taboo against her parents' having intercourse. This, we were told, is because there is no danger of the novice dying or being severely wounded in the course of the ritual. These considerations are responsible for the interdiction on parental intercourse at the boys' circumcision rites.

[1] See my *Chihamba, the White Spirit*, R. L. I. Paper No. 33, p. 56.

Indigenous Exegesis

According to Manyosa, my wife's best informant on *Nkang'a*, the women go round the *mudyi* tree, 'to take away *andumba* witchcraft familiars and bad things, for next day many people

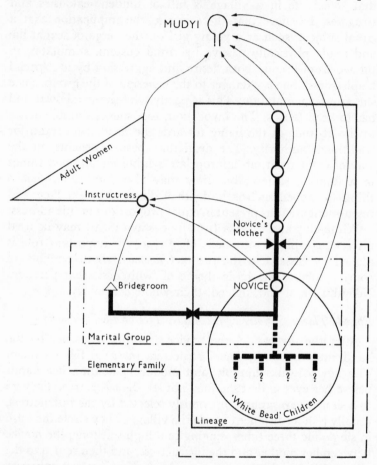

Fig. VI. The groups, categories and relationships associated with the *mudyi* symbol.

will come and bring their familiars with them; the instructress takes only the novice and her mother with her because you cannot be sure there are no witches present when there are many people.' She said that the act of flattening the grass (*ku-bola*) was to 'make the *mudyi* taboo' (*nakujilika* or *nakujilisha mudyi*). It was now the 'elder' (*mukulumpi*) of *Nkang'a* (i.e., the dominant symbol). In other words, they literally 'wove a circle round it thrice' to make a sacred area where the rites might be performed.

I have presented at length elsewhere some indigenous interpretations of the *mudyi* tree,[1] perhaps the pivotal symbol of the whole Ndembu ritual system. It stands for the 'tribe' or 'tribal custom' (*muchidi wetu*, 'our kind'), for matriliny, for the novice's own matrilineage, for the mother-child relationship, for life (*wumi*), for learning (*ku-diza*), for women's breasts and breast-milk, and for initiation. At one stage in *Nkang'a*, we shall see that *mudyi* leaves are said to represent the children desired for the novice. I add here a few further interpretations from various ritual contexts. For example, in the *Wubwang'u* ritual performed for a mother of twins there is an esoteric episode in which two saplings are bound together over a stream to form an arch. One is of the *muhotuhotu* species,[2] here representing 'man' (*iyala*), and the other is of *mudyi*, in this context representing 'woman'. The patient stands on a log in the stream (near its source), and the senior male practitioner blows *mpemba* powder, here representing 'semen', over her, while the senior female practitioner blows powdered *mukundu* (red clay) over her, standing for 'the blood'. *Mudyi*, according to many informants on the spot, stood for 'fruitful womanhood' in this usage.

In the *Musolu* ritual to bring on delayed rains, a miniature bow of *mudyi* wood stands for 'the procreativeness of women' (*lusemu lwawambanda*).

I was also told by a group of women in informal discussion that 'only when a baby has drunk much milk will it have a

[1] 'Ritual Symbolism, Morality and Social Structure among the Ndembu', *R.L.I. Journal* xxx (December 1961), pp. 5–9.

'Three Symbols of Passage in Ndembu Circumcision Rites' in *Essays on the Ritual of Social Relations*, Ed. Gluckman, M. U. P. (1962), pp. 131–7.

White, *Tradition and Change in Luvale Marriage*, op. cit., p. 2, notes that the Luvale may select one of several species of trees for this function, including the *muulya* (= *mudyi* in Chindembu). He relates this to the greater importance of choice and experimentation in Luvale culture.

[2] See above, pp. 17–20, for other meanings of this tree. Bemba, during *cisungu*, stick a *mulombwa* tree in the ground and bend it over to form an arch, while a branch of the *mwenge* tree is crossed over it at right angles to form a double hoop. The *mwenge* is 'a female tree, representing the pliancy of the woman', while the *mulombwa*, a hardwood with red juice represents (1) a male tree; (2) a lion; and (3) a chief. (*Chisungu*, op. cit., pp. 94–96.)

shade (*mukishi*) when it dies. That is why a tiny infant is buried under a *mudyi* tree, so that it may have milk and be born again.'

Fasting

The novice does not eat until the end of the *kwing'ija* dance. This is common practice in ritual. The candidates in *Chihamba* did not eat during the day of chasing. Nor did the *Nkula* patients. A novice's kinswoman explained her fast at *Nkang'a* by saying that it would help her 'to give birth on our (i.e. the matrilineage's) behalf'.[1] Others said that it was part of her 'testing' (*kweseka*) or 'ordeal'.

The Instructress

The *Nkong'u*, or instructress, may be a parents' friend or a relative of the novice. Table 5, p. 307 in Appendix C, shows that out of 36 instructresses in the sample, 10 were called 'older sister' by the novice, and 5 were called 'cross-cousin', making a total of 15 kinswomen of the same genealogical generation; 6 were primary or classificatory 'grandmothers' of the novice (including one own mother's own mother and 4 classificatory mother's mothers). There were 4 affines of the same generation, linked through the novices' brothers, and 3 affines of the same generation, linked through their bridegrooms. Only 5 belonged to the senior adjacent generation, and these were remote kin; 4 of them, in fact, being of slave descent, and slavery neutralizes kinship. Only one instructress could not be linked genealogically with the novice in any way. Thus 30 out of 36 instructresses, or 83·3 per cent, belonged to the same 'linked-generation' category as the novice. There is a rule that a uterine sister should not act as instructress, but we find that in one case a full sister, and in another a uterine sister, undertook this role. According to the rule also, a novice's own mother's mother should not be her *nkong'u*. Nevertheless, I have recorded an instance of this. Anyone who collects quantitative data in the field must expect to find such anomalies, when custom is checked against social reality, as Malinowski pointed out long ago. Few rules are fully observed in any society, and many rules of custom are broken with impunity.

[1] Fasting during labour is the rule.

The Luvale term for the instructress in the girl's puberty rites is *chilombola*,[1] the term, in fact, that is applied to a 'shepherd', a circumcised man who looks after novices, in the circumcision rituals both of Luvale and Ndembu. The instructress's function, however, corresponds more closely with that of the *mfumwa tubwiku*, 'the lodge instructor' in *Mukanda*, than with that of 'shepherd' in these rites. One interesting difference is that in the circumcision rites the instructor may have sons in the lodge, but there is a strong taboo against mothers acting as instructresses of their novice-daughters. Ndembu say that this is because the instructress teaches her charge many of the actual techniques of sexual intercourse, and it would be 'shameful' for a mother to do this. The main instruction received by boys in *Mukanda* is in tribal lore, hunting and fishing, and general moral and social behaviour. Where sexual instruction is given, it is not given by a novice's own father but by other lodge officials, and his own father need not be present. Among the Ndembu, the mother may not be brought directly into contact with her children's sexual activities. Thus, one reason given me for keeping the mothers away from the scene of circumcision was that 'it would be a matter of great shame' for them.

The Taboo on the Novice's Looking at Mudyi

Two explanations were advanced for this taboo. Several informants, including Manyosa, said that 'the instructress might die if the novice saw *mudyi* at *ku-bola mudyi*'. These informants agreed with the interpretation offered by Muchona and many women for the general taboo laid on the novice against looking at *mudyi* in subsequent episodes: 'If she looked, if she uncovered her eyes, she would become stupid. She is like a child at school when she sleeps under *mudyi*, she has not yet slept properly with her husband. If she sees *mudyi* she would become an idiot [*wasupa*].' This statement recalls the taboo laid on the boys at *Mukanda* against seeing the *mudyi* under which the leading novices were circumcised. But it is not

---

[1] See White, C. M. N., *Tradition and Change in Luvale Marriage*, op. cit., p. 2. White notes for the Luvale that, once chosen, an instructress must abstain from sexual intercourse, otherwise the girl to be instructed will become mad or frigid. I failed to collect information upon this point among the Ndembu.

exegesis, merely a statement of the nature of the mystical sanction.[1]

Episode Four: Before Sunrise on the Day of Kwing'ija

About half an hour before sunrise, the instructress and a few close matrilineal kinswomen of the novice—but *not* the novice's mother—wake the village with a shout. They go to the *mudyi* by the nearest village path. The novice goes to the *mudyi* alone, not taking any path but directly through the bush. Some informants say that the novice should properly be carried to the *mudyi*. She wears a small cloth only, just concealing the pudenda, and covers her head with the blanket that will soon be spread over her. Her mother has removed her daughter's usual cloth and will wear it herself.

The instructress kindles a fire near the *mudyi* with peeled, white, dry sticks (usually of *mweya* wood), collected the previous night after the *ku-bola mudyi* rite. She must not use glowing cinders from any other fire, but must light it afresh—nowadays with store matches. At first the novice sits by the fire in silence, looking into the flames. She keeps her head covered with the blanket by holding her clenched fists against her temples. When the fire is burning well, she goes into the bush to relieve herself, for she will not get another chance until sundown. Then she sits on an antelope's hide, usually a duiker's. This must not come from a striped or spotted antelope.

The women circle the *mudyi* twice, singing loudly in the lower register:

'*A kwinka Nkang'o,*
'They are giving you Nkang'a,

Wunakuli mwanami,
You have grown up, my child,

Wunatembeki wakababa.'
[When] you have passed puberty you will be pregnant.'

The novice herself takes part vigorously in the singing. She is joined for a time by several of the younger women who sit round the fire.

---

[1] See my essay 'Symbols in Ndembu Ritual' in *The Forest of Symbols*, op. cit., p. 38 for a discussion of the problem of 'blocked exegesis'.

Indigenous Exegesis

Nakedness of Novice. The novice wears only a small piece of cloth 'on the face' (*kumesu*), i.e. on the pubes in case, according to women informants, anyone should see them if her blanket were removed accidentally during the dance. This would render her barren. Later, in the seclusion hut, she must remain completely naked, 'like the novices', said Muchona, 'before the *chikula* rites of *Mukanda*, the boys' circumcision ritual.'

The New Fire. 'The fire of *mudyi* [*ijiku damudyi*]', said the women, 'resembles the fire of *Mukanda* in that it must not go out all day. Should it by chance go out, this would be unlucky, and another one may not be kindled. The firewood must be white, preferably of *mweya* wood, for *Nkang'a* is a very heavy ritual [*chidyika chasweja kulema*], like those of the hunting cults, *Wuyang'a* and *Wubinda*, where *mweya* firewood is also used. *Mweya* wood is to cause strength [*kukolisha*].' The dryness of the wood, in fact, represents 'strength' (*wukolu*).

The Antelope Skin. The skin most favoured is that of the duiker, though reedbuck and roan antelope skins may be used. Striped and spotted skins, like that of the bushbuck (*mbala*) are taboo, for they might 'give leprosy'.[1] The hides of wild, never domestic, animals must be used. This is because, as Muchona said, 'hunting is important for us, the Lunda'. In the past, he said, the Ndembu of both sexes only wore the skins of wild animals. In the hunting cults, he continued, hunter-candidates wear duiker skins because 'they please the shades of hunters'.

Ritual Silence. Chief Kapenda told me that any woman who has had a sacred fire lit for her by a 'doctor' or adept, whether at initiation or in a ritual of affliction, must be silent. This is because 'spirits do not like to hear people talking loudly'. Silence is a sign of respect, the chief said, both towards those in authority and village elders. Respect is sometimes expressed by snapping the thumb and index finger together (*ku-jiloka*), connected with *ku-jila*, 'to be taboo'. Thus, when a woman 'who has a shade' (*mukishi*) approaches the fire made for her to cook on during seclusion, she must '*jiloka*'. When a chief has intercourse with his wife, she must not speak and must '*jiloka*' afterwards.

[1] Lepers' skins are streaked or spotted with the disease.

Episode Five: Rousing the Villagers by Families

After singing the close matrilineal kinswomen return to the village to rouse the people. First they go to the novice's mother's hut—usually the father is there too—proceed to the back of it, stand close to the wall facing it, and sing into the rafters. Next they go to the headman's hut and stand singing in a row before the door. After this they go to all the other huts in the order of seniority of their owners. They then return to the *mudyi*. They sing the song also sung by novices at *Mukanda*:

'*Chekeli chekeli che-e wadyila muteng'u kwachanyi.*'

'Chekeli, chekeli, cries the drongo bird, it is dawn.'

In effect the men are boisterously roused by the women.

Episode Six: The Preparation of the Ifwilu

As the sun rises the instructress takes the antelope skin and spreads it out close to the *mudyi* tree. The trampled site is now known as *ifwilu* or *chifwilu*, 'the dying-place', or *ihung'u*, 'the suffering-place', terms also applied to the site of circumcision in *Mukanda*. The novice's blanket is then spread over the skin. The elder women carry the novice from the fire and place her on her left side, legs bent back to the buttocks, on the blanket. Her hands are laid on her temples. The blanket is usually provided by the bridegroom. When she is wrapped up out of sight in it, the women hoot in praise—'*Ove-e, ove-e*'—beating their hands on their lips (*ku-bula nyingula*). Sometimes two blankets are used to tuck her up in, and a cloth is provided for a pillow.

The instructress now addresses the novice, telling her that she must not move all day. Were she seen to do so, the women would press their thumbnails into her whole body—a punishment called *ku-jinda*. Even though she may be hungry and feel stiff, she must lie silently without stirring. She must remain covered; for if she looks at the *mudyi* she would become 'witless' (*wasupa*), and would never bear any children.

The instructress then takes the arrow given her by the bridegroom, and inserts it into the ground among the roots of the *mudyi*. She drapes a string of white beads[1] over its feathered end.

---

[1] White beads also have significance among the Bemba and are associated with a major tree symbol at puberty. At the 'rite of the honouring of the *musuku* tree', which Richards describes as 'one of the symbols of womanhood', Bemba women tie two small rings of white beads round twigs of this tree (*Chisungu*, op cit., p. 72).

Then she announces that 'the arrow has come from so-and-so who is going to marry the novice.' He has also provided the beads.

Indigenous Exegesis

'*The Place of Suffering*'. One informant discussed the concept *ihung'u* (*chihung'u*) as follows: '*Chihung'u* (or the plural *yihung'u*) is any sort of trouble (*malwa*). It may be given by a shade (*mukishi*) or a disease (*musong'u*). It may be given because a patient (*muyeji*) has only gone through the *kulembeka* rites of a ritual of affliction, and has not undergone *kutumbuka*.' *Kutumbuka* represents the final stage of a ritual of affliction, such as *Nkula* or *Mukala*, and is usually accompanied by a great public dance (see pp. 70–71). To have 'passed' *kutumbuka* gives a doctor higher status than to have 'passed' *kulembeka*; thus the *chihung'u* ('suffering' or 'affliction') may be regarded, painful though it is, as a mark of election, the sign of a shade's esteem and wish to make the patient a member of its cult. The term *ihung'u* may also be applied to a person who has been 'caught' by a shade: the afflicted one himself. It may also signify the site where novices experience ordeal in the initiation rites of the *Mung'ongi* funerary association. *Chihung'u* is used to denote the hut of the principal patient in the *Chihamba* cult ritual. Finally it is sometimes applied to the place where a woman is in labour. *Chihung'u* is a multivocal concept, connoting such qualities as 'ordeal', 'admonition', 'birth pangs', 'punishment', 'initiation', 'change of status', 'election', and 'trouble'. There is in it the notion that it is right and proper for the novice to suffer before she is admitted into the moral community of adult, married women.

'*The Place of Dying*'. The novice is regarded as someone 'dying'. She must not speak, her fists are clenched—and must not be opened that day—and she may not eat. For this reason she is sometimes spoken of as 'closed up'. Nor may she be seen· by men. She is also separated from her parents during the day-long ritual. Like a baby or a corpse, she lies in the foetal position, wrapped in a blanket.

The White Beads. White beads play a most important role in the novice's life and in different episodes of her *Nkang'a*. It is indeed difficult, therefore, to avoid anticipating what is to come; for like other Ndembu ritual symbols, their meaning in any given episode is partly determined by their meaning and function in other episodes and even rituals. It can be said without exaggeration that in any given context the total meaning of a symbol is felt to be penumbrally present, even though only a single aspect of its total meaning may be stressed in a particular episode.

The white beads are described in everyday usage as *wusang'a watooka*, but in *Nkang'a* are called *kasenzi*. Strictly speaking this term refers to a miniature bow (*kawuta*), made of *mudyi* wood and inserted inside the apex (*muntung'u*) of the novice's hut.[1] The bow is entwined with white beads, and it is the combination of bow and beads to which *kasenzi* properly refers. *Kasenzi* is a symbol which itself signifies an entire class of symbols, and may be described, therefore, as a 'meta-symbol'. This class comprises sacred musical bows, each of which is called *mankunkundimba*, which are played by novices during seclusion to make known their wants and summon attention. We shall consider these presently. In the past the white beads were hung around an arrow in the course of a rite called *chikosa* (or *kukosa*) *kasenzi*, purifying the *kasenzi*. This rite, accompanied by a night-long public dance, took place about midway through the period of seclusion. In the words of one informant: 'At *kukosa kasenzi* they put white beads on an arrow (*nsewu*), to show that the novice was well washed with medicine, would not grow thin, and was pure (*watooka*), free from *chisaku* (evil magic) or witchcraft/sorcery (*wuloji*). After *ku-kosa kasenzi*, she can play the musical bow, which is an instrument with many strings. She is now an elder (*mukulumpi*) and purified (*wunatooki*). If someone took a little piece of *kasenzi* and was caught, the novice's mother could accuse him or her of sorcery or witchcraft. She would say, "This *kasenzi* is kept here so that my child may have children." *Kasenzi* means the production of children (*lusemu*). The beads represent the children the novice will produce.'

Later, at *kwidisha*, when the novice leaves seclusion and dances in public, these white beads are first hung in the smoke of her private fire, then put in water 'to wash them fully white'. Then they are hidden beneath a packing of red earth covering

[1] Among the Bemba, the groom's sister, during the *cisungu* ceremony, at one rite, 'carries a toy bow and arrows, wears red powder (*nkula*), and carries a piece of ant-hill to represent a load' (*Chisungu*, op. cit., pp. 73–74). Compare also the dress of the *Nkula* patients in this book, p. 70.

the novice's head. The mud pack is afterwards criss-crossed by several strings of coloured beads. If the white beads can be seen by other men, it is said that the bridegroom (*kalemba*) will become very angry, for the beads represent the children he will beget.

On the morning after the first night of marriage, if she has been satisfied by her husband, the novice shakes her head vigorously, pulls the *kasenzi* beads out of her hair, and scatters the red 'mud pack' on the sleeping mat, in her husband's presence.

The beads are then taken to the novice's mother, who keeps them for the *Kumutena* ('mentioning him') rite, which is performed when it is certain that the young wife is pregnant for the first time. In the course of this rite, these same white beads are hung around her neck, 'to help her to grow big.' Then they are hung round her stomach, 'on the liver' (*hamuchima*), together with two cowries, which represent here the female genitalia. Two cowries are used 'to represent two children, not just one child'.[1]

Later, when the young wife bears her child, these white beads will be fastened round its wrist.[2] If, during labour, the child's arm should appear before its head, the white beads should be placed in the hand—'then the baby will go back inside, turn round, and be born the right way round.'

But this does not end the tale of the white beads, first given by a woman's bridegroom for her puberty ritual. If her husband should die the widow must give his female kin some white beads, including *kasenzi* beads, to wear around their necks. This is regarded not only as a sign of good will towards her affines, but also as a recognition of her husband's role in the production of her children.

The beads, then, represent the mutual fertility of a woman and her first husband. He is the arrow, she the bow, and the beads themselves are their children.

[1] See Nkula song '*Mwana moye . . .*,' p. 66.

[2] Beidelman records that among the Ngulu of Tanganyika, also a matrilineal people, 'white beads are placed on an infant's neck to celebrate its normal development and, if parents fear that their child may abnormally cut its upper teeth first and thus have to be slain, a doctor may place a wooden fork decorated with white beads upon the infant's gums to counteract this abnormal, disorderly development' ('Pig', op. cit., p. 376).

The Taboo against the Novice's Making Any Sound. Manyosa told
my wife an alarming tale which girls learn just before they
become novices, emphasizing the high value attached to lying
still. It runs: 'Once upon a time, a novice was passing through
her *kwing'ija* rites at the *mudyi* tree. Towards noon, the women
saw her moving under the blanket. But they just went on dancing. Again, she seemed to struggle, but they said: "No, no, we
must just go on dancing." But when they lifted her up later
in the day, they were astonished to see that a chameleon
[*ilong'olu*] had crept into her nose and entered her brain.
Blood was pouring out. She was quite dead. Then there was
wailing and weeping—at *Nkang'a* too! *Nkang'a* became
Chibimbi, a mourning can..., a time for crying.' Manyosa
thought that it was admirable of the wretched girl to refrain
from crying out. But there would seem to be also an implicit
criticism of the women for just enjoying themselves and not
seeing what was the matter. And also for not making sure that
the site was swept clear of pests and insects (*tububu*—a term also
applied to witchcraft familiars).

Episode Seven: The Women's Dance (Until Noon)

Dancing now begins. A girl takes an axe and removes bushes
and stumps in a ring around the *mudyi*. Any *mudyi* roots cleared
during this operation are heaped against the *mudyi* tree in the
centre. In a short while most of the women of the sponsoring
village have assembled; these are usually close maternal or
paternal kin and affines of the novice. They dance slowly in
a circle round the blanket-shrouded novice (see Plate 7*a*).
Within the ring there are commonly two women, who lead the
singing alternately. They dance on either side of the girl,
regularly meeting near the *mudyi* and clapping all four flat
upright palms together (see Plate 7*b*). 'To lead the singing' is
ku-fukishila, to reply in chorus is *kwiteja*, literally 'to agree'.
The singing is loud and aggressive. As the morning advances,
women from neighbouring villages, and even from afar—
kinswomen of the novice who have been informed of the performance by messenger—arrive, many with their babies in
carrying-cloths on their backs, and join the stamping, whirling
circle. The men usually gather in the village shelter and drink
beer. They always make comments most critical of the female

PLATE 7

a. Dawn dance of senior women of novice's lineage round blanket-wrapped novice. Note *mudyi* sapling and bridegroom's arrow.

b. Women lampoon men in song before the novice is turned over.

PLATE 8

b. 'The little drum of thirst'—the only Ndembu drum played regularly by the women.

a. The *chifukaminu* turns the novice at noon.

sex at such times. They are not allowed to dance with the women before noon,[1] although a few rash spirits or buffoons may attempt to do so, miming the women's gestures on the outside of the dance circle. In two different areas I have seen a male transvestite at a performance of *Nkang'a*—both men were said to have 'an inborn propensity' (*chisemwa*) for doing this sort of thing. Dressed as women, they stood near the dancers but did not take part in the dance. The behaviour of these men was said to be idiosyncratic, but when, on the other hand, women wore items of male apparel or mimed male activities in their dances this was said to be 'according to custom'. For example, women often wear men's hats, and solo dancers imitate old men, feigning to have beards and limping with uneven steps. Male cripples and blind men are allowed to sing in the women's circle at this phase in the rites.

Many of the songs mock at marriage and many praise adultery. Some are extraordinarily elliptical and full of topical allusions. Here are a few:

(*a*) '*Nenzang'a neyi nayimbili,*
    'I have come with you to sing to you,
    Kanyinki mukanda,
    Give me a letter [i.e. a receipt for divorce],
    Wumu mukanda chaseka dehi.'
    One letter [divorce papers], [for] one is fed up [with marriage].'

(*b*) '*Tambikenu Kasong'u,*
    'Call Kasong'u [a woman's name],
    Iyayi! kumwinkamu,
    O mother! putting him in! [i.e. she is ready for adultery, an informant explained]
    Mwana waluwa kuwusang'a,
    The girl is making a mistake at the beads [refers to the string of beads worn by women round the waist; i.e. she is committing adultery]
    Eye chingongu chahaChikinta.'
    O the stick for beating the *Chikinta* drum [i.e. the penis].'

---

[1] Richards mentions that Bemba women drove 'a passing man away with mock abuse', during *cisungu*, at the making of the *mbusa* (small pottery emblems), during which the solidarity of women was strongly evident (*Chisungu*, op. cit., p. 69).

(c) '*Fumaku wuluwi kushalili yamweni.*'
    'Leave marriage to stay by yourself.'

This last song was rather curiously explained by one informant to mean, 'Depart from marriage with a polygynous husband; let the favourite wife live alone with her husband.' But it was generally taken as a recommendation of the life of a prostitute.

Other songs about polygynous marriage are highly ironical—as so many African songs are. Take this one, for example.

(d) '*Enu akwetu mumbu hanoshi,*
    'You, my friends, the jackal has called,
    Enu akwetu kuhadyikila kwenu,
    You, my friends, living in your co-marriage,
    Enu akwetu muhadyikila sehenu.'
    You, my friends, who are co-wives [of one husband], laugh!'

Mention of the jackal implies witchcraft, for the jackal is one of the forms assumed by women's necrophagous familiars. The song suggests that one of the co-wives has been bewitched to death by the other.

(e) '*Kubobola kuhadyikila kwenu.*'
    'There is loud chattering in co-marriage' (i.e. 'because of jealousy', one informant said).

(f) '*Eyi welili neyi wayobolang'a, iwu mutong'a wenzeshimu.*'
    'You did [something] when you played with my vulva, here is the *mutong'a* basket, fill it up.'

This was paraphrased by my informants as: 'You said you would beget children when you married me. I do my best. Here is the basket, fill it with children.' When the women sing this song, they gleefully challenge the men standing at a distance by waving the long, open *mutong'a* baskets (used for carrying cassava roots) over their heads.

Other songs extol clandestine love, comparing the pleasure experienced to sparks from a hunter's flint (*ilola dambanji*, literally 'murderer's stone'). Others, again, mention how the housewife steals away from her husband's side when he is asleep, to seek her lover.

The novice's mother rarely approaches the dancers at this

stage. When she does, she tends to be ridiculed. Once my wife heard an old woman call a novice's mother to the ring: When she came, rather reluctantly, she was greeted by the song: 'You have given birth only to eggs!',[1] at which the women laughed immoderately.

Some of the songs mock or censure important local personalities, such as rich men and government chiefs. I once saw one of the song-leaders acting the role of lover of one of the local chief's wives and singing scandalous songs about her. As an example of the extreme allusiveness of such topical songs, the following would be hard to beat. It consists merely of the words, '*Eng'a mwani, munamweni mwamwena dehi*', 'Yes, thanks, you are silent, you were silent already.' The song referred to a court case in which a chief, to whom the Native Court offered large damages for the adultery of his wife, would accept no more than 'a ticky' (a threepenny piece), as a sign that he was not appeased. It was alleged that the adulterer, a schoolmaster at the chief's capital village, then fell ill and died ('he was silent') as the result of the chief's sorcery.

Other songs, however, stress the need for decent conduct. One song, after pointing out that 'stealing, lying, quarrelsomeness, and adultery are no good', goes on:

'*Chenachina chiwelang'a*	'If you carry on like that
Wambakatung'a naneyi hinyi?	Who will build with you?
Wambakashala nawampembi.'	You will stay with goats.'

There are various kinds of dances. On several occasions we saw a dance known as *wuleng'u* or *ku-leng'a*, in which one of the song leaders carries an axe and a cup, while the other holds an axe and a bottle of shredded onions and beans in water. Sometimes one of these dancers borrows a head scarf, drapes it over her head, then flings it among the dancers, one of whom snatches and wears it. In a not uncommon variant of *wuleng'u*, a woman—usually a matrilineal kinswoman of the novice—dances round the women's circle in the opposite direction to the others. She wears a short skirt, holds a small woman's axe, and carries an unstoppered bottle of beer. She flourishes the axe and bottle over her head, spraying the people with beer.

---

[1] Some Ndembu women refrained from eating eggs on the grounds that to do so would make them barren.

Her movements are fast and vigorous. Afterwards she gives the beer to the (male) drummers.

Exegesis

Manyosa explained to my wife the meaning of some of the dances and the objects used in them. The *ku-leng'a* dance, as we have seen, is the name of a dance performed at the *Nkula* ritual (p. 71). Its name seems to be connected with *ku-leng'a*, 'to cut in strips', although no woman could give us an explanation of the strips of onions and bean-pods. Manyosa said: 'There is a song for *wuleng'u*. The dancer goes everywhere, far away and back. She feels happy because the girl has matured [*nakuli dehi*]. It is to teach the girl wisdom. In Angola the novice's mother performs the dance. Her hair hangs down in strips before her eyes and she tosses it about. She wears rattles on her legs. The cup stands for *kapudyi* [thin porridge given to babies].

'Throwing away a cloth means that if the novice's husband gives her only a small, torn cloth, and not a good one, she will throw it away, for she wants a big one. Sometimes the women hand a cloth round. By this [is meant] that each woman is giving the next one a baby.'

Episode Eight: After the Turning of the Novice

At noon the novice is turned by her *chifukaminu*, 'the one who kneels', so that she now lies on her right side. This woman, who may be her instructress but is usually an elderly relative of the novice in the 'grandparent' generation, also rubs her shoulder to remove the stiffness from it (see Plate 8*a*).

A man, carrying a woman's meal basket, comes to the *mudyi* and dances with the women. After he has gone a woman enters the circle, carrying a *mutong'a* basket full of long pieces of termite's nests ('ant-hills') and *ipopu* leaves. The women sing, 'The weight of the basket is killing me.' Then the woman scatters the leaves over all the dancers. Occasionally women take leaves from the bushes round the trodden circle and scatter them throughout the village. These events take place just after noon. Often a bowl of leaves is passed from woman to woman around the ring of dancers.

At this time a great crowd has collected. Men come closer,

and begin to join the circle of dancing women. They are no longer chased away. Young men often form a circle of their own in the village for dancing.

The songs now sung tend to emphasize fertility rather than adultery, and are less critical of men. At some performances a 'water-drum' (*kang'omampwita*, 'the little drum of thirst') is played, always by women, according to our observations—the only type of drum, as far as I know, played by women (see Plate 8*b*). This drum is open at one end, which rests on the player's knee. She beats the skin-covered end with one hand. With the other she grasps a stick, called *iteti*[1] or 'reed'. This stick passes through the interior of the drum to a piece of string which is attached through the drum-skin to a round disk of wood stuck to the outer side of the membrane. A curious grunting sound, said to represent that of a couple during intercourse, is produced by the player grasping the reed firmly with a wet cloth and drawing her hand up and down the reed. The friction of cloth on reed causes the latter to vibrate, and the sound is amplified by the resonating chamber of the drum. The strokes of the arm produce a rhythm at about walking pace. A second drummer beats the side of the drum with two sticks, at a quicker syncopated rhythm. The cloth constantly requires replenishing with water; 'it drinks' (*yapwita*), as Ndembu say. Sometimes the second drummer does the *danse du ventre*, with a circular movement of her stomach muscles.

Indigenous Exegesis

Chifukamihu, from *ku-fukama*, 'to kneel', is applied to the woman who kneels beside the novice and turns her over at noon. Her role is homologous with that of the circumciser's assistant at *Mukanda*, who holds the novice during the circumcision.

Termites' Nests. According to Manyosa, the pieces of termites' nests (*mafwamfwa*) in the *mutong'a* basket are 'to make it heavy, just as a man is heavy'. The leaves are 'to make the women lucky and give them procreative power (*lusemu*). They are very pleased with them.'

Symbolism of Left and Right. At the beginning of the day, the novice was laid on her *left* side; at noon she was turned on her

---

[1] Often used as a euphemism for the penis, as in the *Nkang'a* song, *iteti demana*, 'the reed is standing up'.

right side. As we have seen, among Ndembu the left hand stands for feminity, and the right hand for masculinity; and according to Muchona, this is because an arrow is usually held in the right hand, and a bow in the left hand. The ritual bow at the apex of the seclusion hut represents the 'procreative power' (*lusemu*) of the novice, as does the musical bow she plays during seclusion. On the other hand, the arrow stood for the bridegroom at the *mudyi* site. The bridewealth he will pay is also called *nsewu* or 'arrow'. A woman is said to carry her baby in the crook of her left arm, while a man carries his bow or gun on his right shoulder. When the girl is laid on her left side, this is said to signify that 'the dance is for the women'. When she is turned to the right, this is held to mean that men will enter the ritual. This becomes more evident in the next episode.

Episode Nine: The Erection of the Seclusion Hut

At about 4 p.m., the site of the novice's seclusion hut (*nkunka*) is prepared. It is usually located on the boundary between village and bush, on the opposite side of the village from the *mudyi*. Sometimes it may be sited near her mother's hut, but often it is made merely where there is a convenient place.

First of all, the site is hoed over by the instructress and the novice's mother (see Plate 9*a*). Then the bridegroom, if present, or his male representative, if he is not, marks a circle on the ground with the hoe. Then he traces a semicircle in front of what will be the doorway, to denote the border of the enclosure fence. Four or five young men, kin and friends of the groom, collect rafters and grass for the hut. Meanwhile the groom cuts down two long *mudyi* stems, trimming them into poles with his axe, for the main rafters. The actual work of construction is inaugurated by the bridegroom and his younger uterine brother, who take a *mudyi* pole each and plant it in the ground on opposite sides of the circle. The tops of the two poles are then lashed together. Another pole is added to make a sort of tepee frame. Other rafters are then added by the helpers, and the whole structure is thatched with grass. It is the bridegroom's task to make the fence on another day. When the hut is finished, the groom's younger brother sits on the apex of the roof, one leg on each side, to 'show that the hut is strong' (see Plate 9*b*).

PLATE 9

a. Instructress and novice's mother clear the site where the seclusion hut will be made. Cassava meal is prepared for visitors' feast.

b Bridegroom's younger brother astride novice's seclusion hut. Note *andumba* calabash in entrance (see text).

PLATE 10

Seclusion hut in its enclosure. Note proximity to village of novice's matrilineage.

During the course of construction, arguments over payment take place between the young men, on the one hand, and the instructress and novice's mother, on the other. These women are obliged to pay the groom's assistants, customarily in beer, or with a chicken, but nowadays often in cash. The instructress must pay the groom's brother a small sum of money (3d or 6d) before he will come down from the roof.

Indigenous Exegesis

According to many informants, the inverted V-shape of the *mudyi* poles represents *ipanza* (or *mpanza*), 'the crutch' or 'fork' of the human body, 'where children come from'.

Muchona told me that the groom's younger brother is known as the 'little', or 'lesser', bridegroom (*kalemba kanyanya*). He acts for the bridegroom in various ways. On the morning of *kwidisha*, for example, his washing water is used for washing the novice for her public dance. He and the groom eat the same chicken given by the bride's mother on the marital morning. But he does not sleep with the novice.[1] He acts on behalf of the groom because the latter has to avoid his bride until they at last sleep together.

Comments and Analysis

This episode, the building of the seclusion hut, brings out a number of aspects of the social structure. The mother's role in clearing the site indicates, for instance, the persistence of the mother-daughter tie, even in a ritual which results in a loosening of that tie. But, after all, the major articulating principle of Ndembu social organization is matriliny, and there cannot be a complete rupture of the mother-child tie. It is altered in character, not dissolved. The social equivalence of siblings is strikingly brought out by the co-operation of the bridegroom and his brother in the building of the seclusion hut. In the ritual situation, however, there is an interesting reversal of their secular roles. During the separation ritual the bridegroom must have no contact whatever with the novice, his bride-to-be.

---

[1] There appears to be a mystical sanction against this, for one *Nkang'a* song runs: 'My brother-in-law (*ishaku dami*), you have baked my sweet potatoes. That is why I'm feeling pain and scratching my arm.' But this song is said to refer to adultery and the venereal disease which may be its result.

He may not even perform symbolic actions which have sexual reference to her. Thus, his brother acts as his surrogate when he sits on the completed seclusion hut, i.e. has symbolic intercourse with the novice, representing the marital state. On the other hand, in secular life, his younger brother may joke freely with his wife, but may not have access to her sexually. In related tribes such as the Luvale, it is true, a younger brother may have intercourse with his older brother's wife, but not among the Ndembu. Yet, in the ritual situation, it is the bridegroom who must refrain from the expression of sexuality in his relations with his bride, while his younger brother acts symbolically as surrogate husband. Tension between the bridegroom and the ritual instructress, who is responsible for the maintenance of the taboos of *Nkang'a*, is obliquely expressed in the argumentative bargaining between the bridegroom's brother and the instructress. The bridegroom himself must behave publicly with respect towards the ritual instructress, but his brother can freely express on his behalf the bridegroom's impatience with the restrictions imposed on him. Two structural considerations enter into the wrangling between the bridegroom's friends and the novice's mother and instructress, who are identified in this episode. The first is the general opposition between men and women, portrayed in this ritual. The second is the conflict between bride's kin and bridegroom's kin, which is expressed even more distinctly in the final phase of *Nkang'a*. Ritual expression is also given to the impatience of the bridegroom and his kin with the restrictions, imposed by the life-crisis ritual, on the bridegroom's sexual desires, and on the wish of his kin to incorporate the bride in their village group.

Episode Ten: The Preparation of the Women's Meal

After helping with the preparation of the seclusion hut, the novice's mother, assisted by the groom's mother, organizes the preparation of food for the women visitors. She and her village friends pound, cook, and serve up large quantities of cassava mush and beans. These are set out on several plates. A plate of cassava and a plate of beans are allocated to each of the main villages whose female members are present. Sometimes small fish fry (*anshi*) are provided.

Before the meal begins the instructress holds up a plate of cassava mixed with beans, while the novice's mother lifts a large spoon containing the same mixture. Then, with the instructress leading the way, followed by the novice's mother, a procession of the women concerned with the cooking forms up. Each woman holds aloft a plate of food. They go solemnly to the *mudyi* and encircle it once, singing:

'*Chipwampwilu* [or *chipwampula*], you are the owner of the child [*mwinimwana*].'

Suddenly, the novice's mother shouts, 'Who wants the cassava of *chipwampwilu*?', and holds up the spoonful of food. The women waiting by the *mudyi*, excluding those who helped prepare the food, rush to seize the spoon. The first to grab it, eats from it hastily (see Plate 11*a*). Having eaten, she returns the spoon to the novice's mother.

The plates are then set down a few yards from the *mudyi* tree. The women and their children eat from the plates nearest to their own villages. The sponsoring village is the last to begin eating, in accordance with the Ndembu etiquette of hospitality.

Indigenous Exegesis

Our informants would not, or could not, explain the meaning of the term *chipwampwilu*. But Manyosa told my wife that 'The woman who snatches the spoon of *chipwampwilu* should come from the novice's own village or a neighbouring village, otherwise the mother believes that her child will go far away from her and die there. The novice's mother wants her daughter to stay nearby.'

The term, *chipwampula*,[1] is used as an alternative to *chipwampwilu*, in the song sung during the circling of the *mudyi* with the spoon: '*Chipwampula eyi mwinimwana eyi*', 'You are *chipwampula*, you are the owner of the child', and it seems to refer to the novice's mother.

The person who snatches (*wanukula*) the spoon is called 'the hyaena' (*chimbu*). She is thought to acquire fertility and good luck for herself by triumphing thus in competition with the other women.

The role of *chimbu*, 'hyaena' or, among the Northern

---

[1] I asked whether *chipwampula* was connected with *wupwampu*, 'sorrow, mourning', but this was denied by my informants. It appears to be an archaic term.

Ndembu, 'lion', appears in several kinds of ritual. In *Mukanda*, boys' circumcision, *chimbu* is the name of the officiant who seizes the boys from their mothers and takes them to be circumcised. In hunting ritual, performed to celebrate the prowess of great hunters, an antelope's heart and a ball of cassava are stolen by his young son, called *chimbu* during the episode. *Chimbu*, as we have seen, means 'lion'[1] as well as 'hyaena', and both are 'thieves', say Ndembu, for they steal livestock from the villages. Hunters are also described as 'thieves', who steal animals from the bush. In *Wuyang'a*, the gun-hunters' cult, the son is believed to seize a portion of his father's hunting prowess—in the same way that it is thought the *chimbu* at *Nkang'a* steals some of the novice's mother's fertility. *Chimbu* is a polysemous symbol, with the generic sense of 'an agency of violent change'.

This symbol represents a different kind of ethical evaluation from that which pervades the white symbolism. The morality implicit in the white symbolism stresses conformity to orthodox norms of conduct. Health and good luck are the fruits of dutiful observance. But the *chimbu* symbolism suggests that the good things of life, prestige as a hunter, chieftainship, and fertility, may also be won by aggression and pertinacity. The bold override sanctions. In Ndembu thought two conflicting ideals coexist; blessings may be obtained by co-operation with one's fellows, but may also be snatched by successful competition with them. In *Nkang'a* the woman who becomes *chimbu* and snatches the magically fertilizing cassava follows the second path. But the individualist who snatches power is, in this ritual context, still reckoned to act in a socially approved manner. The bold hunter gets meat for the community, the chief rules for the public benefit, the woman who bests the others in grasping the magic food hopes to produce children for her kin and so to add followers to her village. Nevertheless, the selfish elements in behaviour symbolized by the *chimbu* border on anti-social conduct. The very name, *chimbu*, is used in common speech and especially in anti-witchcraft ritual to mean 'witch',

[1] Among the Bemba, according to Richards (*Chisungu*, op. cit., p. 78), 'the lion is equated throughout [the girl's nubility ceremony] with the bridegroom, the chief, the male principle.' In Ndembu boys' initiation the circumciser is described as a 'lion' in a traditional song.

PLATE 11

a. The 'hyaena' has snatched 'the cassava mush of *chipwampwilu*' and holds it in her hand. (See text.)

b. Instructress plays sacred musical bows in entrance of novice's seclusion hut.

PLATE 12

a. Instructress dresses novice's hair shortly before her coming-out dance.

b. Novice's coming-out dance. Note fly-switch in one hand and cloth in the other (see text).

'sorcerer', or a witch's familiar. The hyaena itself, which is believed to dig up graves and eat corpses, is dreaded and hated.

Episode Eleven: The Women's Formal Meal

At the meal following the *chimbu* episode, the plates of food are arranged in a rough square, each village's share being placed in the corner nearest its site, and that of the sponsoring village being in the middle. The oldest women eat first and the youngest girls last, in order of seniority. Informants told us that long ago men used to eat with the women, but this practice has been discontinued for many years. Villages from which few women have come are not given independent representation, but their members must sit with kin and friends from villages that have come in strength. Prestige accrues, therefore, to those villages sending large contingents to the rites. The village sponsoring *Nkang'a* is fed last, in accordance with the Ndembu rule that guests and strangers should be fed before one's own people.

It is strongly felt that the provision of a large meal by the novice's matrilineal kin is an auspicious indication of her competence as a housewife. Thus Manyosa grumbled that at her daughter-in-law's *Nkang'a*, she and her son's other matrilineal kin 'waited for cassava mush and relish all day, but none came; we waited and waited. I, Manyosa, waited for years and never received cassava mush from Rosa, my son's wife, even when I was ill. Nor would she cook for her husband.' The communion meal stresses once more the collaboration and unity of women, now *including* the novice's mother who provides the meal, as against the competition between women portrayed in the *chimbu* episode. The provision of such a large meal also portrays the high value set on hospitality and generosity in Ndembu culture.

Episode Twelve: Putting the Novice in her Seclusion Hut

At sunset the women go to the *mudyi* tree to lift up the novice. An old woman—usually the classificatory 'grandmother' (of her own matrilineage) who acted as *chifukaminu*—takes her from under the blanket and holds her under the armpits. The instructress stands by, with her hand on the girl's head. The instructress then picks up the girl and carries her on her back, with the girl's arms round her neck, and legs round her stomach.

Other women cover the novice completely with her blanket. No men are allowed anywhere near the *mudyi* at this point. A bunch of *masasa* grass is picked up from under the antelope skin, and put into the novice's left hand. This grass must be taken from the *chifwilu*, 'the place of death', to 'join the *chifwilu* to the seclusion hut'.[1] The women collect branches and lean them against the *mudyi* bush. Each woman takes a leaf from the *mudyi* and hides it in her clenched fist. They sing '*shinke-e pande-e*', 'close up, press in magic'.

When the girl has been lifted on her instructress's back, the women crowd around with the leaves from the *mudyi* tree held tightly in their closed fists. This symbolic act is once more a condensation of several different significances. For the *mudyi* leaves stand for children or foetuses, the closed-up hand is said to stand for 'the womb' (*ivumu*). On the other hand, the leaf is said to stand for the novice, and the closed hand for the seclusion hut and the condition of seclusion.

The whole crowd of women and girls dance, singing, towards the village, while the instructress dances in the middle with the novice on her back. The men await them in a packed throng near the central village shelter. The drums are massed before the shelter and played with thunderous emphasis. Just before the women reach the village they stop; dance, as though marking time; then pack round the novice to hide her as much as possible from the gaze of the men. Next, they approach the men's group and slowly encircle it three times, stopping periodically, then starting again. Now they advance towards the seclusion hut while the singing swells up, hard and jubilant. The instructress turns round, and enters th⸱ seclusion hut backwards while the women crowd around the entrance. She takes the girl to the far side of the hut and gently lets her down on the ground. When she does this all the women trill outside and cry, 'It is finished.' Then they turn round, hold out their fists with the *mudyi* leaves clenched in them, and run as hard as they can towards the throng of men. They circle the men rapidly, then run to the hut of the novice's mother, where

[1] It is possible to see in this symbolic action a representation of the continuity of the ritual process through a series of sites. 'Sacredness' is contained in the purposive, patterned actions of the ritual, and is conferred on the symbolic articles which form the instruments and objects of those actions.

each pushes her *mudyi* leaf into the outside thatch, high up on the roof. These leaves are now said to represent the novice's mother's hoped-for grandchildren. She hopes that her daughter will bear many children who will come to live with their grandmother, as good grandchildren should in Ndembu society. Thus, the women have taken the novice away from her mother only in order to bring back many grandchildren to her. Although the daughter is no longer a dependent member of a matricentric family, she may soon be a link in a matrilineage. The mother, through her daughter's fertility, hopes one day to become a respected elder among her own matrilineal kin.

Indigenous Exegesis

The Grandmother. The role of grandmother is an important one in *Nkang'a*. In the past there used to be a long period of betrothal, and at one of its phases, *ikwachilu*, when the groom made a stack of firewood for his mother-in-law, he would take two sticks to the girl's grandmother. Again, at the end of *Nkang'a* it used to be the custom, not always observed today, for the novice to be led to her grandmother's hut, before she was taken to sleep with her bridegroom.

The Carrying of the Novice. We received various explanations of why the novice had to be carried. Manyosa, for example, said that 'The girl was suffering when she lay still and hungry all day. She felt as if she were dead. So it is troublesome for her to walk. She must be carried to her hut where she will be free to move.' Manyosa then ventured a less commonsense interpretation. 'The place by the *mudyi* is called "the dying place of the novice" [*ifwilu dakankang'a*]. Thus, if she fell, she would become "dead in the hut" [*wafwa mwitala*, i.e., frigid] for her husband.' Muchona, who was prone to generalize from his wide knowledge of Ndembu ritual, told me that 'To lift anybody, or anything, up is a sign that that person is seen and known by everybody. It is also a sign of importance or chiefly authority [*wanta*]. At *Nkang'a*, although the people cannot see the novice under her blanket, they know that she is alive, that she has left the *ifwilu*.' Other informants compared the novice to a 'baby'—'*wafwana neyi mukeki*', 'she resembles a baby' which is carried in a cloth (called *ng'oji*; the same term means 'placenta') on its mother's back.

It would seem that both ideas, high status and childlike dependence, are simultaneously present in the minds of Ndembu when they consider the position of the novice in this episode. There is also the implicit notion that sacred persons and objects must not touch ground trodden by profane feet. Furthermore, there may be here an echo of the symbolism of *Mukanda*, where in several episodes the novices must be held up, or climb up, lest they become impotent. The ground (on which they were circumcised) is a 'place of suffering' or 'death'; to be 'above' it is to be 'alive', 'free from death', 'free from suffering'. A parallelism is asserted between the white-black contrast and the 'above' (*hewulu*)-'below' (*heseki*) contrast. The first term in each is associated with auspicious connotations, the second with inauspicious ones. For example, chiefly authority (*wanta*) is regarded both as 'white' and 'above'. The term *iseki* represents 'the earth' or 'the ground', and it is sometimes used as a circumlocution for a deceased relative, in the phrase, *iseki detu da Kahali*, literally 'our earth of Kahali', i.e. 'our dead kinsman, Kahali'. *Heseki*, 'below', means literally 'on the earth', and shares earth's connotation of death. Thus 'life', 'potency', 'importance' are 'above', while 'death', 'sterility', and 'abasement' are 'below'.

Masasa Grass. According to Muchona, *masasa* is the term applied to grass used by house-mice (*ankunkulu anyizanda ansanza*) for the lining of their nests. 'The novice is brought into her seclusion hut that she may also have a nest in which she will bear many children. Any kind of grass or even leaves may be collected. The *masasa* grass is put in the novice's bed in her seclusion hut.'

Walking Backwards.   Manyosa told my wife that 'the walking backwards' (*kwenda makinkanyima*) of the instructress was to prevent the girl looking up at the apex (*ntung'u*) of her hut, which represented her procreative power (*lusemu*): 'In seclusion, she must never look up, only down. And she must never face anything directly.' In Ndembu rites there are many instances in which sacred objects and shrines are approached backwards.[1]

[1] See, for example, my *Chihamba, the White Spirit*, op. cit., p. 32; and in this book the account of *Nkula*, on p. 64.

Audrey Richards, in *Chisungu*, describes how Bemba girls in one episode 'crawl backwards, covered with blankets'. Her Bemba informant told her that this action meant 'forsaking their old way of life' (p. 64).

Hiding the Mudyi Leaves. Women informants told my wife: 'If the women do not run at top speed, carefully concealing the leaves as they do so, the men might see the leaves. This would be very bad. The leaves are the novice's children. If they are not taken to her mother's thatch, the novice will have no children.' They compared the running of the women with an episode in the *Kumutena*, first pregnancy rite, where the pregnant woman must rush through the door of her hut quickly when she is roused in the middle of the night by her senior female kin with cries of 'fire!', 'a raid [*njita*]!' This is thought to make her baby 'go quickly' through the entrance of the womb at birth. Other instances of the value Ndembu attach to speed in ritual comes to mind: how, for example, they lay emphasis on the circumciser's quickness in operating, and on the running of the candidates at *Chihamba*.[1]

Episode Thirteen: The Night Dance

I have attended many such night dances after *Kwing'ija*. There are generally two rings of dancers: the first consisting mainly of the close kin of the novice, including her father and mother; the other of visitors. The former are often elderly; the latter are younger people. The kin tend to sing traditional songs; the visitors to dance the modern *Chikinta* and sing topical songs. At some dances of this sort new songs are introduced or improvised in the course of the night. *Nkang'a* nights provide occasions for some of the worst quarrels I have seen among the Ndembu, especially between husbands and lovers of the women, who, stimulated by a day's singing of songs extolling sexuality and adultery, are extremely forward in luring sweethearts into the bush. Fights between groups of men from rival villages are by no means uncommon, and I have seen such a nocturnal dance actually brought to an abrupt end by the headman of the sponsoring village because fighting became uncontrollable. This was regarded as bringing 'much shame' on all concerned. Scenes like these attest to the fact that, though people are enjoined to co-operate in performing ritual, nevertheless, conflicts between them in secular life are never completely erased, but break out redoubled when there are

[1] *Chihamba, the White Spirit*, op. cit., p. 31.

relaxations of norms enforcing friendliness. Cleavages determined by custom may be openly expressed in the form of a given ritual, and to some extent may there be 'abreacted' or 'sublimated'. But not all cleavages are brought to light in this way, for no single ritual can reflect or express the total structure of a society. The suppressed, or merely situationally submerged cleavages, tend to come to the fore during the intervals between ritual episodes. It is probably for this reason that one sometimes finds taboos against violent behaviour at such times, which is said to bring mystical danger upon the principal subjects of the ritual.

RESUMÉ OF SEPARATION RITES

The rites of separation, although they constitute only the first of three main phases, have a certain autonomy. Let us recapitulate their main features. The ritual begins quietly just outside the village in the bush, with village women only as participants. The mother of the novice is excluded, and the novice herself becomes the passive subject of the whole subsequent ritual. When the sun is up and until noon, the *mudyi* tree and the recumbent novice are the focus of a feminine rite. Songs celebrating the perilous joys of adultery are sung to tease the smarting husbands of the women of the vicinage whose wives muster in force. The novice herself is teased in song about sexual matters, and popular songs lampoon local celebrities. This period ends at noon when, in the symbolic idiom, the girl is turned from her feminine, left side to her masculine, right side. In the first part of the afternoon men participate more and more in the ritual, and songs and symbols are introduced on the theme of fertility. Popular songs are still sung, but the rebellious tone of the earlier period is somewhat muted. When the seclusion hut is built, at the opposite side of the village to the *mudyi*, with its strictly female connotation, men and women co-operate; the novice's mother and the instructress collaborate once more in clearing bush for the hut, since the mother is to be reunited with her daughter at a new level of social interaction, that of the matrilineage. Both now stand in opposition to the bridegroom's party, for the novice's fertility will always belong to the matrilineage, even though the bridegroom's village mates will enjoy her services and those of her children as long as the marriage lasts. The instructress, who will magically prepare the novice to bear children, is linked here with the mother who desires uterine grandchildren. On the other hand, the instructress has a common interest with the bridegroom in preparing the novice to be sexually adept; in this role she must be isolated from the mother, who must not come into contact with her daughter's sexual life. This role of the instructress will become more prominent in the next two phases of *Nkang'a*. The building of the seclusion hut is followed by the episode of the *chimbu*, which expresses competition between women and conflict between the mother and the adult women, a conflict that arises from the contradiction between familial ties and those of the wider society. Men take no part in this episode. Then follows a reunification of the entire women's group in a communion meal provided by the mothers of the young couple. Finally there is the episode of the removal of the girl from the *mudyi* to the seclusion hut, which is at once the end of the separation phase and the beginning of the seclusion phase. The women once more assert ritual dominance as they encircle the men on their way from one sacred site to another. The encirclement also marks a return of the women to their menfolk and, at the same time, the addition of masculine power, represented by the drums, the men's meeting shelter, and the solid mass of men, to the female fertility principle, symbolized by the *mudyi* leaves. 'Encirclement' in the Ndembu ritual idiom has a sexual connotation, in addition to its other meanings, since the sexual act is performed as a circling movement, known as 'the dance of the bed', and represented in ritual by the *danse du ventre*. The *mudyi* leaves stand for children in general, for the hoped-for children of the novice and grandchildren of the novice's mother, and also for the novice herself. Identifications of various kinds are frequent in *Nkang'a*. In this case, the multiple identifications of the *mudyi* symbolism represent what Radcliffe-Brown calls 'the unity of the lineage'. It also represents its continuity through women. In this episode the girl is taken personally from her mother, but her fertility is given back to the lineage, represented again by the mother. A personal and familial tie is converted into a tie of corporate kinship. Finally, the high value set on female fruitfulness, which is shared by all Ndembu over and above sectional attachments, is expressed by the *mudyi* symbolism (see Fig. VI, p. 206).

SOCIOLOGICAL ANALYSIS OF KWING'IJA

The following sociological aspects of *Nkang'a* have so far emerged. The main participants have been, in order of appearance: the bridegroom, and/or his parents and close senior matrilineal kin, the novice's mother, the instructress, the headman of the village where *Nkang'a* is performed (which is usually the village of the novice's closest matrilineal kin, although sometimes it may be the father's village), the novice herself, and the women of the village. The novice's father, although he may be present at the exchanging of the arrows, has until now remained in the background. He has helped to organize supplies of beer and food for the ritual assembly, but he plays no part in the ritual episodes proper. The bridegroom, too, is virtually excluded from the ritual until the final stage. It is principally to loosen and reshape the tie between the novice and her mother in a matrilineal society that *Nkang'a* is performed, and to deal with the social repercussions of this altered relationship. The headman in his person represents both the male and female members of the village. His prayer recognizes that many social and inter-personal disputes may, in the ritual situation, come to a head. But the headman, like the novice's father and the groom, recedes into the background as stress is laid more and more on the relationships between the women. The 'muted' behaviour of the men, however, is just as important a part of the total ritual situation as the prominent behaviour of the women. *Nkang'a* emphasizes that the main elements of stability in the unstable and labile Ndembu social system are provided by matrilineal descent. Men are, in fact, interlinked with one another by descent most importantly through women. Thus, modifications in the relations between women in a line of descent are of vital importance to men. Men withdraw, as it were, from the centre of ritual attention, in order that such changes may be the more clearly delineated by ritual custom. But this withdrawal itself bears witness to the interest men take in the readjustments that are taking place in the matrilineal framework. And in the end, a man, the novice's husband, will come forward and remove the novice from the sphere of her mother and matrilineage. On the female side of the ritual equation, the instructress is the agent of the novice's transition from one social position to another, and represents the interest of the wider society in the girl's marriage and fertility. The unity of the village women, whether kin or affines of the headman, is expressed in their role on the morning of the phase of separation. Soon the *mudyi* tree will become the focus of the ritual opposition between men and women in *Ndembu* society. The exclusion of the mother from the initial separation rites expresses her coming domestic estrangement from her daughter, and also stands for the incompatibility between their close, inter-personal tie and the daughter's assimilation into the category of mature, married women.

The *mudyi* symbolism absorbs all these relationships in that it stands for matriliny in general, for the matrilineage of the novice, for the novice's link with her mother, and for the ritual unity of adult women led by the instructress. Around this tree are clustered other symbols; the skin and blanket of the novice, the ritual fire, the arrow and beads given by the bridegroom. The social implications of these symbols, some of which express potential[1] conflict between the groom and the novice's matrilineage, are subordinated to those of the *mudyi*, which emphasize the enduring continuities of matrilineal descent.

The rituals performed by societies that possess a considerable degree of cohesion—whose members, moreover, 'feel their unity and perceive their common interest in symbols'[2]—are, beyond doubt, rituals pervaded with affect. People derive emotional satisfaction from the observance of secular customs which ensure the maintenance of the social structure. Any threat to the maintenance of these customary relations arouses strong emotions, so long as the society is a 'going concern'. And certain pivotal ritual symbols, such as *mudyi*, *mpemba*, and *muyombu*, summarize many such customs in a single representation, and mobilize strong emotions in support of the social order. But ritual also recognizes that the psychic nature of man is not

[1] The arrow is, in many ritual contexts, a symbol of taking possession by force.
[2] Fortes, M. and Evans-Pritchard, E. E. (eds.), *African Political Systems*, London: Oxford University Press (1940), p. 17.

infinitely malleable with respect to the forces of social conditioning. To make a human being obey social norms, violence must be done to his natural impulses. These must be repressed or re-directed. If, for example, a society is defined by rules of kinship, persons who might in many ways be mutually incompatible are compelled to enter into close relationships with one another; powerful antagonisms may grow beneath the surface. Again, where incest taboos ban the overt expression of sexual attraction between certain kin categories, such kin may well continue to feel sexually drawn to one another. Hatred and illicit sexual passion may thus be repressed beneath customarily prescribed behaviour and especially where relationships between members of an elementary family are concerned. Now, if this view is correct, that ritual handles modifications and breaches in customarily prescribed social relations, there is a considerable probability, in a society where a high emotional value is attached to the maintenance of the social order, that the members will be subliminally aware of these psychological pressures that menace social cohesion. Many will feel guilty because they feel such pressures within themselves. Furthermore, a breach in the continuity of a socially prescribed relationship, whether caused by the social process itself, as in *Nkang'a*, or by the action of individuals, brings to the surface what has hitherto been repressed by external social pressures and by internal psychic mechanisms of defence against illicit drives. In a public situation even a breach in a single relationship, which has become explicit and can no longer be concealed, may spread to other relationships. Breach is contagious. This is especially the case in simple face-to-face communities, whose members are interlinked by multiple ties of kinship and of political, economic, local, and ritual co-operation. Through the breaches in established customary relations, socially repudiated feelings of animosity and sexual passion may threaten to come to the surface. From the members of the disturbed group there may be a 'feed-back' of disruptive drives into the social system. Ritual has to take this process of psychological 'feedback' into serious account. It must give expression to the illicit drives, bring them into the open, as Ndembu say themselves, in order that they may be purged and exorcised. One way is by the symbols that stand for socially rejected modes of behaviour.

Another device is to prescribe behaviour that portrays typical animosities in culturally defined relationships. Such symbols and stereotyped behavioural expressions of tension and conflict are associated with symbols and behaviour that stand for the ideal values in which the continuity and stability of the system are embodied. Thus, a transference of affective energy is made from socially negative to socially positive symbolism and behaviour. There exists yet another class of symbols which simultaneously express conflict and cohesion—for example, the red symbols which change in meaning from socially negative to socially positive representations in the course of the ritual. Such symbols resemble dreams or neurotic symptoms in that they are compromise-formations between licit values and illicit drives. Where they are used they indicate that psychic conflicts of a serious character tend to break through into the social field and that the social field has been previously subject to acute and dangerous disturbance.

A life-crisis ritual such as *Nkang'a* gives expression to social forces that separate two persons closely interlinked in the kinship structure. A close personal relationship, charged with the ambivalent emotions of the family situation, is radically altered in character. The fact that this alteration is inevitable, in terms of Ndembu social structure, is not immediately accepted in the essentially conservative, unconscious psyches of those concerned. Change is painful and unconsciously resisted: but it must be accepted if the claims of the social structure are to be met. The form of the ritual has to take into account these resistances and overcome them. The resistances feed back into the ritual situation and secure expression in its symbolism, its taboos, and its prescribed behaviour.

In ritual also, primitive society reappraises its ideology and structural form, and finds them good. Refractory behaviour and the expression of conflict are allowed, even in some instances prescribed, to release energies by which social cohesion can be renewed. But social cohesion is recognized to be the outcome of a struggle, often a struggle to overcome cleavages caused by contradictions in the structural principles of the society itself. A struggle may also arise from the resistances of human nature to social conditioning. Or both kinds of struggle may provoke and exacerbate one another. In any case, the

structure of each kind of ritual betrays marks of the struggle in
its symbolisms and enjoined behaviour. But, since ritual is first
and foremost a *social* phenomenon, a system of social facts, what
it portrays are typical or average kinds of struggle. In the long
history of a society certain kinds of conflict become recognized
as regularly occurring in certain enduring social relationships.
As such conflicts impinge on social life, and periodically disturb
it, they become part of the behaviour expected, but not
wanted, in the given relationship. Although they are not
governed by custom, but challenge custom and disturb cohesion, they appear as its *regular antithesis*, as custom's 'dark
shadow'. Thus, when a given relationship is isolated and
scrutinized in ritual, the conflicts and resistances typical of
that relationship also receive recognition and stereotyped
representation. Custom is strengthened by the ritual portrayal
and subsequent transmutation of its self-generated conflicts.
These, though undesired, have become socially accepted as
part of the relationship. Even where conflict is, in fact, absent or
slight in a relationship where it might be socially expected,
symbols and behaviour indicative of conflict in such a relationship are employed in ritual. Ritual takes heed only of the
typical, of the modal, not of the specific or the exceptional.
Whether in any particular case individuals have in fact come
into conflict or not is irrelevant in the ritual situation. In any
case, it is considered likely in most tribal societies that if conflict has not been made explicit in any given instance, it may
well be implicit.

But though there may be a stereotyping of conflicts and
resistances in the form of symbols, this does not mean that
most of those present at a ritual do not feel their emotions
powerfully and variously stirred. In a society that is still fully
functional there is a strong probability that the principal
actors in a ritual actually do feel what they are supposed to feel.
Symbols stimulate emotions in societies where symbolism is
ritually important. And, in a society which has changed little
for centuries, the kinds of conflict depicted in the cultural
structure of ritual are the same as those that occur in the
present. The ritual system is not a meaningless inheritance
from a dead past, but something that meets contemporary
needs. The form of the ritual is consistent with the form of the

society. And the conflicts of that society are the same as those dramatized and symbolized in its ritual. Because people are deeply concerned emotionally about such conflicts, they are moved when they see them ritually portrayed. And when they are ritually resolved, they feel emotional catharsis.

VIII
NKANG'A: PART TWO

KUNKUNKA

Episode One: The Bridegroom Lights the Novice's Fire

On the night of the *kwing'ija* dance, the bridegroom goes into the seclusion hut and lights a fire.[1] In the past he used a fire drill, or friction sticks; today he must use no more than two matches. The fire must be a new one and must not be kindled from the embers of another fire. The novice must hide her eyes with her hands while he is in the hut. It is said that if in the past a bridegroom failed to light a fire, he would not be allowed to marry the novice. The fire is said to represent marriage, and the manner of its kindling to betoken the success or otherwise of the particular marriage.

Episode Two: The Novice's First Night in Seclusion

Shortly after the novice is carried in, food is brought to her. The instructress eats some of it before she does. The novice is fed by hand by the instructress. Before the novice eats her first meal, she must put a small portion of cassava mush on the calabash resonator of the musical bows (*mankunkundimba*) that have been secretly placed in the seclusion hut. Then she puts a dab of mush on the left-hand *mudyi* post, and afterwards another on the right-hand post. She takes off her blanket, removes the cloth covering her pubes, and eats her food. Like the boy novices at *Mukanda*, she may not go covered during this phase. When water or beer is brought, she must sprinkle some on the resonator before drinking.

At some, but not all, performances of *Nkang'a*, the instructress puts a blob of mush at the point of junction of the *mudyi* posts. Where this is practised, it must be done before every meal thereafter.

The novice's best friend usually brings her a present of fish to eat.

[1] Richards, in *Chisungu*, relates that in Bemba puberty ritual, 'fire is equated with generation' (op. cit., p. 78).

After eating, she is given medicine (*yitumbu*) to 'produce children'. This consists of seeds from a round prickly cucumber (*katanda*), pounded and mixed with cassava. First she takes some in her mouth and spits it out to the right. She takes more and spits it to the left. Then she swallows a small quantity.

That night the instructress puts her to bed, 'as though she were a baby (*neyi mukeki*)'. Shortly after this, a small, uninitiated girl is introduced into the hut. She will be the novice's attendant or 'handmaid'. Her title in *Nkang'a* is *kansonselelu*, from *ku-sonsela*, 'to make up a fire' or 'add wood to a fire'.

The seclusion hut contains scant furnishings—only the novice's sleeping mat and blanket and, at night, those of her handmaid.

Indigenous Exegesis

The musical bow, as we have noted above, is called *mankunkundimba*. Ndembu derive this term from *nkunku* meaning 'early', since it is characteristically played at dawn during seclusion. The novice also plays it when she is hungry, or if she is afraid that wild animals, especially lions, are prowling about. She is forbidden to call out, and must speak only in whispers or a low voice. In a crisis, she may summon help by playing her bow. The calabash resonator is known as *kashinakaji*, 'the old woman'. The blobs of cassava mush are each called *ndambi*, a name also give to the pieces of mush thrown over the side of the lodge by the boy novices at *Mukanda*. The mush placed on the resonator is said by my wife's women informants to be 'for the *andumba* [familiars] of witches', for it is feared that some of the old women who come to visit the novice during seclusion may try to bewitch her. Ndembu believe that the familiars will be content with the mush and leave the girl alone.

The cassava mush on the *mudyi* poles is for the shades of the matrilineal ancestresses of the novice. Little pieces of mush are put on the posts and the resonator by the instructress before every meal during seclusion.

Manyosa said the cucumber seeds are eaten 'to produce children'. The novices at *Mukanda* mime copulation with a *katanda* cucumber just before they emerge from seclusion. When the novice spits to the left and right, women informants said that this is 'to keep the *ayikodjikodji* spirits of sterile and malevolent people away from the novice'.

The nakedness of the novice symbolizes her ritual infancy. She is as though newly born. The arch of *mudyi* posts, or rafters, like an inverted V represents the position of a woman during intercourse. The apex stands for the female genitalia. Placing the cassava near the apex recalls once more the connection Ndembu make between nourishment and procreation. The *mankunkundimba* musical bow is yet another symbol of female fertility, recalling the bow-symbolism mentioned above. The white beads that during the phase of separation had been draped over the arrow inserted near the foot of the *mudyi* tree are now tied around a tiny replica of a bow, called *kasenzi* or *kawuta* (literally, 'little bow'), made by the instructress from *mudyi* wood. The *kasenzi* is placed in the *muntung'u*, the apex of the hut. My wife's informant said that *kasenzi* stands for the production of children (*lusemu*). The white beads also stand for fertility. In the past, it is said, the seclusion period was broken by a rite called *Ku-kosa kasenzi*, 'the cleansing or washing of *kasenzi*'. During this ritual, which is no longer performed, the white beads from the *kasenzi* are draped once more on the bridegroom's arrow. This indicated that the novice 'was well washed with medicine, would not grow thin, and was pure, free from the *chisaku* ['the inimical action'] of witchcraft or sorcery [both are called *wuloji*].' It was only after this ritual that she could play the *mankunkundimba*, an instrument of many strings (representing many offspring). 'She is now an elder [*mukulumpi*], and purified [*wunatooki*, literally 'she has been white', or *anamutookeshi dehi*, 'they have already caused her to be white or purified'].' The same informants, who were women, told my wife that if a person took a little piece of *kasenzi* and was caught with it, the novice's mother could accuse her of witchcraft. One woman said 'this *kasenzi* is kept in the seclusion hut so that my child will have children. If anyone tries to steal a piece of it, this shows that she wants to eat those children', i.e. at a necrophagous feast. A close affinity appears to exist between the *kasenzi* bow with its many beads and the musical bow with its many strings. Both stand for female fertility, as we have seen. The same white beads will reappear on other important occasions in the novice's life—at her coming-out dance, at her first pregnancy ritual, and at the birth of her first child. Like the *mudyi* tree itself, beside which they have been placed during the separation ritual, they represent female fertility, motherhood, and observance of the norms of kinship and marital behaviour that lead to fertility, good luck, health, and strength.

The novice must not call out aloud to summon people to attend to her wants during seclusion. Instead she must play the musical bow. Different tunes on the bow indicate different requirements. She must also play this bow at dawn and at sunset. If she is aware that her instructress or other senior women are approaching, she must play it to greet them. But in practice the novice usually sends her handmaid on errands and with messages, and confines her playing of the bow to greeting the sunrise and sunset. It must on no account be taken out of the seclusion hut, not even into the enclosure. Men must never see it. If they do, it is believed that she may become barren. The bow is 'a mystery of the women', say Ndembu women (see Plate 11*b*; special permission was given to take this posed photograph in the seclusion area).

As I have mentioned, seclusion was formerly divided into two periods—before and after the rites of *chikosa kasenzi*, comparable to the *Chikula chanyanya* or *Chikosa chikula* rites in *Mukanda*. Before these rites the novice was formerly supposed to remain most of the time in the enclosure. Her movements were limited to visits to the bush, led by her handmaid, to relieve herself, for she 'must not soil the seclusion hut'. After *chikosa kasenzi* she was allowed to visit friends in the village, although she had to be covered by her blanket all the time. Nowadays, however, the two periods of seclusion are merged, and there are no public rites separating them. The girl is not washed until *kwidisha*.

Ritual Interdictions of Seclusion

(*a*)   The novice must not look upwards, see the *kasenzi* bow and beads at the apex of her hut, or face anything directly (see Frontispiece).

(*b*)   She must look down and whenever possible keep her fists pressed against her temples.

(*c*)   She must not sing, nor must she laugh unless she hides her face.

17

(*d*)   She must not speak loudly, but only in whispers, 'lest she should cause the death of her relatives'.

(*e*)   She must play the musical bow if she sees the instructress or other elders approaching.

(*f*)   She must not refuse food; for 'the women want her to get fat for her husband. She must be fat and beautiful for her *kwidisha* dance.'

(*g*)   She must not become angry during instruction, or no one will come to her *kwidisha* dance.

(*h*)   She must obey all the commands of her elders.

(*i*)   She must not act boldly or cheekily.

(*j*)   If her mother or a classificatory 'mother' enter the enclosure or seclusion hut, she must sit well away from them. No one called 'mother' must teach the girl or dance before her. It would be a shameful matter were they to do so.

(*k*)   She must not wear anything at all under her blanket, not even a string of beads, except when dancing.

(*l*)   When she greets elders she must do so by passing her closed hand—never open—along the elder's hand. But she may greet uninitiated girls with an open hand.

(*m*)   She must not light, or even touch, fire, or it will 'bite' her. This might cause the death of one of her relatives.

(*n*)   She must not cook in the seclusion hut. No cooking pot or basket may be brought into it. Her food is brought to her from her mother's kitchen.

(*o*)   If she takes food in her own hands to put into her mouth, one of her relatives will die. This taboo applied in the past to the period *before chikosa kasenzi*. It is not observed today.

(*p*)   She must not look at the food when it is brought through the doorway.

(*q*)   She must not look at any performances of ritual that may be going on in her village or in any village she may visit.

(*r*)   She must not see a dead body, otherwise she will become barren or bear dead children.

If she breaks either of the last two taboos, she is removed from the seclusion hut, and *Nkang'a* is brought to an end.

(*s*)   If one of her relatives dies while she is in seclusion, she may be told that she must have broken a taboo. If this is confirmed by divination, she is led out of the seclusion hut by a porridge stirrer, and the initiation is immediately terminated without a *kwidisha* dance.

(*t*)   When she goes on visits, she must keep her blanket well over her head, and walk bent right over 'like a sheep'. If she does not, and sees the huts of her village, 'her mother will die'.

(*u*)   She must creep round the outside of the village when visiting.

(*v*)   She must not do any kind of work.[1]

Observations on an Nkang'a Terminated by a Novice's Taboo-breaking

When my wife visited a village where a girl was secluded, she found to her surprise that the *nkunka* had been abandoned and that the girl had returned to the routine of village life. She was told that a matrilineal relative of the novice had died and that the death had been attributed to the novice's having seen part of an *Nkula* ritual. She was taken out of her hut, led by a porridge stirrer as described, and the *Nkang'a* was declared at an end. My wife was told that this would not prevent the girl from getting married later, but her parents might receive only a small amount of bridewealth for her, since it was feared she might have become barren, as well as unlucky.

The Handmaid (Kansonselelu). From the first night until the end of *kwidisha*, the novice is accompanied in all she does by her handmaid. This little girl is preferably the novice's sister or classificatory sister. She must normally belong to the novice's genealogical generation. It is her duty to keep the fire in the seclusion hut burning until the end of seclusion, to bring the novice her food and drinking water, and to summon the novice's relatives if she is in need or afraid of anything. She leads the novice out to relieve herself in the bush, sleeps beside her in the seclusion hut, and accompanies her on visits to women and girl friends in her own and adjacent villages. When the novice is

---

[1] Many of these interdictions correspond with those laid on a Luvale girl novice. White mentions, in addition, that a Luvale novice must not cut her nails or hair, cultivate, or cut firewood. He also mentions food prohibitions. Luvale novices, for example, may not eat certain species of fish, or any fish dried on a pointed stick (which will cause frigidity). Others include beer, honey (said to be symbolic of tears, and hence of mourning), locusts (said to cause madness), zebra, tortoise, and eggs (White, *Tradition and Change in Luvale Marriage*, op. cit., pp. 7 and 16). Similar food prohibitions apply to Ndembu women after undergoing rituals of affliction (see, for example, those of the *Nkulu* rites, pp. 77–78 of this book).

taught various kinds of dances, the handmaid is taught with her, and at *kwidisha* her performance, as well as that of the novice, is carefully watched and critically assessed. The handmaid sleeps in the seclusion hut near the novice. It is thought fitting to assign this role to girls of about seven to ten years old. They thus get the opportunity to learn much of the mystery (*mpang'u*) of *Nkang'a* before their own initiation.

Instruction. During seclusion the novice is instructed more by example and practice than by precept. Training in dancing and sexual techniques takes up the greater part of her education. The instructress is assisted in both kinds of teaching by many women from the surrounding villages. In seclusion the novice herself, rather than abstract womanhood, provides the main focus of symbolic action.

Dancing. The novice practices dancing in her enclosure. She spends a very great deal of her time learning and perfecting the steps. Before she became a novice she had already begun to learn some of them from older girls in the village play groups. But now she knows that she will face the exacting tests of *kwidisha*, the 'coming-out' rites, where she has to dance before the eyes of several hundred people. The girl removes her blanket for dancing in her enclosure. She is lent a cloth by one of the women who come to train her. She passes it between her legs and under a waist-string, back and front. The overlapping ends are drawn round to form a skirt. Rattles are tied round her calves, and a pad of rattles is fastened to the small of her back. Her nascent breasts are left uncovered. While she is being dressed she remains quite passive, giving no assistance to her instructress.

The main dance steps taught her are:

(1) *Chimbayeka*, which is a very rapid stamping action to make all the rattles sussurate continuously and the breasts shake up and down.

(2) The 'bee dance' (*mpuka*), in which the novice mimes the masculine and hazardous task of cutting honey from a wild bees' nest on a tree. She pretends to be stung, to lick up honey, and to hand honey, represented by grass and leaves, round to all the onlookers. She mimes a more than womanly courage; for it is said that 'novices, unlike other girls and women, do not fear bees'.

(3) She pretends to catch fish in a stooping dance, using a large rag to represent a fishing basket.[1]

(4) Another dance portrays a woman receiving a small, tattered piece of cheap blue cloth (*kawulombu*) from her husband. She holds it up disparagingly before the assembled women, crumples it up in her hand, and throws it away over her head. This represents criticism of a mean or poor husband.

(5) Yet another dance portrays the action of 'sweeping'. This is the *kukombakomba* dance: her feet are close together, her body is nearly bent double. She jumps from side to side, and her head flops loosely in time from one shoulder to the other.

(6) In addition, she is taught traditional dances, such as *wuleng'u*, and even men's dances, like the hunters' dance in the *Wubinda* cult; for she may be called upon to show her skill in any of these at *kwidisha*. While resting between dances she puts her closed fists on her temples.

Sexual Instruction. The instructress and other older women teach the novice sexual techniques. My wife was once shown by women of Mukanza Village how novices were trained. It was hoped that a novice in seclusion at a nearby village would come, but she was 'too shy', the women regretfully explained. They told my wife that as they were all mothers, they were not too modest to show her what was done. Two women lay on the hut floor facing one another. Both were on their sides. The younger of the two kept her legs together, while the other clasped hers around those of her partner. The older woman's arms were around the younger one's neck, while the latter held her partner round the small of the back. They then began to do 'the dance of the bed' (*ku-hang'ana hakadidi*), i.e. a circular movement of the abdomen, in perfect time with one another. The same movements, those of the *danse du ventre*, are exhibited by old women at *Nkang'a* public dances. Then the younger woman got up, and the other showed how, after a few moments of the smooth circling rhythm, there followed a rapid shaking of the buttocks backwards and forwards—representing the orgasm. Then she rolled back her eyes and laid back her head to burlesque the reaction of the man.

Another position demonstrated was 'the sitting dance', in

---

[1] According to Richards, Bemba women, at *cisungu*, sing a song about setting fish traps. This they explained as follows: 'The fish has many children and so will the girl'. 'It represents the organ of the man' (*Chisungu*, op. cit., p. 65).

which the partners sat facing each other, one astride the other's
thighs. In this, too, the circling motif prevailed. Training in
sexual matters, said the women, generally took place at night.
It is absolutely taboo for the novice's mother to be present on
such occasions. After her *Nkang'a* is over, they said, a woman is
forbidden to sleep in the same hut as her mother.

The instructress widens the girl's vagina by inserting three
fingers in it, using castor oil as a lubricant. To accustom her to
a large erection, a peeled sweet potato or cassava root is
shaped like a phallus and inserted by the instructress into the
novice's vagina. Sometimes the roots of *kambanjibanji* and
matooka plants are used for this purpose. Castor oil and the sap
of the *ilala* plant are used as lubricants by the instructress when
she does this. She also lengthens the novice's labia, massaging
them to make them long and supple. The sooty outer coat on
the bark of a well grown *mudyi* tree is employed to blacken the
girl's vulva. This is said to enhance her sexual attractiveness. All
this training is to overcome any tendency the novice may have
to frigidity. *Kambanjibanji* roots, for example, when peeled are
'hot' and 'stinging'. Sexual techniques constitute a part of what
Manyosa calls 'women's wisdom or sense' (*mana wawambanda*).
Other aspects of this wisdom include advice to go to the menstruation hut during periods, and to throw the water used for
washing the cloth used at such times in the river, not in the bush,
where it might impair hunters' medicines or be used by sorcerers.

If a novice has her first menstruation during seclusion, she
continues to live in the *nkunka* hut; for this itself stands for the
menstruation hut (*itala dikwawu*, literally 'other hut'), even
though many novices do not menstruate until after marriage.

Cicatrization.[1] During seclusion the novice is cicatrized by a
woman skilled in the work. The novice is said to experience
much pain while the incisions are being made, but after the
operation she is allowed to revile the operator, just as boys are
entitled to swear at the circumciser. Groups of horizontal
incisions (*nyikaka*) converge on the navel from either side, like
several sentences of braille. Other cicatrices are made beneath
the navel towards the pubes and on the small of the back.
Black wood ash, mixed with castor oil, is rubbed into the cuts

---

[1] White gives an account of very similar practices among the Luvale (White,
Tradition and Change in Luvale Marriage, op. cit., p. 7).

to make them black. Manyosa told my wife that the marks near the pubes are usually done in childhood. The raised cicatrices beside the navel constitute a sort of erotic braille, and are 'to catch a man' (*nakukwata iyala*) by giving him enhanced sexual pleasure. He plays his hand over them. The general term for 'to cicatrize' is *ku-tapala ntapu*, connected with *ku-tapa*, 'to stab, kill'. A vertical tattoo mark is called *nchatu*, said to be a borrowing from Luvale. *Ku-chata* is the Luvale word for 'to tattoo'. Ndembu use *mubemba* or *chibemba* for 'tattoo mark', but this term is being ousted by *nchatu*. Those novices who can stand the pain are also tattooed on the mid-chest, above the line of the breasts. Two cuts are made, known jointly as *kashatu kawambanda*. According to Muchona, these marks mean 'to deny the lover' (*nakudikala ndowa*). The first *nchatu* stands for a girl's lover before marriage, the second for her husband. When the marks have been made, the instructress tells the girl not to mention her former lover's name to her husband. The two men will then 'remain friends', and not fight one another.

Verbal Instruction. There does not appear to be a great deal of homiletic instruction, at least nowadays; for our informants have told us that the novice learns most of her household duties from her husband's female relatives *after* she has gone to live with him in his village. But she is taught during seclusion by her instructress, who repeats these admonitions to her solemnly just before she sleeps with her bridegroom after *kwidisha*, that she must be a good wife and avoid adultery, obey her husband, keep her hut and marital bed clean, be always ready to cook for him, greet his guests hospitably and bring them food, help him in his gardens, and 'run away to the other hut' during her periods. She must refrain from stealing the crops in her neighbours' gardens, from being a shrew and a tittle-tattle, and from paying overlong visits to her mother's village, for by so doing she might incur her husband's jealous anger.

REAGGREGATION: KWIDISHA OR BRINGING-OUT

Episode One: The Arrival of the Bridegroom's Party

About an hour after sunset on the eve of *kwidisha*, a group of the bridegroom's male relatives, accompanied by their kinswomen and wives who carry baskets of cassava meal and calabashes of beer, arrive at the village where the novice is being secluded. They are led by the bridegroom, who bears a calabash of beer on his left shoulder and carries an arrow in his right hand. When they reach the centre of the village, a party of the novice's male kin, followed by their womenfolk also carrying calabashes of beer, go forward to meet them, headed by the novice's mother with a calabash. She says to the groom, 'I have ten [or any greater number of] calabashes. How many have you?' He must have brought at least an equal number.

During the encounter drums are played, and a special song is sung:

'*Enikalemba enza eyeyeye eyeya wenza eyeyeye*'
'The bridegroom's group comes, he comes.'

Next the men of each group confront and begin taunting one another. The novice's party shout, 'If you are strong men, come now, show us your strength!' The novice's mother, according to Muchona, 'wants her daughter to be married by a strong, and not by a weak, group.' If the groom's party then succeeds in pushing their opponents right back, the novice's mother and her kin are delighted. The novice's mother praises them, according to Muchona, saying, 'If any other village attacks you, O bridegroom's party (*enikalemba*), you will defeat them because you are strong.' The bridegroom himself does not take part in this 'push-of-war', in case he gets hurt before his bridal night. Muchona said that in the past derisive remarks by the novice's kin, if they defeated the groom's party, would often provoke real fighting with spears.

After the push-of-war, the bridegroom exchanges calabashes of beer with the novice's mother. The groom's younger brother, the 'little *kalemba*', takes to the novice's seclusion hut the one received by the groom, and inserts the groom's arrow in the ground beside it. This beer is for the instructress to drink.

According to Musona of Mukanza Village, the marriage payment was formerly handed over at about midnight that same night. I have myself, however, seen this payment made only after the novice has danced a *kwidisha*. In Musona's words, '*Kalemba* is brought from *katewu* (where he is shaved around the hair line) while the women trill *nying'ula*. His father takes five or ten four-yard lengths of cloth, and gives them to the father, mother, and mother's brother of the novice. The groom's father gives all the cloths to the bride's father, who then gives half to his brother-in-law, the girl's maternal uncle. The girl's father and maternal uncle are the only ones who can enter the novice's enclosure during seclusion, though they cannot enter her hut. They are very important men for her.' It was Musona who told me that in the past the father or uncle of a man who wanted to marry a girl would negotiate on behalf of his son with her father or uncle. This was corroborated by many other informants.

Episode Two: Public Night Dance

A big fire is made, drums are played, and the usual Ndembu night dance takes place, full of brawls and jollity and adultery. It ends at dawn. Often sleeping mats are considerately put down by the sponsoring village for the older people to doze on.

Episode Three: The Bridegroom's Younger Brother Washes and Shaves

Before dawn the 'little bridegroom' washes himself. The water he uses is then taken to the seclusion hut to be used by the instructress for washing the novice. He shaves around the hairline, and then anoints himself with castor oil provided by the bridegroom.

About this time the bridegroom gives a cock and a young fowl to the novice's mother.

Episode Four: Taking the Novice from Her Seclusion Hut

At dawn the instructress and other senior women come to the seclusion hut. The novice is lying down, facing the door, half covered with her blanket. She crooks one arm and rests her head on the hand. She performs the 'dance of the bed', undulating her hips, and sings a song in praise of the sunrise. The women lead her away, covered by her blanket, to a place in the bush known as katewu, 'the shaving-place', just outside the village. This is often located behind an ant-hill or a large shrub, and is further protected from view by a screen of reed mats.

Episode Five: Preparation of the Novice in Katewu

The novice is seated on a mat behind the screens. She holds her closed fists to her temples as in previous episodes, and bows

her head. Her handmaid sits beside her, dressed normally. The
novice wears only her blanket. The instructress places round
her neck and over her shoulder a string with an amulet hanging
from it, made of the skin of a galago (*katontu*). This contains
medicines (including the root of the *katawa* plant) to help her
overcome the feeling of shyness and nakedness when she makes
her first public appearance as an initiated woman. Sometimes
she takes a *mudyi* leaf in her mouth, 'to make her strong if she
is sick'. The amulet is also intended as protection against the
bad medicine of her enemies and rivals, for some women may
be jealous of her if she is a good dancer. Such enemies try,
when no-one is noticing, to rub medicine on the novice's right
foot to make her dance awkwardly. But at some performances
the amulet is not allowed, for the women say that their preparations are adequate to protect the girl.

The instructress takes the miniature bow down from the apex
of the seclusion hut, removes the *kasenzi* white beads from it,
and places them in a bowl of water on one side of the *katewu*.
She brings leg-rattles and back-rattles for the novice, and puts
the back-rattles behind her ('to make her strong') until the
time comes for putting them on.

Next the instructress begins to comb out and plait the
novice's hair. Another woman attends to the handmaid's hair.
While they are doing so, many women and girls gather around
behind the screen and begin to sing. First the instructress sings
very softly the circumcision song of *Mukanda*. Then all join in
singing 'the plaiting song':

'*Yindenu eye yindenu, akwenu hiyakuyinda akankang'a ami nukuyi-
vinda mwanami.*'

'Plait the hair, plait the hair, your friends will plait the
novice's hair,
I will plait your hair, my child.'

After this the women sing the usual songs of the moment,
with a few traditional ones, such as:

'Giving birth is a hard matter,
Rearing children is hard,
But bringing a woman to her
husband is good,
Getting a marriage payment of
sixty shillings is good.'

The last line of this song is obviously a modern touch!

Beer is sometimes drunk by the women on this occasion. Some of them do impromptu solo dances, shaking the novice's rattles.

After plaiting the girl's hair, the instructress fetches in a large vessel, the water used by the bridegroom's brother. Often she has to drive away small boys who try to peep at what is going on. She removes the novice's blanket and also her amulet, so that she is quite naked. The novice sits, head down, with her hands over her pubes. The instructress washes her all over. The novice evinces extreme modesty. After washing the girl, the instructress replaces her amulet. The handmaid is also undressed completely by her own mother, except for her peraminal string—the novice does not wear one at this time. She is then washed with the same water. But she shows no signs of shyness.

Then the instructress shaves the novice around her hair line, and the handmaid is also shaved. The novice's pubic hair, too, is shaved off.

Many of the women now remove large strings of beads from their necks and under their clothes from their waists, and hand them to the instructress, who displays them by holding them up high. She places the white *kasenzi* beads along the wide central parting she has made in the girl's hair. Then some of the coloured beads that had belonged to the women are put on the girl's head and shoulders by the instructress, while others are looped over her breasts, which are well developed by this time.

The instructress next rubs the novice all over with castor oil and red earth,[1] being careful to rub her cicatrices carefully with the oil. Meanwhile, the women sing, '*Ching'a chawayila manji*', 'oil must be rubbed in'. The oil and also the soap used for the washing are provided by the bridegroom. The novice's ears are stuffed with leaves, and she covers her pubes with her hands when the red earth is applied. Her hair is thickly packed with oil and red earth, which completely conceals the white *kasenzi* beads. The beads on her body are reddened as much as

---

[1] In the Bemba *cisungu* rites, red powder (*nkula*) is rubbed on the older women present during one of the earlier separation rites. Bemba say that this powder used to be rubbed on returning warriors and men who had passed successfully through the poison ordeal. It is still daubed on lion-killers (*Chisungu*, op. cit., p. 66).

possible. The handmaid is also oiled and rubbed with red earth. This part of the ceremony almost exactly resembles the corresponding Luvale rites (White, op. cit., p. 11).

The women find, or borrow, two large cloths, which are held up for display. One is folded to make a girdle, and this is fastened round the novice's waist. The other cloth is passed between her legs, led up at the back and front under the girdle, then drawn over and round to serve as a skirt. While she is thus being dressed, she stands up, with bowed head and fists pressed to the temples. An ordinary cloth is fastened round her handmaid's waist, not passed through her legs. Throughout these preparations it is noticeable that the novice shows shyness, even fear, while the handmaid seems perfectly confident. This observation holds good for a number of performances at which my wife was present.

Indigenous Exegesis

The Novice's Modesty. Informants told my wife that 'it is good for a novice to be shy and quiet. *Nkang'a* is truly the time for her to be quiet. A wife in the hut is sometimes angry and talks loudly. That, too, is good, for her husband is not always clever.' At this point there was much laughter.

The clenching of the fists represents the 'closed-up' state of the novice (see Frontispiece). She is not yet properly married, and is termed *mujiki*, from *ku-jika*, 'to be closed'. The fists also stand for '*nkunka*', the seclusion hut and the state of being secluded.

Washing and Shaving. Both these actions are to 'purify' (*ku-tookesha*) a person from a state of biological or ritual impurity. Thus, at the end of the mortuary ritual a widow is washed and oiled, shaved around the hair line, and given a new white cloth and white beads to wear. Again, when a woman's baby dies, the mother's head is shaved completely, she is washed in a river, and given a new white cloth and beads. At *Mukanda*, boys' circumcision, the novices at *kwidisha* are taken to wash themselves in a stream, then shaved at a *katewu*, oiled and given beads to wear, as well as new clothes. At the *ku-jilola* rites of *Chihamba*, too, the candidates are shaved around the hair line. Indeed, shaving is an integral part of the culminating rites of all cults of affliction, where it is said to have the function of 'letting everyone see that the patient is cured and that painful diseases have been shaved off'. Shaving and washing, and also nail paring, seem to represent a change in the ritual state of the subject. The past and its adhering uncleanness are eliminated; a new life can begin without impediment.

Oil and Red Earth. I have spoken at length with many informants about this mode of decoration. All insisted that the red earth did *not* here represent menstrual blood. It is not called *mukundu* as in many Ndembu rituals, but *ndeng'i.* Some said that the mud head dressing, now seen only in *Nkang'a,* was once widely used by women 'to please men with beauty (*nakuwahisha amayala lubanji*)'. These informants held that the decoration was 'to make the novice appear to be well washed and well anointed [*ku-wayisha*]'. Other informants, including Manyosa, compared the *Nkang'a* decoration with the practice of rubbing red earth and oil into the faces of patients at *Nkula.* I did not observe this at *Nkula,* but I was assured by these informants that it was an essential traditional part of *Nkula.* They said that it was 'a sign of the *ilembu* medicine'. Now this medicine, as we have seen, represents female fertility and maternal blood. It also stands for the coagulation of menstrual blood. I am, therefore, inclined to think that the view which regards the oil and red earth as merely decoration is a superficial one. It is possible that the general stress on white symbolism in *Nkang'a* has led to a suppression of those aspects of the ritual which refer to the red symbolism of menstruation. For even those informants that compared *Nkang'a* with *Nkula,* with reference to the decoration in each, denied that the *Nkang'a* decoration had any connection with any kind of blood. Yet the hiding of the white beads, representing children, under the red mud-pack, and their subsequent disclosure to the bridegroom, have obvious analogies to the *ilembu* and *ikinda* rites at Nkula (see pp. 74–5), and seem consistent with the Ndembu theory of procreation.

Passing the Skirt through the Novice's Legs. The above opinion is reinforced when taken in conjunction with informants' unanimous interpretations of the passing of the novice's dancing skirt between her legs—whereas the handmaid's skirt is merely fastened round her waist. They say that 'The cloth is like a menstrual cloth—it is important that the novice's private parts should not be seen when she is dancing.' It is possible

that these items—red decoration and skirt—refer to a period
in the past when *Nkang'a* was performed at the onset of the
menses. Alternatively, these symbols may merely indicate that
the novice has 'matured' (*nakuli*), a sense which may be used interchangeably with 'she has undergone her first menstrual period'.

Episode Six: The Communal Meal at Katewu

The novice kneels and sits back on her heels, placing her
upturned fists on her lap. The cock given to her mother by the
bridegroom is brought in boiled, together with a plate of
cassava mush, both cooked by the novice's mother. Sometimes
duiker-antelope meat is brought, in which case the women sing,
'*nkayi yakusema*', 'the duiker of giving birth'. The cock's head,
cut off before cooking, is put into the novice's lap. She takes it
in her hand and cries, 'Why have you given me only the head?'
The women laugh and say, 'This is your husband in your hut
tonight.' Then she cries or feigns to cry, looking frightened.

Next the instructress washes the novice's hands, and then
feeds her by hand, while she resumes her head-hanging posture,
crossing her fists in her lap. The handmaid feeds herself.
Afterwards the instructress presents all the little girls in the
crowd with lumps of cassava mush and small pieces of chicken,
calling out their names in order of age as she does so. It is said
that they are entitled to their share 'because they were the
novice's companions in seclusion'.

Rings of white clay are now drawn around the heads of the
novice and her handmaid. The female relatives of the novice,
'mothers', 'sisters', and 'cross-cousins', anoint themselves
beside the orbits 'because they are happy that she is coming out'.

Now the novice stands up, and the women tell her to put
her fists to her temples once more, saying that this should be
her posture whenever she stands, unless she is dancing, until
the following morning. The instructress gives her a short
harangue, reminding her of the correct dancing steps. She is
now ready to 'come out'.

Indigenous Exegesis

'*The Duiker of Giving Birth*'. The duiker represents hunting
and virility in many different kinds of ritual. It is the animal
most commonly hunted by Ndembu men.

The Ritual Meal. At *Mukanda*, the boys' circumcision ritual, the novices eat a meal of cassava and chicken at a similar *katewu* before their coming-out dance. The little girls who eat with the girl novice were her companions in the enclosure, just as the group of boys were companions together in the circumcision lodge. The big difference between these girls and the boy novices of course is that the former are not yet initiated. But this very difference indicates, I think, that the transition between infancy and adulthood is less sharply marked in the case of females, who have, in any case, more to do with children throughout their lives than adult males.

The Cock's Head. Manyosa told my wife that teasing the novice with the cock's head was to teach her 'to respect her husband'. The cock 'has a beard like a man', and symbolizes 'her husband (*mfumwindi*)'. Hunters keep portions of the head of their kill for themselves, and those portions of the animal reserved for hunters are called either *mutu* ('the head') or *yijila* (the sacred or tabooed) portions.

Episode Seven: The Kwidisha Dance (at approximately 10.30 a.m.)

The women trill to warn the men in their shelter that the novice is coming. The men shout in answer. Two women pick up the blanket or a mat, and screen the novice from view with it as she is led to the village *chisela*, or dancing place. She goes round the outside of the village. Meanwhile the instructress, the handmaid, and all the other women proceed to the village dancing place, led by a woman with an axe held aloft in her hand. The men have brought the drums into position, including, if possible, a drum that has been used in a performance of *Mukanda*. The village headman, elders, and important guests sit on stools near the drums.

A circle of men and women forms up around the handmaid, and she begins to dance to the drums while the people sing. Suddenly the novice and her companions, having circled half the village, bear down upon the crowd. Now the handmaid and the instructress dance out of the circle to meet her. The screen is whisked aside, while the people sing, as at *Mukanda*, 'we have revealed her to public view'. Novice, handmaid, and instructress dance into the circle. I have seen mothers dancing there too. The novice dances in a crouching position until she reaches and touches the drums. Then she abruptly straightens up. She is given the eland-tail switch of authority belonging to the village headman. Then she and her handmaid kneel before the drums and dance in a kneeling position. The novice rises and dances swiftly and dramatically across the diameter of the circle. She returns to the drums and spits on the ground before them in blessing and thanksgiving. Or else she may put spittle on her hands and smear it on the ground in front of the drums.

Her first dance is *Chimbayeka* (see Plate 12*b*). At the climax of the rattling and quivering, the women onlookers trill *nying'ula*, and a man goes forward and places a coin on her head. The instructress takes it off and keeps it for herself. Then the hand-maid takes the switch and dances round the ring begging for gifts for the novice. The headman usually gives her a small present such as a comb, and she displays it to all the people. Two bowls are then placed in the middle of the circle, one containing a thin layer of cassava meal, the other a layer of gunpowder. People come forward and ostentatiously throw money or small gifts into the bowls. All matrilineal kin, however distant, are supposed to give more than patrilateral kin of any degree. No matrilineal kinsman is expected to give less than threepence, while paternal kin can 'get away with' a half-penny. The instructress collects up the money afterwards. She will retain the largest share for herself, but some will go to the handmaid, and some to the novice's parents to help equip her with various implements and utensils (her *'yipwepu'*, literally 'pieces of calabash') that she will bring to her marriage.

During the dance the handmaid takes an axe, and the novice mimes pleading for it, then snatches it for herself, has it taken from her again, and recovers it, until finally the girls embrace in reconciliation. They portray similar quarrels over gifts of cloth thrown in by onlookers. These dances mime the quarrels of co-wives, who call one another 'older and younger sister', and express the hope that they will live together amicably. The novice sometimes covers her younger brothers and sisters with cloths, to show that siblings should be generous towards one another.

The novice also performs the fishing dance, pretending to offer fish (representing 'children' as well as fish) to the assembly in general. She also hands a cloth to important men in the crowd, who are expected, in return for being singled out as eminent, to give it back to her with a gift inside. She is given a gun and does the *Wuyang'a* hunters' dance. Some novices, more sophisticatedly, take pencil and paper and hand these to educated men, who write on the paper before handing it back with small amounts of money.

After dancing for well over an hour, at about noon the novice is led away by her instructress, and the gathering disperses. She is then given a leg of the boiled cock saved for her from the ritual meal. If her husband has not yet come to the village to sleep with her, she goes to her maternal grandmother's hut to rest and sleep.

Episode Eight: The Novice Is Taken to the Bridegroom's Hut

The first night in which the novice and bridegroom share the same bed after *kwidisha* is the occasion of a test of the groom's virility. For this reason he is given aphrodisiac medicines before his bride is brought to him. He usually sits in the bush a little to the side of the village with his men friends and male doctors, who treat him with medicines. Three species of trees used in the *Mukanda* circumcision rites, *kapwipu*, *mubang'a*, and *chikoli*, are said to provide ingredients for a medicine to produce a strong erection. Another aphrodisiac is prepared as follows: the roots of the *mundoyi* plant are boiled, and the resulting liquid is poured into a folded leaf funnel. A hollow grass or a reed is drawn through the leaf and inserted in the opening of the bridegroom's penis. The medicine is then blown into it. This is said to guarantee a protracted orgasm. After this the root of the *kapepi kachana* tree (literally 'the *kapepi* tree of the plain') is boiled in water and given to the groom to drink, so that he will have a strong erection. Roots of a species of grass found on plains are also used for this purpose. Another root to induce erection rejoices in the name *kafwahankokola*, 'little elbow-bone'.

The bridegroom then goes to the hut where he is staying, or if he has returned to his own village, to his own hut, and awaits the arrival of his bride. He must sit on the bed, bent forward in an attitude of modesty. The bride is carried over the threshold by her instructress. She is carried in backwards, just as she entered her seclusion hut. If she faces the doorway now, it is said, just as it was then, that she will be barren. The bridegroom must stand upright when the bride sits on the bed. Otherwise, say Ndembu, he will fail to have an erection. The handmaid accompanies the bride. The bridegroom pays her a few shillings for her services, and she goes away.

The two arrows exchanged before *Nkang'a* by the parents of the couple are fixed in the ground at either end of the bridal bed. The instructress tells them that she has done whatever was necessary, and that it is their responsibility, not hers, what happens henceforward. She then leaves them by themselves. Men have told me that the bride then often asks for two or three shillings. When she gets paid she removes her clothes. The couple have intercourse as many times as the bridegroom can manage. *Coitus reservatus* is the rule. If the bride is pleased she blows in her husband's ears. After the first act of intercourse the bride wipes the man's penis with her hands and rubs the fluids over her chest. During this night no fore-play is indulged in, for it is a direct test of potency.

Well before dawn the husband puts four small coins, three pennies and a sixpenny piece for example, under the sleeping mat, one under the pillow, two beneath the bodies of himself and his bride, and one at the foot of the bed. These are presents for the instructress.

Episode Nine: The Arrival of the Instructress

While it is still fairly dark, the instructress enters the hut with a bowl of washing water mixed with the dregs (*nshikwa*) of millet beer. Before entering she knocks and waits for the husband's permission. She tries to meet the bride's eyes. If the latter nods, she knows that matters have gone satisfactorily. If the bridegroom proved sexually unsatisfactory, the bride angrily twists a piece of reed or grass stalk in her hands, behind his back. The instructress then withdraws with the washing water. She returns every morning until the bride nods. Men feel great shame if they are treated in this way.

Chief Kapenda told me of a man who committed suicide after enduring it for more than a week.

On the other hand, the husband is entitled to rebuke the instructress if his wife is sexually incompetent or frigid. This is put down to her faulty training. In practice, however, it is very rare for a bride to register disapproval. Too many interests are involved between her kin and her husband's, social, financial, and even political. It is a myth rather than a practice, but an interesting one in that it suggests that the onus of proving sexual adequacy falls on the man in Ndembu society.

It is said that the instructress is very pleased if she hears that things have gone all right. She shakes both of them by the hand, collects her coins from under the mat, and leaves them the water to purify themselves with. Now she brings some black mud (*malowa*) that she has collected from the bottom of a stream the previous night and hidden away in a secret place. She tiptoes into the village and throws a small portion of the mud on every doorway.[1]

Meanwhile the bride, having washed, pulls the white *kasenzi* beads out of her hair, and shakes the red earth covering it over the sleeping mat in her husband's presence. When she returns, the instructress takes the water in which the couple have washed and the beads to the bride's mother's hut. There she throws the water under the mother's bed, for she is forbidden to throw it away in the bush. She gives the mother the white beads; to keep until her daughter's first pregnancy rites.

Indigenous Exegesis

The Beer Dregs. Muchona explained this as follows: 'The woman's hands are bad and smelling after sleeping with her husband and after wiping his penis. She washes in beer dregs because she slept with her husband after he had been given beer to drink. The dregs of this same beer are used in her washing water. Beer dregs are very good for taking away a smell and removing dirt from the hands.'

Black Mud. Once more I rely on Muchona's explanation. It is confirmed, like most of his statements, by other informants. He said: '*Malowa*, black clay, is a symbol of love (*nkeng'i*) in *Nkang'a*. A young girl and her husband are now loving one another. Everyone in the village must be connected with the same love. *Malowa* also means that their marriage should be

---

[1] White writes that, among the Luvale, a novice, during her seclusion, 'goes round the village throwing mud on the roofs of houses, and in the early morning she picks up earth and scatters it in the village' (White, *Tradition and Change in Luvale Marriage*, op. cit., p. 8).

peaceful, because it is cold from the river.' When I asked him if black mud also meant trouble and bad luck, as it does in some other contexts, he replied, 'No, it does not mean bad luck here in *Nkang'a*.'

Episode Ten: Ritual Meal after Consummation

The instructress returns, bringing some fowls to the bridegroom. It is correct etiquette for him to say, 'No, give a live fowl to my maternal uncle, another to my father, and two to my friends; cook them, and serve them up with cassava mush.' The bridal pair later eat their first meal together, which consists of a boiled hen and cassava. They are careful not to break any of its bones, for it is believed that if they do so, their children will not be strong. The bones are put back into the pot in which the hen was brought, and sent back to the bride's mother. I have heard two versions of their subsequent fate. According to one, the bride may later use them as an ingredient in a fertility medicine. According to the other, the bride's mother buries them beneath her daughter's *mudyi* tree. In both cases they are believed to assist the bride magically to produce children.

In an interesting alternative account of the post-bridal meal, the bridegroom and his younger brother eat together, sharing a fowl given by the bride's mother, while the bride and her girl companions eat in another place, sharing a fowl presented to her by the groom's mother.

Episode Eleven: The End of the Instructress's Task

That evening the instructress returns, and tells the couple: 'Tonight you will be undisturbed. I will not let anyone come near you.' They can now indulge in sexual play. The bridegroom is said to derive great enjoyment from 'playing the fingers of his left hand over three cicatrices made just over the bride's vulva when she was a child.'

Next morning the instructress returns, and jokes familiarly with the couple. She says, 'Now my work is really finished. But you will see me again in two weeks' time.' The bridegroom, if he is a polite man, tells her to wait a little, and goes to his friends to collect presents for her. Helped by his relatives, he himself will give her a substantial present, typically two four-yard lengths of cloth.

If the groom has been staying at his wife's village he remains there for another two weeks. He works for his parents-in-law during this period. In the past he might have been obliged to remain for a whole year, digging a garden for his mother-in-law and even making a new hut for his in-laws. Eventually, he made a special payment, known as *kazundu*, 'to take the bride from her mother's knee', as Ndembu put it, and removed her to his own village. In the more distant past the bride's relatives would fabricate symbolic shapes out of magic stalks and grasses. These are called *nyishing'a*, although today this term is widely applied to cash payments made in ritual situations both as gifts and in order to secure access to the more esoteric episodes. Maize stalks and chicken's feathers are shaped to represent a chief's crown (*chibang'ulu* or *nsala yakalong'u*, 'the red feather of a grey parrot', an important element in a chief's insignia), a hoe (*itemwa*), an axe (*chizembi*), a pot of salt (*ndehu yamung'wa*), a basket of cassava (*mutong'a wamakamba*), meat (*mbiji*), fish (*inshi*), and a goat (*mpembi*), represented by a stick. They might also add a stick called *mutondu wekumi* ('the stick of ten'), standing for ten separate articles, beads, bracelets, food, etc. Another stick stood for a mat (*chikang'a*). A messenger from the bride's party would take each of these items in turn to the groom's party, and each would be haggled over. Payment would be made in terms of the article represented or in a bargaining compromise. Today *kazundu* is commuted into an overall cash payment varying with the wealth and status of the groom. This same set of *nyishing'a* was formerly paid, and I have seen it paid today—though mainly in terms of cash for each separate item—to the doctor-adepts after the performance of an important ritual of affliction. But the payment *kazundu* by the groom and his kin was never as extensive as *nyishing'a* paid by the kin of the subject of an important ritual of affliction. In the past first marriage could be broken down into five main components: 1) a series of exchanges of food between groom and bride's kin, rather to the advantage of the latter; 2) the joint participation of bride and groom in *Nkang'a*; 3) the passage of symbolic items from groom to bride's mother; 4) the groom's labour service for his mother-in-law; and 5) the payment of *kazundu* in kind. Today first marriage is largely a matter of three cash payments, the small betrothal fee (*chijika muchisu*), bridewealth proper (*nsewu*)—easily the largest payment—and the removal fee (*kazundu*). Today, with labour migration, the groom is very often unable to attend *Nkang'a*, and labour service is usually omitted. But in the past *Nkang'a* was incomplete without his participation.

Analysis

The time has now come to pass under review the dominant features of *Nkang'a* as a whole. Firstly, and most importantly, we must consider the role of this ritual in bringing about adjustments in a field of social relations which has experienced stress and the possibility of conflict as a result of the transition of one of its members from girlhood to womanhood. Because in the past this transition was almost invariably associated with marriage, an act which allied two discrete groups, the ritual had political value as an integrative mechanism. But because at the same time it deprived other groups, such as the elementary family, the minimal matrilineage, and often the village, of a useful member, it involved loss and disturbance in a local field of kinship relations. To strengthen the cohesion of the wider field of politico-kinship relations, *Nkang'a* necessarily upset the equilibrium of the local field; the girl's puberty and marriage theoretically conferring benefits on the former and short term disabilities on the latter. But indemnification was made in a number of ways. Firstly, direct payments in cash, kind, and labour service were made by the husband's group to the girl's father, representing the elementary family, and to the mother and the mother's brother, representing the matrilineage. Here the husband's group acted, in a sense, not only on their own behalf but on behalf of the Ndembu as a whole; for any link between villages might be the precursor of further links of kinship and affinity within and between vicinages and chiefdoms in the loose, decentralized polity. Secondly, it was made clear in the symbolic idiom of the ritual that long-term benefits would accrue to the lineage and village of the novice if she were fruitful. Her children would come back to the lineage of her mother, and would not belong permanently to that of her husband. Thus, today's loss would be tomorrow's gain. The permeating symbolism of birth and death reflects the sociological change: the girl 'dies' as an active member of her own family group, and is 'born' into membership of her husband's village and the adult tribe. Much of the cultural structure of *Nkang'a* is concerned with the conflicts arising from this change of social relations. The norms governing her behaviour in her former status as a dependent on mother, father, and mother's brother no longer apply during her seclusion, and new norms appropriate to her future status are taught to her by precept, example, mime, and symbol.

But *Nkang'a* brings to light not only conflicts between groups but also contradictions between the principles on which such groups are organized. A major contradiction exists between *matrilineal descent*, which governs residential affiliation, succession to office, and inheritance of property, and *virilocal marriage*, which determines the post-marital residential affiliation of women. A man takes a woman away from her mother and keeps her away from her matrilineal kin. Let us first examine the formulation, 'a man takes a woman away from her mother, another woman'. This, I believe, is at the basis of the sharp opposition between women and men so vividly portrayed throughout the entire ritual. Men as a sex destroy the consanguineal cohesion of women and scatter them throughout the land, to work for them and bear children. Women lose and men gain through marriage. Nevertheless, the bond of matrilineal kinship persists through time as the articulating principle of politico-kinship groupings. Through their children, women are ultimately triumphant. Thus, *Nkang'a* is not only a 'ritual of rebellion', to use Professor Gluckman's term. It is also an expression of woman's ultimate structural dominance. The *mudyi* tree is not merely an emblem of womanhood: it also represents the value set on matriliny as the hub around which the whole society revolves. Between various categories of female relationship *Nkang'a* demonstrates keen conflict: between the mother and daughter, between senior and junior women, between the mother and adult female society, between mother and instructress. But the *mudyi* stands for their widest common interest and their ultimate solidarity as the seed-bearers of Ndembu society. It opposes them to men as a sex before it reunites them with men as joint producers of children, in the concluding episode of the phase of separation.

Nkang'a also reveals this opposition between men and

women at the heart of marriage itself. The psychological conflict between men and women, based on anatomical differences as interpreted by culture, receives added strength from this social opposition and finds dramatic expression on the first night of marriage. Before the couple can establish pleasurable free-and-easy sexual relations, the husband must undergo an ordeal in which he must prove his virility to his wife and to the women as a whole, who are here represented by the instructress. He must be put on trial before he can enjoy the privileges of virilocal marriage.

But the novice herself must suffer before she is considered worthy of entry into the adult world. She is harshly conditioned in the behavioural patterns of a gerontocratic society. She is shown that she must respect older women even when she has become a wife. She must even submit to them sexually during seclusion. But an outlet is given to her suppressed individuality on the day of her 'coming-out' dance, when she becomes the observed of all observers. On this day she holds the switch of male political authority in her hand and is showered with presents. That night she can pronounce sentence on her husband's virility. In previous chapters we have seen that running through most Ndembu rituals is the belief that one must suffer to obtain benefits. Psychoanalysts claim that many of their patients unconsciously think that any voluntary suffering entitles them to the privilege of a compensating pleasure. The same ideas are expressed in the attitudes of sacrifice and prayer in the higher religions. In both practices the sympathy of God is bought, and more intense punishments are avoided by accepting an unpleasantness as 'prophylactic punishment'.

Now let us look at the formulation, 'a man keeps a woman away from her maternal kin'. The conflict implicit in this situation is made explicit in the 'push-of-war' that precedes the transmission of bridewealth between the groom's group and the bride's male matrilineal kin. That hostility is felt against the groom himself is signalized by his absence from the scene of struggle. Antagonism is indeed so intense that he may suffer injury if he takes part. Conflict is also expressed in the bargaining between the groom's party and the novice's mother and instructress at the building of the seclusion hut.

Reference has already been made to several other kinds of

conflict dramatized or symbolized in *Nkang'a*: between co-wives, between individual and society, between the novice and her village kin, between the married pair and the bride's village. But all the conflicts, great or small, overtly expressed or concealed under symbolic guise, are made to subserve the great aim of the ritual, to convert a girl into a fruitful married woman, fully aware of the rights and duties of her adult status. All members of the ritual assembly, whatever their internecine dissensions, feel that they have a common interest in furthering this aim, and they co-operate in ritual to bring it about. But part of their ritual collaboration consists of the mimesis of conflict: each conflict being resolved within the wider framework of the whole ritual. At the phase of separation women oppose men but are later reunited with them. The mother is at first excluded from the women's group and afterwards gives them food. Taboos demonstrate hostility between mother and daughter, who later dance within the same circle at the phase of reintegration. Novice and handmaid mime in dance the conflicts of co-wives, and their subsequent friendship. And so on. I have already ventured the hypothesis that ritual affects individual members of a ritual assembly in such a way as to change the quality of certain of their emotional drives while preserving the original energy of those drives. Hostility is transformed into unanimity, conflict into cohesion, hate into friendship. As we have seen, certain basic principles according to which a society is organized may ultimately be in contradiction with one another, and groups or individuals may become victims of such a contradiction. In Ndembu society, for instance, if matriliny were consistently and unilaterally applied as a means of recruiting and maintaining social groups, this would mean that female matrilineal kin would continue to reside together for the whole of their lives. The corollary of this arrangement would be that, given the incest barrier against marriage between members of the elementary family, marriage would be uxorilocal; husbands would reside in the villages of their wives. On the other hand, if stable and permanent virilocal marriage were the rule, sons would never leave their fathers, and patriliny would become established in rights to residence, succession to office, and inheritance of property. But, in fact, both matriliny and virilocality coexist in Ndembu society, and the process of social life discloses a series of attempts to adjust their contending claims on individual allegiance. For example, we have noted the emphasis on unity within a genealogical generation of bilateral kin, and alliance between alternate generations in opposition to the intermediate generation. Conflicts arising from divergent maternal and paternal allegiance are reduced by allying bilateral kin belonging to the same generation against members of adjacent generations, although the latter may be linked to them by close lineal and familial ties. But, despite this compromise mode of grouping (and others I will not mention here), the fundamental contradiction remains, a contradiction which asserts itself strongly in the situation of marriage. Marriage is an exceptionally 'sore spot' in the Ndembu social structure; for it represents the mutual confrontation of irreconcilable principles of social organization which cannot be glossed over. Most of the conflicts represented in the girl's puberty ritual stem from this basic contradiction between matriliny and virilocality. Each of the antagonists in these various sets of conflicts competes with its opposite number in terms of rights over persons, goods, or economic resources. During the process of competition, there arise in the individual participants hostile and aggressive impulses to attain their own ends, regardless of the bonds which ultimately interlink them as members of a single society. If these impulses did not become subject to control, the wider society would be disrupted. Now, ritual is not merely a means of repressing these impulses and compelling members of the group that performs it to accept the top-level values in which its overall unity is expressed. Nor does it simply effect a 'cathartic' discharge of socially dangerous impulses by means of their dramatization, or by their symbolization if they are too obnoxious to be represented directly. Ritual among the Ndembu is neither a crusher nor a safety-valve. Rather does it utilize the power or energy of mutual hostility in particular relationships to promote reunification in these relationships, and mobilize and direct the total energy released by *all* the specific conflicts. Ritual, then, invests with that energy the quintessential symbols of the solidarity of the widest effective social group, of the whole Ndembu people. The dramatization, or symbolization, of conflict is the means wherewith such symbols are endued with warmth and desirability.

IX
RITUALS AND SOCIAL PROCESSES

I have described the ritual symbol as a factor in social action, associated with collective ends and means, whether explicitly formulated or not.[1] We are now in a position to consider the validity of this formulation. There is no doubt that Ndembu, by their religious activities, call public attention to axioms of conduct which are rendered all the more impressive by their association with mystical power. These axioms are endowed with renewed vitality, and the great passions underlying reproduction and personal survival are domesticated and subordinated to the social virtues. But, in arguing thus, we are perhaps laying stress on the parts rather than the whole of ritual. For each kind of ritual is itself a unit. Just as the symbol, its ultimate unit of specific structure, from its Greek root, συμβάλλειν, signifies throwing or putting together, so does the ritual put together many apparently separated things. So let us now examine closely how ritual organizes both men and their social experience into a kind of order.

The unity of a given ritual is a dramatic unity. It is in this sense a kind of work of art. It differs from the organized game or the duel, though both are institutionalized processes, in that its rules leave little scope for competition, the outcome of which is uncertain. Sometimes, of course, rituals may contain ordeals or contests, like the push-of-war at *Nkang'a*, without preordained outcome, but it is rare for such episodes to have central significance. Even in that class of rituals—called by Professor Gluckman, 'rituals of rebellion'—when participants express hostility to one another, they do so in obedience to traditional rules. This is indeed characteristic; at all costs the rubrics should be observed. For it is felt that only by staying within the channels marked out by custom, through which collective action should flow (note here the derivation of the Latin *ritus* from the Indo-European root meaning 'flow'), will the peace and harmony typically promised to ritual participants finally be achieved. To complete a ritual, as I have

---

[1] See 'Symbols in Ndembu Ritual' in *The Forest of Symbols*, op. cit., p. 20

shown, is to overcome cleavages. It is collective man's conquest of himself. For in pursuit of personal and factional ends, men are divided, and in loyalty to their sub-groups, men are set at odds, but before what they conceive to be the eternal or eternally recurrent, these divisions and animosities are annihilated.

If unity, then, must be regarded as the product, and not the premise, of ritual action, it must further be supposed that a ritual sequence arises out of some condition of social disunity, actual or potential. It may be held that the decision to perform a ritual is itself a mark of unity among the intending participants. But a wish to unite is not the same as a lively sentiment of unity. There may be an agreement to attend a performance, but it is an agreement between those who differ and wish to transmute their differences into an authentic solidarity. A minimum of initial consensus must become a maximum of ultimate concordance. That is why we find, in analysing the successive stages of many kinds of ritual, an increasing disclosure (either explicitly in confessions of mutual ill-feeling, or implicitly in the guise of symbolic actions and articles) of all wishes, ideas, and feelings which threaten to obstruct the progress towards the ideal unity. The many professions of mutual brotherliness and regard, the common use of the first person plural whilst addressing the deities or shades, the care that should be bestowed on the suffering and the unlucky—all these attest to the need for community that is expressed in the liturgical forms of most religious practices. We see here social processes of unification couched in the idiom of individual psychology. But it is an old error to attempt to explain them in terms of such a psychology. For ritual is pre-eminently concerned with the health of the corporate body, with securing balance and harmony between its parts, which are groups, categories, roles, and statuses, rather than individual men and women. This is not to say that ritual takes no cognizance of the individual, but it does so by prescribing that he subordinates his individuality to his multiple social roles. If the individual is to be reconciled to this, however, he must be promised some rewards. That is why, in the semantic cluster represented by Ndembu white symbolism, we find not only a reference to the genial and social virtues of generosity, hospitality, and truthfulness, but also to health, strength, and long life. The morally upright man, it is implied, is the fortunate man.

It is only if every individual is strongly induced to act in conformity with social norms that the component groupings of his society will be in something like the right relation. I say 'something like', because it is one of the major theses of my studies of the Ndembu that the very norms of the social structure themselves produce disputes. In fact, there can be no such thing as 'structural integration' for Ndembu society; it cannot constitute a differentiated *whole*. It is for this reason, in my opinion, that Ndembu ritual is so poor in symbols representing corporate groups or principles of political organization. Some African societies, such as the Tallensi, Swazi, and Fon, reflect in their ritual the articulated unity of their social arrangements. But the kind of unity embodied in Ndembu ritual and symbols tends to be homogeneous, 'structure'-less. What appears to be aimed at is the formation in the individual of a general sense of acceptance of social norms. In other words, through ritual he is moved to collaborate with his fellows in many forms of social relations, but not in a specifically designated set of relations.

What I have called 'a ritual mechanism of redress' may be further subdivided into two stages, each of which is susceptible of further subdivision. The first is divination; the second, remedial ritual prescribed by the diviner. The decision to go to a diviner is already the sign both of a recognition of hidden group tensions and of a wish to restore unity. Ndembu tell numerous tales of people who delayed consulting a diviner on behalf of a sick kinsman until it was too late and the neglected one died. They draw from this the invariable moral that the procrastinators bear an equal share of guilt with the witch or sorcerer directly responsible for the death. In these tales they recognize the reluctance of members of a corporate kin-group to take action, which almost always brings to light the ill will in relationships ideally supposed to be amicable. Further, when the group has reached that point in its developmental cycle when fission is imminent, divination is almost certain to make public the dominant structural cleavage, which once stated, cannot be glossed over any longer for the sake of social appearances. In this instance, there may be reluctance to go to a diviner, even when severe illness strikes a village member. Such a delay is considered morally reprehensible in the highest degree, precisely because there are powerful inducements to procrastinate. Here the value set on human life is in direct contradiction to the value attached to maintaining at least the appearance of social unity. Nevertheless, once this first step is taken with full knowledge of what it may entail, Ndembu feel strongly induced to overcome their divisions and reaffirm their unity. There is always the risk, during this ritual sequence, of quarrels so violent that they may not be restrained. But, from the Ndembu point of view, the longer the delay, the greater the risk of hidden malice turning into the use of lethal witchcraft or sorcery.

Thus, the typical development of a ritual sequence is from the public expression of a wish to cure a patient and redress breaches in the social structure, through exposure of hidden animosities, to the renewal of social bonds in the course of a protracted ritual full of symbolism. We have seen in the case of Nswanamundong'u Village how Kamahasanyi's kin delayed going to a diviner and how eventually he and his wife had to go by themselves. This was clearly associated with the state of conflict in the village. We have also seen how the successive diviners gave public utterance to what just could not be said under ordinary circumstances. Finally, we have seen how Kamahasanyi, apparently cured of his illness, eventually came to be accepted as a full village member, while the members of the Konkoto group one by one moved out of the village, leaving there only its matrilineal nucleus. Unity had, in other words, been restored among those who really mattered—the matrikin who inherit from and succeed one another. Events had followed the classical pattern. I could cite many similar instances of the pattern from other villages. Indeed, to my mind it is the clue to the dramatic form of the remedial ritual itself.

The views of Durkheim and his disciples, which tend to stress reciprocity at the expense of competition, still have a wide currency. For example, Albert Salomon[1] considers that Marcel Mauss's studies 'verify the thesis that the diverse reciprocities

[1] 'Symbols and Images in the Constitution of Society', *Symbols and Society*. Eds. L. Bryson, L. Finkelstein, H. Hoagland and R. M. Maciver (New York 1955), p. 120.

which make up the social fabric find their ultimate significance in religious symbols which refer to the meaning of unity, peace, and correspondences'. Now, this is a half truth and apt to be misleading. For while the theory of exchange, with its ethics of giving, receiving, and reciprocating, may well be one source of ritual unity, another and more important one consists in the mutual recognition of differences and failures to reciprocate. The *pathos* of the ritual situation arises from human antagonisms which may themselves be provoked by the very rules which men make to establish peace among themselves. If the gods of Olympus may be taken as authentic personifications of human values and laws, it is not surprising to find them so often disputing among themselves. For human life is lived on many levels, and norms appropriate to one level tend to be transplanted to others where they are inappropriate. It is difficult to restrict the competence of a norm once it has been established, for rules by their very essence tend to become universals. Yet torn from their native context, they may promote conflict at the alien levels to which they have been transferred. A case in point among the Ndembu is when a village headman, belonging to the matrilineage of the senior chief, insists on treating his villagers as subordinates rather than as blood kin with rights over as well as duties towards him. A relationship of *primus inter pares* has been misconstrued, as a result of what we may call norm migration, as one of ruler over subjects, and the result has been the exacerbation of conflicts that would otherwise have lain dormant for a long time. Yet the headman could with some justification invoke the aid of traditional ways of thought. He is, after all, a leader and a blood kinsman of the senior chief and, therefore, in Ndembu thought in some respects identified with him. But this mystical and ceremonial identification has transgressed its contextual limits. For ·a village headman's role is not a chief's, and the attempt to universalize a specific norm has merely precipitated trouble.

One thing that ritual does is to specify the proper provenance of a norm. Another is *dramatically* to represent the rights, obligations, and cultural context of a social status. This notion of 'drama' is crucial to the understanding of ritual. Both in its plot and its symbolism, a ritual is an epitome of the wider and spontaneous social process in which it is embodied and which ideally it controls. Here we should consider briefly the fact that a drama of any kind, whether natural or artificial, profane or sacred, is likely to be connected with what Gluckman calls a cyclical and repetitive social system.[1] He writes that 'a repetitive social system is one in which conflicts can be wholly resolved and cooperation wholly achieved within the pattern of the system'. In such a system we may find rivalry between individuals and interest groups for authority, prestige, wealth, and other sources of power, but we do not find reformers or revolutionaries. There is an unquestioning adherence to certain axiomatic values, which gives the social structure itself almost the character of a creed. When we study conflict in such societies, we are, I think, justified in applying the term 'drama' to public crises. For the minimal definition of drama would probably include the playing of roles, the employment of a rhetorical style of diction, and at least some sense of an audience. A drama also implies knowledge and acceptance of a single set of rules, and the expectation of a progress of events towards a climax. All these criteria are present in both the Ndembu social drama and ritual sequence. In the social drama individuals don their social *personae* and become typical headmen, typical lineage heads, typical fathers, cross-cousins, sister's children. They bless, curse, inveigh, argue, and pronounce judgement in what may be termed 'the grand manner', using ceremonious forms of speech seldom heard in ordinary conversation. Moreover, they seek to bring about a denouement, a resolution of crisis. For audience they have representatives of other sub-groups of Ndembu society or even of the wider society, called in as arbiters, judges, diviners, or ritual officiants. A public dispute soon comes to exhibit these basic features of all drama in a repetitive social system where there is the belief, to quote Gluckman again, that there is 'no change possible in the character of the parts of the system or the pattern of their interdependence'.

This can be even more clearly seen when one considers the second class in Gluckman's scheme, 'changing social systems'. In this class 'new types of groups and social personalities, in ever-changing relationships with one another, are emerging

---

[1] *Analysis of a Social Situation in Modern Zululand*, Rhodes–Livingstone Paper No. 28, Manchester University Press (1958), p. 54.

constantly'. Changes take place in the 'character of the relationships which constitute the parts of the system' and in 'the pattern of their interdepende ice, with its conflicts and cohesion'. Now, the point I wish to make is that in such changing systems one may find quarrels, disputes, faction struggles, but not dramas. For the drama implies consensus as to the values and principles of the social structure. Indeed, it is these very values and principles that dictate the form and course that quarrels and disputes will follow in repetitive systems. In such systems social disputes tend, when prolonged, to become 'social dramas', in which men establish identity, not as solitary individuals, but through their roles in traditional groups and sub-groups. In changing systems, however, disputes do not become dramas. They may well remain in what I call the phase of 'crisis', for customary modes of redress cannot always grapple successfully with novel and unprecedented stresses. These problems of social change do not concern us here, but it may be worth saying a few words about the relations between social drama, ritual, and cyclical societies. Both ritual and judicial processes may themselves be termed 'dramatic', for they have their roles, their characteristic 'exalted' style of utterance, their 'audience'. Ritual provides a stage on which roles are enacted and the conflicts of the secular drama reflected in symbol, mime, and precept. Both ritual and judicial dramas are ways in which a society's members become conscious of the values and laws that bind them together, and the nature of the forces that put these in jeopardy.

A repetitive social system is constituted by customs that make for recurrent series of social events, like the rebellion cycle in the Zulu kingship, described by Gluckman, or the developmental cycle of the Yao village, discussed by Mitchell. But a cycle of social events does not complete its course smoothly. We are dealing with the periodic, not with the unvarying. And the periodic has phases of conflict. In the repetitive system of the Ndembu, certain principles of organization, which appeared in the abstract to give rise to consistent norms, in practice initiated processes that worked against one another.[1] Over a period of time, these conflicting processes led to the breaking of particular relationships and schism in particular groups,

[1] See *Schism and Continuity*, op. cit., p. 124.

although new relationships and groups according to the old pattern were eventually established. The contrary processes, in fact, compensated one another within the structure of the changing but repetitive social field. Conflict and change were both *contained* within the repetitive cycle. A drama, social or ritual, exhibits a similar development, expressed in terms of a mounting conflict between its protagonists, which is at the same time a reduplication. A drama has a kind of circularity of form and intention. There is an intention of restoring an antecedent condition, in this case a condition of dynamic equilibrium between the parts of a society. But any process that involves conflict has its 'victims', and any process that reaffirms norms implies condemnation of norm-breakers. It also implies punishment of the innovator as well as the law-breaker, since the introduction of radical novelty would prevent the ultimate closure of the circle. This 'victimizing' and punitive tendency of a cyclical system is reflected in its ritual dramas, for most of them contain a sacrifice. A sacrifice may be regarded as restorative, regenerative; at the moment when the wheel has come a full circle, it sets the cycle going again, the victim is held to be at once innocent and guilty: innocent because the conflicts that have gone before are not the victim's fault, but guilty because a scapegoat is required to atone for those conflicts. In the victim extremes meet.

This view of sacrifice as symbolically constituting at once the end and the beginning of cycles of social development is reinforced by the fact that in Ndembu ritual the act of blood-spilling seldom concludes a performance, but occurs somewhere within it. For example, the symbolic slaying of the demi-god *Kavula*[1] is followed by several significant ritual episodes. In the rites of *Nkula*, the beheading of a red fowl is essential for the preparation of fertility medicine that follows. Circumcision, which in my opinion may be regarded as a species of sacrifice, is followed among the Ndembu by a period in which the secluded novices are taught behaviour and lore appropriate to their new status. The sacrifice, then, represents 'the high spot' rather than the termination of a ritual. It is a 'spot' where, in native belief, the visible and invisible components of the cosmic order interpenetrate and exchange qualities. For

[1] See *Chihamba, the White Spirit*, op. cit.

it is before sacrifice that the shades are most feelingly invoked, and, indeed, in several kinds of sacrifice it is believed that the representative or embodiment of a spiritual being is the victim. Thus, at crucial points of transition from one status or state of being to another, it is felt necessary to renew the developmental cycles by bringing them into contact with the invisible world of the shades, the powers, and the obscure self-subsistent Being behind them all.

Wherever a cyclical repetitive social system is found, the social drama, as I have defined it, will also be found. And where the social drama is found, ritual or ceremonial institutions of redress are likely to be present. And where these are present, the shedding of blood, conceived of as having mystical and purifying significance, will probably constitute one of their main features. This is as true of Islamic circumcision and feud as of animal sacrifice among the Bantu. In strongly horticultural and ideologically vegetarian societies, the shedding of blood may be replaced by the destruction or immolation of symbolic articles connoting life and fertility. But in all instances, the social group must symbolically renounce its complex commitment to the specific relationships and affectual ties of the previous structural cycle, the good with the bad, the pleasant with the unpleasant, in order to begin a new cycle free from the past, purified from its ills and sins, and in complete conformity with the ideas and moral tenets of the culture. It is hard to give up the past in which there has been so great an emotional investment. But in all societies which are cyclical, progressive changes are inadmissible, norms must be maintained at the expense of novel ways of thinking and acting, and the network of actually existing social relations must appear to duplicate the 'structural relations' in Evans-Pritchard's sense, i.e. those which are consistent and constant. Thus sacrifice, as representing the end of a cycle, is a 'sacrifice' indeed, a death of many personal and sectional strivings and desires for the sake of social renewal. But sacrifice, as representing the beginning of a cycle, is also a birth and a hope for the future; a future which will follow the same general course as the past. It is hard for us, in a Western culture dominated by change and devoted to novelty, fully to appreciate the deep sense of security and stability that is induced by ritual and symbol in a primitive society surrounded by dangers and afflicted by disease. For if ritual does not promise the better, it insures against the worst. One of the compensations of opting out of history is the possession of a stable background for the human drama of individual interaction. The plot is known, the actors know their parts, and honour is theirs if they play them well and vividly. Society does not allow itself to be clogged by the detritus of events, but periodically purges itself by ritual sacrifice.

The reader may wonder whether Ndembu ritual may properly be termed 'cyclical' at all, in view of the contingent and occasional character of its performance. There are no major seasonal rites, celebrating crucial changes in the eco-logical cycle. Even *Musolu*, a ritual to hasten tardy rains, is only performed rarely, for the rains are usually on time. But the factor of recurrence is to be found in the developmental cycles of such social groups as families, lineages, villages, and vicinages, and in the life cycles of individuals: it springs from the complex interaction of structural growth and biological development, in the context of a mobile social system made up of small groups. Ideally, we should record the micro-histories of many such small groups, record every performance of ritual in which their members played leading roles, and consider whether such performances tended to occur in critical periods of their developmental cycles. Middleton's penetrating study of a Lugbara community[1] and its use of ritual tends to support the hypothesis that in many African tribes rituals are per-formed most frequently when a small community is in danger of splitting up. Indeed, it is only among societies which have long enjoyed a settled ecological pattern that we would expect to find the dominance of rites performed according to the calendar. Ndembu ecology has little of the regularity associated with a relatively advanced agriculture, residential stability, or even limited access to economic resources. They practise shifting cultivation, their hunting is fitful and individualistic, and their villages and families move widely and split often. The regu-larities which receive most recognition in rite and symbol are those of human and animal biology, wild nature, and the division between inhabited and uninhabited territory. These have a universal rather than a local-cultural quality. A society

[1] Middleton, J., *Lugbara Religion*, London: Oxford University Press (1961).

whose structure does not closely follow a fixed ecological pattern finds its archetypes of regularity in biological processes; it places the emphasis on man himself, rather than on his works. Thus, we find that the fluids of the human body quite literally colour much of Ndembu symbolism. Blood, milk, semen, urine, the black fluid of physical decay—all these become associated with, and give vigour to, concepts of morality, social organization, meteorological processes such as the sequence of night and day, the onset of the rains, and the growth of vegetation.

THE BASIC CONTRADICTION

As we have seen, there is a basic incompatibility in Ndembu society between matrilineal descent and virilocal marriage. Virilocal marriage harmonizes with patrilineal descent, a harmony which is often found in association with residential stability and deep lineages. But where virilocal marriage is coupled with matrilineal descent under conditions of shifting cultivation, an acute tension is set up in the local community when a certain relatively low population threshold has been reached. Historically it is quite likely that Ndembu society is the product of a crossing between a small, but politically superior, society of patrilineal, virilocal invaders and a numerically preponderant, but organizationally inferior, society of matrilineal, uxorilocal natives. Culturally, therefore, they may perhaps represent a transitional social type, structurally unstable, and 'overcompensating' for this structural instability by a proliferation of ritual mechanisms of redress.

The contradiction between modes of descent and affinity is at the heart of the social and ritual dramas discussed in this book. We have seen how it dominates *Nkang'a*. Almost every episode betrays the contradiction. The bridegroom's aggressive arrow, his brother's argument with the instructress, the push-of-war between groom's and bride's wedding parties, and the harsh testing of the groom's virility by the bride and her instructress—all these attest directly to the opposition between virilocality and matriliny. But it has less direct consequences too: the opposition of male and female, of the women of the bride's mother's village and the women of other villages, and even of the bride and her mother, all express this basic contradiction which sharpens the battle of the sexes, causes villages to compete for personnel, and confers independence on a daughter only by separating her from her mother to follow her man.

In *Nkang'a* these conflicts are stereotyped, and their resolution is stereotyped too. Furthermore, the ultimate pre-eminence of matriliny is underlined by the importance of the *mudyi* tree itself and by a number of other symbols, such as *kasenzi* and the novice's white beads. In these rites the public representation and stylization of structural conflict and opposition undoubtedly function both as a warning to the participants and as a prophylactic remedy against structurally induced animosities. Not only the novice and her bridegroom but also their kin and neighbours learn, by performing ritual roles or observing their performance, what are likely to be the major strains in corporate and personal relationships resulting from marriage in Ndembu society.

Rituals of affliction, on the other hand, do not anticipate strains and tensions, but seem almost 'designed' to contain or redress them once they have begun to impair seriously the orderly functioning of group life. If we take, for example, the extended case history of Kamahasanyi and his kin, we find that the same contradiction between matriliny and virilocality significantly affects the quarrelsome and neurotic behaviour we have noted therein. For one of the results of virilocality is that a son may often reside in his father's village until he is quite mature, especially if his parents enjoy a stable marriage. This would be an ideal situation in many patrilineal societies, but what would there be considered the virtue of *pietas* may be considered a fault by the matrilineal Ndembu. For as we have seen, the Ndembu hold that an adult man's proper place is in the village of his close matrilineal kin, helping them economically, supporting them in their jural affairs, and, in the past at least, lending them the help of his spear and bow in feuds and raids. It is in this corporate group, too, that he may hope to succeed to office and inherit property. It is from the shades of this group that he may expect mystical help in the hunt, and protection against illness, ill luck, and witchcraft. On the other hand, every Ndembu knows that it is precisely among his own matrilineal kin that he must encounter rivalry and envy, which may be exacerbated to the point of fomenting sorcery or witchcraft. For the very principle that joins them also divides them, because their common blood makes all eligible for only a single office. Fear of the jealousy of matrilineal kin is the reason very often given by Ndembu for living with patrilateral relatives or affines. Yet it is generally considered the mark of a proper man to face the difficulties and disadvantages of living with those of his kin whose maternal grandmothers or great-grandmothers were suckled at the same pair of breasts.

Kamahasanyi remained with his father well into his middle years. I suspect that his mother and perhaps even his grandmother were slaves of his father's matrilineage in Konkoto chiefdom. This would have made Kamahasanyi himself a slave by matrilineal inheritance of status, although a slave whose father is an important headman often enjoys many benefits in Ndembu society. But it would also mean that he was unable to go to seek his fortune among his matrilineal kin, and was left in unnatural dependence upon the father and his kin. But even when there is no question of slavery, one often finds middle-aged men residing with their fathers, especially if the latter ɪre chiefs or headmen. In most cases the sons are unaggressive, even timid, men. The major crisis of their lives occurs when their fathers die, for custom decrees that they should then leave their paternal villages and live with their maternal kin. This custom does not affect slaves, who pass to their fathers' heirs, but in this case it is common to find matrilineages of slave descent growing up within their owners' village, so that the slave's son still remains with his maternal kin.

It is the case of the older man who returns to his matrikin which often brings to a head the perpetual tension between matriliny and patrifiliation. In Kamahasanyi's case the tension was peculiarly exacerbated by the presence in his matrilineal village of a number of his patrilateral kin, who were, moreover, matrilineally interconnected among themselves. They dwelt in a separate section of the village. It would seem that Kamahasanyi tried from the beginning to maintain a foot in both camps, and he chose for his own hut a site between the two groups of kin. His reward was to be cuckolded by a paternal kinsman, and to earn the dislike of his matrilineal kinsmen, who no doubt felt that his return to his own village had been long overdue. It appears that Kamahasanyi's relations with his paternal kin had been by no means cordial for some time before he left Konkoto, and he had even been accused by them of practising sorcery against his wife, a patrilateral cross-cousin closely related to his father. When she died he had paid no *mpepi*, the traditional death payment to the kin of the deceased spouse. As cross-cousin of the deceased, this would not normally have been required of him; that it was required suggests that he was being treated as a stranger and was no longer welcome. The fact that he next married a matrilateral cross-cousin suggests that Kamahasanyi himself had at last resolved to throw in his lot with his matrilineal kin. His fourth wife Maria was, indeed, daughter of the acting headman of his matrilineal village, a strong personality in her own right, and largely instrumental in breaking Kamahasanyi's attachment to his father's country. It must be remembered that Kamahasanyi had shown himself to be sterile, and was consequently not much of an asset to any group of corporate kin seeking a sire for their future members. As he had no children he would always be regarded in certain respects as no better than an unmarried youngster. But he could have obtained prestige by showing especial skill in some profession or craft, such as hunting, doctoring, or blacksmithing, or by exceptional assiduity in cultivating. From the standpoint of individual psychology, it is perhaps not surprising that he should undergo so many performances of curative ritual; for it is as the patient that an Ndembu acquires membership, and eventually the status of practitioner, in a cult of affliction.

With a history first of dependence on his father's kin and later of rejection by them, Kamahasanyi must have felt that his cool reception by his matrilineal kin excluded him from a normal social life. His matrilateral cousin-wife's adultery with a patrilateral kinsman of his must have been the final blow. In him the basic contradiction of Ndembu society, unmitigated by countervailing tendencies, was deeply internalized, and led for a time to a total withdrawal from the field of social relations. Unable to master his social surroundings, he withdrew to his hut, to the bed no longer shared with his wife. Unable to play the man, he played the woman in fantasy. But it is to his credit, and to the credit of the institutional arrangements of his culture, that he found a way out of his impasse. He went to a diviner, and succeeded in getting his wife to go with him, thereby setting in train a series of ritual events, at the end of which he entered the path of ritual eminence, became to some extent integrated with his matrilineal kin, precipitated the departure from the village first of his wife's lover, then of his other patrilateral kin, and finally preserved his marriage. Contradictions, which may not be resolved on the level of politico-kinship relations among the Ndembu, may yet be resolved, or rather transcended, on the plane of ritual. By setting in motion ritual mechanisms of redress, Kamahasanyi compelled his kin to take notice of him and invest time, money, and energy in public rites which demanded their full participation and prescribed that 'their livers should be white' towards him. It is the presence of such ritual institutions in Ndembu society that makes it possible to assimilate into the social life of villages persons who, though kin, are for all practical purposes strangers to the majority of their members.

APPENDIX A

Ndembu Concepts of 'Shade', 'Shadow', and 'Ghost'

To understand how a people think and feel, it is best to let them speak for themselves first. I shall, therefore, give some informants' views on the nature of the shades and related concepts, translated as literally as possible.

The Concept of Shade (mukishi)

I asked a number of older Ndembu men to explain the term *mukishi* (shade) to me. Here are some of their answers:

Texts

A. '*Mukishi chinalumbuluki neyi wunayi mwisang'a wunalozi kanyama henohu,*

   ' "Shade" may be explained as follows: if you have gone into the bush [and] have shot an animal at that time,
   neyi mukishi wami wunankwashi. Hukwinza nakwanyama hukumu-shikijila
   you [think] "My shade has helped me." When you come with an animal you put it near
   kunyiyombu yeyi hukuonona mashi hukusansa kunyiyombu. Hukuyinka
   your [ancestral] shrine-trees, you take blood and sprinkle [it] on the shrine-trees. You give
   antu ejima mbiji yakuteleka.'
   everybody meat to cook.'

B. '*Mukishi wanetu twabulang'a kujiha neyi wakata hukunona mpemba hukutwala*

   'The shade for [those of] us who do not kill [animals] [may be explained thus:] If you are sick you take powdered white clay, bring it
   kunyiyombu hukukomba hukupeshela neyi mukishi wami nkwachiluku nendeng'a
   to the shrine-trees, sweep [dirt from the base of the trees], and make invocation, saying, "My shade keep me upright with your help that I may continue to walk
   wukolu. Hukuwaya hukwinka ninyaneyi nuwena yakuwaya.'
   [in] strength." You rub [white clay on your arms] and give your children [some] too to rub on.'

C. '*Twalondang'a ona mukishi wami ayi nakunlombela kudi Chinyaweji (hela Nzambi[1])*

'We want that shade of mine to go to ask [pray] on my behalf to God

neyi Chinyaweji nang'iteji yang'anakeni. Neyi nang'anakeni dehi hinukwenda

if God agrees with me [or 'accepts my prayer'], he has felt compassion for me. If he has felt pity for me I will walk

chachiwahi. Hinukuhosha nami komana mukishi wami walala.'

well. Then indeed I will say "My shade is true [with overtones of 'honest', 'loyal', 'constant']." '

D. '*Wena akishi ashakamang'a kwoku kumajamu awu nuwena endolang'a kwejima*

'They [the] shades remain [or 'reside'] in the sites of their graves and walk about everywhere

ilang'a twabulang'a kwakuyimona. Neyi wukumumona ching'a wufwi hela

but we fail to see them. If you [will] see one you must die or

wukushike namukukata kweneni nankashi. Ching'a akeng'i chimbanda

you will fall into a very great sickness. You must seek out a doctor

weluka dehi nsompu wenzi wakunwishi. Kuyimona chakubula kukata ching'a

who knows [pounded leaf-] medicine that he may come and give it to you to drink. To see them without becoming sick you must

wunamuloti. Neyi wunamuloti dehi hukutong'ojoka neyi mukishi wami nawani

have dreamed of one. If you have dreamed of one you think: "I have found my shade

kutulu. Neyi walozang'a hukunona mpemba hukupeshela neyi mukishi wami

in sleep." If you shoot [i.e. hunt] you take white clay and invoke [the shade]: "My shade,

lelu ching'a wunkwashi niyi mwisang'a nakuloza kanyama kulonda nenzi

today you must help me that I may go into the bush to kill an animal so that I may come [back]

nambiji. Neyi wudi nawalwa wumwang'ili nikunyiyombu hikuya nimwisang'a

with meat." If you have beer you should pour it out at the shrine-trees and then go into the bush.

---

[1] *Chinyaweji* is the ancient term; *Nzambi* was perhaps introduced by missionaries.

Neyi mukishi weyi nakwiteji mwalala hukujiha kanyama hukwinza ninayu

If your shade has accepted [or 'agreed with'] you truly, you will kill an animal and come with it

hamukala. Antu ejima hiyakwiluka nawu komana mukishi windi walala.'

to the village. Everybody will know, "Indeed, his shade is true [genuine, veracious, not deceptive]." '

E. *'Nsang'u yamukishi yafuma hana hitwakambamang'a mutulu dihu twalotang'a*

'The explanation [or 'narrative'] of the shade sets out from [the point] when we are asleep and dreaming.

kulota hitukumona muntu wafwa dehi hakwinza hakuhosha hakulomba walwa

[We] dream we [will] see a person who is already dead coming, speaking begging for beer,

nindi nyinkuhu walwa hela kudya. Chitwahindukang'ana twatong'ojo-kang'a

he says, "Give me beer or food." When we are awake we think

netu kawusoku wami wafwa dehi lelu nenzi nakulomba kudya hela walwa.

"My relative who is already dead has come today to ask for food or beer."

Neyi mufu nakeng'i kukukatisha wukukukatisha, wukukata mumujimba.

If the dead [person] wanted to make you ill, he will make you ill, you will be ill in the body.

Hakuya nakuhong'a kung'ombu yamwishi kutiya mukwakuhong'a, nindi owu muntu

They go to consult a pounding pole diviner[1]; the diviner tells them: "That person

wakata wudi namukishi windi, ching'a mwakayi kunyiyombu mwaka-mupesheli mpemba

who is sick has his shade. You must go to the shrine-trees and pray to him [i.e. the shade] with white clay

mwakamwinki niwalwa kunyiyombu kulonda mwakamwanuki mukishi windi

and give him beer too at the shrine-trees so that you may remember his shade

nakumukombelela kulonda muntu akakoli.'

and entreat him that the person may be strong [or 'healthy']." '

---

[1]See *Ndembu Divination, op. cit.,* pp. 72 et seq. for an account of this technique.

F. '*Mukishi hekalang'a hampinji yaduwu eyala namumbanduku. Ilang'a Nzambi*

'A shade is not present at the time of intercourse between a man and a woman. But God

diyu wahanang'a antu niakishi hamu nindi eyi muntu tambulaku mwana.

is the one who gives [or 'bestows'] both [living] people and shades. He says: "You person, receive a child."

Ni mukishi windi nindi nineyi tambulaku mukishi hamu.'

And his shade[1] says "As for you, receive a shade together with [it]." '

Another text describes the behaviour of the shades:

G. '*Hiyakadiwana kumajamu hiyakudisambilila kunahu. Nukuyimona nehi;*

'They will meet one another at the graves and will greet one another, that is all. I will not see them;

anashakami dehi kanka wawu. Etu tunayiluki netu atemuka nakuhema

they have already remained on their own. We have known them, we [say that] they run to play

nakubobola hiyakuseha neyi chochu chitwasehang'a etu amumi. Engang'a

and talk loudly and they laugh just as we the living are wont to laugh. They come

hamukala nawufuku. Hiyakuyimona kudi akulumpi anabawuka dehi hela

to the village at night. They are seen by elders who practise sorcery [or 'witchcraft'] or

ana anwa dehi nsompu. Hiyakuyimona neyi nyevulu hohu; kumumona chikupu

by those who have already drunk pounded leaf-medicine. They are seen like shadows only; to see one fully

namesu nehi. Wamumona namesu neyi wunafwi dehi hela wukwikala wakata hama.'

with the eyes is impossible. You see one with the eyes if you have died or if you become very ill indeed.'

The Concept of 'Shade' in Relation to Other Concepts of the Soul and the Dead

Before the concept of 'shade' can be discussed adequately, it must be examined with reference to related concepts, for it is an element in a system of thought that draws much of its meaning from its conceptual context. For example, we must consider the term '*mukishi*' ('shade') in connection with the terms '*mwevulu*' ('shadow' or 'reflection'), '*musalu*' ('ghost'), and '*mufu*' ('a dead person'). I present texts explaining these:

[1] i.e. the father's (or mother's) tutelary shade—'his' or 'her shade'.

The Concept of Shadow (mwevulu)

H. *'Mwevulu wetu diwu wumi wutunakwenda nachu; wabula mwevulu wukwiluka nehi,*

'Our shadow is the life with which we walk; [if] you lack a shadow, you know nothing,

wunafwi dehi, mulong'a diwu watulamang'a hela neyi wunafwi mwevulu weyi

you have already died, because he is the one who looks after us— although when you have died your shadow

waya dehi kwacheng'i nakwendalaku. Chinafwani neyi wudi kwakulehi hukumulota

goes elsewhere and walks about there. It is as if you are far away and dream

kawusoku weyi. Wudi nindi wunenzi dehi himukukisambilila. Henohu

of your relative. You are with him, you have already come, you will greet one another. Then

eyi wudi mutulu chinafwani neyi wuna mwevulu windi diwu wunakuwani kumutu weyi.'

you are asleep [and] it seems that that shadow of his has found you in your head.'

I. *'Neyi wunafwi dehi mwevulu weyi hukuya kwaNzambi. Chinafwani neyi wunanati*

'When you have died your shadow goes to *Nzambi* [the High God]. It is as though you have thrown away

nsewu yinawili heseki wukuyimona kumwevulu wayu hinaholokileng'a

an arrow which has landed on the ground; you will see it by its shadow when it is falling

wukuyimona wuna mwevulu wayu diwu wumi wayu kuwunayimoni.

you will see it because of its shadow which is its life where you have seen it.

Neyi kumona wuna mwevulu wayu nehi yinajimbali dehi. Chinafwani neyi wowu wumi

If you don't see its shadow it's already lost. [In this] it is like the life

wamuntu ona wunafwi. Chinafwani neyi nyevulu yejima hohamu.'

of that person who has died. It's just like all shadows [in this respect].'

J. *'Mwevulu watachikang'a hohu hafwang'ayi muntu. Antu ahoshang'a nawu mwevulu*

'The shadow begins only when a person dies. People say that the shadow

wunayi dehi mwiwulu hela nawu mwevulu wunatuki dehi mwiwulu.
Akulumpi

has already gone into the sky or has already flown into the sky.
Elders

ahoshang'a nawu mwevulu diyu ijina dakusemuka; neyi muntu wukufwa
wukusemuka

say that the shadow is the "birth-name"; when a person dies he
will be born

nawa cheng'i. Mwevulu wudi neyi mpepela yakunkang'a. Chitwaka-
mang'a

yet again. The shadow is like the wind that blows. When we are
asleep

nawufuku twalotang'a akwetu afwa dehi, tudinashakama nawu tudi-
nakuhosha

at night we dream of our friends who are already dead, we are
sitting together, talking together

nawu tudinakuseha nawu, ilang'a chitukutona hitwayimonang'aku, dichi
chadifwana

and laughing with them, but when we wake up we do not see
them, it is just as

neyi akishi nawa.'

if they are shades.'

The Concept of 'Ghost' (musalu or mufu)
(i) *Musalu*

K. '*Musalu hitwamumonang'aku. Kumumona ching'a wanwa dehi nsompu*
jawafu

'We do not [usually] see a ghost. To see one you must have
already drunk pounded-leaf medicines of the dead,

jamusalu. Musalu himuntu wafwa dehi. Chakufwayi neyi wanwini

of the ghost. The ghost is a person dead already. When he died,
if he drank

nsompu jamusalu wukusaluka. Musalu wambukang'a mwiyedi, wumi
wumu

the medicines of the ghost, he will rise again. The "ghost"
divides into two parts, one "life"

wayang'a kwiwulu kudi Nzambi, wumi wukwawu washalang'a namu-
jimba

goes to the sky to God, the other "life" stays for the body

mwijamu—diwu wasalukang'a huwukuya munyikala nakujaha antu

in the grave—this one rises again and goes into the villages to
kill people

nakunonajola yuma yakuteleka.'

and drags away things to be cooked [and eaten]'.

Further Notes on Musalu (translated account collected early in my field-work).

'A "shadow" (*mwevulu*) does not stay in the grave. But a "ghost" (*musalu*) does stay in the grave. It has long legs and arms and long finger nails. It has a strange appearance from living a long time in the grave. A "ghost" may kill a person who has a grudge (*chitela*) by hitting him with a stick.'

This last sentence probably refers to the belief that a person who drinks *mwiyanawu* medicine may take revenge against the witch or sorcerer who slays him (the 'person with a grudge') by rising from the grave and killing the death-dealer.

A *musalu* clearly has vampire-like characteristics. *Ku-saluka* from which *musalu* is derived, means to 'rise up after death'—sometimes 'to change into an animal after death'.

(ii) *Mufu* (Literally 'dead one'). .

L. '*Mufu wacheng'i chinambukili. Hakwila mufu hakusaluka nakwendo-lang'a*
'A ghost is different and must be distinguished from [a shade]. For a ghost rises [from the grave] and roams about
mujinjila. Hamu nahamu tukumuwana mufu wudi nachimuni chakesi. Hitukwiluka
in many paths. Often we will find a ghost who has a burning hank of grass [literally 'light of fire']. Then we know
netu tunahumang'ani namufu, ilang'a mukishi hitwamumonang'aku,
that we have met with a ghost. But we do not see a shade; it stays
nwiwulu kwaNzambi, diyi watulombelang'a wumi wetu kudi Nzambi. Mufu
in the sky with God, it is the one who prays for our life [*wumi*] to God. A ghost
chinafwani neyi hohamu namukwawu Satana. Neyi wukuhumang'ana ching'a
is exactly the same as that other one [i.e. of the Christian faith], Satan. If you meet a ghost, you must
wushikeni kukata mulong'a mufu dichi hitunayibombeli hamu naSatana.
return home sick because of the ghost. That is why we have linked together the ghost and Satan.'

This is an attempt by a pagan to make the distinction between 'shade' and 'ghost' intelligible on what he assumes to be Christian terms.

APPENDIX B

Synopses of Some Performances of Ihamba

I outline some of the main features of performances of *Ihamba* which I have seen myself or have had well described to me, laying main stress on the social relations.

A. *From my Observations*

(1) *Ihamba at Mukeyi Farm (27.11.51)*

This, *Ihamba* was performed for Nyasapatu (D18, see Fig. X, p. 312) wife of Mukeyi,[1] and classificatory 'sister' of Ihembi and Matembu, the headman of the village in which Ihembi and Mundoyi resided and where Mukeyi and Nyasapatu had until recently lived. Mukeyi had built a 'farm', or small settlement, of his own shortly before the performance.

Nyasapatu had been suffering from an acute pain under her right shoulder blade, and Ihembi suggested that he should 'do *Ihamba*' for her without waiting to consult a diviner. It is interesting that *Ihamba* may be performed for a close relative and affine of its practitioners, for they must be presumed to keep the secret of the tooth's removal from the patient. Cult loyalties here prevail over kinship and marital ties.

The doctors were the 'old firm' of Ihembi, Mundoyi and Mukeyi, assisted by Mungwayanga, a headman, originally from Nyamwana Chiefdom but now resident in Kapenda Area and a famed specialist in many kinds of ritual.

On this occasion the shrine was constructed just before the drumming began. There was a coolness between Matembu and Mukeyi as a result of the latter's departure from Matembu Village. Tension also existed in the relationship between Matembu and Ihembi; for Ihembi was the older man and might have become headman if he had not spent so many years away from the village in Balovale District. The headmanship of Matembu, it will be recalled, was an important office in the political structure of Kapenda Chiefdom, and members of its matrilineal core were eligible for election to the chieftainship.

The tension between Ihembi and Matembu became visible when Matembu arrived late. The following dialogue ensued:

Ihembi: 'I am very angry with you, Matembu. It is your plain duty to see that many of your people come to this *Ihamba*, leaving

---

[1] One of the doctors in the long Kamahasanyi case. See pp. 115–16.

their work in the gardens, if need be. Also you have come late yourself.'

Matembu: 'You should be sure of what you say before you scold. I was seeing to everything necessary to make *Ihamba* come quickly [I was told that this referred to 'the making of some kind of medicine']. Moreover I have been trying to buy beer for Mukeyi.'

Ihembi: 'I still see no people here. What is the matter? You may be headman of the village but I am your "older brother" [classificatory] by birth order and am therefore entitled to your respect. [Sarcastically] Thank you very much!'

Divination as Part of the Performance

Ihembi scattered some powdered red clay in the meal-mortar full of pounded medicines (identical with those collected at Kamahasanyi's *Ihamba*) and water. 'If the powder dispersed,' he said, 'the *ihamba* comes from a distant relative.' If it coagulated in clumps, a near relative was indicated. In this case it did coagulate in clumps. This prompted Ihembi to say: 'The late Chief Kapenda Kamong'a was the patient's father. Perhaps it is his *ihamba* that has come.' When Nyasapatu failed to quiver after this remark, Ihembi went on: 'Perhaps it is Kamong'a. But if it were he, he would have come quickly. Perhaps it is one who died in Matembu Village. If it was Kamong'a we have been playing the wrong drum music [At *Ihamba* drum music beloved by the deceased in his lifetime is played]. If you came from Matembu, come quickly to your sister.'

A little later Ihembi said firmly: 'It is the shade of Mpoku Kahehu, my mother's brother (*mandumi*) [A distant 'mother's brother': see skeleton genealogy].'

Nyasapatu did not quiver violently, and her air of lassitude produced the impression that there was no *ihamba* in her. After a long time Headman Mungwayanga asserted: 'There is no *ihamba*.' Ihembi disagreed: 'There is truly an *ihamba* here. But women may be sending their *tuyebela* [familiars] as well. If this is so, patient, do not quiver [*ku-zakuka*].'

Much later, Nyasapatu fell twitching on her side, and Ihembi personally removed the horns affixed to her back. When he did not 'find' an *ihamba* tooth in them he said: 'Previously, this *ihamba* [in Nyasapatu] was taken from another woman and sealed into a small calabash. But it escaped, for that calabash is now empty. Now it has entered Nyasapatu. Mpoku is annoyed because no one has inherited his name. If this tooth is removed, his name should be given to someone in Matembu.'

Mundoyi added: 'This shade [*mukishi*] is not coming for the reason that there has been quarrelling in Matembu Village [an oblique reference to the headman's irritation at the departure of Nyasapatu and Mukeyi]. But if he has been angry, nevertheless he should just stay quiet now.'

After this several of the women present suggested that they should sing the song of the modern *Tukuka* cult—imported from the Chokwe and Luvale tribes—to make Nyasapatu quiver (*ku-zakuka*), and help her to rid herself of the *ihamba*. Mundoyi scornfully disagreed with them. Then an old woman came forward, twitching, and stuttering in a tongue said by some to be Portuguese and by others to be 'nonsense'. Women said that she was possessed by a spirit that urged the people to perform *Masandu*, a Luvale ritual, full of tremblings and 'speaking with tongues', introduced into Ndembu territory a year or two before. There was clearly a cleavage in the ritual assembly between traditionalists and 'moderns', and also one between men and women; the women on the whole favouring the recently introduced rituals with their hysterical behavioural manifestations.

While they were wrangling, Nyasapatu herself broke in quietly to say that Matembu and his fellow villagers never took any notice of her during her long illness, and never went to diviners to find out whose shade was troubling her. Since she had no 'brother' apart from Matembu, and no other near relatives, why, this was clearly the reason why '*ihamba* was not coming out'. After this she 'quivered' a little, but Ihembi still did not 'find' an *ihamba*. Mundoyi said that the women's ill-judged attempt to 'change the medicines in the middle of *Ihamba*' was responsible for this.

Finally, as evening drew on, Ihembi, after one last attempt to dredge out a tooth from the medicines in which the cupping horns had been shaken, pronounced gloomily: 'Just as I said before, Mpoku's *ihamba* has escaped. It was there all right, but it has flown away. At any rate it is no longer in Nyasapatu. But it is hard luck.'

In the four performances over which I saw Ihembi officiate, this was the first time that he failed to produce a tooth to view. I got the impression that he wanted to make Headman Matembu believe that the bad feeling in his village was to blame for this failure. He may also have implied that the interference of the women who wanted *Tukuka* and *Masandu* performed had led to the disappearance of the *ihamba*—with the implication that it would swiftly strike again.

It might perhaps be mentioned that Nyasapatu was much older than Mukeyi, and was the classificatory 'mother' of Mukeyi's seminal brother Mundoyi, so that Mukeyi would normally have addressed her by the term '*mama*', 'mother'. She was also barren and undergoing the change in life. Her husband Mukeyi also had no living children, for his only son, Nduwa, named after his and

Mundoyi's father, had died at birth. Nduwa was the son of an earlier divorced wife of Kaonde origin.

(2) *Ihamba at Nswanandong'a Village* (31.1.52)

This *Ihamba*, over which Ihembi once more presided, was performed for Fwaila, the wife of Makwayanga, younger brother of the headman of Nswanandong'a Village in Chief Kapenda's area. It was a sad occasion, for Fwaila was clearly dying of tuberculosis, and, in fact, she survived for only a few months after the performance. Her husband had consulted a basket-diviner in Angola on her behalf, who had diagnosed that her father's father Inzala, from Chimbila Village, also in Kapenda Area, had 'caught her in *Ihamba*'. Inzala had been a renowned hunter in his day. 'But let them not forget *Tulemba*,' the diviner went on, 'for they might be troubling her also.' *Tulemba* is a ritual of affliction performed for women with wasting diseases, leprosy, or reproductive troubles. It may be performed for those with anaemia and tuberculosis. It is conspicuous for its emphasis on white symbolism. It is most commonly referred to by the singular form *Kalemba*. The diviner advised Makwayanga to have first *Ihamba* then *Kalemba* performed for Fwaila. He stipulated that *Ihamba* must be performed at the crossing of two paths near Nswanandong'a Village. Ihembi was called in by Makwayanga to conduct the rites. He brought with him Mukeyi, but not his other assistant Mundoyi; for Mundoyi had recently picked a quarrel with Ihembi, accusing the old man of using sorcery against him and his family. Mundoyi, in fact, was changing his allegiance from Ihembi to Headman Matembu in the complex factional pattern of Matembu Village. In Mundoyi's place Ihembi brought along his own sister's daughter's son to train him in *Ihamba* techniques.

Many people came from Chimbila Village, where both Fwaila's father and mother belonged to the matrilineal nucleus. I arrived about an hour and a half after the performance had begun. Fwaila's cross-cousin Musonda, the senior male representative of Chimbila Village when present, was making an address at the shrine (a *chishing'a* of *kapwipu* wood). He said: 'Her *nkaka* [grandfather] Inzala is making her sick. At first she was very fat and lovely, now she is thin and wasted away. I would like to know why. We know that she was once given a baby out of marriage by a certain person, but truly that is not a heavy reason for troubling our kinswoman. But if it is Inzala in *Ihamba*, he should come quickly so that she may get well. If there is a well grown chicken in this village it should be given [to the doctors]. We want her to get well. *Maheza, maheza, ngambu yafwa!*'

Fwaila hardly quivered at all, even when the drums were brought close to her. Eventually Ihembi pronounced: 'It seems that there are many *mahamba* in her. Inzala therefore feels ashamed—he will not come out quickly. Indeed it is hard to catch such an *ihamba*.'

A little later he spoke again. 'One part of her body is giving her great pain [it was her right lung]. If it were really an *ihamba* it would not just stay there: it would come out so that everyone could see it!'

Ihembi was referring to the belief that an *ihamba* does not kill its victim, but only causes him or her pain, usually as a reprimand for breach of taboo, neglect to make offering to the shade, or quarrelsome behaviour in the kin-group.

Next the mother of the patient made a statement: 'My mother's brother [*mandumi*],[1] Inzala, come out quickly. If an animal is killed they should feed you with it. [This expression refers to the offering of blood made at a dead hunter's grave—often made near a crossing of paths—when his living kin have made a kill. The blood is poured through an aperture in the grave.] Truly if it is not Inzala, nothing at all will come out of her.'

The drumming continued with Fwaila's husband Makwayanga playing a carved and narrow waisted *itumba* drum, and his brother Headman Nswanandong'a—who was a renowned hunter— a stridulator. Still Fwaila did not quiver. A murmuring arose, and the people insisted that Nswanandong'a himself should speak, for a coolness had arisen between his village and Chimbila over Fwaila's state of health. He went to the shrine and said: 'Fwaila became ill when Makwayanga was away working as a Capitao [foreman] on the government motor roads. At that time Headman Chimbila and I were both looking after her. But just lately Chimbila has very obviously kept away from Nswanandong'a Village. Why has he done this? I would like to know.'

Headman Chimbila, who had recently arrived, a very old and conservative Ndembu, groped his way to the shrine—he had lost the sight of one eye—and replied: 'If Fwaila had died during the time I was paying frequent visits, wouldn't people have said that I had killed her with medicine? But truly I have no ill will in my liver against the people of Nswanandong'a, whatever they may say.'

Towards the end of the afternoon, Ihembi stated at the shrine: 'This person who has come in *Ihamba* murdered someone when he was alive. Therefore, I should first make the medicine of *Mbanii*

[1] Inzala was her late husband's father, as well as her own classificatory mother's brother, since it was a cross-cousin marriage. She used the consanguineal, and not the official, term of address because Fwaila's illness primarily concerned the Chimbila matrilineage.

[the ritual to purify homicides], before I carry on with *Ihamba*.'
But there was no response to this from the congregation. Ihembi
went on speculating: 'I think he is angry at the small size of the
chicken given by this village.' The chicken was indeed a scrawny,
hardly hatched bird, and by custom it is given to the senior practitioner himself for his services!

Eventually Fwaila herself spoke: 'I have a bad pain in my right
side. If it is an *ihamba*, it ought to come out and stop hurting me.
If it is not, then let the pain kill me and put an end to my suffering.'

Chimbila followed her: 'If this is the shade, may she quiver that
we may know for certain that it is. If she does not quiver, it may be
that she is being troubled by a shade from her mother's side.'

But by now the general feeling was '*ihamba kwosi*', 'There's no
ihamba'. After a few more songs Ihembi indicated that the performance was at an end. Mukeyi splashed medicine over Fwaila, then
Ihembi asked a woman to feel about in the medicine container to
prove to herself and everyone that he did not keep an incisor tooth
concealed in it to cheat them. Then the other medicines were
buried under the shrine. Whispers of '*wuloji*', 'witchcraft/sorcery',
were distinctly audible in the congregation. Chimbila himself, I
gathered, was suspected. Makwayanga then announced that another
diviner should be consulted. But, he went on, Chimbila, or someone
to represent him, should accompany him this time and help to pay
the fee, for he had gone alone many times on Fwaila's behalf. After
all, they were her matrilineal relatives. Chimbila continued to
hedge, probably because he could see that Fwaila was doomed, and
that the trip would be a waste of time and money, both precious to
subsistence cultivators. Fwaila, as I have said, did not in fact survive
much longer.

(3) *Ihamba at Mukanza Village* (15.1.54)

This village, in Mukang'ala Area, was the scene of several
extended-case histories in *Schism and Continuity*. Some of the actors
in them appear in this *Ihamba* performance.

The patient was Nyamukola, wife of Headman Mukanza and
sister of his nominated successor Sakazao. The doctor, Koshita,
came from Chikang'a Village. The night before the performance
he had insisted that the *chota*, or men's meeting place, should be the
scene of a beer drink at his expense. I was present and heard the
villagers 'under the influence' give vent to their grievances, mostly
in connection with the succession jealousies discussed in *Schism and
Continuity*. It would soon have become clear to Koshita where the
quarrels lay.

At the rites there were twenty-one men and fourteen women

attenders, nearly all of them from the autochthonous 'Kawiko' villages, including the headmen of Nsang'anyi, Nswanamatung'a, Kamawu, and Makumela.

There was much discussion as to the identity of the *ihamba*, and it was put to the divinatory test of '*ku-zakuka*', the 'quivering' of the patient. The names of Ibeleka, mother's mother's brother of Nyamukola, Kahali Chandenda, the mother's mother's mother's mother's sister's daughter's son of Nyamukola (but her husband's first parallel cousin), and Sanjing'a, her own older brother, were put to the patient, for these had all been famous hunters. When the name of Sanjing'a was mentioned, Nyamukola began to tremble violently. It was thereupon agreed that the *ihamba* was his, and when Koshita eventually 'extracted' a tooth it was declared to be Sanjing'a's.

The tooth was sealed up in a small calabash stopped by a maize-cob. It already contained other *mahamba*, claimed to 'come from' other members of the Mukanza Village matrilineage. Headman Mukanza paid for his wife's *Ihamba*.

B. *From Informants' Accounts*

(1) An account of *Ihamba* given to me by an attender. It concerned a young man called Chain, who lived with his father, Mboyunga, in Nswanamatung'a Village in Mukang'ala Area. I had been unable to attend the performance.

'*Chain wafuma kumukala waMakumela kukamama yindi diku kunafumi*
'Chain comes from the village of Makumela where his matrikin are and where

mukishi wehamba. Nkaka yindi diyi mukishi, mandumi yamama yindi,
the shade of the *Ihamba* [sic] came from. His grandfather is the shade, his mother's mother's brother,

diyi wunaholokeli mwijikulwindi Chain Mbunji, wunalondi mashi kudi
he is the one who has fallen upon his grandchild, Chain Mbunji, who has followed blood to

mwijikulwindi, wunenzi kulonda amwiluki. Nawu diyu nkaka yindi
his grandchild, who has come in order to be known. They say: "It is his grandfather

namuholokeli kulonda amwiluki chachiwahi.'
who has fallen on him in order to be well known." '

This same informant told me of a common form of *mukunyi* (pl. *nyikunyi*), i.e. the 'address' made from time to time during *Ihamba* to the shade by his living kin. It ran thus: 'If your relatives are the people who killed you, we will be grateful if you will show us your quivering [i.e. we will see the patient shivering]; if we are not the people who killed you, the patient must not quiver [*ku-zakuka*] now.'

Another *mukunyi* went as follows: 'If we are not the people who killed you, let us suppose that our neighbours [*antung'i netu*] killed you. Please quiver if this is so. If the neighbours didn't kill you, you must not quiver.' Another *mukunyi*, which is really a mode of divination built into the ritual ran thus: 'If the grudge [*chitela*] which caused you to die came from the father's side [*kutata*], will you please show us your quivering. If not please stay quiet.'

These comments throw an interesting light on one of the motives for shade-affliction. Few deaths are ascribed by Ndembu to natural causes: in nearly every case witchcraft or sorcery is suspected. Since the vast majority of accusations concern close kin of the dead, it is widely presumed that death is caused by the ill will or grudge-bearing of close kin, developing into recourse to witch craft/sorcery. All shades, therefore, are assumed to harbour wrath against the kin-group, most frequently the *matrilineal* kin-group, one of whose members bewitched them to death. By the principle of corporate responsibility, which also operates in blood-vengeance cases, *any* member of the kin-group may be smitten with troubles by a vengeful shade. Other reasons are usually alleged for shade-affliction, as we have seen, such as neglect of the shade's memory and quarrels in the kin-group, etc., but this general factor must be considered to operate in the background of most instances of affliction. In this way the history of specific quarrels and disputes in a group finds admission into the religious field, and links the dead with the living in a network of idiosyncratic quarrels as well as by blood ties.

My informant told me that there is always suspicion that it is not *Ihamba* but *wuloji* (witchcraft/sorcery) that is to blame for the patient's troubles. 'If it is *Ihamba*, the shade [*mukishi*] can listen to the words of the address. If there is no quivering, there may be no *ihamba*, but witchcraft.' On the other hand, there may be 'only a disease'.[1] Thus there is a well known song, '*Wihamba indi wumusong'u?*', 'Is it an *ihamba* or a disease?'

(2) Chikasa, of Mpawu Village in Ntambu Area, told me that he was 'bitten' by an *ihamba* when he was a young man of about twenty-five. He had headache and toothache. The *Ihamba* was divined to be that of his father's brother's son, a great hunter. He gave a goat in payment to the doctor, who was a classificatory 'father'.

(3) Nyamuwang'a, a woman of Mukanza Village, then living with her husband in Shika Village in Sailunga Area, was 'bitten' by an *ihamba* in her right buttock. This case was somewhat unusual,

---

[1] See my *Lunda Medicine and Treatment of Disease*, Rhodes-Livingstone Museum Occasional Paper No. 15 (1963), pp. 1–4, for a discussion of the Ndembu concept of 'disease'.

for the shade was that of her own mother. Her mother had been a hunter's wife, and women of this status may return 'in *Ihamba*'.

(4) Nyakalusa, of Mukanza Village, had bad earache, and divination indicated that *Ihamba* was responsible. It was found that her husband's mother's mother's brother was the afflicting shade. Nyakalusa was a slave inherited by her husband from his mother's brother. She had been paid as compensation in a homicide case. That is probably why she was thought to have been afflicted by the shade of an affine, for slaves may be treated as surrogates for their owners. Thus, in the past an important man's slave might undergo the poison ordeal on his master's behalf.

(5) Headman Mukanza had 'bad pains in the hip joint and leg', and *Ihamba* was divined. The *Ihamba* was his own younger brother, Kanyombu, who had recently died. It was alleged by the diviner that Kanyombu's shade was angry because Mukanza had kept for himself some money that I had given him to send Kanyombu to the Mission Hospital and maintain him there in food. Kanyombu died and then 'troubled the village' in various ways, as mentioned in *Schism and Continuity*.

(6) Muchona, my best informant, had undergone no less than eight performances of *Ihamba* to rid him of the tooth of a deceased mother's brother whom he had never seen! I discuss this case in terms of Muchona's personality in an article, 'Muchona the Hornet' in *In the Company of Man*, Ed. J. Casagrande, New York: Harper Brothers (1960).

APPENDIX C

Table 1
Classified Inventory of Ndembu Cults of Affliction

Cult	Modes of Affliction	Mode of Manifestation	Main Ritual Features	Origin
A. HUNTING TROUBLES				
Wubinda				Ndembu
1 *Mukala* or *Kaluwi*	Shade chases game away	Elusive 'will o' the wisp', clad in skins; whistles	Libation of blood on a stone; *chishing'a* shrine of *musoli* on top of large ant-hill	
2 *Chitampakasa*	Causes animals not to appear	May later emerge as *ihamba* tooth	Washing with *nsompu* medicine	
3 *Kalombu*	Hunter persistently fails to find game	?	Small effigy of snake made	
4 *Mundeli*	Hunter misses aim through trembling	Appears in dreams as water-bleached European or snake	Clearing made near stream; snake modelled there in clay; peeled *mukula* branches across stream; libation of blood at *chishing'a*	
5 *Ntambu*	Hunter fails to kill animals	Appears in dreams as lion	Effigy of lion made on mound; hunter practitioner and candidate mime actions of lion	
Wuyang'a	(For celebration of hunter's success)			Western Bantu, Ovimbundu?
1 *Ku-welesha*			Washing for entry into cult	
2 *Ku-sukula*			Offering of blood	
3 *Ku-telekesha*			Celebrates taking of hunter name; feast of meat for attenders	
4 *Mwima*			Celebration of supreme achievement; feast; special shrine planted	

Table 1—*contd.*

Cult	Modes of Affliction	Mode of Manifestation	Main Ritual Features	Origin
A. HUNTING TROUBLES (cont'd.)				
Ihamba	'Biting' pains in body	Upper front incisor tooth 'inside body' = materialization of hunter shade	Extraction of 'tooth' with cupping horns; public confessions	Luvale, Chokwe
B. SICKNESS CULTS				
Kayong'u	Respiratory disorders	Patient dreams of deceased diviner relative	Ritual trembling; beheading of goat and cock at dawn; for would-be diviners, test of divinatory skill	Luvale
Ku-swanika	Any sickness	Patient dreams of shade of close kin	Planting of *muyombu* quickset pole; stress on white symbolism	Ndembu
Kaneng'a	Severe and sudden illness	Witchcraft or sorcery of living person	Collection of medicine from around graveyard; slaughter of black goat; practitioner enters a grave	Luba or Mbwela
Ku-kupula or *Lukupu*	Illness	Witchcraft or sorcery	Construction of effigy of hyaena; aspersion of patient seated upon it, to exorcise familiars	Luba or Mbwela
Tukuka	Wasting or respiratory troubles	Patient dreams of spirits of Europeans	Trembling; speaking with tongues; simulation of European behaviour	Luvale, Chokwe, Ovimbundu
Wukang'a	Fever and headaches	?	Night ceremony; three cocks killed	Luvale
Mbaloli	Sores and boils on feet from heat of ground	'Fire of God'	Ceremony in doorway traversed by many feet	? (not Ndembu)
Tulemba or *Kalemba*	Wasting or reproductive troubles; leprosy	Shade appears decorated in white and dancing in characteristic position	Food plants used, maize, etc., communion meal	Ndembu

Table 1—contd.

Cult	Modes of Affliction	Mode of Manifestation	Main Ritual Features	Origin
B. SICKNESS CULTS (cont'd.)				
Chihamba	Any sickness, reproductive troubles, crop failure, bad luck at hunting	Patient dreams of shades of former *Chihamba* adepts	Chasing and interrogation of candidates; symbolic slaying of demi-god, in secret site; construction of personal *kantong'a* shrine; prevalence of white symbolism	Ndembu
C. REPRODUCTIVE CULTS				
Nkula	Various menstrual disorders; barrenness; miscarriages; ill health of infant	Shade appears in dream dressed as hunter wearing genet skin, carrying bow and arrow	Candidate has male 'helper'; wears hunter's dress; *mukula* tree carved into figurine of infant and placed in calabash symbolizing womb; red symbolism	Ndembu
Isoma or *Tubwiza*	Miscarriages; abortions; still births; barrenness; menstrual disorders; illness of infants	In dreams, appears as *Mvweng'i*, masked dancer at circumcision rites; costume with much string; sways about	Candidate and husband washed with medicine while seated in holes in the ground connected by a tunnel	Ndembu
Wubwang'u	Causes twin pregnancies; infant disorders; barrenness; miscarriages; menstrual disorders	Dreams of deceased who was parent of twins	Prevalence of dual symbols; ribald cross-sexual joking	Ndembu
Mwana Apana	Baby born in caul; delayed birth	Foreign spirit seen in dreams	? (branched stump of tree in doorway of hut)	Congo, Kasai?

Table 2

Experience of Ritual Performances, Classified by Area and Sex

Ritual	Number of Performances						
	Kapenda Area 'progressive'		Mukang'ala Area 'traditional'		Total Men: 21	Total Women: 26	Total 47 persons
	Sample of 11 men	Sample of 16 women	Sample of 10 men	Sample of 10 women			
Hunting Troubles							
Wubinda							
Mukala	—	—	3	—	3	—	3
Chitampakasa	—	—	1	—	1	—	1
Kalombu	—	—	1	—	1	—	1
Mundeli	—	—	1	—	1	—	1
Ntambu	—	—	1	—	1	—	1
Wuyang'a	—	—	2	—	2	—	2
Ihamba[1]	1	—	10	9	11	9	20
Sickness							
Kayong'u	1	1	3	3	4	4	8
Ku-swanika	—	—	2	3	2	3	5
Kaneng'a	8	4	1	3	9	7	16
Ku-kupula	—	1	—	—	—	1	1
Tukuka	—	—	—	2	—	2	2
Wukang'a	1	—	—	—	1	—	1
Mbaloli	—	1	—	—	—	1	1
Tulemba	—	—	1	—	1	—	1
Chihamba[2]	1	8	3	8	4	16	20
Reproductive Troubles							
Nkula	—	10	5	9	5	19	24
Isoma	1	5	2	7	3	12	15
Wubwang'u	2	8	1	4	3	12	15
Mwana Apana	—	—	—	1	—	1	1
Total	15	38	37	49	52	87	139
Average No. of Performances per person	1.4	2.4	3.7	4.9	2.5	3.3	3.0

[1] May be also classified under 'Sickness'.
[2] May be also classified under 'Reproductive Troubles'.

Table 3

Incidence of Shade Affliction in 'traditional' Mukang'ala Area—Men

Sample of 10 Men

Relation-ship of Shade	Mode of Affliction											
	Hunting Troubles					Sickness			Reproductive Ills			Total
	Wubinda	Wuyang'a	Ihamba	Kayong'u	Ku-svanika	Kaneng'a (witches)	Tulemba	Chihamba	Nkula	Isoma	Wub-wang'u	
(female)												
m	—	—	—	1	—	—	—	—	—	1	1	3
mm	—	—	—	—	—	—	—	1	1	—	—	2
mmm	—	—	—	—	—	—	—	1	—	—	—	1
z	—	—	—	—	—	1	—	—	—	—	—	1
mmz	—	—	—	—	—	—	1	—	—	—	—	1
wm	—	—	—	—	—	—	—	—	—	1	—	1
distant affine	—	—	—	—	—	—	—	—	3	—	—	3
not known	—	—	—	—	—	—	—	—	1	—	—	1
Total	—	—	—	1	—	1	1	2	5	2	1	13
(male)												
F	3	—	—	1	—	—	—	—	—	—	—	4
FF	—	—	—	—	—	—	—	1	—	—	—	1
B	—	1	1	—	1	—	—	—	—	—	—	3
mB	1	—	8	1	1	—	—	—	—	—	—	11
mzS	—	—	1	—	—	—	—	—	—	—	—	1
FmmB	1	—	—	—	—	—	—	—	—	—	—	1
Cl.mF	2	—	—	—	—	—	—	—	—	—	—	2
not known	—	1	—	—	—	—	—	—	—	—	—	1
Total	7	2	10	2	2	—	—	1	—	—	—	24
Grand total	7	2	10	3	2	1	1	3	5	2	1	37

Incidence of Shade Affliction in 'traditional' Mukang'ala Area—Women

Sample of 10 Women

Mode of Affliction

Relationship of Shade	Hunting			Sickness				Reproductive Troubles			Total
	Ihamba	Kayong'u	Ku-swanika	Kaneng'a	Tukuka	Chihamba	Nkula	Isoma	Wub-wang'u	Mwana Apana	
(female)											
m	1	—	2	—	—	—	2	—	—	—	5
mm	—	—	—	—	—	2	4	—	1	—	7
mmm	1	—	—	—	—	2	—	2	1	—	6
mmmm	—	—	—	—	—	1	—	—	—	—	1
mz	—	—	1	—	—	—	—	—	—	—	1
mmmmz	—	—	—	—	—	—	—	1	1	—	2
mmzd	—	—	—	—	—	—	—	—	1	—	1
Cl.mm	—	—	—	—	—	2	—	—	—	—	2
Cl.mmm	—	—	—	—	—	—	1	—	—	—	1
Fm	—	—	—	—	—	1	1	—	—	—	2
Fz	—	—	—	—	—	—	1	4	—	—	5
not known	—	—	—	—	—	—	—	—	—	1	1
Total	2	—	3	—	—	8	9	7	4	1	34
(male)											
B	1	1	—	—	—	—	—	—	—	—	2
mmB	2	—	—	—	—	—	—	—	—	—	2
Cl.F	—	1	—	—	—	—	—	—	—	—	1
Cl.mB	2	—	—	—	—	—	—	—	—	—	2
m2ndH	1	—	—	—	—	—	—	—	—	—	1
distant affine	—	—	—	—	1	—	—	—	—	—	1
other tribe	—	1	—	—	1	—	—	—	—	—	2
not known	1	—	—	3	—	—	—	—	—	—	4
Total	7	3	—	3	2	—	—	—	—	—	15
Grand total	9	3	3	3	2	8	9	7	4	1	49

Key: m = mother, z = sister, d = daughter, w = wife, F = father, B = brother, S = son, H = husband, cl = classificatory

Table 3—(contd.)

Incidence of Shade Affliction in 'progressive' Kapenda Area

Relationship of Shade	Hunting		Sickness					Reproductive Troubles			Total
	Ihamba	Kayong'u	Kaneng'a (witches)	Ku-kupula	Wukang'a	Mbaloli	Chihamba	Nkula	Isoma	Wub-wang'u	
Sample of 11 Men											
(female)											
m	—	1	—	—	—	—	—	—	—	—	1
mm	—	—	1	—	—	—	—	—	—	—	1
w	—	—	1	—	—	—	—	—	—	—	1
mFw	—	—	1	—	—	—	—	—	—	—	1
remote affine	—	—	—	—	—	—	—	—	—	2	2
(male)											
F	—	—	—	—	—	—	1	—	—	—	1
mB	1	—	—	—	1	—	—	—	—	—	2
not known	—	—	5	—	—	—	—	—	1	—	6
Total	1	1	8	—	1	—	1	—	1	2	15
Sample of 16 Women											
(female)											
m	—	—	—	—	—	—	—	—	—	1	1
mm	—	—	—	—	—	—	—	3	—	1	4
mmm	—	1	—	—	—	—	6	3	2	1	13
Hz	—	—	—	—	—	—	—	1	—	—	1
not known	—	—	4	—	—	—	1	3	3	—	11
(male)											
B	—	—	—	—	—	1	—	—	—	—	1
not known	—	—	—	1	—	—	1	—	—	5	7
Total	—	1	4	1	—	1	8	10	5	8	38

Key: m = mother, z = sister, d = daughter, w = wife, F = father, B = brother, S = son, H = husband, cl = classificatory

Table 4

Numerical Data for Nkang'a

Location of Nkang'a	No. of cases recorded
In village of novice's mother's matrilineage	13
In village of novice's mother's present husband	3
In village of novice's own father	2
In village of novice's elder sister	1
In village of novice's mother's mother's husband	1
In village of novice's husband (novice was slave)	1
TOTAL	21

Table 5

Relationship of Instructress to Novice

Relationship	No. of cases recorded
Full sister	1
Uterine sister	1
Paternal sister	1
Classificatory sisters	7
"Cross-cousins"	5
Mother's mother	1
"Father's mother"	1
Classificatory mother's mothers	4
Affines of grandparent generation	2
Affines of same generation, through brother	4
Affines of same generation, through husband	3
Total from linked-generation segment	30
Adjacent generation[1]	5
No relationship	1
TOTAL	36

[1] These comprise four slaves and one woman who had inherited the position of her mother.

Table 6
Relationship of Handmaid to Novice

Relationship	No. of cases recorded
Full sisters	3
Classificatory sisters	6
Cross-cousin	1
"Husband's sister"	1
Sister's daughter	1
TOTAL	12

Table 7
Betrothal

Betrothal	No. of cases recorded
Betrothed before *Nkang'a*	26
Not yet betrothed, at *Nkang'a*	7
TOTAL	33

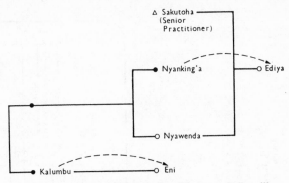

Fig. VII. Genealogy showing shade affliction at Shika village.

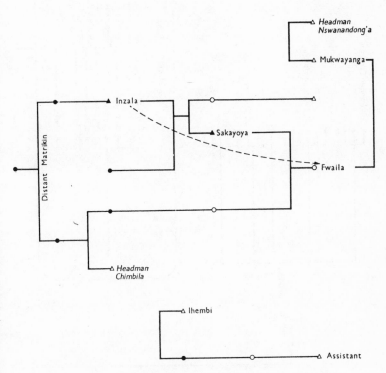

Fig. VIII. Skeleton genealogy for *Ihamba* at Nswanandong'a.

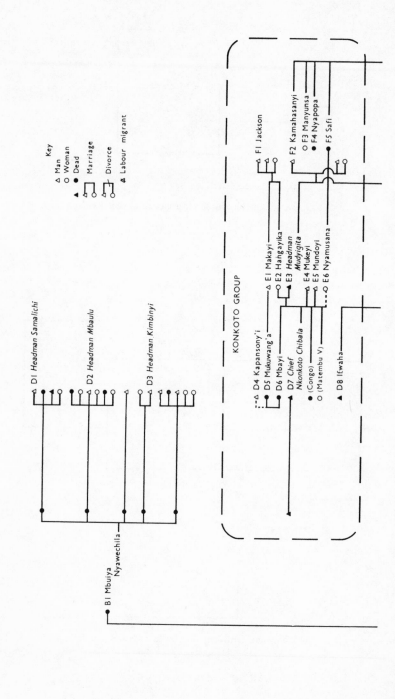

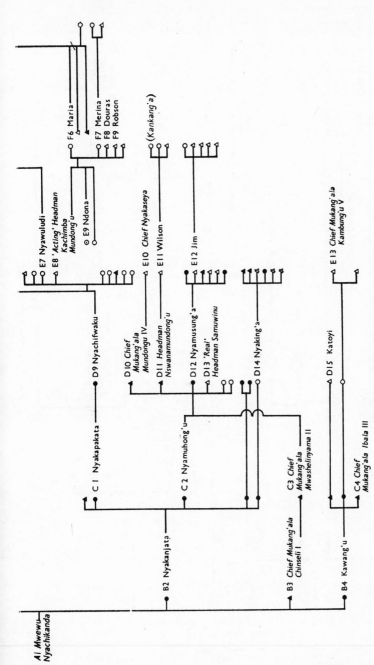

Fig. IX. Nswanamundong'u genealogy.

21

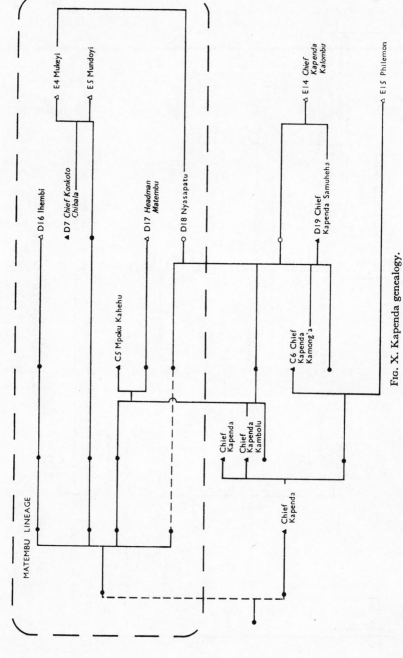

FIG. X. Kapenda genealogy.

BIBLIOGRAPHY

BEALS, A. R., and SIEGEL, B. J. (1966). *Divisiveness: Conflict within the Group*. Stanford University Press.

BEIDELMAN, T. O. (1964). 'Pig (Guluwe): an Essay on Ngulu Sexual Symbolism and Ceremony', *Southwestern Journal of Anthropology*, 20, 4.

BETTELHEIM, B. (1954). *Symbolic Wounds*. Glencoe: Free Press.

FORTES, M., and EVANS-PRITCHARD, E. E. (eds.) (1940). *African Political Systems*. London: Oxford University Press.

GEERTZ, CLIFFORD (1957). 'Ritual and Social Change: a Javanese Example', *American Anthropologist*, 49.

GLUCKMAN, M. G. (1955a). *The Judicial Process among the Barotse of Northern Rhodesia*. Manchester University Press for the Rhodes–Livingstone Institute.

—— (1955b). *Custom and Conflict in Africa*. Oxford: Blackwell.

—— (1958). *Analysis of a Social Situation in Modern Zululand*, Rhodes–Livingstone Paper No. 28, Manchester University Press.

HUBERT, H., and MAUSS, M. (1964). *Essay on Sacrifice* (tr. by W. D. Halls). London: Cohen and West.

JUNOD, H. (1927). *The Life of a South African Tribe*. London: Macmillan.

LEACH, E. (1966). 'A Discussion on Ritualization of Behaviour in Animals and Man', *Philosophical Transactions of the Royal Society of London*, Series B, No. 772, Vol. 251.

LLEWELLYN, K. N., and HOEBEL, E. A. (1941). *The Cheyenne Way*. University of Oklahoma Press.

MELLAND, F. (1923). *In Witchbound Africa*. London: Seely Service and Co.

MIDDLETON, J. (1961). *Lugbara Religion*. London: Oxford University Press.

RICHARDS, A. I. (1956). *Chisungu*. London: Faber and Faber.

SALOMON, ALBERT (1955). 'Symbols and Images in the Constitution of Society' in BRYSON, L., FINKELSTEIN, L., HOAGLAND, H., and MACIVER, R. M. (eds.), *Symbols and Society*. New York.

TURNER, V. W. (1953). *Lunda Rites and Ceremonies*. Rhodes–Livingstone Museum Occasional Paper No. 10. Livingstone.

—— (1955). 'A Lunda Love Story and its Consequences', *Rhodes–Livingstone Journal*, 19.

—— (1957). *Schism and Continuity in an African Society*. Manchester University Press for the Rhodes–Livingstone Institute.

TURNER, V. W. (1961). *Ndembu Divination: its Symbolism and Techniques*. Rhodes–Livingstone Paper No. 31. Manchester University Press.

—— (1962a). *Chihamba, the White Spirit*, Rhodes–Livingstone Paper No. 33. Manchester University Press.

—— (1962b). 'Three Symbols of Passage in Ndembu Circumcision Ritual' in GLUCKMAN, M. (ed.), *Essays in the Ritual of Social Relations*. Manchester University Press.

—— (1967). *The Forest of Symbols*. Cornell University Press.

VERHULPEN, J. (1936). *Baluba et Balubaises de Katanga*. Anvers: L'Avenir Belge.

WHITE, C. M. N. (1947). 'Witchcraft, Divination and Magic among the Balovale Tribes', *Africa*, 18.

—— (1961). *Elements of Luvale Beliefs and Rituals*, Rhodes–Livingstone Paper No. 32. Manchester University Press.

—— (1962). *Tradition and Change in Luvale Marriage*, Rhodes–Livingstone Paper No. 34. Manchester University Press.

WILSON, M. (1957). *Rituals of Kinship among the Nyakyusa*. London: Oxford University Press for the International African Institute.

INDEX

above, below, 169, 178, 230
address, to a tree, 59, 159–160, 186; to a shade, 297, 298
adultery, a subject of *Nkang'a* songs, 217–219
adult female society, 233, 235, 265–266
affinity, 279
affliction by shades, 29, 31, 42–43, 68, 78–79, table of, 303–306, *see also* shades *and* rituals of affliction
African Political Systems, 235
aggression: and sorcery, 154; expressed by *ihamba* symbol, 182; of women in *Nkang'a*, 216; symbolized by *chimbu*, hyaena, 226; and arrow of bridegroom, 279
Akalumpi, *see* Elders
albino, 74–75, 177
alliance between out-of-office factions, 109–111
ambiguous position, 116
ancestor spirits, 14, 20–21; and transmission of jurality, 79; *see also* shades
andumba, *see* familiars
antelope, duiker, in ritual, 256; hide of, 161, 210
apex of hut symbolizing procreative power, 214, 222–223, 230, 242
aphrodisiacs, 259
arrows in Nkang'a: exchange of, 201–202; at *mudyi*, 212–214, 222, 242; brought at *kwidisha*, 250; at bridal night, 260
artifact, symbol as, 84
associational relationships in ritual, 4, 53–4
axe: dance with at *Nkula*, 67; held up at *Nkang'a*, 257–258; blades, clinked at *Ihamba*, 165, 174–175

backwards, entering, a symbol of childbirth: in *Nkula*, 64, 67, 77; in *Nkang'a*, 228, 230, 259–260
bark rope, avoided in fertility medicine, 61
beads, representing children: string of white, at *Nkang'a*, 40n., 212–215; red at *Nkula*, 64–65, 76–77
Beals, A. R. and Siegel, B. J. on divisiveness, 45n.
beer: finger millet, 10, 260–261; white maize, libation of, 69, 73; honey, sacralized, 162
beetle, goliath, for strength, 177

behaviour, ritual, 1; rigid character of, 5–6
Beidelman, T., on Ngulu puberty rites, 199n, 215n.
betrothal: fee, 263; table giving occasion of, 308
biological processes and symbolism, 279
bi-polarity of reference in symbol's meaning, 18–19
black fruit, *muneku*, in *Ihamba*, 189
black goat symbol, 135
black mud symbol, 34, 261–262
blackness, 279; of charcoal, 28; and evil, 49; and witchcraft, 188; and sexual attractiveness, 248–249
blood: symbolism, 18, 56, 175, 279; of huntmanships, 177, 179; of motherhood, 179; and sorcery, 203; ritual shedding of, 276–277; in prayer to shades, 284
bones of bridal meal, 262
bow and arrow; in *Nkula* ritual, 70
bow, miniature, in *Nkang'a*, 314, 222, 242, 252
breach, in social drama, 89, 236
breast-milk, 279; a meaning of *mudyi*, 18–19, 207
bridegroom; 201, 222–224, 240, 250, 253, 266; at bridal night, 259–264; test of virility of, 260–261, 266, 279; used to give labour service to in-laws, 263; younger brother of, 222–224, 250–251
bride's kin and bridegroom's kin, conflict between, 224, 249–250
bridewealth, *see* marriage payment
British, establishment of chiefs by, 10
brittle segmentation of divinatory symbol, 44
brothers: solidarity between, 12; equivalence of, 222–224, 250–251
bullets to shoot were-lion, 177
bush and stream distinctions in medicines, 68–69

calabash resonator of musical bows, 240–241
calabash symbol: representing matriliny, 39–40; representing marriage, 40
carrying novice, 212, 229–230, 259
cassava, 9; used for invocation, 202, 204–205
castor oil: at *Nkang'a*, 248, 251, 253–255
leaves of, in *Ihamba*, 161, 166

menstruation: circumcision an analogue of, 84; onset of and puberty
ritual, 199–200, 248, 255–256
menstruation hut, 64, 248
mfumwa tubwiku, lodge instructor, 209
Middleton, John, on the Lugbara, 278
milk tree, *see mudyi*
missions, 91, 95, 97; and ritual, 170
Mitchell, Clyde, on the Yao, 275
mobility among the Ndembu, 10
models for social life portrayed by
ritual, 7
modesty, ritual: in *Nkula*, 69; in
Nkang'a, 205, 243–245, 254, 259
mongoose symbol, 66
mother-child relationship, 207
mother, daughter: relationship, 20,
223, 234; conflict between, 265, 267
mother of novice, 201, 205; forbidden
to train novice at *Nkang'a*, 209, 244,
248; wears daughter's cloth, 210; excluded from dance, 218–219; clears
seclusion hut site, 222–223; given
fowl by bridegroom, 251; conflict
between adult female society and,
265, 267; conflict between instructress and, 265
mother's brother negotiates marriage
payment, 250–251
mpelu, magical substances, 177–178
mpemba, see white clay
mpepi, see death payment
mubang'a tree which stands stiffly, 259
mucha: fruit stone, symbolizing time,
40–41; in *Nkula* fertility rite, 69
mucheki, tree with white wood, for
Nkula, 60, 62, 69
muchikachika, medicine for *Ihamba*, 160
Muchona, the informant: on *Nkula*,
57–59, 62–65, 70, 74–75, 77–78;
on sorcery, 137; on *Ihamba*, 181, 187;
on *Nkang'a*, 209, 211, 222–223, 229,
249–250, 261–262; undergoes *Ihamba*,
299
mudeng'udeng'u, tree with many fruits,
for *Nkula*, 60–61
mudyi, *Diplorryncus condylocarpon*, tree
with milky latex: meanings of, 17–20,
82, 207, 265; in Ihamba, 165–166,
170, 196; in leaf-clapping rite, 167;
in *Wubwang'u*, 207; in *Musolu*, 207;
at separation phase of *Nkang'a*,
205–214, 216, 220; sanction of madness against novice's looking at, 205,
209, 212; novice laid at foot of, 212;
used to make *kasenzi* bow, 214;
dance around, 216–222; used for
poles for seclusion hut, 222–223,
240–242; picking up novice from,
227–228; leaves from, representing

mudyi (contd.)—
children, 228–229, 231; bark used
for blackening vulva, 248; leaf used
for strength, 252
mudyidyi, wood used for ritual stridulator, 165
Mudyigita, Kamahasanyi's dead father:
afflicts him, 122, 125–126, 144, 157;
invoked, 164, 167
Mufu, figurine representing a dead
person, 36
mufu, a ghost, 287, 290
mufung'u, 'gathering' medicine, for
Ihamba, 160, 189
muhang'andumba, 'witch-chasing' medicine, for *Ihamba*, 174, 191
muhotuhotu broom leaves, anti-witchcraft medicine: in *Nkula*, 59–61, 69;
in *Wubwang'u*, 207
mujiwu, tree with many roots, for *Nkula*,
60–61
Mukala, hunters' 'whistling' shade, and
ritual, 120–121, 140
Mukanda, see circumcision
Mukang'ala: chiefdom, 91, 93, 98–99,
105; *see also* Chief
Mukang'ala-Kapenda dichotomy, 98,
105–108, 112
Mukang'ala matrilineage, 98, 132, 142
Mukanza headman's *Ihamba*, 299
Mukanza Village, 57, 71, 296–297
mukata, pouch for *ihamba* tooth, 178–179
Mukeyi, an *Ihamba* doctor, 115–116,
122, 159, 161–167, 171, 292–296
mukishi: ancestor spirit, 32; mode of,
manifestation, 53; *see also* shade
mukombukombu broom leaves: in *Nkula*,
59, 61, 68; in *Ihamba*, 187–188
mukula, *Pterocarpus angolensis*, tree with
red gum: first for *Nkula*, 59–60, 62n.,
68–69, 71–74; semantic structure of,
82–87; for *Ihamba*, 160; in sorcery,
203
muloji, see witches
multivocality of ritual symbols, 17, 21,
44, 213
mulundu bird, for *Ihamba*, 175
Mundoyi, an *Ihamba* doctor: performs
Ihamba, 115–116, 122, 159–165,
167–168, 170–172, 291–293; invokes
shade of brother, 167
mundoyi roots, as aphrodisiac, 259
muneku, tree with black fruit, in *Ihamba*,
160, 189
Mung'ong'i funerary association, 213
munjimbi, 'forgetting' medicine, for
Ihamba, 160, 189
muntung'ulu, tree with many roots, for
Nkula, 59, 61
Musandu, trembling ritual, 293